The Ruby Programming Language

Other resources from O'Reilly

Related titles	Ruby Cookbook™	Ruby Pocket Reference
	Learning Ruby	Ajax on Rails
	Advanced Rails	Ruby on Rails: Up and
	Rails Cookbook™	Running

oreilly.com
oreilly.com is more than a complete catalog of O'Reilly books. You'll also find links to news, events, articles, weblogs, sample chapters, and code examples.

oreillynet.com is the essential portal for developers interested in open and emerging technologies, including new platforms, programming languages, and operating systems.

Conferences
O'Reilly Media brings diverse innovators together to nurture the ideas that spark revolutionary industries. We specialize in documenting the latest tools and systems, translating the innovator's knowledge into useful skills for those in the trenches. Visit *conferences.oreilly.com* for our upcoming events.

Safari Bookshelf (*safari.oreilly.com*) is the premier online reference library for programmers and IT professionals. Conduct searches across more than 1,000 books. Subscribers can zero in on answers to time-critical questions in a matter of seconds. Read the books on your Bookshelf from cover to cover or simply flip to the page you need. Try it today for free.

The Ruby Programming Language

David Flanagan and Yukihiro Matsumoto

O'REILLY®

Beijing · Cambridge · Farnham · Köln · Paris · Sebastopol · Taipei · Tokyo

The Ruby Programming Language
by David Flanagan and Yukihiro Matsumoto
with drawings by *why the lucky stiff*

Published by O'Reilly Media, Inc., 1005 Gravenstein Highway North, Sebastopol, CA 95472

O'Reilly books may be purchased for educational, business, or sales promotional use. Online editions are also available for most titles (*http://safari.oreilly.com*). For more information, contact our corporate/institutional sales department: (800) 998-9938 or *corporate@oreilly.com*.

Editor: Mike Loukides
Production Editor: Sarah Schneider
Proofreader: Sarah Schneider

Indexer: Joe Wizda
Cover Designer: Karen Montgomery
Interior Designer: David Futato
Illustrators: Rob Romano and *why the lucky stiff*

Printing History:
   January 2008:   First Edition.

This book uses RepKover™, a durable and flexible lay-flat binding.

ISBN-13: 978-0-596-51617-8

[M] [04/08]

Table of Contents

Preface

This book is an updated and expanded version of *Ruby in a Nutshell* (O'Reilly) by Yukihiro Matsumoto, who is better known as Matz. It is loosely modeled after the classic *The C Programming Language* (Prentice Hall) by Brian Kernighan and Dennis Ritchie, and aims to document the Ruby language comprehensively but without the formality of a language specification. It is written for experienced programmers who are new to Ruby, and for current Ruby programmers who want to take their understanding and mastery of the language to the next level.

You'll find a guide to the structure and organization of this book in Chapter 1.

Acknowledgments

David Flanagan

Before anything else, I must thank Matz for the beautiful language he has designed, for his help understanding that language, and for the *Nutshell* that this book grew out of.

Thanks also to:

- *why the lucky stiff* for the delightful drawings that grace these pages (you'll find them on the chapter title pages) and, of course, for his own book on Ruby, *why's (poignant) guide to Ruby*, which you can find online at *http://poignantguide.net/ruby/*.

- My technical reviewers: David A. Black, director of Ruby Power and Light, LLC (*http://www.rubypal.com*); Charles Oliver Nutter of the JRuby team (*http://www.jruby.org*) at Sun Microsystems; Shyouhei Urabe, the maintainer of the Ruby 1.8.6 branch; and Ken Cooper. Their comments helped improve the quality and clarity of the book. Any errors that remain are, of course, my own.

- My editor, Mike Loukides, for asking and persistently encouraging me to write this book, and for his patience while I did so.

Finally, of course, my love and thanks to my family.

—David Flanagan

http://www.davidflanagan.com

January 2008

Yukihiro Matsumoto

In addition to the people listed by David (except myself), I appreciate the help from community members all around the world, especially from Japan: Koichi Sasada, Nobuyoshi Nakada, Akira Tanaka, Shugo Maeda, Usaku Nakamura, and Shyouhei Urabe to name a few (not in any particular order).

And finally, I thank my family, who hopefully forgive their husband and father for dedicating time to Ruby development.

—Yukihiro Matsumoto

January 2008

Conventions Used in This Book

The following typographical conventions are used in this book:

Italic

Indicates new terms, URLs, email addresses, filenames, and file extensions.

`Constant width`

Used for program listings, as well as within paragraphs to refer to program elements such as variable or function names, datatypes, environment variables, statements, and keywords.

`Constant width bold`

Shows commands or other text that should be typed literally by the user.

`Constant width italic`

Shows text that should be replaced with user-supplied values or by values determined by context.

Using Code Examples

This book is here to help you get your job done. In general, you may use the code in this book in your programs and documentation. You do not need to contact us for permission unless you're reproducing a significant portion of the code. For example, writing a program that uses several chunks of code from this book does not require permission. Selling or distributing a CD-ROM of examples from O'Reilly books does require permission. Answering a question by citing this book and quoting example code does not require permission. Incorporating a significant amount of example code from this book into your product's documentation does require permission.

We appreciate, but do not require, attribution. An attribution usually includes the title, author, publisher, and ISBN. For example: "*The Ruby Programming Language* by David Flanagan and Yukihiro Matsumoto. Copyright 2008 David Flanagan and Yukihiro Matsumoto, 978-0-596-51617-8."

If you feel your use of code examples falls outside fair use or the permission given above, feel free to contact us at *permissions@oreilly.com*.

How to Contact Us

Please address comments and questions concerning this book to the publisher:

O'Reilly Media, Inc.
1005 Gravenstein Highway North
Sebastopol, CA 95472
800-998-9938 (in the United States or Canada)
707-829-0515 (international or local)
707 829-0104 (fax)

We have a web page for this book, where we list errata, examples, and any additional information. You can access this page at:

http://www.oreilly.com/catalog/9780596516178

To comment or ask technical questions about this book, send email to:

bookquestions@oreilly.com

For more information about our books, conferences, Resource Centers, and the O'Reilly Network, see our web site at:

http://www.oreilly.com

Safari® Enabled

Safari When you see a Safari® Enabled icon on the cover of your favorite tech-
Books Online nology book, that means the book is available online through the O'Reilly Network Safari Bookshelf.

Safari offers a solution that's better than e-books. It's a virtual library that lets you easily search thousands of top tech books, cut and paste code samples, download chapters, and find quick answers when you need the most accurate, current information. Try it for free at *http://safari.oreilly.com*.

## CHAPTER 1

Introduction

Ruby is a dynamic programming language with a complex but expressive grammar and a core class library with a rich and powerful API. Ruby draws inspiration from Lisp, Smalltalk, and Perl, but uses a grammar that is easy for C and Java™ programmers to learn. Ruby is a pure object-oriented language, but it is also suitable for procedural and functional programming styles. It includes powerful metaprogramming capabilities and can be used to create domain-specific languages or DSLs.

Matz on Ruby

Yukihiro Matsumoto, known as Matz to the English-speaking Ruby community, is the creator of Ruby and the author of *Ruby in a Nutshell* (O'Reilly) (which has been updated and expanded into the present book). He says:

> I knew many languages before I created Ruby, but I was never fully satisfied with them. They were uglier, tougher, more complex, or more simple than I expected. I wanted to create my own language that satisfied me, as a programmer. I knew a lot about the language's target audience: myself. To my surprise, many programmers all over the world feel very much like I do. They feel happy when they discover and program in Ruby.

> Throughout the development of the Ruby language, I've focused my energies on making programming faster and easier. All features in Ruby, including object-oriented features, are designed to work as ordinary programmers (e.g., me) expect them to work. Most programmers feel it is elegant, easy to use, and a pleasure to program.

Matz's guiding philosophy for the design of Ruby is summarized in an oft-quoted remark of his:

> Ruby is designed to make programmers happy.

1.1 A Tour of Ruby

This section is a guided, but meandering, tour through some of the most interesting features of Ruby. Everything discussed here will be documented in detail later in the book, but this first look will give you the flavor of the language.

1.1.1 Ruby Is Object-Oriented

We'll begin with the fact that Ruby is a *completely* object-oriented language. Every value is an object, even simple numeric literals and the values true, false, and nil (nil is a special value that indicates the absence of value; it is Ruby's version of null). Here we invoke a method named class on these values. Comments begin with # in Ruby, and the => arrows in the comments indicate the value returned by the commented code (this is a convention used throughout this book):

```
1.class      # => Fixnum: the number 1 is a Fixnum
0.0.class    # => Float: floating-point numbers have class Float
```

```
true.class   # => TrueClass: true is a the singleton instance of TrueClass
false.class  # => FalseClass
nil.class    # => NilClass
```

In many languages, function and method invocations require parentheses, but there are no parentheses in any of the code above. In Ruby, parentheses are usually optional and they are commonly omitted, especially when the method being invoked takes no arguments. The fact that the parentheses are omitted in the method invocations here makes them look like references to named fields or named variables of the object. This is intentional, but the fact is, Ruby is very strict about encapsulation of its objects; there is no access to the internal state of an object from outside the object. Any such access must be mediated by an accessor method, such as the `class` method shown above.

1.1.2 Blocks and Iterators

The fact that we can invoke methods on integers isn't just an esoteric aspect of Ruby. It is actually something that Ruby programmers do with some frequency:

```
3.times { print "Ruby! " }    # Prints "Ruby! Ruby! Ruby! "
1.upto(9) {|x| print x }      # Prints "123456789"
```

`times` and `upto` are methods implemented by integer objects. They are a special kind of method known as an *iterator*, and they behave like loops. The code within curly braces —known as a *block*—is associated with the method invocation and serves as the body of the loop. The use of iterators and blocks is another notable feature of Ruby; although the language does support an ordinary `while` loop, it is more common to perform loops with constructs that are actually method calls.

Integers are not the only values that have iterator methods. Arrays (and similar "enumerable" objects) define an iterator named `each`, which invokes the associated block once for each element in the array. Each invocation of the block is passed a single element from the array:

```
a = [3, 2, 1]     # This is an array literal
a[3] = a[2] - 1   # Use square brackets to query and set array elements
a.each do |elt|   # each is an iterator. The block has a parameter elt
  print elt+1     # Prints "4321"
end               # This block was delimited with do/end instead of {}
```

Various other useful iterators are defined on top of `each`:

```
a = [1,2,3,4]              # Start with an array
b = a.map {|x| x*x }       # Square elements: b is [1,4,9,16]
c = a.select {|x| x%2==0 } # Select even elements: c is [2,4]
a.inject do |sum,x|        # Compute the sum of the elements => 10
  sum + x
end
```

Hashes, like arrays, are a fundamental data structure in Ruby. As their name implies, they are based on the hashtable data structure and serve to map arbitrary key objects to value objects. (To put this another way, we can say that a hash associates arbitrary value objects with key objects.) Hashes use square brackets, like arrays do, to query and set values in the hash. Instead of using an integer index, they expect key objects within the square brackets. Like the Array class, the Hash class also defines an each iterator method. This method invokes the associated block of code once for each key/value pair in the hash, and (this is where it differs from Array) passes both the key and the value as parameters to the block:

```ruby
h = {                   # A hash that maps number names to digits
  :one => 1,            # The "arrows" show mappings: key=>value
  :two => 2             # The colons indicate Symbol literals
}
h[:one]                 # => 1.  Access a value by key
h[:three] = 3           # Add a new key/value pair to the hash
h.each do |key,value|   # Iterate through the key/value pairs
  print "#{value}:#{key}; "   # Note variables substituted into string
end                     # Prints "1:one; 2:two; 3:three; "
```

Ruby's hashes can use any object as a key, but Symbol objects are the most commonly used. Symbols are immutable, interned strings. They can be compared by identity rather than by textual content (because two distinct Symbol objects will never have the same content).

The ability to associate a block of code with a method invocation is a fundamental and very powerful feature of Ruby. Although its most obvious use is for loop-like constructs, it is also useful for methods that only invoke the block once. For example:

```ruby
File.open("data.txt") do |f| # Open named file and pass stream to block
  line = f.readline            # Use the stream to read from the file
end                            # Stream automatically closed at block end

t = Thread.new do        # Run this block in a new thread
  File.read("data.txt")  # Read a file in the background
end                      # File contents available as thread value
```

As an aside, notice that the Hash.each example previously included this interesting line of code:

```ruby
print "#{value}:#{key}; "    # Note variables substituted into string
```

Double-quoted strings can include arbitrary Ruby expressions delimited by #{ and }. The value of the expression within these delimiters is converted to a string (by calling its to_s method, which is supported by all objects). The resulting string is then used to replace the expression text and its delimiters in the string literal. This substitution of expression values into strings is usually called *string interpolation*.

1.1.3 Expressions and Operators in Ruby

Ruby's syntax is expression-oriented. Control structures such as if that would be called statements in other languages are actually expressions in Ruby. They have values like other simpler expressions do, and we can write code like this:

```ruby
minimum = if x < y then x else y end
```

Although all "statements" in Ruby are actually expressions, they do not all return meaningful values. while loops and method definitions, for example, are expressions that normally return the value nil.

As in most languages, expressions in Ruby are usually built out of values and operators. For the most part, Ruby's operators will be familiar to anyone who knows C, Java, JavaScript, or any similar programming language. Here are examples of some commonplace and some more unusual Ruby operators:

```
1 + 2                   # => 3: addition
1 * 2                   # => 2: multiplication
1 + 2 == 3              # => true: == tests equality
2 ** 1024               # 2 to the power 1024: Ruby has arbitrary size ints
"Ruby" + " rocks!"      # => "Ruby rocks!": string concatenation
"Ruby! " * 3            # => "Ruby! Ruby! Ruby! ": string repetition
"%d %s" % [3, "rubies"] # => "3 rubies": Python-style, printf formatting
max = x > y ? x : y     # The conditional operator
```

Many of Ruby's operators are implemented as methods, and classes can define (or redefine) these methods however they want. (They can't define completely new operators, however; there is only a fixed set of recognized operators.) As examples, notice that the + and * operators behave differently for integers and strings. And you can define these operators any way you want in your own classes. The << operator is another good example. The integer classes Fixnum and Bignum use this operator for the bitwise left-shift operation, following the C programming language. At the same time (following C++), other classes—such as strings, arrays, and streams—use this operator for an append operation. If you create a new class that can have values appended to it in some way, it is a very good idea to define <<.

One of the most powerful operators to override is [ ]. The Array and Hash classes use this operator to access array elements by index and hash values by key. But you can define [ ] in your classes for any purpose you want. You can even define it as a method that expects multiple arguments, comma-separated between the square brackets. (The Array class accepts an index and a length between the square brackets to indicate a subarray or "slice" of the array.) And if you want to allow square brackets to be used on the lefthand side of an assignment expression, you can define the corresponding [ ]= operator. The value on the righthand side of the assignment will be passed as the final argument to the method that implements this operator.

1.1.4 Methods

Methods are defined with the def keyword. The return value of a method is the value of the last expression evaluated in its body:

```
def square(x)   # Define a method named square with one parameter x
  x*x           # Return x squared
end             # End of the method
```

When a method, like the one above, is defined outside of a class or a module, it is effectively a global function rather than a method to be invoked on an object. (Technically, however, a method like this becomes a private method of the Object class.) Methods can also be defined on individual objects by prefixing the name of the method with the object on which it is defined. Methods like these are known as *single-tonmethods*, and they are how Ruby defines class methods:

```
def Math.square(x)  # Define a class method of the Math module
  x*x
end
```

The Math module is part of the core Ruby library, and this code adds a new method to it. This is a key feature of Ruby—classes and modules are "open" and can be modified and extended at runtime.

Method parameters may have default values specified, and methods may accept arbitrary numbers of arguments.

1.1.5 Assignment

The (nonoverridable) = operator in Ruby assigns a value to a variable:

```
x = 1
```

Assignment can be combined with other operators such as + and -:

```
x += 1          # Increment x: note Ruby does not have ++.
y -= 1          # Decrement y: no -- operator, either.
```

Ruby supports parallel assignment, allowing more than one value and more than one variable in assignment expressions:

```
x, y = 1, 2     # Same as x = 1; y = 2
a, b = b, a     # Swap the value of two variables
x,y,z = [1,2,3] # Array elements automatically assigned to variables
```

Methods in Ruby are allowed to return more than one value, and parallel assignment is helpful in conjunction with such methods. For example:

```
# Define a method to convert Cartesian (x,y) coordinates to Polar
def polar(x,y)
  theta = Math.atan2(y,x)   # Compute the angle
  r = Math.hypot(x,y)       # Compute the distance
  [r, theta]                # The last expression is the return value
end

# Here's how we use this method with parallel assignment
distance, angle = polar(2,2)
```

Methods that end with an equals sign (=) are special because Ruby allows them to be invoked using assignment syntax. If an object o has a method named x=, then the following two lines of code do the very same thing:

```
o.x=(1)          # Normal method invocation syntax
o.x = 1          # Method invocation through assignment
```

1.1.6 Punctuation Suffixes and Prefixes

We saw previously that methods whose names end with = can be invoked by assignment expressions. Ruby methods can also end with a question mark or an exclamation point. A question mark is used to mark predicates—methods that return a Boolean value. For example, the `Array` and `Hash` classes both define methods named `empty?` that test whether the data structure has any elements. An exclamation mark at the end of a method name is used to indicate that caution is required with the use of the method. A number of core Ruby classes define pairs of methods with the same name, except that one ends with an exclamation mark and one does not. Usually, the method without the exclamation mark returns a modified copy of the object it is invoked on, and the one with the exclamation mark is a mutator method that alters the object in place. The `Array` class, for example, defines methods `sort` and `sort!`.

In addition to these punctuation characters at the end of method names, you'll notice punctuation characters at the start of Ruby variable names: global variables are prefixed with $, instance variables are prefixed with @, and class variables are prefixed with @@. These prefixes can take a little getting used to, but after a while you may come to appreciate the fact that the prefix tells you the scope of the variable. The prefixes are required in order to disambiguate Ruby's very flexible grammar. One way to think of variable prefixes is that they are one price we pay for being able to omit parentheses around method invocations.

1.1.7 Regexp and Range

We mentioned arrays and hashes earlier as fundamental data structures in Ruby. We demonstrated the use of numbers and strings as well. Two other datatypes are worth mentioning here. A `Regexp` (regular expression) object describes a textual pattern and has methods for determining whether a given string matches that pattern or not. And a `Range` represents the values (usually integers) between two endpoints. Regular expressions and ranges have a literal syntax in Ruby:

```
/[Rr]uby/        # Matches "Ruby" or "ruby"
/\d{5}/          # Matches 5 consecutive digits
1..3             # All x where 1 <= x <= 3
1...3            # All x where 1 <= x < 3
```

`Regexp` and `Range` objects define the normal == operator for testing equality. In addition, they also define the === operator for testing matching and membership. Ruby's `case` statement (like the `switch` statement of C or Java) matches its expression against each of the possible cases using ===, so this operator is often called the *case equality operator*. It leads to conditional tests like these:

```
# Determine US generation name based on birth year
# Case expression tests ranges with ===
generation = case birthyear
              when 1946..1963: "Baby Boomer"
              when 1964..1976: "Generation X"
              when 1978..2000: "Generation Y"
              else nil
              end

# A method to ask the user to confirm something
def are_you_sure?                    # Define a method. Note question mark!
  while true                         # Loop until we explicitly return
    print "Are you sure? [y/n]: "    # Ask the user a question
    response = gets                  # Get her answer
    case response                    # Begin case conditional
    when /^[yY]/                     # If response begins with y or Y
      return true                    # Return true from the method
    when /^[nN]/, /^$/               # If response begins with n,N or is empty
      return false                   # Return false
    end
  end
end
```

1.1.8 Classes and Modules

A class is a collection of related methods that operate on the state of an object. An object's state is held by its instance variables: variables whose names begin with @ and whose values are specific to that particular object. The following code defines an example class named Sequence and demonstrates how to write iterator methods and define operators:

```
#
# This class represents a sequence of numbers characterized by the three
# parameters from, to, and by. The numbers x in the sequence obey the
# following two constraints:
#
#    from <= x <= to
#    x = from + n*by, where n is an integer
#
class Sequence
  # This is an enumerable class; it defines an each iterator below.
  include Enumerable   # Include the methods of this module in this class

  # The initialize method is special; it is automatically invoked to
  # initialize newly created instances of the class
  def initialize(from, to, by)
    # Just save our parameters into instance variables for later use
    @from, @to, @by = from, to, by  # Note parallel assignment and @ prefix
  end

  # This is the iterator required by the Enumerable module
  def each
    x = @from      # Start at the starting point
    while x <= @to # While we haven't reached the end
```

```
      yield x          # Pass x to the block associated with the iterator
      x += @by         # Increment x
    end
  end

  # Define the length method (following arrays) to return the number of
  # values in the sequence
  def length
    return 0 if @from > @to      # Note if used as a statement modifier
    Integer((@to-@from)/@by) + 1 # Compute and return length of sequence
  end

  # Define another name for the same method.
  # It is common for methods to have multiple names in Ruby
  alias size length  # size is now a synonym for length

  # Override the array-access operator to give random access to the sequence
  def[](index)
    return nil if index < 0 # Return nil for negative indexes
    v = @from + index*@by   # Compute the value
    if v <= @to             # If it is part of the sequence
      v                     # Return it
    else                    # Otherwise...
      nil                   # Return nil
    end
  end

  # Override arithmetic operators to return new Sequence objects
  def *(factor)
    Sequence.new(@from*factor, @to*factor, @by*factor)
  end

  def +(offset)
    Sequence.new(@from+offset, @to+offset, @by)
  end
end
```

Here is some code that uses this **Sequence** class:

```
s = Sequence.new(1, 10, 2) # From 1 to 10 by 2's
s.each {|x| print x }      # Prints "13579"
print s[s.size-1]          # Prints 9
t = (s+1)*2                # From 4 to 22 by 4's
```

The key feature of our **Sequence** class is its **each** iterator. If we are only interested in the iterator method, there is no need to define the whole class. Instead, we can simply write an iterator method that accepts the **from**, **to**, and **by** parameters. Instead of making this a global function, let's define it in a module of its own:

```
module Sequences                # Begin a new module
  def self.fromtoby(from, to, by) # A singleton method of the module
    x = from
    while x <= to
      yield x
      x += by
    end
```

```
    end
  end
```

With the iterator defined this way, we write code like this:

```
Sequences.fromtoby(1, 10, 2) {|x| print x }  # Prints "13579"
```

An iterator like this makes it unnecessary to create a `Sequence` object to iterate a sequence of numbers. But the name of the method is quite long, and its invocation syntax is unsatisfying. What we really want is a way to iterate numeric `Range` objects by steps other than 1. One of the amazing features of Ruby is that its classes, even the built-in core classes, are *open*: any program can add methods to them. So we really can define a new iterator method for ranges:

```
class Range                     # Open an existing class for additions
  def by(step)                  # Define an iterator named by
    x = self.begin              # Start at one endpoint of the range
    if exclude_end?             # For ... ranges that exclude the end
      while x < self.end        # Test with the < operator
        yield x
        x += step
      end
    else                        # Otherwise, for .. ranges that include the end
      while x <= self.end       # Test with <= operator
        yield x
        x += step
      end
    end
  end                           # End of method definition
end                             # End of class modification

# Examples
(0..10).by(2) {|x| print x}   # Prints "0246810"
(0...10).by(2) {|x| print x}  # Prints "02468"
```

This `by` method is convenient but unnecessary; the `Range` class already defines an iterator named `step` that serves the same purpose. The core Ruby API is a rich one, and it is worth taking the time to study the platform (see Chapter 9) so you don't end up spending time writing methods that have already been implemented for you!

1.1.9 Ruby Surprises

Every language has features that trip up programmers who are new to the language. Here we describe two of Ruby's surprising features.

Ruby's strings are mutable, which may be surprising to Java programmers in particular. The []= operator allows you to alter the characters of a string or to insert, delete, and replace substrings. The << operator allows you to append to a string, and the `String` class defines various other methods that alter strings in place. Because strings are mutable, string literals in a program are not unique objects. If you include a string literal within a loop, it evaluates to a new object on each iteration of the loop. Call the freeze method on a string (or on any object) to prevent any future modifications to that object.

Ruby's conditionals and loops (such as if and while) evaluate conditional expressions to determine which branch to evaluate or whether to continue looping. Conditional expressions often evaluate to true or false, but this is not required. The value of nil is treated the same as false, and *any other value is the same as* true. This is likely to surprise C programmers who expect 0 to work like false, and JavaScript programmers who expect the empty string "" to be the same as false.

1.2 Try Ruby

We hope our tour of Ruby's key features has piqued your interest and you are eager to try Ruby out. To do that, you'll need a Ruby interpreter, and you'll also want to know how to use three tools—*irb*, *ri*, and *gem*—that are bundled with the interpreter. This section explains how to get and use them.

1.2.1 The Ruby Interpreter

The official web site for Ruby is *http://www.ruby-lang.org*. If Ruby is not already installed on your computer, you can follow the download link on the *ruby-lang.org* home page for instructions on downloading and installing the standard C-based reference implementation of Ruby.

Once you have Ruby installed, you can invoke the Ruby interpreter with the ruby command:

```
% ruby -e 'puts "hello world!"'
hello world!
```

The -e command-line option causes the interpreter to execute a single specified line of Ruby code. More commonly, you'd place your Ruby program in a file and tell the interpreter to invoke it:

```
% ruby hello.rb
hello world!
```

Other Ruby Implementations

In the absence of a formal specification for the Ruby language, the Ruby interpreter from *ruby-lang.org* is the reference implementation that defines the language. It is sometimes known as MRI, or "Matz's Ruby Implementation." For Ruby 1.9, the original MRI interpreter was merged with YARV ("Yet Another Ruby Virtual machine") to produce a new reference implementation that performs internal compilation to bytecode and then executes that bytecode on a virtual machine.

The reference implementation is not the only one available, however. At the time of this writing, there is one alternative implementation (JRuby) released and several other implementations under development:

JRuby

> JRuby is a Java-based implementation of Ruby, available from *http://jruby.org*. At the time of this writing, the current release is JRuby 1.1, which is compatible with Ruby 1.8. A 1.9-compatible release of JRuby may be available by the time you read this. JRuby is open source software, developed primarily at Sun Microsystems.

IronRuby

> IronRuby is Microsoft's implementation of Ruby for their .NET framework and DLR (Dynamic Language Runtime). The source code for IronRuby is available under the Microsoft Permissive License. At the time of this writing, IronRuby is not yet at a 1.0 release level. The project home page is *http://www.ironruby.net*.

Rubinius

> Rubinius is an open source project that describes itself as "an alternative Ruby implementation written largely in Ruby. The Rubinius virtual machine, named shotgun, is based loosely on the Smalltalk-80 VM architecture." At the time of this writing, Rubinius is not at version 1.0. The home page for the Rubinius project is *http://rubini.us*.

Cardinal

> Cardinal is a Ruby implementation intended to run on the Parrot VM (which aims to power Perl 6 and a number of other dynamic languages). At the time of this writing, neither Parrot nor Cardinal have released a 1.0 version. Cardinal does not have its own home page; it is hosted as part of the open source Parrot project at *http://www.parrotcode.org*.

1.2.2 Displaying Output

In order to try out Ruby features, you need a way to display output so that your test programs can print their results. The `puts` function—used in the "hello world" code earlier—is one way to do this. Loosely speaking, `puts` prints a string of text to the console and appends a newline (unless the string already ends with one). If passed an object that is not a string, `puts` calls the `to_s` method of that object and prints the string returned by that method. `print` does more or less the same thing, but it does not append a newline. For example, type the following two-line program in a text editor and save it in a file named *count.rb*:

```
9.downto(1) {|n| print n }    # No newline between numbers
puts " blastoff!"             # End with a newline
```

Now run the program with your Ruby interpreter:

```
% ruby count.rb
```

It should produce the following output:

```
987654321 blastoff!
```

You may find the function `p` to be a useful alternative to `puts`. Not only is it shorter to type, but it converts objects to strings with the `inspect` method, which sometimes returns more programmer-friendly representations than to_s does. When printing an array, for example, p outputs it using array literal notation, whereas puts simply prints each element of the array on a line by itself.

1.2.3 Interactive Ruby with irb

irb (short for "interactive Ruby") is a Ruby shell. Type any Ruby expression at its prompt and it will evaluate it and display its value for you. This is often the easiest way to try out the language features you read about in this book. Here is an example *irb* session, with annotations:

```
$ irb --simple-prompt     # Start irb from the terminal
>> 2**3                   # Try exponentiation
=> 8                      # This is the result
>> "Ruby! " * 3           # Try string repetition
=> "Ruby! Ruby! Ruby! "   # The result
>> 1.upto(3){|x| puts x } # Try an iterator
1                         # Three lines of output
2                         # Because we called puts 3 times
3
=> 1                      # The return value of 1.upto(3)
>> quit                   # Exit irb
$                         # Back to the terminal prompt
```

This example session shows you all you need to know about *irb* to make productive use of it while exploring Ruby. It does have a number of other important features, however, including subshells (type "irb" at the prompt to start a subshell) and configurability.

1.2.4 Viewing Ruby Documentation with ri

Another critical Ruby tool is the *ri*[*] documentation viewer. Invoke *ri* on the command line followed by the name of a Ruby class, module, or method, and *ri* will display documentation for you. You may specify a method name without a qualifying class or module name, but this will just show you a list of all methods by that name (unless the method is unique). Normally, you can separate a class or module name from a method name with a period. If a class defines a class method and an instance method by the same name, you must instead use :: to refer to the class method or # to refer to the instance method. Here are some example invocations of *ri*:

```
ri Array
ri Array.sort
ri Hash#each
ri Math::sqrt
```

---

[*] Opinions differ as to what "ri" stands for. It has been called "Ruby Index," "Ruby Information," and "Ruby Interactive."

This documentation displayed by *ri* is extracted from specially formatted comments in Ruby source code. See §2.1.1.2 for details.

1.2.5 Ruby Package Management with gem

Ruby's package management system is known as RubyGems, and packages or modules distributed using RubyGems are called "gems." RubyGems makes it easy to install Ruby software and can automatically manage complex dependencies between packages.

The frontend script for RubyGems is *gem*, and it's distributed with Ruby 1.9 just as *irb* and *ri* are. In Ruby 1.8, you must install it separately—see *http://rubygems.org*. Once the *gem* program is installed, you might use it like this:

```
# gem install rails
Successfully installed activesupport-1.4.4
Successfully installed activerecord-1.15.5
Successfully installed actionpack-1.13.5
Successfully installed actionmailer-1.3.5
Successfully installed actionwebservice-1.2.5
Successfully installed rails-1.2.5
6 gems installed
Installing ri documentation for activesupport-1.4.4...
Installing ri documentation for activerecord-1.15.5...
...etc...
```

As you can see, the `gem install` command installs the most recent version of the gem you request and also installs any gems that the requested gem requires. *gem* has other useful subcommands as well. Some examples:

```
gem list              # List installed gems
gem enviroment        # Display RubyGems configuration information
gem update rails      # Update a named gem
gem update            # Update all installed gems
gem update --system   # Update RubyGems itself
gem uninstall rails   # Remove an installed gem
```

In Ruby 1.8, the gems you install cannot be automatically loaded by Ruby's `require` method. (See §7.6 for more about loading modules of Ruby code with the `require` method.) If you're writing a program that will be using modules installed as gems, you must first require the `rubygems` module. Some Ruby 1.8 distributions are preconfigured with the RubyGems library, but you may need to download and install this manually. Loading this `rubygems` module alters the `require` method itself so that it searches the set of installed gems before it searches the standard library. You can also automatically enable RubyGems support by running Ruby with the `-rubygems` command-line option. And if you add `-rubygems` to the `RUBYOPT` environment variable, then the RubyGems library will be loaded on every invocation of Ruby.

The `rubygems` module is part of the standard library in Ruby 1.9, but it is no longer required to load gems. Ruby 1.9 knows how to find installed gems on its own, and you do not have to put `require 'rubygems'` in your programs that use gems.

When you load a gem with `require` (in either 1.8 or 1.9), it loads the most recent installed version of the gem you specify. If you have more specific version requirements, you can use the `gem` method before calling `require`. This finds a version of the gem matching the version constraints you specify and "activates" it, so that a subsequent `require` will load that version:

```
require 'rubygems'             # Not necessary in Ruby 1.9
gem 'RedCloth', '> 2.0', '< 4.0' # Activate RedCloth version 2.x or 3.x
require 'RedCloth'             # And now load it
```

You'll find more about `require` and gems in §7.6.1. Complete coverage of RubyGems, the *gem* program, and the `rubygems` module are beyond the scope of this book. The `gem` command is self-documenting—start by running `gem help`. For details on the `gem` method, try `ri gem`. And for complete details, see the documentation at *http://ruby gems.org*.

1.2.6 More Ruby Tutorials

This chapter began with a tutorial introduction to the Ruby language. You can try out the code snippets of that tutorial using *irb*. If you want more tutorials before diving into the language more formally, there are two good ones available by following links on the *http://www.ruby-lang.org* home page. One *irb*-based tutorial is called "Ruby in Twenty Minutes."[*] Another tutorial, called "Try Ruby!", is interesting because it works in your web browser and does not require you to have Ruby or *irb* installed on your system.[†]

1.2.7 Ruby Resources

The Ruby web site (*http://www.ruby-lang.org*) is the place to find links to other Ruby resources, such as online documentation, libraries, mailing lists, blogs, IRC channels, user groups, and conferences. Try the "Documentation," "Libraries," and "Community" links on the home page.

1.3 About This Book

As its title implies, this book covers the Ruby programming language and aspires to do so comprehensively and accessibly. This edition of the book covers language versions 1.8 and 1.9. Ruby blurs the distinction between language and platform, and so our coverage of the language includes a detailed overview of the core Ruby API. But this book is not an API reference and does not cover the core classes comprehensively. Also,

---

[*] At the time of this writing, the direct URL for this tutorial is *http://www.ruby-lang.org/en/documentation/quickstart/*.

[†] If you can't find the "Try Ruby!" link on the Ruby home page, try this URL: *http://tryruby.hobix.com*.

this is not a book about Ruby frameworks (like Rails), nor a book about Ruby tools (like *rake* and *gem*).

This chapter concludes with a heavily commented extended example demonstrating a nontrivial Ruby program. The chapters that follow cover Ruby from the bottom up:

- Chapter 2 covers the lexical and syntactic structure of Ruby, including basic issues like character set, case sensitivity, and reserved words.

- Chapter 3 explains the kinds of data—numbers, strings, ranges, arrays, and so on —that Ruby programs can manipulate, and it covers the basic features of all Ruby objects.

- Chapter 4 covers primary expressions in Ruby—literals, variable references, *method* invocations, and assignments—and it explains the operators used to combine primary expressions into compound expressions.

- Chapter 5 explains conditionals, loops (including blocks and iterator methods), exceptions, and the other Ruby expressions that would be called statements or control structures in other languages.

- Chapter 6 formally documents Ruby's method definition and invocation syntax, and it also covers the invocable objects known as procs and lambdas. This chapter includes an explanation of closures and an exploration of functional programming techniques in Ruby.

- Chapter 7 explains how to define classes and modules in Ruby. Classes are fundamental to object-oriented programming, and this chapter also covers topics such as inheritance, method visibility, mixin modules, and the method name resolution algorithm.

- Chapter 8 covers Ruby's APIs that allow a program to inspect and manipulate itself, and then demonstrates metaprogramming techniques that use those APIs to make programming easier. The chapter includes an example of domain-specific language.

- Chapter 9 demonstrates the most important classes and methods of the core Ruby platform with simple code fragments. This is not a reference but a detailed overview of the core classes. Topics include text processing, numeric computation, collections (such as arrays and hashes), input/output, networking, and threads. After reading this chapter, you'll understand the breadth of the Ruby platform, and you'll be able to use the *ri* tool or an online reference to explore the platform in depth.

- Chapter 10 covers the top-level Ruby programming environment, including global variables and global functions, command-line arguments supported by the Ruby interpreter, and Ruby's security mechanism.

1.3.1 How to Read This Book

It is easy to program in Ruby, but Ruby is not a simple language. Because this book documents Ruby comprehensively, it is not a simple book (though we hope that you find it easy to read and understand). It is intended for experienced programmers who want to master Ruby and are willing to read carefully and thoughtfully to achieve that goal.

Like all similar programming books, this book contains forward and backward references throughout. Programming languages are not linear systems, and it is impossible to document them linearly. As you can see from the chapter outline, this book takes a bottom-up approach to Ruby: it starts with the simplest elements of Ruby's grammar and moves on to document successively higher-level syntactic structures—from tokens to values to expressions and control structures to methods and classes. This is a classic approach to documenting programming languages, but it does not avoid the problem of forward references.

The book is intended to be read in the order it is written, but some advanced topics are best skimmed or skipped on the first reading; they will make much more sense when you come back to them after having read the chapters that follow. On the other hand, don't let every forward reference scare you off. Many of them are simply informative, letting you know that more details will be presented later. The reference does not necessarily imply that those future details are required to understand the current material.

1.4 A Sudoku Solver in Ruby

This chapter concludes with a nontrivial Ruby application to give you a better idea of what Ruby programs actually look like. We've chosen a Sudoku[*] solver as a good short to medium-length program that demonstrates a number of features of Ruby. Don't expect to understand every detail of Example 1-1, but do read through the code; it is very thoroughly commented, and you should have little difficulty following along.

Example 1-1. A Sudoku solver in Ruby

```
#
# This module defines a Sudoku::Puzzle class to represent a 9x9
# Sudoku puzzle and also defines exception classes raised for
# invalid input and over-constrained puzzles. This module also defines
# the method Sudoku.solve to solve a puzzle. The solve method uses
# the Sudoku.scan method, which is also defined here.
#
# Use this module to solve Sudoku puzzles with code like this:
```

---

[*] Sudoku is a logic puzzle that takes the form of a 9 × 9 grid of numbers and blank squares. The task is to fill each blank with a digit 1 to 9 so that no row or column or 3 × 3 subgrid includes the same digit twice. Sudoku has been popular in Japan for some time, but it gained sudden popularity in the English-speaking world in 2004 and 2005. If you are unfamiliar with Sudoku, try reading the Wikipedia entry (*http://en.wikipedia.org/ wiki/Sudoku*) and try an online puzzle (*http://websudoku.com/*).

```
#
# require 'sudoku'
# puts Sudoku.solve(Sudoku::Puzzle.new(ARGF.readlines))
#
module Sudoku

  #
  # The Sudoku::Puzzle class represents the state of a 9x9 Sudoku puzzle.
  #
  # Some definitions and terminology used in this implementation:
  #
  # - Each element of a puzzle is called a "cell".
  # - Rows and columns are numbered from 0 to 8, and the coordinates [0,0]
  #   refer to the cell in the upper-left corner of the puzzle.
  # - The nine 3x3 subgrids are known as "boxes" and are also numbered from
  #   0 to 8, ordered from left to right and top to bottom. The box in
  #   the upper-left is box 0. The box in the upper-right is box 2. The
  #   box in the middle is box 4. The box in the lower-right is box 8.
  #
  # Create a new puzzle with Sudoku::Puzzle.new, specifying the initial
  # state as a string or as an array of strings. The string(s) should use
  # the characters 1 through 9 for the given values, and '.' for cells
  # whose value is unspecified. Whitespace in the input is ignored.
  #
  # Read and write access to individual cells of the puzzle is through the
  # [] and []= operators, which expect two-dimensional [row,column] indexing.
  # These methods use numbers (not characters) 0 to 9 for cell contents.
  # 0 represents an unknown value.
  #
  # The has_duplicates? predicate returns true if the puzzle is invalid
  # because any row, column, or box includes the same digit twice.
  #
  # The each_unknown method is an iterator that loops through the cells of
  # the puzzle and invokes the associated block once for each cell whose
  # value is unknown.
  #
  # The possible method returns an array of integers in the range 1..9.
  # The elements of the array are the only values allowed in the specified
  # cell. If this array is empty, then the puzzle is over-specified and
  # cannot be solved. If the array has only one element, then that element
  # must be the value for that cell of the puzzle.
  #
  class Puzzle

    # These constants are used for translating between the external
    # string representation of a puzzle and the internal representation.
    ASCII = ".123456789"
    BIN = "\000\001\002\003\004\005\006\007\010\011"

    # This is the initialization method for the class. It is automatically
    # invoked on new Puzzle instances created with Puzzle.new. Pass the input
    # puzzle as an array of lines or as a single string. Use ASCII digits 1
    # to 9 and use the '.' character for unknown cells. Whitespace,
    # including newlines, will be stripped.
    def initialize(lines)
```

```ruby
  if (lines.respond_to? :join)    # If argument looks like an array of lines
    s = lines.join                # Then join them into a single string
  else                            # Otherwise, assume we have a string
    s = lines.dup                 # And make a private copy of it
  end

  # Remove whitespace (including newlines) from the data
  # The '!' in gsub! indicates that this is a mutator method that
  # alters the string directly rather than making a copy.
  s.gsub!(/\s/, "")   # /\s/ is a Regexp that matches any whitespace

  # Raise an exception if the input is the wrong size.
  # Note that we use unless instead of if, and use it in modifier form.
  raise Invalid, "Grid is the wrong size" unless s.size == 81

  # Check for invalid characters, and save the location of the first.
  # Note that we assign and test the value assigned at the same time.
  if i = s.index(/[^123456789\.]/)
    # Include the invalid character in the error message.
    # Note the Ruby expression inside #{} in string literal.
    raise Invalid, "Illegal character #{s[i,1]} in puzzle"
  end

  # The following two lines convert our string of ASCII characters
  # to an array of integers, using two powerful String methods.
  # The resulting array is stored in the instance variable @grid
  # The number 0 is used to represent an unknown value.
  s.tr!(ASCII, BIN)     # Translate ASCII characters into bytes
  @grid = s.unpack('c*') # Now unpack the bytes into an array of numbers

  # Make sure that the rows, columns, and boxes have no duplicates.
  raise Invalid, "Initial puzzle has duplicates" if has_duplicates?
end

# Return the state of the puzzle as a string of 9 lines with 9
# characters (plus newline) each.
def to_s
  # This method is implemented with a single line of Ruby magic that
  # reverses the steps in the initialize() method. Writing dense code
  # like this is probably not good coding style, but it demonstrates
  # the power and expressiveness of the language.
  #
  # Broken down, the line below works like this:
  # (0..8).collect invokes the code in curly braces 9 times--once
  # for each row--and collects the return value of that code into an
  # array. The code in curly braces takes a subarray of the grid
  # representing a single row and packs its numbers into a string.
  # The join() method joins the elements of the array into a single
  # string with newlines between them. Finally, the tr() method
  # translates the binary string representation into ASCII digits.
  (0..8).collect{|r| @grid[r*9,9].pack('c9')}.join("\n").tr(BIN,ASCII)
end

# Return a duplicate of this Puzzle object.
# This method overrides Object.dup to copy the @grid array.
```

```ruby
def dup
  copy = super          # Make a shallow copy by calling Object.dup
  @grid = @grid.dup     # Make a new copy of the internal data
  copy                  # Return the copied object
end

# We override the array access operator to allow access to the
# individual cells of a puzzle. Puzzles are two-dimensional,
# and must be indexed with row and column coordinates.
def [](row, col)
  # Convert two-dimensional (row,col) coordinates into a one-dimensional
  # array index and get and return the cell value at that index
  @grid[row*9 + col]
end

# This method allows the array access operator to be used on the
# lefthand side of an assignment operation. It sets the value of
# the cell at (row, col) to newvalue.
def []=(row, col, newvalue)
  # Raise an exception unless the new value is in the range 0 to 9.
  unless (0..9).include? newvalue
    raise Invalid, "illegal cell value"
  end
  # Set the appropriate element of the internal array to the value.
  @grid[row*9 + col] = newvalue
end

# This array maps from one-dimensional grid index to box number.
# It is used in the method below. The name BoxOfIndex begins with a
# capital letter, so this is a constant. Also, the array has been
# frozen, so it cannot be modified.
BoxOfIndex = [
  0,0,0,1,1,1,2,2,2,0,0,0,1,1,1,2,2,2,0,0,0,1,1,1,2,2,2,
  3,3,3,4,4,4,5,5,5,3,3,3,4,4,4,5,5,5,3,3,3,4,4,4,5,5,5,
  6,6,6,7,7,7,8,8,8,6,6,6,7,7,7,8,8,8,6,6,6,7,7,7,8,8,8
].freeze

# This method defines a custom looping construct (an "iterator") for
# Sudoku puzzles.  For each cell whose value is unknown, this method
# passes ("yields") the row number, column number, and box number to the
# block associated with this iterator.
def each_unknown
  0.upto 8 do |row|                       # For each row
    0.upto 8 do |col|                     # For each column
      index = row*9+col                   # Cell index for (row,col)
      next if @grid[index] != 0           # Move on if we know the cell's value
      box = BoxOfIndex[index]             # Figure out the box for this cell
      yield row, col, box                 # Invoke the associated block
    end
  end
end

# Returns true if any row, column, or box has duplicates.
# Otherwise returns false. Duplicates in rows, columns, or boxes are not
# allowed in Sudoku, so a return value of true means an invalid puzzle.
```

```ruby
def has_duplicates?
  # uniq! returns nil if all the elements in an array are unique.
  # So if uniq! returns something then the board has duplicates.
  0.upto(8) {|row| return true if rowdigits(row).uniq! }
  0.upto(8) {|col| return true if coldigits(col).uniq! }
  0.upto(8) {|box| return true if boxdigits(box).uniq! }

  false  # If all the tests have passed, then the board has no duplicates
end


# This array holds a set of all Sudoku digits. Used below.
AllDigits = [1, 2, 3, 4, 5, 6, 7, 8, 9].freeze

# Return an array of all values that could be placed in the cell
# at (row,col) without creating a duplicate in the row, column, or box.
# Note that the + operator on arrays does concatenation but that the -
# operator performs a set difference operation.
def possible(row, col, box)
  AllDigits - (rowdigits(row) + coldigits(col) + boxdigits(box))
end


private  # All methods after this line are private to the class

# Return an array of all known values in the specified row.
def rowdigits(row)
  # Extract the subarray that represents the row and remove all zeros.
  # Array subtraction is set difference, with duplicate removal.
  @grid[row*9,9] - [0]
end

# Return an array of all known values in the specified column.
def coldigits(col)
  result = []              # Start with an empty array
  col.step(80, 9) {|i|     # Loop from col by nines up to 80
    v = @grid[i]           # Get value of cell at that index
    result << v if (v != 0) # Add it to the array if non-zero
  }
  result                   # Return the array
end

# Map box number to the index of the upper-left corner of the box.
BoxToIndex = [0, 3, 6, 27, 30, 33, 54, 57, 60].freeze

# Return an array of all the known values in the specified box.
def boxdigits(b)
  # Convert box number to index of upper-left corner of the box.
  i = BoxToIndex[b]
  # Return an array of values, with 0 elements removed.
  [
    @grid[i],    @grid[i+1],  @grid[i+2],
    @grid[i+9],  @grid[i+10], @grid[i+11],
    @grid[i+18], @grid[i+19], @grid[i+20]
  ] - [0]
end
end  # This is the end of the Puzzle class
```

```ruby
# An exception of this class indicates invalid input,
class Invalid < StandardError
end

# An exception of this class indicates that a puzzle is over-constrained
# and that no solution is possible.
class Impossible < StandardError
end

#
# This method scans a Puzzle, looking for unknown cells that have only
# a single possible value. If it finds any, it sets their value. Since
# setting a cell alters the possible values for other cells, it
# continues scanning until it has scanned the entire puzzle without
# finding any cells whose value it can set.
#
# This method returns three values. If it solves the puzzle, all three
# values are nil. Otherwise, the first two values returned are the row and
# column of a cell whose value is still unknown. The third value is the
# set of values possible at that row and column. This is a minimal set of
# possible values: there is no unknown cell in the puzzle that has fewer
# possible values. This complex return value enables a useful heuristic
# in the solve() method: that method can guess at values for cells where
# the guess is most likely to be correct.
#
# This method raises Impossible if it finds a cell for which there are
# no possible values. This can happen if the puzzle is over-constrained,
# or if the solve() method below has made an incorrect guess.
#
# This method mutates the specified Puzzle object in place.
# If has_duplicates? is false on entry, then it will be false on exit.
#
def Sudoku.scan(puzzle)
  unchanged = false  # This is our loop variable

  # Loop until we've scanned the whole board without making a change.
  until unchanged
    unchanged = true        # Assume no cells will be changed this time
    rmin,cmin,pmin = nil    # Track cell with minimal possible set
    min = 10                # More than the maximal number of possibilities

    # Loop through cells whose value is unknown.
    puzzle.each_unknown do |row, col, box|
      # Find the set of values that could go in this cell
      p = puzzle.possible(row, col, box)

      # Branch based on the size of the set p.
      # We care about 3 cases: p.size==0, p.size==1, and p.size > 1.
      case p.size
      when 0  # No possible values means the puzzle is over-constrained
        raise Impossible
      when 1  # We've found a unique value, so set it in the grid
        puzzle[row,col] = p[0] # Set that position on the grid to the value
        unchanged = false       # Note that we've made a change
```

```ruby
        else   # For any other number of possibilities
          # Keep track of the smallest set of possibilities.
          # But don't bother if we're going to repeat this loop.
          if unchanged && p.size < min
            min = p.size            # Current smallest size
            rmin, cmin, pmin = row, col, p  # Note parallel assignment
          end
        end
      end
    end
  end

  # Return the cell with the minimal set of possibilities.
  # Note multiple return values.
  return rmin, cmin, pmin
end

# Solve a Sudoku puzzle using simple logic, if possible, but fall back
# on brute-force when necessary. This is a recursive method. It either
# returns a solution or raises an exception. The solution is returned
# as a new Puzzle object with no unknown cells. This method does not
# modify the Puzzle it is passed. Note that this method cannot detect
# an under-constrained puzzle.
def Sudoku.solve(puzzle)
  # Make a private copy of the puzzle that we can modify.
  puzzle = puzzle.dup

  # Use logic to fill in as much of the puzzle as we can.
  # This method mutates the puzzle we give it, but always leaves it valid.
  # It returns a row, a column, and set of possible values at that cell.
  # Note parallel assignment of these return values to three variables.
  r,c,p = scan(puzzle)

  # If we solved it with logic, return the solved puzzle.
  return puzzle if r == nil

  # Otherwise, try each of the values in p for cell [r,c].
  # Since we're picking from a set of possible values, the guess leaves
  # the puzzle in a valid state. The guess will either lead to a solution
  # or to an impossible puzzle. We'll know we have an impossible
  # puzzle if a recursive call to scan throws an exception. If this happens
  # we need to try another guess, or re-raise an exception if we've tried
  # all the options we've got.
  p.each do |guess|       # For each value in the set of possible values
    puzzle[r,c] = guess    # Guess the value

    begin
      # Now try (recursively) to solve the modified puzzle.
      # This recursive invocation will call scan() again to apply logic
      # to the modified board, and will then guess another cell if needed.
      # Remember that solve() will either return a valid solution or
      # raise an exception.
      return solve(puzzle)  # If it returns, we just return the solution
    rescue Impossible
      next                  # If it raises an exception, try the next guess
    end
```

```
    end

    # If we get here, then none of our guesses worked out
    # so we must have guessed wrong sometime earlier.
    raise Impossible
  end
end
```

Example 1-1 is 345 lines long. Because the example was written for this introductory chapter, it has particularly verbose comments. Strip away the comments and the blank lines and you're left with just 129 lines of code, which is pretty good for an object-oriented Sudoku solver that does not rely on a simple brute-force algorithm. We hope that this example demonstrates the power and expressiveness of Ruby.

## CHAPTER 2

The Structure and Execution of Ruby Programs

This chapter explains the structure of Ruby programs. It starts with the lexical structure, covering tokens and the characters that comprise them. Next, it covers the syntactic structure of a Ruby program, explaining how expressions, control structures, methods, classes, and so on are written as a series of tokens. Finally, the chapter describes files of Ruby code, explaining how Ruby programs can be split across multiple files and how the Ruby interpreter executes a file of Ruby code.

2.1 Lexical Structure

The Ruby interpreter parses a program as a sequence of *tokens*. Tokens include comments, literals, punctuation, identifiers, and keywords. This section introduces these types of tokens and also includes important information about the characters that comprise the tokens and the whitespace that separates the tokens.

2.1.1 Comments

Comments in Ruby begin with a # character and continue to the end of the line. The Ruby interpreter ignores the # character and any text that follows it (but does not ignore the newline character, which is meaningful whitespace and may serve as a statement terminator). If a # character appears within a string or regular expression literal (see Chapter 3), then it is simply part of the string or regular expression and does not introduce a comment:

```
# This entire line is a comment
x = "#This is a string"            # And this is a comment
y = /#This is a regular expression/  # Here's another comment
```

Multiline comments are usually written simply by beginning each line with a separate # character:

```
#
# This class represents a Complex number
# Despite its name, it is not complex at all.
#
```

Note that Ruby has no equivalent of the C-style /*...*/ comment. There is no way to embed a comment in the middle of a line of code.

2.1.1.1 Embedded documents

Ruby supports another style of multiline comment known as an *embedded document*. These start on a line that begins =begin and continue until (and include) a line that begins =end. Any text that appears after =begin or =end is part of the comment and is also ignored, but that extra text must be separated from the =begin and =end by at least one space.

Embedded documents are a convenient way to comment out long blocks of code without prefixing each line with a # character:

```
=begin Someone needs to fix the broken code below!
    Any code here is commented out
=end
```

Note that embedded documents only work if the = signs are the first characters of each line:

```
# =begin This used to begin a comment. Now it is itself commented out!
    The code that goes here is no longer commented out
# =end
```

As their name implies, embedded documents can be used to include long blocks of documentation within a program, or to embed source code of another language (such as HTML or SQL) within a Ruby program. Embedded documents are usually intended to be used by some kind of postprocessing tool that is run over the Ruby source code, and it is typical to follow =begin with an identifier that indicates which tool the comment is intended for.

2.1.1.2 Documentation comments

Ruby programs can include embedded API documentation as specially formatted comments that precede method, class, and module definitions. You can browse this documentation using the *ri* tool described earlier in §1.2.4. The *rdoc* tool extracts documentation comments from Ruby source and formats them as HTML or prepares them for display by *ri*. Documentation of the *rdoc* tool is beyond the scope of this book; see the file *lib/rdoc/README* in the Ruby source code for details.

Documentation comments must come immediately before the module, class, or method whose API they document. They are usually written as multiline comments where each line begins with #, but they can also be written as embedded documents that start =begin rdoc. (The *rdoc* tool will not process these comments if you leave out the "rdoc".)

The following example comment demonstrates the most important formatting elements of the markup grammar used in Ruby's documentation comments; a detailed description of the grammar is available in the *README* file mentioned previously:

```
#
# Rdoc comments use a simple markup grammar like those used in wikis.
#
# Separate paragraphs with a blank line.
#
# = Headings
#
# Headings begin with an equals sign
#
# == Sub-Headings
# The line above produces a subheading.
# === Sub-Sub-Heading
# And so on.
#
# = Examples
```

```
#
#   Indented lines are displayed verbatim in code font.
#     Be careful not to indent your headings and lists, though.
#
# = Lists and Fonts
#
# List items begin with * or -. Indicate fonts with punctuation or HTML:
# * _italic_ or <i>multi-word italic</i>
# * *bold* or <b>multi-word bold</b>
# * +code+ or <tt>multi-word code</tt>
#
# 1. Numbered lists begin with numbers.
# 99. Any number will do; they don't have to be sequential.
# 1. There is no way to do nested lists.
#
# The terms of a description list are bracketed:
# [item 1]  This is a description of item 1
# [item 2]  This is a description of item 2
#
```

2.1.2 Literals

Literals are values that appear directly in Ruby source code. They include numbers, strings of text, and regular expressions. (Other literals, such as array and hash values, are not individual tokens but are more complex expressions.) Ruby number and string literal syntax is actually quite complicated, and is covered in detail in Chapter 3. For now, an example suffices to illustrate what Ruby literals look like:

```
1                    # An integer literal
1.0                  # A floating-point literal
'one'                # A string literal
"two"                # Another string literal
/three/              # A regular expression literal
```

2.1.3 Punctuation

Ruby uses punctuation characters for a number of purposes. Most Ruby operators are written using punctuation characters, such as + for addition, * for multiplication, and || for the Boolean OR operation. See §4.6 for a complete list of Ruby operators. Punctuation characters also serve to delimit string, regular expression, array, and hash literals, and to group and separate expressions, method arguments, and array indexes. We'll see miscellaneous other uses of punctuation scattered throughout Ruby syntax.

2.1.4 Identifiers

An *identifier* is simply a name. Ruby uses identifiers to name variables, methods, classes, and so forth. Ruby identifiers consist of letters, numbers, and underscore characters, but they may not begin with a number. Identifiers may not include whitespace or nonprinting characters, and they may not include punctuation characters except as described here.

Identifiers that begin with a capital letter A–Z are constants, and the Ruby interpreter will issue a warning (but not an error) if you alter the value of such an identifier. Class and module names must begin with initial capital letters. The following are identifiers:

```
i
x2
old_value
_internal    # Identifiers may begin with underscores
PI           # Constant
```

By convention, multiword identifiers that are not constants are written with underscores like_this, whereas multiword constants are written LikeThis or LIKE_THIS.

2.1.4.1 Case sensitivity

Ruby is a case-sensitive language. Lowercase letters and uppercase letters are distinct. The keyword end, for example, is completely different from the keyword END.

2.1.4.2 Unicode characters in identifiers

Ruby's rules for forming identifiers are defined in terms of ASCII characters that are not allowed. In general, all characters outside of the ASCII character set are valid in identifiers, including characters that appear to be punctuation. In a UTF-8 encoded file, for example, the following Ruby code is valid:

```
def ×(x,y)  # The name of this method is the Unicode multiplication sign
   x*y      # The body of this method multiplies its arguments
end
```

Similarly, a Japanese programmer writing a program encoded in SJIS or EUC can include Kanji characters in her identifiers. See §2.4.1 for more about writing Ruby programs using encodings other than ASCII.

The special rules about forming identifiers are based on ASCII characters and are not enforced for characters outside of that set. An identifier may not begin with an ASCII digit, for example, but it may begin with a digit from a non-Latin alphabet. Similarly, an identifier must begin with an ASCII capital letter in order to be considered a constant. The identifier Å, for example, is not a constant.

Two identifiers are the same only if they are represented by the same sequence of bytes. Some character sets, such as Unicode, have more than one codepoint that represents the same character. No Unicode normalization is performed in Ruby, and two distinct codepoints are treated as distinct characters, even if they have the same meaning or are represented by the same font glyph.

2.1.4.3 Punctuation in identifiers

Punctuation characters may appear at the start and end of Ruby identifiers. They have the following meanings:

$ Global variables are prefixed with a dollar sign. Following Perl's example, Ruby defines a number of global variables that include other punctuation characters, such as $_ and $-K. See Chapter 10 for a list of these special globals.

@   Instance variables are prefixed with a single at sign, and class variables are prefixed with two at signs. Instance variables and class variables are explained in Chapter 7.

?   As a helpful convention, methods that return Boolean values often have names that end with a question mark.

!   Method names may end with an exclamation point to indicate that they should be used cautiously. This naming convention is often to distinguish mutator methods that alter the object on which they are invoked from variants that return a modified copy of the original object.

=   Methods whose names end with an equals sign can be invoked by placing the method name, without the equals sign, on the left side of an assignment operator. (You can read more about this in §4.5.3 and §7.1.5.)

Here are some example identifiers that contain leading or trailing punctuation characters:

```
$files        # A global variable
@data         # An instance variable
@@counter     # A class variable
empty?        # A Boolean-valued method or predicate
sort!         # An in-place alternative to the regular sort method
timeout=      # A method invoked by assignment
```

A number of Ruby's operators are implemented as methods, so that classes can redefine them for their own purposes. It is therefore possible to use certain operators as method names as well. In this context, the punctuation character or characters of the operator are treated as identifiers rather than operators. See §4.6 for more about Ruby's operators.

2.1.5 Keywords

The following keywords have special meaning in Ruby and are treated specially by the Ruby parser:

```
__LINE__      case      ensure    not       then
__ENCODING__  class     false     or        true
__FILE__      def       for       redo      undef
BEGIN         defined?  if        rescue    unless
END           do        in        retry     until
alias         else      module    return    when
and           elsif     next      self      while
begin         end       nil       super     yield
break
```

In addition to those keywords, there are three keyword-like tokens that are treated specially by the Ruby parser when they appear at the beginning of a line:

```
=begin    =end       __END__
```

As we've seen, =begin and =end at the beginning of a line delimit multiline comments. And the token __END__ marks the end of the program (and the beginning of a data section) if it appears on a line by itself with no leading or trailing whitespace.

In most languages, these words would be called "reserved words" and they would be never allowed as identifiers. The Ruby parser is flexible and does not complain if you prefix these keywords with @, @@, or $ prefixes and use them as instance, class, or global variable names. Also, you can use these keywords as method names, with the caveat that the method must always be explicitly invoked through an object. Note, however, that using these keywords in identifiers will result in confusing code. The best practice is to treat these keywords as reserved.

Many important features of the Ruby language are actually implemented as methods of the Kernel, Module, Class, and Object classes. It is good practice, therefore, to treat the following identifiers as reserved words as well:

```
# These are methods that appear to be statements or keywords
at_exit         catch           private         require
attr            include         proc            throw
attr_accessor   lambda          protected
attr_reader     load            public
attr_writer     loop            raise

# These are commonly used global functions
Array           chomp!          gsub!           select
Float           chop            iterator?       sleep
Integer         chop!           load            split
String          eval            open            sprintf
URI             exec            p               srand
abort           exit            print           sub
autoload        exit!           printf          sub!
autoload?       fail            putc            syscall
binding         fork            puts            system
block_given?    format          rand            test
callcc          getc            readline        trap
caller          gets            readlines       warn
chomp           gsub            scan

# These are commonly used object methods
allocate        freeze          kind_of?        superclass
clone           frozen?         method          taint
display         hash            methods         tainted?
dup             id              new             to_a
enum_for        inherited       nil?            to_enum
eql?            inspect         object_id       to_s
equal?          instance_of?    respond_to?     untaint
extend          is_a?           send
```

2.1.6 Whitespace

Spaces, tabs, and newlines are not tokens themselves but are used to separate tokens that would otherwise merge into a single token. Aside from this basic token-separating function, most whitespace is ignored by the Ruby interpreter and is simply used to format programs so that they are easy to read and understand. Not all whitespace is ignored, however. Some is required, and some whitespace is actually forbidden. Ruby's grammar is expressive but complex, and there are a few cases in which inserting or removing whitespace can change the meaning of a program. Although these cases do not often arise, it is important to know about them.

2.1.6.1 Newlines as statement terminators

The most common form of whitespace dependency has to do with newlines as statement terminators. In languages like C and Java, every statement must be terminated with a semicolon. You can use semicolons to terminate statements in Ruby, too, but this is only required if you put more than one statement on the same line. Convention dictates that semicolons be omitted elsewhere.

Without explicit semicolons, the Ruby interpreter must figure out on its own where statements end. If the Ruby code on a line is a syntactically complete statement, Ruby uses the newline as the statement terminator. If the statement is not complete, then Ruby continues parsing the statement on the next line. (In Ruby 1.9, there is one exception, which is described later in this section.)

This is no problem if all your statements fit on a single line. When they don't, however, you must take care that you break the line in such a way that the Ruby interpreter cannot interpret the first line as a statement of its own. This is where the whitespace dependency lies: your program may behave differently depending on where you insert a newline. For example, the following code adds x and y and assigns the sum to total:

```
total = x +    # Incomplete expression, parsing continues
  y
```

But this code assigns x to total, and then evaluates y, doing nothing with it:

```
total = x # This is a complete expression
  + y       # A useless but complete expression
```

As another example, consider the return and break statements. These statements may optionally be followed by an expression that provides a return value. A newline between the keyword and the expression will terminate the statement before the expression.

You can safely insert a newline without fear of prematurely terminating your statement after an operator or after a period or comma in a method invocation, array literal, or hash literal.

You can also escape a line break with a backslash, which prevents Ruby from automatically terminating the statement:

```
var total = first_long_variable_name + second_long_variable_name \
  + third_long_variable_name # Note no statement terminator above
```

In Ruby 1.9, the statement terminator rules change slightly. If the first nonspace character on a line is a period, then the line is considered a continuation line, and the newline before it is not a statement terminator. Lines that start with periods are useful for the long method chains sometimes used with "fluent APIs," in which each method invocation returns an object on which additional invocations can be made. For example:

```
animals = Array.new
  .push("dog")    # Does not work in Ruby 1.8
  .push("cow")
  .push("cat")
  .sort
```

2.1.6.2 Spaces and method invocations

Ruby's grammar allows the parentheses around method invocations to be omitted in certain circumstances. This allows Ruby methods to be used as if they were statements, which is an important part of Ruby's elegance. Unfortunately, however, it opens up a pernicious whitespace dependency. Consider the following two lines, which differ only by a single space:

```
f(3+2)+1
f (3+2)+1
```

The first line passes the value 5 to the function f and then adds 1 to the result. Since the second line has a space after the function name, Ruby assumes that the parentheses around the method call have been omitted. The parentheses that appear after the space are used to group a subexpression, but the entire expression (3+2)+1 is used as the method argument. If warnings are enabled (with -w), Ruby issues a warning whenever it sees ambiguous code like this.

The solution to this whitespace dependency is straightforward:

- Never put a space between a method name and the opening parenthesis.
- If the first argument to a method begins with an open parenthesis, always use parentheses in the method invocation. For example, write f((3+2)+1).
- Always run the Ruby interpreter with the -w option so it will warn you if you forget either of the rules above!

2.2 Syntactic Structure

So far, we've discussed the tokens of a Ruby program and the characters that make them up. Now we move on to briefly describe how those lexical tokens combine into the larger syntactic structures of a Ruby program. This section describes the syntax of Ruby programs, from the simplest expressions to the largest modules. This section is, in effect, a roadmap to the chapters that follow.

The basic unit of syntax in Ruby is the *expression*. The Ruby interpreter *evaluates* expressions, producing values. The simplest expressions are *primary expressions*, which represent values directly. Number and string literals, described earlier in this chapter, are primary expressions. Other primary expressions include certain keywords such as true, false, nil, and self. Variable references are also primary expressions; they evaluate to the value of the variable.

More complex values can be written as compound expressions:

```
[1,2,3]                # An Array literal
{1=>"one", 2=>"two"}   # A Hash literal
1..3                   # A Range literal
```

Operators are used to perform computations on values, and compound expressions are built by combining simpler subexpressions with operators:

```
1         # A primary expression
x         # Another primary expression
x = 1     # An assignment expression
x = x + 1 # An expression with two operators
```

Chapter 4 covers operators and expressions, including variables and assignment expressions.

Expressions can be combined with Ruby's keywords to create *statements*, such as the if statement for conditionally executing code and the while statement for repeatedly executing code:

```
if x < 10 then   # If this expression is true
  x = x + 1      # Then execute this statement
end              # Marks the end of the conditional

while x < 10 do  # While this expression is true...
  print x        # Execute this statement
  x = x + 1      # Then execute this statement
end              # Marks the end of the loop
```

In Ruby, these statements are technically expressions, but there is still a useful distinction between expressions that affect the control flow of a program and those that do not. Chapter 5 explains Ruby's control structures.

In all but the most trivial programs, we usually need to group expressions and statements into parameterized units so that they can be executed repeatedly and operate on varying inputs. You may know these parameterized units as functions, procedures, or subroutines. Since Ruby is an object-oriented language, they are called *methods*. Methods, along with related structures called *procs* and *lambdas*, are the topic of Chapter 6.

Finally, groups of methods that are designed to interoperate can be combined into *classes*, and groups of related classes and methods that are independent of those classes can be organized into *modules*. Classes and modules are the topic of Chapter 7.

ucture. Module, class, and method definitions, and
de blocks of nested code. These blocks are delimited
, by convention, are indented two spaces relative to
ds of blocks in Ruby programs. One kind is formally
re the chunks of code associated with or passed to

l the code inside them are the block associated with
.times. Formal blocks of this kind may be delimited
delimited with the keywords do and end:

ised when the block is written on more than one line.
the code within the block. Blocks are covered in §5.4.

ie blocks, we can call the other kind of block a *body*
block" is often used for both). A body is just the list
body of a class definition, a method definition, a
ire never delimited with curly braces in Ruby—key-
ers instead. The specific syntax for statement bodies,
dule bodies are documented in Chapters 5, 6, and 7.

within each other, and Ruby programs typically have
several levels of nested code, made readable by their relative indentation. Here is a
schematic example:

```ruby
module Stats                      # A module
  class Dataset                   # A class in the module
    def initialize(filename)      # A method in the class
      IO.foreach(filename) do |line|  # A block in the method
        if line[0,1] == "#"       # An if statement in the block
          next                    # A simple statement in the if
        end                       # End the if body
      end                         # End the block
    end                           # End the method body
  end                             # End the class body
end                               # End the module body
```

2.3 File Structure

There are only a few rules about how a file of Ruby code must be structured. These
rules are related to the deployment of Ruby programs and are not directly relevant to
the language itself.

First, if a Ruby program contains a "shebang" comment, to tell the (Unix-like) operating system how to execute it, that comment must appear on the first line.

Second, if a Ruby program contains a "coding" comment (as described in §2.4.1), that comment must appear on the first line or on the second line if the first line is a shebang.

Third, if a file contains a line that consists of the single token __END__ with no whitespace before or after, then the Ruby interpreter stops processing the file at that point. The remainder of the file may contain arbitrary data that the program can read using the IO stream object DATA. (See Chapter 10 and §9.7 for more about this global constant.)

Ruby programs are not required to fit in a single file. Many programs load additional Ruby code from external libraries, for example. Programs use require to load code from another file. require searches for specified modules of code against a search path, and prevents any given module from being loaded more than once. See §7.6 for details.

The following code illustrates each of these points of Ruby file structure:

```
#!/usr/bin/ruby -w          shebang comment
# -*- coding: utf-8 -*-      coding comment
require 'socket'             load networking library

    ...                     program code goes here

__END__                     mark end of code
    ...                     program data goes here
```

2.4 Program Encoding

At the lowest level, a Ruby program is simply a sequence of characters. Ruby's lexical rules are defined using characters of the ASCII character set. Comments begin with the # character (ASCII code 35), for example, and allowed whitespace characters are horizontal tab (ASCII 9), newline (10), vertical tab (11), form feed (12), carriage return (13), and space (32). All Ruby keywords are written using ASCII characters, and all operators and other punctuation are drawn from the ASCII character set.

By default, the Ruby interpreter assumes that Ruby source code is encoded in ASCII. This is not required, however; the interpreter can also process files that use other encodings, as long as those encodings can represent the full set of ASCII characters. In order for the Ruby interpreter to be able to interpret the bytes of a source file as characters, it must know what encoding to use. Ruby files can identify their own encodings or you can tell the interpreter how they are encoded. Doing so is explained shortly.

The Ruby interpreter is actually quite flexible about the characters that appear in a Ruby program. Certain ASCII characters have specific meanings, and certain ASCII characters are not allowed in identifiers, but beyond that, a Ruby program may contain any characters allowed by the encoding. We explained earlier that identifiers may contain characters outside of the ASCII character set. The same is true for comments and string and regular expression literals: they may contain any characters other than the delimiter character that marks the end of the comment or literal. In ASCII-encoded files, strings may include arbitrary bytes, including those that represent nonprinting control characters. (Using raw bytes like this is not recommended, however; Ruby string literals support escape sequences so that arbitrary characters can be included by numeric code instead.) If the file is written using the UTF-8 encoding, then comments, strings, and regular expressions may include arbitrary Unicode characters. If the file is encoded using the Japanese SJIS or EUC encodings, then strings may include Kanji characters.

2.4.1 Specifying Program Encoding

By default, the Ruby interpreter assumes that programs are encoded in ASCII. In Ruby 1.8, you can specify a different encoding with the -K command-line option. To run a Ruby program that includes Unicode characters encoded in UTF-8, invoke the interpreter with the -Ku option. Programs that include Japanese characters in EUC-JP or SJIS encodings can be run with the -Ke and -Ks options.

Ruby 1.9 also supports the -K option, but it is no longer the preferred way to specify the encoding of a program file. Rather than have the user of a script specify the encoding when they invoke Ruby, the author of the script can specify the encoding of the script by placing a special "coding comment" at the start of the file.[*] For example:

```
# coding: utf-8
```

The comment must be written entirely in ASCII, and must include the string `coding` followed by a colon or equals sign and the name of the desired encoding (which cannot include spaces or punctuation other than hyphen and underscore). Whitespace is allowed on either side of the colon or equals sign, and the string `coding` may have any prefix, such as `en` to spell `encoding`. The entire comment, including `coding` and the encoding name, is case-insensitive and can be written with upper- or lowercase letters.

Encoding comments are usually written so that they also inform a text editor of the file encoding. Emacs users might write:

```
# -*- coding: utf-8 -*-
```

And vi users can write:

```
# vi: set fileencoding=utf-8 :
```

An encoding comment like this one is usually only valid on the first line of the file. It may appear on the second line, however, if the first line is a shebang comment (which makes a script executable on Unix-like operating systems):

```
#!/usr/bin/ruby -w
# coding: utf-8
```

---

[*] Ruby follows Python's conventions in this; see *http://www.python.org/dev/peps/pep-0263/*.

Encoding names are not case-sensitive and may be written in uppercase, lowercase, or a mix. Ruby 1.9 supports at least the following source encodings: ASCII-8BIT (also known as BINARY), US-ASCII (7-bit ASCII), the European encodings ISO-8859-1 through ISO-8859-15, the Unicode encoding UTF-8, and the Japanese encodings SHIFT_JIS (also known as SJIS) and EUC-JP. Your build or distribution of Ruby may support additional encodings as well.

As a special case, UTF-8-encoded files identify their encoding if the first three bytes of the file are 0xEF 0xBB 0xBF. These bytes are known as the BOM or "Byte Order Mark" and are optional in UTF-8-encoded files. (Certain Windows programs add these bytes when saving Unicode files.)

In Ruby 1.9, the language keyword __ENCODING__ (there are two underscores at the beginning and at the end) evaluates to the source encoding of the currently executing code. The resulting value is an Encoding object. (See §3.2.6.2 for more on the Encoding class.)

2.4.2 Source Encoding and Default External Encoding

In Ruby 1.9, it is important to understand the difference between the *source encoding* of a Ruby file and the *default external encoding* of a Ruby process. The source encoding is what we described earlier: it tells the Ruby interpreter how to read characters in a script. Source encodings are typically set with coding comments. A Ruby program may consist of more than one file, and different files may have different source encodings. The source encoding of a file affects the encoding of the string literals in that file. For more about the encoding of strings, see §3.2.6.

The default external encoding is something different: this is the encoding that Ruby uses by default when reading from files and streams. The default external encoding is global to the Ruby process and does not change from file to file. Normally, the default external encoding is set based on the locale that your computer is configured to. But you can also explicitly specify the default external encoding with command-line options, as we'll describe shortly. The default external encoding does not affect the encoding of string literals, but it is quite important for I/O, as we'll see in §9.7.2.

We described the -K interpreter option earlier as a way to set the source encoding. In fact, what this option really does is set the default external encoding of the process and then uses that encoding as the default source encoding.

In Ruby 1.9, the -K option exists for compatibility with Ruby 1.8 but is not the preferred way to set the default external encoding. Two new options, -E and --encoding, allow you to specify an encoding by its full name rather than by a one-character abbreviation. For example:

```
ruby -E utf-8          # Encoding name follows -E
ruby -Eutf-8           # The space is optional
ruby --encoding utf-8  # Encoding following --encoding with a space
ruby --encoding=utf-8  # Or use an equals sign with --encoding
```

See §10.1 for complete details.

You can query the default external encoding with `Encoding.default_external`. This class method returns an `Encoding` object. Use `Encoding.locale_charmap` to obtain the name (as a string) of the character encoding derived from the locale. This method is always based on the locale setting and ignores command-line options that override the default external encoding.

2.5 Program Execution

Ruby is a scripting language. This means that Ruby programs are simply lists, or scripts, of statements to be executed. By default, these statements are executed sequentially, in the order they appear. Ruby's control structures (described in Chapter 5) alter this default execution order and allow statements to be executed conditionally or repeatedly, for example.

Programmers who are used to traditional static compiled languages like C or Java may find this slightly confusing. There is no special `main` method in Ruby from which execution begins. The Ruby interpreter is given a script of statements to execute, and it begins executing at the first line and continues to the last line.

(Actually, that last statement is not quite true. The Ruby interpreter first scans the file for `BEGIN` statements, and executes the code in their bodies. Then it goes back to line 1 and starts executing sequentially. See §5.7 for more on `BEGIN`.)

Another difference between Ruby and compiled languages has to do with module, class, and method definitions. In compiled languages, these are syntactic structures that are processed by the compiler. In Ruby, they are statements like any other. When the Ruby interpreter encounters a class definition, it executes it, causing a new class to come into existence. Similarly, when the Ruby interpreter encounters a method definition, it executes it, causing a new method to be defined. Later in the program, the interpreter will probably encounter and execute a method invocation expression for the method, and this invocation will cause the statements in the method body to be executed.

The Ruby interpreter is invoked from the command line and given a script to execute. Very simple one-line scripts are sometimes written directly on the command line. More commonly, however, the name of the file containing the script is specified. The Ruby interpreter reads the file and executes the script. It first executes any `BEGIN` blocks. Then it starts at the first line of the file and continues until one of the following happens:

- It executes a statement that causes the Ruby program to terminate.
- It reaches the end of the file.
- It reads a line that marks the logical end of the file with the token `__END__`.

Before it quits, the Ruby interpreter typically (unless the `exit!` method was called) executes the bodies of any `END` statements it has encountered and any other "shutdown hook" code registered with the `at_exit` function.

## CHAPTER 3

Datatypes and Objects

In order to understand a programming language, you have to know what kinds of data it can manipulate and what it can do with that data. This chapter is about the values manipulated by Ruby programs. It begins with comprehensive coverage of numeric and textual values. Next, it explains arrays and hashes—two important data structures that are a fundamental part of Ruby. The chapter then moves on to explain ranges, symbols, and the special values true, false, and nil. All Ruby values are objects, and this chapter concludes with detailed coverage of the features that all objects share.

The classes described in this chapter are the fundamental datatypes of the Ruby language. This chapter explains the basic behavior of those types: how literal values are written in a program, how integer and floating-point arithmetic work, how textual data is encoded, how values can serve as hash keys, and so on. Although we cover numbers, strings, arrays, and hashes here, this chapter makes no attempt to explain the APIs defined by those types. Instead, Chapter 9 demonstrates those APIs by example, and it also covers many other important (but nonfundamental) classes.

3.1 Numbers

Ruby includes five built-in classes for representing numbers, and the standard library includes three more numeric classes that are sometimes useful. Figure 3-1 shows the class hierarchy.

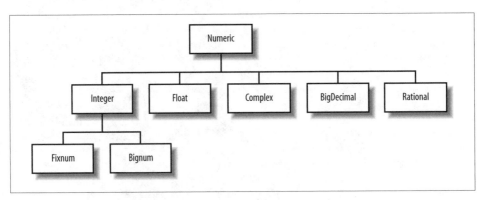

Figure 3-1. Numeric class hierarchy

All number objects in Ruby are instances of Numeric. All integers are instances of Integer. If an integer value fits within 31 bits (on most implementations), it is an instance of Fixnum. Otherwise, it is a Bignum. Bignum objects represent integers of arbitrary size, and if the result of an operation on Fixnum operands is too big to fit in a Fixnum, that result is transparently converted to a Bignum. Similarly, if the result of an operation on Bignum objects falls within the range of Fixnum, then the result is a Fixnum. Real numbers are approximated in Ruby with the Float class, which uses the native floating-point representation of the platform.

The `Complex` class represents complex numbers, of course. `BigDecimal` represents real numbers with arbitrary precision, using a decimal representation rather than a binary representation. And `Rational` represents rational numbers: one integer divided by another. In Ruby 1.8 these classes are in the standard library. In Ruby 1.9, `Complex` and `Rational` are built-in.

All numeric objects are *immutable*; there are no methods that allow you to change the value held by the object. If you pass a reference to a numeric object to a method, you need not worry that the method will modify the object. `Fixnum` objects are commonly used, and Ruby implementations typically treat them as immediate values rather than as references. Because numbers are immutable, however, there is really no way to tell the difference.

3.1.1 Integer Literals

An integer literal is simply a sequence of digits:

```
0
123
12345678901234567890
```

If the integer values fit within the range of the `Fixnum` class, the value is a `Fixnum`. Otherwise, it is a `Bignum`, which supports integers of any size. Underscores may be inserted into integer literals (though not at the beginning or end), and this feature is sometimes used as a thousands separator:

```
1_000_000_000    # One billion (or 1,000 million in the UK)
```

If an integer literal begins with zero and has more than one digit, then it is interpreted in some base other than base 10. Numbers beginning with `0x` or `0X` are hexadecimal (base 16) and use the letters `a` through `f` (or `A` through F) as digits for 10 through 15. Numbers beginning `0b` or `0B` are binary (base 2) and may only include digits `0` and `1`. Numbers beginning with `0` and no subsequent letter are octal (base 8) and should consist of digits between `0` and `7`. Examples:

```
0377         # Octal representation of 255
0b1111_1111  # Binary representation of 255
0xFF         # Hexadecimal representation of 255
```

To represent a negative number, simply begin an integer literal with a minus sign. Literals may also begin with a plus sign, although this never changes the meaning of the literal.

3.1.2 Floating-Point Literals

A floating-point literal is an optional sign followed by one or more decimal digits, a decimal point (the `.` character), one or more additional digits, and an optional exponent. An exponent begins with the letter `e` or `E`, and is followed by an optional sign and one or more decimal digits. As with integer literals, underscores may be used within floating-point literals. Unlike integer literals, it is not possible to express floating-point values in any radix other than base 10. Here are some examples of floating-point literals:

```
0.0
-3.14
6.02e23      # This means 6.02 × 10²³
1_000_000.01 # One million and a little bit more
```

Ruby requires that digits appear before and after the decimal point. You cannot simply write `.1`, for example; you must explicitly write `0.1`. This is necessary to avoid ambiguity in Ruby's complex grammar. Ruby differs from many other languages in this way.

3.1.3 Arithmetic in Ruby

All numeric types in Ruby define standard +, -, *, and / operators for addition, subtraction, multiplication, and division. When an integer result is too large for a `Fixnum`, Ruby automatically converts to a `Bignum`, and as a result, integer arithmetic in Ruby never overflows as it does in many other languages. Floating-point numbers (at least on platforms that use the standard IEEE-754 floating-point representation) overflow to special positive or negative infinity values, and underflow to zero.

The division operator depends on the class of the operands: if both operands are integers, then truncating integer division is performed. If either operand is a `Float`, then floating-point division is performed. There are also three division methods: `div` performs integer division, `fdiv` performs floating-point division, and `quo` returns a `Rational` when possible, and otherwise returns a `Float` (this requires the "rational" module in Ruby 1.8):

```
[5/2, 5.0/2, 5/2.0]              # => [2, 2.5, 2.5]
[5.0.div(2), 5.0.fdiv(2), 5.quo(2)] # => [2, 2.5, Rational(5,2)]
```

Integer division by zero causes a `ZeroDivisionError` to be thrown. Floating-point division by zero does not cause an error; it simply returns the value `Infinity`. The case of `0.0/0.0` is special; on most modern hardware, and with most operating systems, it evaluates to another special floating-point value known as NaN, or Not-a-Number.

The modulo (%) operator (and the synonymous `modulo` method) compute the remainder after integer division. They can also be used with `Float` and `Rational` operands. The `divmod` method returns both quotient and modulo :

```
x = 5%2         # => 1: quotient is 2, with 1 left over
q,r = 10.divmod 3 # => [3,1]: quotient is 3, remainder is 1
```

Ruby uses the ** operator for exponentiation. Exponents need not be integers:

```
x**4        # This is the same thing as x*x*x*x
x**-1       # The same thing as 1/x
x**(1/3.0)  # The cube root of x. Use Math.cbrt in Ruby 1.9
x**(1/4)    # Oops! Integer division means this is x**0, which is always 1
x**(1.0/4.0) # This is the fourth-root of x
```

When multiple exponentiations are combined into a single expression, they are evaluated from right to left. Thus, 4**3**2 is the same as 4**9, not 64**2.

Exponentiation can result in very large values. Remember that integers can become arbitrarily large, but `Float` objects cannot represent numbers larger than `Float::MAX`. Thus, the expression 10**1000 yields an exact integer result, but the expression 9.9**1000 overflows to the `Float` value `Infinity`.

`Fixnum` and `Bignum` values support the standard bit-manipulation operators—~, &, |, ^, >>, and <<—that are common in C, Java, and many other languages. (See §4.6 for details.) In addition, integer values can also be indexed like arrays to query (but not set) individual bits. The index 0 returns the least significant bit:

```
even = (x[0] == 0)   # A number is even if the least-significant bit is 0
```

Division, Modulo, and Negative Numbers

When one (but not both) of the operands is negative, Ruby performs the integer division and modulo operations differently than languages like C, C++, and Java do (but the same as the languages Python and Tcl). Consider the quotient -7/3. Ruby rounds toward negative infinity and returns –3. C and related languages round toward zero instead and return –2. In Ruby, -a/b equals a/-b but may not equal -(a/b).

Ruby's definition of the modulo operation also differs from that of C and Java. In Ruby, -7%3 is 2. In C and Java, the result is -1 instead. The magnitude of the result differs, because the quotient differed. But the sign of the result differs, too. In Ruby, the sign of the result is always the sign of the second operand. In C and Java, the sign of the result is always the sign of the first operand. (Ruby's `remainder` method behaves like the C modulo operator.)

3.1.4 Binary Floating-Point and Rounding Errors

Most computer hardware and most computer languages (including Ruby) approximate real numbers using a floating-point representation like Ruby's `Float` class. For hardware efficiency, most floating-point representations are binary representations, which can exactly represent fractions like 1/2, 1/4, and 1/1024. Unfortunately, the fractions we use most commonly (especially when performing financial calculations) are 1/10, 1/100, 1/1000, and so on. Binary floating-point representations cannot exactly represent numbers as simple as 0.1.

`Float` objects have plenty of precision and can approximate 0.1 very well, but the fact that this number cannot be represented exactly leads to problems. Consider the following simple Ruby expression:

```
0.4 - 0.3 == 0.1    # Evaluates to false in most implementations
```

Because of rounding error, the difference between the approximations of 0.4 and 0.3 is not quite the same as the approximation of 0.1. This problem is not specific to Ruby:

C, Java, JavaScript, and all languages that use IEEE-754 floating-point numbers suffer from it as well.

One solution to this problem is to use a decimal representation of real numbers rather than a binary representation. The `BigDecimal` class from Ruby's standard library is one such representation. Arithmetic on `BigDecimal` objects is many times slower than arithmetic on `Float` values. It is fast enough for typical financial calculations, but not for scientific number crunching. §9.3.3 includes a short example of the use of the `BigDecimal` library.

3.2 Text

Text is represented in Ruby by objects of the `String` class. Strings are mutable objects, and the `String` class defines a powerful set of operators and methods for extracting substrings, inserting and deleting text, searching, replacing, and so on. Ruby provides a number of ways to express string literals in your programs, and some of them support a powerful string interpolation syntax by which the values of arbitrary Ruby expressions can be substituted into string literals. The sections that follow explain string and character literals and string operators. The full string API is covered in §9.1.

Textual patterns are represented in Ruby as `Regexp` objects, and Ruby defines a syntax for including regular expressions literally in your programs. The code `/[a-z]\d+/`, for example, represents a single lowercase letter followed by one or more digits. Regular expressions are a commonly used feature of Ruby, but regexps are not a fundamental datatype in the way that numbers, strings, and arrays are. See §9.2 for documentation of regular expression syntax and the `Regexp` API.

Text in Ruby 1.8 and Ruby 1.9

The biggest change between Ruby 1.8 and Ruby 1.9 is that 1.9 offers comprehensive built-in support for Unicode and other multibyte text representations. The ramifications of this change are extensive and will be mentioned throughout this section, especially in §3.2.6.

3.2.1 String Literals

Ruby provides quite a few ways to embed strings literally into your programs.

3.2.1.1 Single-quoted string literals

The simplest string literals are enclosed in single quotes (the apostrophe character). The text within the quote marks is the value of the string:

```
'This is a simple Ruby string literal'
```

If you need to place an apostrophe within a single-quoted string literal, precede it with a backslash so that the Ruby interpreter does not think that it terminates the string:

```
'Won\'t you read O\'Reilly\'s book?'
```

The backslash also works to escape another backslash, so that the second backslash is not itself interpreted as an escape character. Here are some situations in which you need to use a double backslash:

```
'This string literal ends with a single backslash: \\'
'This is a backslash-quote: \\\''
'Two backslashes: \\\\'
```

In single-quoted strings, a backslash is not special if the character that follows it is anything other than a quote or a backslash. Most of the time, therefore, backslashes need not be doubled (although they can be) in string literals. For example, the following two string literals are equal:

```
'a\b' == 'a\\b'
```

Single-quoted strings may extend over multiple lines, and the resulting string literal includes the newline characters. It is not possible to escape the newlines with a backslash:

```
'This is a long string literal \
that includes a backslash and a newline'
```

If you want to break a long single-quoted string literal across multiple lines without embedding newlines in it, simply break it into multiple adjacent string literals; the Ruby interpreter will concatenate them during the parsing process. Remember, though, that you must escape the newlines (see Chapter 2) between the literals so that Ruby does not interpret the newline as a statement terminator:

```
message =
'These three literals are '\
'concatenated into one by the interpreter. '\
'The resulting string contains no newlines.'
```

3.2.1.2 Double-quoted string literals

String literals delimited by double quotation marks are much more flexible than single-quoted literals. Double-quoted literals support quite a few backslash escape sequences, such as \n for newline, \t for tab, and \" for a quotation mark that does not terminate the string:

```
"\t\"This quote begins with a tab and ends with a newline\"\n"
"\\"  # A single backslash
```

In Ruby 1.9, the \u escape embeds arbitrary Unicode characters, specified by their codepoint, into a double-quoted string. This escape sequence is complex enough that we'll describe it in its own section (see §3.2.1.3). Many of the other backslash escape sequences are obscure and are used for encoding binary data into strings. The complete list of escape sequences is shown in Table 3-1.

More powerfully, double-quoted string literals may also include arbitrary Ruby expressions. When the string is created, the expression is evaluated, converted to a string, and inserted into the string in place of the expression text itself. This substitution of an expression with its value is known in Ruby as "string interpolation." Expressions within double-quoted strings begin with the # character and are enclosed within curly braces:

```
"360 degrees=#{2*Math::PI} radians" # "360 degrees=6.28318530717959 radians"
```

When the expression to be interpolated into the string literal is simply a reference to a global, instance, or class variable, then the curly braces may be omitted:

```
$salutation = 'hello'     # Define a global variable
"#$salutation world"      # Use it in a double-quoted string
```

Use a backslash to escape the # character if you do not want it to be treated specially. Note that this only needs to be done if the character after # is {, $, or @:

```
"My phone #: 555-1234"                  # No escape needed
"Use \#{ to interpolate expressions"  # Escape #{ with backslash
```

String Interpolation with sprintf

C programmers may be happy to know that Ruby also supports printf and sprintf[*] functions for interpolating formatted values into strings:

```
sprintf("pi is about %.4f", Math::PI) # Returns "pi is about 3.1416"
```

The advantage of this style of interpolation is that the format string can specify options, such as the number of decimal places to display in a Float. In true Ruby style, there is even an operator form of the sprintf method: simply use a % operator between a format string and the arguments to be interpolated into it:

```
"pi is about %.4f" % Math::PI # Same as example above
"%s: %f" % ["pi", Math::PI]   # Array on righthand side for multiple args
```

Double-quoted string literals may span multiple lines, and line terminators become part of the string literal, unless escaped with a backslash:

```
"This string literal
has two lines \
but is written on three"
```

You may prefer to explicitly encode the line terminators in your strings—in order to enforce network CRLF (Carriage Return Line Feed) line terminators, as used in the HTTP protocol, for example. To do this, write all your string literals on a single line and explicitly include the line endings with the \r and \n escape sequences. Remember that adjacent string literals are automatically concatenated, but if they are written on *separate* lines, the newline between them must be escaped:

[*] Use *ri* to learn more: ri Kernel.sprintf

```
"This string has three lines.\r\n" \
"It is written as three adjacent literals\r\n" \
"separated by escaped newlines\r\n"
```

Table 3-1. Backslash escapes in double-quoted strings

Escape sequence	Meaning
\ *x*	A backslash before any character *x* is equivalent to the character *x* by itself, unless *x* is a line terminator or one of the special characters abcefnrstuvxCM01234567. This syntax is useful to escape the special meaning of the \, #, and " characters.
\a	The BEL character (ASCII code 7). Rings the console bell. Equivalent to \C-g or \007.
\b	The Backspace character (ASCII code 8). Equivalent to \C-h or \010.
\e	The ESC character (ASCII code 27). Equivalent to \033.
\f	The Form Feed character (ASCII code 12). Equivalent to \C-l and \014.
\n	The Newline character (ASCII code 10). Equivalent to \C-j and \012.
\r	The Carriage Return character (ASCII code 13). Equivalent to \C-m and \015.
\s	The Space character (ASCII code 32).
\t	The TAB character (ASCII code 9). Equivalent to \C-i and \011.
\u *nnnn*	The Unicode codepoint *nnnn*, where each *n* is one hexadecimal digit. Leading zeros may not be dropped; all four digits are required in this form of the \u escape. Supported in Ruby 1.9 and later.
\u{ *hexdigits* }	The Unicode codepoint(s) specified by *hexdigits*. See the description of this escape in the main text. Ruby 1.9 and later.
\v	The vertical tab character (ASCII code 11). Equivalent to \C-k and \013.
\ *nnn*	The byte *nnn*, where *nnn* is three octal digits between 000 and 377.
\ *nn*	Same as \0*nn*, where *nn* is two octal digits between 00 and 77.
\ *n*	Same as \00*n*, where *n* is an octal digit between 0 and 7.
\x *nn*	The byte *nn*, where *nn* is two hexadecimal digits between 00 and FF. (Both lowercase and uppercase letters are allowed as hexadecimal digits.)
\x *n*	Same as \x0*n*, where *n* is a hexadecimal digit between 0 and F (or f).
\c *x*	Shorthand for \C-*x*.
\C- *x*	The character whose character code is formed by zeroing the sixth and seventh bits of *x*, retaining the high-order bit and the five low bits. *x* can be any character, but this sequence is usually used to represent control characters Control-A through Control-Z (ASCII codes 1 through 26). Because of the layout of the ASCII table, you can use either lowercase or uppercase letters for *x*. Note that \c*x* is shorthand. *x* can be any single character or an escape other than \C \u, \x, or *nnn*.
\M- *x*	The character whose character code is formed by setting the high bit of the code of *x*. This is used to represent "meta" characters, which are not technically part of the ASCII character set. *x* can be any single character or an escape other than \M \u, \x, or *nnn*. \M can be combined with \C as in \M-\C-A.
\ *eol*	A backslash before a line terminator escapes the terminator. Neither the backslash nor the terminator appear in the string.

3.2.1.3 Unicode escapes

In Ruby 1.9, double-quoted strings can include arbitrary Unicode characters with \u escapes. In its simplest form, \u is followed by exactly four hexadecimal digits (letters can be upper- or lowercase), which represent a Unicode codepoint between 0000 and FFFF. For example:

```
"\u00D7"    # => "×": leading zeros cannot be dropped
"\u20ac"    # => "€": lowercase letters are okay
```

A second form of the \u escape is followed by an open curly brace, one to six hexadecimal digits, and a close curly brace. The digits between the braces can represent any Unicode codepoint between 0 and 10FFFF, and leading zeros can be dropped in this form:

```
"\u{A5}"        # => "¥": same as "\u00A5"
"\u{3C0}"       # Greek lowercase pi: same as "\u03C0"
"\u{10ffff}"    # The largest Unicode codepoint
```

Finally, the \u{} form of this escape allows multiple codepoints to be embedded within a single escape. Simply place multiple runs of one to six hexadecimal digits, separated by a single space or tab character, within the curly braces. Spaces are not allowed after the opening curly brace or before the closing brace:

```
money = "\u{20AC A3 A5}"  # => "€£¥"
```

Note that spaces within the curly braces do not encode spaces in the string itself. You can, however, encode the ASCII space character with Unicode codepoint 20:

```
money = "\u{20AC 20 A3 20 A5}"  # => "€ £ ¥"
```

Strings that use the \u escape are encoded using the Unicode UTF-8 encoding. (See §3.2.6 for more on the encoding of strings.)

\u escapes are usually, but not always, legal in strings. If the source file uses an encoding other than UTF-8, and a string contains multibyte characters in that encoding (literal characters, not characters created with escapes), then it is not legal to use \u in that string—it is just not possible for one string to encode characters in two different encodings. You can always use \u if the source encoding (see §2.4.1) is UTF-8. And you can always use \u in a string that only contains ASCII characters.

\u escapes may appear in double-quoted strings, and also in other forms of quoted text (described shortly) such as regular expressions, characters literals, %- and %Q-delimited strings, %W-delimited arrays, here documents, and backquote-delimited command strings. Java programmers should note that Ruby's \u escape can only appear in quoted text, not in program identifiers.

3.2.1.4 Arbitrary delimiters for string literals

When working with text that contains apostrophes and quotation marks, it is awkward to use it as single- and double-quoted string literals. Ruby supports a generalized quoting syntax for string literals (and, as we'll see later, for regular expression and array literals as well). The sequence %q begins a string literal that follows single-quoted string rules, and the sequence %Q (or just %) introduces a literal that follows double-quoted string rules. The first character following q or Q is the delimiter character, and the string literal continues until a matching (unescaped) delimiter is found. If the opening delimiter is (, [, {, or <, then the matching delimiter is),], }, or >. (Note that the backtick ` and apostrophe ' are not a matched pair.) Otherwise, the closing delimiter is the same as the opening delimiter. Here are some examples:

```
%q(Don't worry about escaping ' characters!)
%Q|"How are you?", he said|
%-This string literal ends with a newline\n-  # Q omitted in this one
```

If you find that you need to escape the delimiter character, you can use a backslash (even in the stricter %q form) or just choose a different delimiter:

```
%q_This string literal contains \_underscores\__
%Q!Just use a _different_ delimiter\!!
```

If you use paired delimiters, you don't need to escape those delimiters in your literals, as long as they appear in properly nested pairs:

```
# XML uses paired angle brackets:
%<<book><title>Ruby in a Nutshell</title></book>>  # This works
# Expressions use paired, nested parens:
%((1+(2*3)) = #{(1+(2*3))})                         # This works, too
%(A mismatched paren \( must be escaped)            # Escape needed here
```

3.2.1.5 Here documents

For long string literals, there may be no single character delimiter that can be used without worrying about remembering to escape characters within the literal. Ruby's solution to this problem is to allow you to specify an arbitrary sequence of characters to serve as the delimiter for the string. This kind of literal is borrowed from Unix shell syntax and is historically known as a *here document*. (Because the document is right here in the source code rather than in an external file.)

Here documents begin with << or <<-. These are followed immediately (no space is allowed, to prevent ambiguity with the left-shift operator) by an identifier or string that specifies the ending delimiter. The text of the string literal begins on the next line and continues until the text of the delimiter appears on a line by itself. For example:

```
document = <<HERE         # This is how we begin a here document
This is a string literal.
It has two lines and abruptly ends...
HERE
```

The Ruby interpreter gets the contents of a string literal by reading a line at a time from its input. This does not mean, however, that the << must be the last thing on its own line. In fact, after reading the content of a here document, the Ruby interpreter goes back to the line it was on and continues parsing it. The following Ruby code, for example, creates a string by concatenating two here documents and a regular single-quoted string:

```
greeting = <<HERE + <<THERE + "World"
Hello
HERE
There
THERE
```

The `<<HERE` on line 1 causes the interpreter to read lines 2 and 3. And the `<<THERE` causes the interpreter to read lines 4 and 5. After these lines have been read, the three string literals are concatenated into one.

The ending delimiter of a here document really must appear on a line by itself: no comment may follow the delimiter. If the here document begins with `<<`, then the delimiter must start at the beginning of the line. If the literal begins with `<<-` instead, then the delimiter may have whitespace in front of it. The newline at the beginning of a here document is not part of the literal, but the newline at the end of the document is. Therefore, every here document ends with a line terminator, except for an empty here document, which is the same as `""`:

```
empty = <<END
END
```

If you use an unquoted identifier as the terminator, as in the previous examples, then the here document behaves like a double-quoted string for the purposes of interpreting backslash escapes and the `#` character. If you want to be very, very literal, allowing no escape characters whatsoever, place the delimiter in single quotes. Doing this also allows you to use spaces in your delimiter:

```
document = <<'THIS IS THE END, MY ONLY FRIEND, THE END'
.
. lots and lots of text goes here
. with no escaping at all.
.
THIS IS THE END, MY ONLY FRIEND, THE END
```

The single quotes around the delimiter hint that this string literal is like a single-quoted string. In fact, this kind of here document is even stricter. Because the single quote is not a delimiter, there is never a need to escape a single quote with a backslash. And because the backslash is never needed as an escape character, there is never a need to escape the backslash itself. In this kind of here document, therefore, backslashes are simply part of the string literal.

You may also use a double-quoted string literal as the delimiter for a here document. This is the same as using a single identifier, except that it allows spaces within the delimiter:

```
document = <<-"# # #"    # This is the only place we can put a comment
<html><head><title>#{title}</title></head>
<body>
<h1>#{title}</h1>
```

```
        #{body}
        </body>
        </html>
                   # # #
```

Note that there is no way to include a comment within a here document except on the first line after the << token and before the start of the literal. Of all the # characters in this code, one introduces a comment, three interpolate expressions into the literal, and the rest are the delimiter.

3.2.1.6 Backtick command execution

Ruby supports another syntax involving quotes and strings. When text is enclosed in backquotes (the ` character, also known as backticks), that text is treated as a double-quoted string literal. The value of that literal is passed to the specially named `Kernel.`` method. This method executes the text as an operating system shell command and returns the command's output as a string.

Consider the following Ruby code:

```
`ls`
```

On a Unix system, these four characters yield a string that lists the names of the files in the current directory. This is highly platform-dependent, of course. A rough equivalent in Windows might be `` `dir` ``.

Ruby supports a generalized quote syntax you can use in place of backticks. This is like the %Q syntax introduced earlier, but uses %x (for execute) instead:

```
%x[ls]
```

Note that the text within the backticks (or following %x) is processed like a double-quoted literal, which means that arbitrary Ruby expressions can be interpolated into the string. For example:

```
if windows
  listcmd = 'dir'
else
  listcmd = 'ls'
end
listing = `#{listcmd}`
```

In a case like this, however, it is simpler just to invoke the backtick method directly:

```
listing = Kernel.`(listcmd)
```

3.2.1.7 String literals and mutability

Strings are mutable in Ruby. Therefore, the Ruby interpreter cannot use the same object to represent two identical string literals. (If you are a Java programmer, you may find this surprising.) Each time Ruby encounters a string literal, it creates a new object. If you include a literal within the body of a loop, Ruby will create a new object for each iteration. You can demonstrate this for yourself as follows:

```
10.times { puts "test".object_id }
```

For efficiency, you should avoid using literals within loops.

3.2.1.8 The String.new method

In addition to all the string literal options described earlier, you can also create new strings with the `String.new` method. With no arguments, this method returns a newly created string with no characters. With a single string argument, it creates and returns a new `String` object that represents the same text as the argument object.

3.2.2 Character Literals

Single characters can be included literally in a Ruby program by preceding the character with a question mark. No quotation marks of any kind are used:

```
?A    # Character literal for the ASCII character A
?"    # Character literal for the double-quote character
??    # Character literal for the question mark character
```

Although Ruby has a character literal syntax, it does not have a special class to represent single characters. Also, the interpretation of character literals has changed between Ruby 1.8 and Ruby 1.9. In Ruby 1.8, character literals evaluate to the integer encoding of the specified character. ?A, for example, is the same as 65 because the ASCII encoding for the capital letter A is the integer 65. In Ruby 1.8, the character literal syntax only works with ASCII and single-byte characters.

In Ruby 1.9 and later, characters are simply strings of length 1. That is, the literal ?A is the same as the literal 'A', and there is really no need for this character literal syntax in new code. In Ruby 1.9, the character literal syntax works with multibyte characters and can also be used with the \u Unicode escape (though not with the multicodepoint form \u{a b c}):

```
?\u20AC == ?€    # => true: Ruby 1.9 only
?€ == "\u20AC"   # => true
```

The character literal syntax can actually be used with any of the character escapes listed earlier in Table 3-1:

```
?\t      # Character literal for the TAB character
?\C-x    # Character literal for Ctrl-X
?\111    # Literal for character whose encoding is 0111 (octal)
```

3.2.3 String Operators

The `String` class defines several useful operators for manipulating strings of text. The + operator concatenates two strings and returns the result as a new `String` object:

```
planet = "Earth"
"Hello" + " " + planet    # Produces "Hello Earth"
```

Java programmers should note that the + operator does not convert its righthand operand to a string; you must do that yourself:

```
"Hello planet #" + planet_number.to_s  # to_s converts to a string
```

Of course, in Ruby, string interpolation is usually simpler than string concatenation with +. With string interpolation, the call to **to_s** is done automatically:

```
"Hello planet ##{planet_number}"
```

The << operator appends its second operand to its first, and should be familiar to C++ programmers. This operator is very different from +; it alters the lefthand operand rather than creating and returning a new object:

```
greeting = "Hello"
greeting << " " << "World"
puts greeting   # Outputs "Hello World"
```

Like +, the << operator does no type conversion on the righthand operand. If the right-hand operand is an integer, however, it is taken to be a character code, and the corresponding character is appended. In Ruby 1.8, only integers between 0 and 255 are allowed. In Ruby 1.9, any integer that represents a valid codepoint in the string's encoding can be used:

```
alphabet = "A"
alphabet << ?B   # Alphabet is now "AB"
alphabet << 67   # And now it is "ABC"
alphabet << 256  # Error in Ruby 1.8: codes must be >=0 and < 256
```

The * operator expects an integer as its righthand operand. It returns a **String** that repeats the text specified on the lefthand side the number of times specified by the righthand side:

```
ellipsis = '.'*3    # Evaluates to '...'
```

If the lefthand side is a string literal, any interpolation is performed just once before the repetition is done. This means that the following too-clever code does not do what you might want it to:

```
a = 0;
"#{a=a+1} " * 3   # Returns "1 1 1 ", not "1 2 3 "
```

String defines all the standard comparison operators. == and != compare strings for equality and inequality. Two strings are equal if—and only if—they have the same length and all characters are equal. <, <=, >, and >= compare the relative order of strings by comparing the character codes of the characters that make up a string. If one string is a prefix of another, the shorter string is less than the longer string. Comparison is based strictly on character codes. No normalization is done, and natural language collation order (if it differs from the numeric sequence of character codes) is ignored.

String comparison is case-sensitive.[*] Remember that in ASCII, the uppercase letters all have lower codes than the lowercase letters. This means, for example, that "Z" < "a". For case-insensitive comparison of ASCII characters, use the **casecmp** method (see

§9.1) or convert your strings to the same case with downcase or upcase methods before comparing them. (Keep in mind that Ruby's knowledge of upper- and lowercase letters is limited to the ASCII character set.)

3.2.4 Accessing Characters and Substrings

Perhaps the most important operator supported by String is the square-bracket array-index operator [], which is used for extracting or altering portions of a string. This operator is quite flexible and can be used with a number of different operand types. It can also be used on the lefthand side of an assignment, as a way of altering string content.

In Ruby 1.8, a string is like an array of bytes or 8-bit character codes. The length of this array is given by the length or size method, and you get or set elements of the array simply by specifying the character number within square brackets:

```
s = 'hello';    # Ruby 1.8
s[0]            # 104: the ASCII character code for the first character 'h'
s[s.length-1]   # 111: the character code of the last character 'o'
s[-1]           # 111: another way of accessing the last character
s[-2]           # 108: the second-to-last character
s[-s.length]    # 104: another way of accessing the first character
s[s.length]     # nil: there is no character at that index
```

Notice that negative array indexes specify a 1-based position from the end of the string. Also notice that Ruby does not throw an exception if you try to access a character beyond the end of the string; it simply returns nil instead.

Ruby 1.9 returns single-character strings rather than character codes when you index a single character. Keep in mind that when working with multibyte strings, with characters encoded using variable numbers of bytes, random access to characters is less efficient than access to the underlying bytes:

```
s = 'hello';    # Ruby 1.9
s[0]            # 'h': the first character of the string, as a string
s[s.length-1]   # 'o': the last character 'o'
s[-1]           # 'o': another way of accessing the last character
s[-2]           # 'l': the second-to-last character
s[-s.length]    # 'h': another way of accessing the first character
s[s.length]     # nil: there is no character at that index
```

To alter individual characters of a string, simply use brackets on the lefthand side of an assignment expression. In Ruby 1.8, the righthand side may be an ASCII character code or a string. In Ruby 1.9, the righthand side must be a string. You can use character literals in either version of the language:

---

[*] In Ruby 1.8, setting the deprecated global variable $= to true makes the ==, <, and related comparison operators perform case-insensitive comparisons. You should not do this, however; setting this variable produces a warning message, even if the Ruby interpreter is invoked without the -w flag. And in Ruby 1.9, $= is no longer supported.

```
s[0] = ?H        # Replace first character with a capital H
s[-1] = ?O       # Replace last character with a capital O
s[s.length] = ?! # ERROR! Can't assign beyond the end of the string
```

The righthand side of an assignment statement like this need not be a character code: it may be any string, including a multicharacter string or the empty string. Again, this works in both Ruby 1.8 and Ruby 1.9:

```
s = "hello"      # Begin with a greeting
s[-1] = ""       # Delete the last character; s is now "hell"
s[-1] = "p!"     # Change new last character and add one; s is now "help!"
```

More often than not, you want to retrieve substrings from a string rather than individual character codes. To do this, use two comma-separated operands between the square brackets. The first operand specifies an index (which may be negative), and the second specifies a length (which must be nonnegative). The result is the substring that begins at the specified index and continues for the specified number of characters:

```
s = "hello"
s[0,2]           # "he"
s[-1,1]          # "o": returns a string, not the character code ?o
s[0,0]           # "": a zero-length substring is always empty
s[0,10]          # "hello": returns all the characters that are available
s[s.length,1]    # "": there is an empty string immediately beyond the end
s[s.length+1,1]  # nil: it is an error to read past that
s[0,-1]          # nil: negative lengths don't make any sense
```

If you assign a string to a string indexed like this, you replace the specified substring with the new string. If the righthand side is the empty string, this is a deletion, and if the lefthand side has zero-length, this is an insertion:

```
s = "hello"
s[0,1] = "H"                # Replace first letter with a capital letter
s[s.length,0] = " world"    # Append by assigning beyond the end of the string
s[5,0] = ","                # Insert a comma, without deleting anything
s[5,6] = ""                 # Delete with no insertion; s == "Hellod"
```

Another way to extract, insert, delete, or replace a substring is by indexing a string with a Range object. We'll explain ranges in detail in §3.5 later. For our purposes here, a Range is two integers separated by dots. When a Range is used to index a string, the return value is the substring whose characters fall within the Range:

```
s = "hello"
s[2..3]          # "ll": characters 2 and 3
s[-3..-1]        # "llo": negative indexes work, too
s[0..0]          # "h": this Range includes one character index
s[0...0]         # "": this Range is empty
s[2..1]          # "": this Range is also empty
s[7..10]         # nil: this Range is outside the string bounds
s[-2..-1] = "p!"      # Replacement: s becomes "help!"
s[0...0] = "Please "  # Insertion: s becomes "Please help!"
s[6..10] = ""         # Deletion: s becomes "Please!"
```

Don't confuse string indexing with two comma-separated integers with this form that uses a single Range object. Although both involve two integers, there is an important difference: the form with the comma specifies an index and a length; the form that uses a Range object specifies two indexes.

It is also possible to index a string with a string. When you do this, the return value is the first substring of the target string that matches the index string, or nil, if no match is found. This form of string indexing is really only useful on the lefthand side of an assignment statement when you want to replace the matched string with some other string:

```
s = "hello"        # Start with the word "hello"
while(s["l"])      # While the string contains the substring "l"
   s["l"] = "L";    # Replace first occurrence of "l" with "L"
end                # Now we have "heLLo"
```

Finally, you can index a string using a regular expression. (Regular expression objects are covered in §9.2.) The result is the first substring of the string that matches the pattern, and again, this form of string indexing is most useful when used on the lefthand side of an assignment:

```
s[/[aeiou]/] = '*'     # Replace first vowel with an asterisk
```

3.2.5 Iterating Strings

In Ruby 1.8, the String class defines an each method that iterates a string line-by-line. The String class includes the methods of the Enumerable module, and they can be used to process the lines of a string. You can use the each_byte iterator in Ruby 1.8 to iterate through the bytes of a string, but there is little advantage to using each_byte over the [] operator because random access to bytes is as quick as sequential access in 1.8.

The situation is quite different in Ruby 1.9, which removes the each method, and in which the String class is no longer Enumerable. In place of each, Ruby 1.9 defines three clearly named string iterators: each_byte iterates sequentially through the individual bytes that comprise a string; each_char iterates the characters; and each_line iterates the lines. If you want to process a string character-by-character, it may be more efficient to use each_char than to use the [] operator and character indexes:

```
s = "¥1000"
s.each_char {|x| print "#{x} " }         # Prints "¥ 1 0 0 0". Ruby 1.9
0.upto(s.size-1) {|i| print "#{s[i]} "}  # Inefficient with multibyte chars
```

3.2.6 String Encodings and Multibyte Characters

Strings are fundamentally different in Ruby 1.8 and Ruby 1.9:

- In Ruby 1.8, strings are a sequence of bytes. When strings are used to represent text (instead of binary data), each byte of the string is assumed to represent a single

ASCII character. In 1.8, the individual elements of a string are not characters, but numbers—the actual byte value or character encoding.

- In Ruby 1.9, on the other hand, strings are true sequences of characters, and those characters need not be confined to the ASCII character set. In 1.9, the individual elements of a string are characters—represented as strings of length 1—rather than integer character codes. Every string has an encoding that specifies the correspondence between the bytes in the string and the characters those bytes represent. Encodings such as the UTF-8 encoding of Unicode characters use variable numbers of bytes for each character, and there is no longer a 1-to-1 (nor even a 2-to-1) correspondence between bytes and characters.

The subsections that follow explain the encoding-related features of strings in Ruby 1.9, and also demonstrate rudimentary support for multibyte characters in Ruby 1.8 using the jcode library.

3.2.6.1 Multibyte characters in Ruby 1.9

The String class has been rewritten in Ruby 1.9 to be aware of and properly handle multibyte characters. Although multibyte support is the biggest change in Ruby 1.9, it is not a highly visible change: code that uses multibyte strings just works. It is worth understanding why it works, however, and this section explains the details.

If a string contains multibyte characters, then the number of bytes does not correspond to the number of characters. In Ruby 1.9, the length and size methods return the number of characters in a string, and the new bytesize method returns the number of bytes. The [] and []= operators allow you to query and set the characters of a string, and the new methods getbyte and setbyte allow you to query and set individual bytes (though you should not often need to do this):

```
# -*- coding: utf-8 -*-   # Specify Unicode UTF-8 characters

# This is a string literal containing a multibyte multiplication character
s = "2×2=4"

# The string contains 6 bytes which encode 5 characters
s.bytesize                              # => 6
s.bytesize.times {|i| print s.getbyte(i), " "} # Prints "50 195 151 50 61 52"
s.length                                # => 5
s.length.times { |i| print s[i], " "}   # Prints "2 × 2 = 4"
s.setbyte(5, s.getbyte(5)+1);           # s is now "2×2=5"
```

Note that the first line in this code is a coding comment that sets the source encoding (see §2.4.1) to UTF-8. Without this comment, the Ruby interpreter would not know how to decode the sequence of bytes in the string literal into a sequence of characters.

When a string contains characters encoded with varying numbers of bytes, it is no longer possible to map directly from character index to byte offset in the string. In the string above, for example, the second character begins at the second byte. But the third character begins at the fourth byte. This means that you cannot assume that random access to arbitrary characters within a string is a fast operation. When you use the [ ] operator, as we did in the code above, to access a character or substring within a multibyte string, the Ruby implementation must internally iterate sequentially through the string to find the desired character index. In general, therefore, you should try to do your string processing using sequential algorithms when possible. That is: use the each_char iterator when possible instead of repeated calls to the [ ] operator. On the other hand, it is usually not necessary to worry too much about this. Ruby implementations optimize the cases that can be optimized, and if a string consists entirely of 1-byte characters, random access to those characters will be efficient. If you want to attempt your own optimizations, you can use the instance method ascii_only? to determine whether a string consists entirely of 7-bit ASCII characters.

The Ruby 1.9 String class defines an encoding method that returns the encoding of a string (the return value is an Encoding object, which is described below):

```
# -*- coding: utf-8 -*-
s = "2×2=4"     # Note multibyte multiplication character
s.encoding      # => <Encoding: UTF-8>
t = "2+2=4"     # All characters are in the ASCII subset of UTF-8
t.encoding      # => <Encoding: US-ASCII>
```

The encoding of a string literal is based on the source encoding of the file it appears within. But its encoding is not always the same as the source encoding. If a string literal contains only 7-bit ASCII characters, then its encoding method will return ASCII, even if the source encoding is UTF-8 (a superset of ASCII), for example. This optimization lets string methods know that all characters in the string are one byte long. Also, if a string literal contains \u escapes, then its encoding will be UTF-8, even if the source encoding is something different.

ASCII and BINARY encodings

The "ASCII-8BIT" encoding shown earlier is Ruby 1.9's name for the legacy encoding used by Ruby 1.8; it is the ASCII character set with no restrictions on the use of non-printing and control characters. In this encoding, one byte always equals one character, and strings can hold binary data or character data.

Certain Ruby 1.9 methods require you to specify an encoding name (or Encoding object —see below). You can specify this ASCII encoding as "ASCII-8BIT" or by its alias "BINARY". This may seem surprising, but it's true: as far as Ruby is concerned, a sequence of bytes with no encoding ("BINARY") is the same as a sequence of 8-bit ASCII characters.

Ruby 1.9 also supports an encoding named "US-ASCII", which is true 7-bit ASCII; it differs from ASCII-8BIT in that it does not allow any bytes with their 8th bit set. The encoding name "ASCII" is an alias for "US-ASCII".

Certain string operations, such as concatenation and pattern matching, require that two strings (or a string and a regular expression) have compatible encodings. If you concatenate an ASCII string with a UTF-8 string, for example, you obtain a UTF-8 string. It is not possible, however, to concatenate a UTF-8 string and an SJIS string: the encodings are not compatible, and an exception will be raised. You can test whether two strings (or a string and a regular expression) have compatible encodings by using the class method `Encoding.compatible?`. If the encodings of the two arguments are compatible, it returns the one that is the superset of the other. If the encodings are incompatible, it returns `nil`.

You can explicitly set the encoding of a string with `force_encoding`. This is useful if you have a string of bytes (read from an I/O stream, perhaps) and want to tell Ruby how they should be interpreted as characters. Or, if you have a string of multibyte characters, but you want to index individual bytes with [ ]:

```
text = stream.readline.force_encoding("utf-8")
bytes = text.dup.force_encoding(nil)   # nil encoding means binary
```

`force_encoding` does not make a copy of its receiver; it modifies the encoding of the string and returns the string. This method does not do any character conversion—the underlying bytes of the string are not changed, only Ruby's interpretation of them is changed. As shown above, the argument to `force_encoding` can be the name of an encoding or `nil` to specify binary encoding. You can also pass an `Encoding` object to specify the encoding.

`force_encoding` does no validation; it does not check that the underlying bytes of the string represent a valid sequence of characters in the specified encoding. Use `valid_encoding?` to perform validation. This instance method takes no arguments and checks whether the bytes of a string can be interpreted as a valid sequence of characters using the string's encoding:

```
s = "\xa4".force_encoding("utf-8")  # This is not a valid UTF-8 string
s.valid_encoding?                   # => false
```

The `encode` method (and the mutating `encode!` variant) of a string is quite different from `force_encoding`. It returns a string that represents the same sequence of characters as its receiver, but using a different encoding. In order to change the encoding of—or *transcode*—a string like this, the `encode` method must alter the underlying bytes that make up the string. Here is an example:

```
# -*- coding: utf-8 -*-
euro1 = "\u20AC"                       # Start with the Unicode Euro character
puts euro1                             # Prints "€"
euro1.encoding                         # => <Encoding:UTF-8>
euro1.bytesize                         # => 3

euro2 = euro1.encode("iso-8859-15")    # Transcode to Latin-15
puts euro2.inspect                     # Prints "\xA4"
euro2.encoding                         # => <Encoding:iso-8859-15>
euro2.bytesize                         # => 1

euro3 = euro2.encode("utf-8")          # Transcode back to UTF-8
euro1 == euro3                         # => true
```

Note that you should not often need to use the encode method. The most common time to transcode strings is before writing them to a file or sending them across a network connection. And, as we'll see in §9.7.2, Ruby's I/O stream classes support the automatic transcoding of text when it is written out.

If the string that you are calling encode on consists of unencoded bytes, you need to specify the encoding by which to interpret those bytes before transcoding them to another encoding. Do this by passing two arguments to encode. The first argument is the desired encoding, and the second argument is the current encoding of the string. For example:

```
# Interpret a byte as an iso-8859-15 codepoint, and transcode to UTF-8
byte = "\xA4"
char = byte.encode("utf-8", "iso-8859-15")
```

That is, the following two lines of code have the same effect:

```
text = bytes.encode(to, from)
text = bytes.dup.force_encoding(from).encode(to)
```

Character encodings differ not only in their mapping from bytes to characters, but in the set of characters that they can represent. Unicode (also known as UCS—the Universal Character Set) tries to allow all characters, but character encodings not based on Unicode can only represent a subset of characters. It is not possible, therefore, to transcode all UTF-8 strings to EUC-JP (for example); Unicode characters that are neither Latin nor Japanese cannot be translated.

If the encode or encode! method encounters a character that it cannot transcode, it raises an exception:

```
"\u20AC".encode("iso-8859-1") # No euro sign in Latin-1, so raise exception
```

encode and encode! accept a hash of transcoding options as their final argument. At the time of this writing, the only defined option name is :invalid, and the only defined value for that key is :ignore. "ri String.encode" will give details when more options are implemented.

3.2.6.2 The Encoding class

The Encoding class of Ruby 1.9 represents a character encoding. Encoding objects act as opaque identifiers for an encoding and do not have many methods of their own. The name method returns the name of an encoding. to_s is a synonym for name, and inspect converts an Encoding object to a string in a more verbose way than name does.

Ruby defines a constant for each of the built-in encodings it supports, and these are the easiest way to specify a hardcoded encoding in your program. The predefined constants include at least the following:

```
Encoding::ASCII_8BIT     # Also ::BINARY
Encoding::UTF_8          # UTF-8-encoded Unicode characters
Encoding::EUC_JP         # EUC-encoded Japanese
Encoding::SHIFT_JIS      # Japanese: also ::SJIS, ::WINDOWS_31J, ::CP932
```

Note that because these are constants, they must be written in uppercase, and hyphens in the encoding names must be converted to underscores. Ruby 1.9 also supports the US-ASCII encoding, the European encodings ISO-8859-1 through ISO-8859-15, and the Unicode UTF-16 and UTF-32 encodings in big-endian and little-endian variants.

If you have an encoding name as a string and want to obtain the corresponding Encoding object, use the Encoding.find factory method:

```
encoding = Encoding.find("utf-8")
```

Using Encoding.find causes the named encoding to be dynamically loaded, if necessary. Encoding.find accepts encoding names that are in either upper- or lowercase. Call the name method of an Encoding to obtain the name of the encoding as a string.

Encoding.list returns an array of all available encoding objects. Encoding.name_list returns an array of the names (as strings) of all available encodings. Many encodings have more than one name in common use, and Encoding.aliases returns a hash that maps encoding aliases to the official encoding names for which they are synonyms. The array returned by Encoding.name_list includes the aliases in the Encoding.aliases hash.

Use Encoding.default_external to obtain the Encoding object that represents the default external encoding (see §2.4.2). To obtain the encoding for the current locale, call Encoding.locale_charmap and pass the resulting string to Encoding.find.

Most methods that expect an Encoding object will also accept a case-insensitive encoding name (such as ascii, binary, utf-8, euc-jp, or sjis) in place of an Encoding object.

3.2.6.3 Multibyte characters in Ruby 1.8

Normally, Ruby 1.8 treats all strings as sequences of 8-bit bytes. There is rudimentary support for multibyte characters (using the UTF-8, EUC, or SJIS encodings) in the jcode module of the standard library.

To use this library, require the jcode module, and set the global $KCODE variable to the encoding that your multibyte characters use. (Alternatively, use the -K command-line option when you start the Ruby interpreter.) The jcode library defines a new jlength method for String objects: it returns the length of the string in characters rather than in bytes. The existing 1.8 length and size methods are unchanged—they return the string length in bytes.

The jcode library does not modify the array indexing operator on strings, and does not allow random access to the characters that comprise a multibyte string. But it does define a new iterator named each_char, which works like the standard each_byte but passes each character of the string (as a string instead of as a character code) to the block of code you supply:

```
$KCODE = "u"        # Specify Unicode UTF-8, or start Ruby with -Ku option
require "jcode"     # Load multibyte character support

mb = "2\303\2272=4" # This is "2×2=4" with a Unicode multiplication sign
```

```
mb.length           # => 6: there are 6 bytes in this string
mb.jlength          # => 5: but only 5 characters
mb.mbchar?          # => 1: position of the first multibyte char, or nil
mb.each_byte do |c| # Iterate through the bytes of the string.
  print c, " "      # c is Fixnum
end                 # Outputs "50 195 151 50 61 52 "
mb.each_char do |c| # Iterate through the characters of the string
  print c, " "      # c is a String with jlength 1 and variable length
end                 # Outputs "2 × 2 = 4 "
```

The jcode library also modifies several existing String methods, such as chop, delete, and tr, to work with multibyte strings.

3.3 Arrays

An array is a sequence of values that allows values to be accessed by their position, or *index*, in the sequence. In Ruby, the first value in an array has index 0. The size and length methods return the number of elements in an array. The last element of the array is at index size-1. Negative index values count from the end of the array, so the last element of an array can also be accessed with an index of –1. The second-to-last has an index of –2, and so on. If you attempt to read an element beyond the end of an array (with an index >= size) or before the beginning of an array (with an index < -size), Ruby simply returns nil and does not throw an exception.

Ruby's arrays are untyped and mutable. The elements of an array need not all be of the same class, and they can be changed at any time. Furthermore, arrays are dynamically resizeable; you can append elements to them and they grow as needed. If you assign a value to an element beyond the end of the array, the array is automatically extended with nil elements. (It is an error, however, to assign a value to an element before the beginning of an array.)

An array literal is a comma-separated list of values, enclosed in square brackets:

```
[1, 2, 3]           # An array that holds three Fixnum objects
[-10...0, 0..10,]   # An array of two ranges; trailing commas are allowed
[[1,2],[3,4],[5]]   # An array of nested arrays
[x+y, x-y, x*y]     # Array elements can be arbitrary expressions
[]                  # The empty array has size 0
```

Ruby includes a special-case syntax for expressing array literals whose elements are short strings without spaces:

```
words = %w[this is a test] # Same as: ['this', 'is', 'a', 'test']
open = %w| ( [ { < |       # Same as: ['(', '[', '{', '<']
white = %W(\s \t \r \n)    # Same as: ["\s", "\t", "\r", "\n"]
```

%w and %W introduce an array literal, much like %q and %Q introduce a String literal. In particular, the delimiter rules for %w and %W are the same as for %q and %Q. Within the delimiters, no quotation marks are required around the array element strings, and no commas are required between the elements. Array elements are delimited by whitespace.

You can also create arrays with the **Array.new** constructor, and this provides options for programmatically initializing the array elements:

```
empty = Array.new       # []: returns a new empty array
nils = Array.new(3)     # [nil, nil, nil]: new array with 3 nil elements
zeros = Array.new(4, 0) # [0, 0, 0, 0]: new array with 4 0 elements
copy = Array.new(nils)  # Make a new copy of an existing array
count = Array.new(3) {|i| i+1}  # [1,2,3]: 3 elements computed from index
```

To obtain the value of an array element, use a single integer within square brackets:

```
a = [0, 1, 4, 9, 16]  # Array holds the squares of the indexes
a[0]         # First element is 0
a[-1]        # Last element is 16
a[-2]        # Second to last element is 9
a[a.size-1]  # Another way to query the last element
a[-a.size]   # Another way to query the first element
a[8]         # Querying beyond the end returns nil
a[-8]        # Querying before the start returns nil, too
```

All of the expressions above, except for the last, can also be used on the lefthand side of an assignment:

```
a[0] = "zero"   # a is ["zero", 1, 4, 9, 16]
a[-1] = 1..16   # a is ["zero", 1, 4, 9, 1..16]
a[8] = 64       # a is ["zero", 1, 4, 9, 1..16, nil, nil, nil, 64]
a[-10] = 100    # Error: can't assign before the start of an array
```

Like strings, arrays can also be indexed with two integers that represent a starting index and a number of elements, or a **Range** object. In either case, the expression returns the specified subarray:

```
a = ('a'..'e').to_a  # Range converted to ['a', 'b', 'c', 'd', 'e']
a[0,0]      # []: this subarray has zero elements
a[1,1]      # ['b']: a one-element array
a[-2,2]     # ['d','e']: the last two elements of the array
a[0..2]     # ['a', 'b', 'c']: the first three elements
a[-2..-1]   # ['d','e']: the last two elements of the array
a[0...-1]   # ['a', 'b', 'c', 'd']: all but the last element
```

When used on the lefthand side of an assignment, a subarray can be replaced by the elements of the array on the righthand side. This basic operation works for insertions and deletions as well:

```
a[0,2] = ['A', 'B']       # a becomes ['A', 'B', 'c', 'd', 'e']
a[2...5]=['C', 'D', 'E']  # a becomes ['A', 'B', 'C', 'D', 'E']
a[0,0] = [1,2,3]          # Insert elements at the beginning of a
a[0..2] = []              # Delete those elements
a[-1,1] = ['Z']           # Replace last element with another
a[-1,1] = 'Z'             # For single elements, the array is optional
a[-2,2] = nil  # Delete last 2 elements in 1.8; replace with nil in 1.9
```

In addition to the square bracket operator for indexing an array, the **Array** class defines a number of other useful operators. Use + to concatenate two arrays:

```
a = [1, 2, 3] + [4, 5]      # [1, 2, 3, 4, 5]
a = a + [[6, 7, 8]]         # [1, 2, 3, 4, 5, [6, 7, 8]]
a = a + 9                   # Error: righthand side must be an array
```

The + operator creates a new array that contains the elements of both its operands. Use << to append an element to the end of an existing array, and use concat to append the elements of an array:

```
a = []          # Start with an empty array
a << 1          # a is [1]
a << 2 << 3     # a is [1, 2, 3]
a << [4,5,6]    # a is [1, 2, 3, [4, 5, 6]]
a.concat [7,8]  # a is [1, 2, 3, [4, 5, 6], 7, 8]
```

The - operator subtracts one array from another. It begins by making a copy of its lefthand array, and then removes any elements from that copy if they appear anywhere in the righthand array:

```
['a', 'b', 'c', 'b', 'a'] - ['b', 'c', 'd']      # ['a', 'a']
```

Like the String class, Array also uses the multiplication operator for repetition:

```
a = [0] * 8     # [0, 0, 0, 0, 0, 0, 0, 0]
```

The Array class borrows the Boolean operators | and & and uses them for union and intersection. | concatenates its arguments and then removes all duplicate elements from the result. & returns an array that holds elements that appear in both of the operand arrays. The returned array does not contain any duplicate elements:

```
a = [1, 1, 2, 2, 3, 3, 4]
b = [5, 5, 4, 4, 3, 3, 2]
a | b    # [1, 2, 3, 4, 5]: duplicates are removed
b | a    # [5, 4, 3, 2, 1]: elements are the same, but order is different
a & b    # [2, 3, 4]
b & a    # [4, 3, 2]
```

Note that these operators are not transitive: a|b is not the same as b|a, for example. If you ignore the ordering of the elements, however, and consider the arrays to be unordered sets, then these operators make more sense. Note also that the algorithm by which union and intersection are performed is not specified, and there are no guarantees about the order of the elements in the returned arrays.

The Array class defines quite a few useful methods. The only one we'll discuss here is the each iterator, used for looping through the elements of an array:

```
a = ('A'..'Z').to_a    # Begin with an array of letters
a.each {|x| print x }  # Print the alphabet, one letter at a time
```

Other Array methods you may want to look up include clear, compact!, delete_if, each_index, empty?, fill, flatten!, include?, index, join, pop, push, reverse, reverse_each, rindex, shift, sort, sort!, uniq!, and unshift.

We'll see arrays again when we consider parallel assignment in §4.5.5 and method invocation in Chapter 6. And we'll explore the Array API in detail in §9.5.2.

3.4 Hashes

A *hash* is a data structure that maintains a set of objects known as *keys*, and associates a value with each key. Hashes are also known as *maps* because they map keys to values. They are sometimes called *associative arrays* because they associate values with each of the keys, and can be thought of as arrays in which the array index can be any object instead of an integer. An example makes this clearer:

```
# This hash will map the names of digits to the digits themselves
numbers = Hash.new      # Create a new, empty, hash object
numbers["one"] = 1      # Map the String "one" to the Fixnum 1
numbers["two"] = 2      # Note that we are using array notation here
numbers["three"] = 3

sum = numbers["one"] + numbers["two"]  # Retrieve values like this
```

This introduction to hashes documents Ruby's hash literal syntax and explains the requirements for an object to be used as a hash key. More information on the API defined by the Hash class is provided in §9.5.3.

3.4.1 Hash Literals

A hash literal is written as a comma-separated list of key/value pairs, enclosed within curly braces. Keys and values are separated with a two-character "arrow": =>. The Hash object created earlier could also be created with the following literal:

```
numbers = { "one" => 1, "two" => 2, "three" => 3 }
```

In general, Symbol objects work more efficiently as hash keys than strings do:

```
numbers = { :one => 1, :two => 2, :three => 3 }
```

Symbols are immutable interned strings, written as colon-prefixed identifiers; they are explained in more detail in §3.6 later in this chapter.

Ruby 1.8 allows commas in place of arrows, but this deprecated syntax is no longer supported in Ruby 1.9:

```
numbers = { :one, 1, :two, 2, :three, 3 } # Same, but harder to read
```

Both Ruby 1.8 and Ruby 1.9 allow a single trailing comma at the end of the key/value list:

```
numbers = { :one => 1, :two => 2, } # Extra comma ignored
```

Ruby 1.9 supports a very useful and succinct hash literal syntax when the keys are symbols. In this case, the colon moves to the end of the hash key and replaces the arrow:[*]

```
numbers = { one: 1, two: 2, three: 3 }
```

Note that there may not be any space between the hash key identifier and the colon.

---

[*] The result is a syntax much like that used by JavaScript objects.

3.4.2 Hash Codes, Equality, and Mutable Keys

Ruby's hashes are implemented, unsurprisingly, with a data structure known as a *hash table*. Objects used as keys in a hash must have a method named hash that returns a Fixnum *hashcode* for the key. If two keys are equal, they must have the same hashcode. Unequal keys may also have the same hashcode, but hash tables are most efficient when duplicate hashcodes are rare.

The Hash class compares keys for equality with the eql? method. For most Ruby classes, eql? works like the == operator (see §3.8.5 for details). If you define a new class that overrides the eql? method, you must also override the hash method, or else instances of your class will not work as keys in a hash. (We'll see examples of writing a hash method in Chapter 7.)

If you define a class and do not override eql?, then instances of that class are compared for object identity when used as hash keys. Two distinct instances of your class are distinct hash keys even if they represent the same content. In this case, the default hash method is appropriate: it returns the unique object_id of the object.

Note that mutable objects are problematic as hash keys. Changing the content of an object typically changes its hashcode. If you use an object as a key and then alter that object, the internal hash table becomes corrupted, and the hash no longer works correctly.

Because strings are mutable but commonly used hash keys, Ruby treats them as a special case and makes private copies of all strings used as keys. This is the only special case, however; you must be very cautious when using any other mutable object as a hash key. Consider making a private copy or calling the freeze method. If you must use mutable hash keys, call the rehash method of the Hash every time you mutate a key.

3.5 Ranges

A Range object represents the values between a start value and an end value. Range literals are written by placing two or three dots between the start and end value. If two dots are used, then the range is *inclusive* and the end value is part of the range. If three dots are used, then the range is *exclusive* and the end value is not part of the range:

```
1..10     # The integers 1 through 10, including 10
1.0...10.0 # The numbers between 1.0 and 10.0, excluding 10.0 itself
```

Test whether a value is included in a range with the include? method (but see below for a discussion of alternatives):

```
cold_war = 1945..1989
cold_war.include? birthdate.year
```

Implicit in the definition of a range is the notion of ordering. If a range is the values between two endpoints, there obviously must be some way to compare values to those endpoints. In Ruby, this is done with the comparison operator <=>, which compares its two operands and evaluates to -1, 0, or 1, depending on their relative order (or equality). Classes such as numbers and strings that have an ordering define the <=> operator. A value can only be used as a range endpoint if it responds to this operator. The endpoints of a range and the values "in" the range are typically all of the same class. Technically, however, any value that is compatible with the <=> operators of the range endpoints can be considered a member of the range.

The primary purpose for ranges is comparison: to be able to determine whether a value is in or out of the range. An important secondary purpose is iteration: if the class of the endpoints of a range defines a `succ` method (for successor), then there is a discrete set of range members, and they can be iterated with `each`, `step`, and `Enumerable` methods. Consider the range 'a'..'c', for example:

```
r = 'a'..'c'
r.each {|l| print "[#{l}]"}    # Prints "[a][b][c]"
r.step(2) { |l| print "[#{l}]"} # Prints "[a][c]"
r.to_a                         # => ['a','b','c']: Enumerable defines to_a
```

The reason this works is that the `String` class defines a `succ` method and 'a'.succ is 'b' and 'b'.succ is 'c'. Ranges that can be iterated like this are *discrete* ranges. Ranges whose endpoints do not define a `succ` method cannot be iterated, and so they can be called *continuous*. Note that ranges with integer endpoints are discrete, but floating-point numbers as endpoints are continuous.

Ranges with integer endpoints are the most commonly used in typical Ruby programs. Because they are discrete, integer ranges can be used to index strings and arrays. They are also a convenient way to represent an enumerable collection of ascending values.

Notice that the code assigns a range literal to a variable, and then invokes methods on the range through the variable. If you want to invoke a method directly on a range literal, you must parenthesize the literal, or the method invocation is actually on the endpoint of the range rather than on the `Range` object itself:

```
1..3.to_a    # Tries to call to_a on the number 3
(1..3).to_a  # => [1,2,3]
```

3.5.1 Testing Membership in a Range

The `Range` class defines methods for determining whether an arbitrary value is a member of (i.e., is included in) a range. Before going into detail on these methods, it is necessary to explain that range membership can be defined in two different ways that are related to the difference between continuous and discrete ranges. A value x is a member of the range `begin..end` by the first definition if:

```
begin <= x <= end
```

And x is a member of the range `begin...end` (with three dots) if:

```
begin <= x < end
```

All range endpoint values must implement the <=> operator, so this definition of membership works for any `Range` object and does not require the endpoints to implement the `succ` method. We'll call this the continuous membership test.

The second definition of membership—discrete membership—does depend on `succ`. It treats a `Range` begin..end as a set that includes `begin`, `begin.succ`, `begin.succ.succ`, and so on. By this definition, range membership is set membership, and a value x is included in a range only if it is a value returned by one of the `succ` invocations. Note that testing for discrete membership is potentially a much more expensive operation than testing for continuous membership.

With that as background, we can describe the `Range` methods for testing membership. Ruby 1.8 supports two methods, `include?` and `member?`. They are synonyms, and both use the continuous membership test:

```
r = 0...100      # The range of integers 0 through 99
r.member? 50     # => true: 50 is a member of the range
r.include? 100   # => false: 100 is excluded from the range
r.include? 99.9  # => true: 99.9 is less than 100
```

The situation is different in Ruby 1.9. That version of the language introduces a new method, `cover?`, which works like `include?` and `member?` do in Ruby 1.8: it always uses the continuous membership test. `include?` and `member?` are still synonyms in Ruby 1.9. If the endpoints of the range are numbers, these methods use the continuous membership test, just as they did in Ruby 1.8. If the endpoints are not numeric, however, they instead use the discrete membership test. We can illustrate these changes with a discrete range of strings (you may want to use *ri* to understand how `String.succ` works):

```
triples = "AAA".."ZZZ"
triples.include? "ABC"       # true; fast in 1.8 and slow in 1.9
triples.include? "ABCD"      # true in 1.8, false in 1.9
triples.cover?   "ABCD"      # true and fast in 1.9
triples.to_a.include? "ABCD" # false and slow in 1.8 and 1.9
```

In practice, most ranges have numeric endpoints, and the `Range` API changes between Ruby 1.8 and 1.9 have little impact.

3.6 Symbols

A typical implementation of a Ruby interpreter maintains a symbol table in which it stores the names of all the classes, methods, and variables it knows about. This allows such an interpreter to avoid most string comparisons: it refers to method names (for example) by their position in this symbol table. This turns a relatively expensive string operation into a relatively cheap integer operation.

These symbols are not purely internal to the interpreter; they can also be used by Ruby programs. A `Symbol` object refers to a symbol. A symbol literal is written by prefixing an identifier or string with a colon:

```
:symbol                    # A Symbol literal
:"symbol"                  # The same literal
:'another long symbol'     # Quotes are useful for symbols with spaces
s = "string"
sym = :"#{s}"              # The Symbol :string
```

Symbols also have a %s literal syntax that allows arbitrary delimiters in the same way that %q and %Q can be used for string literals:

```
%s["]     # Same as :'"'
```

Symbols are often used to refer to method names in reflective code. For example, suppose we want to know if some object has an **each** method:

```
o.respond_to? :each
```

Here's another example. It tests whether a given object responds to a specified method, and, if so, invokes that method:

```
name = :size
if o.respond_to? name
  o.send(name)
end
```

You can convert a String to a Symbol using the intern or to_sym methods. And you can convert a Symbol back into a String with the to_s method or its alias id2name:

```
str = "string"        # Begin with a string
sym = str.intern      # Convert to a symbol
sym = str.to_sym      # Another way to do the same thing
str = sym.to_s        # Convert back to a string
str = sym.id2name     # Another way to do it
```

Two strings may hold the same content and yet be completely distinct objects. This is never the case with symbols. Two strings with the same content will both convert to exactly the same Symbol object. Two distinct Symbol objects will always have different content.

Whenever you write code that uses strings not for their textual content but as a kind of unique identifier, consider using symbols instead. Rather than writing a method that expects an argument to be either the string "AM" or "PM", for example, you could write it to expect the symbol :AM or the symbol :PM. Comparing two Symbol objects for equality is much faster than comparing two strings for equality. For this reason, symbols are generally preferred to strings as hash keys.

In Ruby 1.9, the Symbol class defines a number of String methods, such as length, size, the comparison operators, and even the [ ] and =~ operators. This makes symbols somewhat interchangeable with strings and allows their use as a kind of immutable (and not garbage-collected) string.

3.7 True, False, and Nil

We saw in §2.1.5 that true, false, and nil are keywords in Ruby. true and false are
the two Boolean values, and they represent truth and falsehood, yes and no, on and
off. nil is a special value reserved to indicate the absence of value.

Each of these keywords evaluates to a special object. true evaluates to an object that is
a singleton instance of TrueClass. Likewise, false and nil are singleton instances of
FalseClass and NilClass. Note that there is no Boolean class in Ruby. TrueClass and
FalseClass both have Object as their superclass.

If you want to check whether a value is nil, you can simply compare it to nil, or use
the method nil?:

```
o == nil    # Is o nil?
o.nil?      # Another way to test
```

Note that true, false, and nil refer to objects, not numbers. false and nil are not the
same thing as 0, and true is not the same thing as 1. When Ruby requires a Boolean
value, nil behaves like false, and any value other than nil or false behaves like true.

3.8 Objects

Ruby is a very pure object-oriented language: all values are objects, and there is no
distinction between primitive types and object types as there are in many other languages. In Ruby, all objects inherit from a class named Object and share the methods
defined by that class. This section explains the common features of all objects in Ruby.
It is dense in parts, but it's required reading; the information here is fundamental.

3.8.1 Object References

When we work with objects in Ruby, we are really working with object *references*. It
is not the object itself we manipulate but a reference to it.* When we assign a value to
a variable, we are not copying an object "into" that variable; we are merely storing a
reference to an object into that variable. Some code makes this clear:

```
s = "Ruby"  # Create a String object. Store a reference to it in s.
t = s       # Copy the reference to t. s and t both refer to the same object.
t[-1] = ""  # Modify the object through the reference in t.
print s     # Access the modified object through s. Prints "Rub".
t = "Java"  # t now refers to a different object.
print s,t   # Prints "RubJava".
```

---

* If you are familiar with C or C++, you can think of a reference as a pointer: the address of the object in
memory. Ruby does not use pointers, however. References in Ruby are opaque and internal to the
implementation. There is no way to take the address of a value, dereference a value, or do pointer arithmetic.

When you pass an object to a method in Ruby, it is an object reference that is passed to the method. It is not the object itself, and it is not a reference to the reference to the object. Another way to say this is that method arguments are passed *by value* rather than *by reference*, but that the values passed are object references.

Because object references are passed to methods, methods can use those references to modify the underlying object. These modifications are then visible when the method returns.

3.8.1.1 Immediate values

We've said that all values in Ruby are objects and all objects are manipulated by reference. In the reference implementation, however, Fixnum and Symbol objects are actually "immediate values" rather than references. Neither of these classes have mutator methods, so Fixnum and Symbol objects are immutable, which means that there is really no way to tell that they are manipulated by value rather than by reference.

The existence of immediate values should be considered an implementation detail. The only practical difference between immediate values and reference values is that immediate values cannot have singleton methods defined on them. (Singleton methods are explained in §6.1.4.)

3.8.2 Object Lifetime

The built-in Ruby classes described in this chapter have literal syntaxes, and instances of these classes are created simply by including their values literally in your code. Objects of other classes need to be explicitly created, and this is most often done with a method named new:

```
myObject = myClass.new
```

new is a method of the Class class. It allocates memory to hold the new object, then it initializes the state of that newly allocated "empty" object by invoking its initialize method. The arguments to new are passed directly on to initialize. Most classes define an initialize method to perform whatever initialization is necessary for instances.

The new and initialize methods provide the default technique for creating new classes, but classes may also define other methods, known as "factory methods," that return instances. We'll learn more about new, initialize, and factory methods in §7.4.

Ruby objects never need to be explicitly deallocated, as they do in languages like C and C++. Ruby uses a technique called *garbage collection* to automatically destroy objects that are no longer needed. An object becomes a candidate for garbage collection when it is *unreachable*—when there are no remaining references to the object except from other unreachable objects.

The fact that Ruby uses garbage collection means that Ruby programs are less susceptible to memory leaks than programs written in languages that require objects and memory to be explicitly deallocated and freed. But garbage collection does not mean that memory leaks are impossible: any code that creates long-lived references to objects that would otherwise be short-lived can be a source of memory leaks. Consider a hash used as a cache. If the cache is not pruned using some kind of least-recently-used algorithm, then cached objects will remain reachable as long as the hash itself is reachable. If the hash is referenced through a global variable, then it will be reachable as long as the Ruby interpreter is running.

3.8.3 Object Identity

Every object has an object identifier, a `Fixnum`, that you can obtain with the `object_id` method. The value returned by this method is constant and unique for the lifetime of the object. While the object is accessible, it will always have the same ID, and no other object will share that ID.

The method `id` is a deprecated synonym for `object_id`. Ruby 1.8 issues a warning if you use it, and it has been removed in Ruby 1.9.

`__id__` is a valid synonym for `object_id`. It exists as a fallback, so you can access an object's ID even if the `object_id` method has been undefined or overridden.

The `Object` class implements the `hash` method to simply return an object's ID.

3.8.4 Object Class and Object Type

There are several ways to determine the class of an object in Ruby. The simplest is simply to ask for it:

```
o = "test"  # This is a value
o.class     # Returns an object representing the String class
```

If you are interested in the class hierarchy of an object, you can ask any class what its superclass is:

```
o.class                       # String: o is a String object
o.class.superclass            # Object: superclass of String is Object
o.class.superclass.superclass # nil: Object has no superclass
```

In Ruby 1.9, `Object` is no longer the true root of the class hierarchy:

```
# Ruby 1.9 only
Object.superclass            # BasicObject: Object has a superclass in 1.9
BasicObject.superclass       # nil: BasicObject has no superclass
```

See §7.3 for more on `BasicObject`.

So a particularly straightforward way to check the class of an object is by direct comparison:

```
o.class == String     # true if o is a String
```

The `instance_of?` method does the same thing and is a little more elegant:

```
o.instance_of? String   # true if o is a String
```

Usually when we test the class of an object, we would also like to know if the object is an instance of any subclass of that class. To test this, use the is_a? method, or its synonym kind_of?:

```
x = 1                    # This is the value we're working with
x.instance_of? Fixnum    # true: is an instance of Fixnum
x.instance_of? Numeric   # false: instance_of? doesn't check inheritance
x.is_a? Fixnum           # true: x is a Fixnum
x.is_a? Integer          # true: x is an Integer
x.is_a? Numeric          # true: x is a Numeric
x.is_a? Comparable       # true: works with mixin modules, too
x.is_a? Object           # true for any value of x
```

The Class class defines the === operator in such a way that it can be used in place of is_a?:

```
Numeric === x            # true: x is_a Numeric
```

This idiom is unique to Ruby and is probably less readable than using the more traditional is_a? method.

Every object has a well-defined class in Ruby, and that class never changes during the lifetime of the object. An object's *type*, on the other hand, is more fluid. The type of an object is related to its class, but the class is only part of an object's type. When we talk about the type of an object, we mean the set of behaviors that characterize the object. Another way to put it is that the type of an object is the set of methods it can respond to. (This definition becomes recursive because it is not just the name of the methods that matter, but also the types of arguments that those methods can accept.)

In Ruby programming, we often don't care about the class of an object, we just want to know whether we can invoke some method on it. Consider, for example, the << operator. Arrays, strings, files, and other I/O-related classes define this as an append operator. If we are writing a method that produces textual output, we might write it generically to use this operator. Then our method can be invoked with any argument that implements <<. We don't care about the class of the argument, just that we can append to it. We can test for this with the respond_to? method:

```
o.respond_to? :"<<"  # true if o has an << operator
```

The shortcoming of this approach is that it only checks the name of a method, not the arguments for that method. For example, Fixnum and Bignum implement << as a left-shift operator and expect the argument to be a number instead of a string. Integer objects appear to be "appendable" when we use a respond_to? test, but they produce an error when our code appends a string. There is no general solution to this problem, but an ad-hoc remedy, in this case, is to explicitly rule out Numeric objects with the is_a? method:

```
o.respond_to? :"<<" and not o.is_a? Numeric
```

Another example of the type-versus-class distinction is the StringIO class (from Ruby's standard library). StringIO enables reading from and writing to string objects as if they were IO objects. StringIO mimics the IO API—StringIO objects define the same methods that IO objects do. But StringIO is not a subclass of IO. If you write a method that expects a stream argument, and test the class of the argument with is_a? IO, then your method won't work with StringIO arguments.

Focusing on types rather than classes leads to a programming style known in Ruby as "duck typing." We'll see duck typing examples in Chapter 7.

3.8.5 Object Equality

Ruby has a surprising number of ways to compare objects for equality, and it is important to understand how they work, so you know when to use each method.

3.8.5.1 The equal? method

The equal? method is defined by Object to test whether two values refer to exactly the same object. For any two distinct objects, this method always returns false:

```
a = "Ruby"          # One reference to one String object
b = c = "Ruby"      # Two references to another String object
a.equal?(b)         # false: a and b are different objects
b.equal?(c)         # true: b and c refer to the same object
```

By convention, subclasses never override the equal? method.

Another way to determine if two objects are, in fact, the same object is to check their object_id:

```
a.object_id == b.object_id   # Works like a.equal?(b)
```

3.8.5.2 The == operator

The == operator is the most common way to test for equality. In the Object class, it is simply a synonym for equal?, and it tests whether two object references are identical. Most classes redefine this operator to allow distinct instances to be tested for equality:

```
a = "Ruby"     # One String object
b = "Ruby"     # A different String object with the same content
a.equal?(b)    # false: a and b do not refer to the same object
a == b         # true: but these two distinct objects have equal values
```

Note that the single equals sign in this code is the assignment operator. It takes two equals signs to test for equality in Ruby (this is a convention that Ruby shares with many other programming languages).

Most standard Ruby classes define the == operator to implement a reasonable definition of equality. This includes the Array and Hash classes. Two arrays are equal according to == if they have the same number of elements, and if their corresponding elements are all equal according to ==. Two hashes are == if they contain the same number of key/value pairs, and if the keys and values are themselves equal. (Values are compared with the == operator, but hash keys are compared with the eql? method, described later in this chapter.)

Equality for Java Programmers

If you are a Java programmer, you are used to using the == operator to test if two objects are the same object, and you are used to using the equals method to test whether two distinct objects have the same value. Ruby's convention is just about the opposite of Java's.

The Numeric classes perform simple type conversions in their == operators, so that (for example) the Fixnum 1 and the Float 1.0 compare as equal. The == operator of classes, such as String and Array, normally requires both operands to be of the same class. If the righthand operand defines a to_str or to_ary conversion function (see §3.8.7), then these operators invoke the == operator defined by the righthand operand, and let that object decide whether it is equal to the lefthand string or array. Thus, it is possible (though not common) to define classes with string-like or array-like comparison behavior.

!= ("not-equal") is used in Ruby to test for inequality. When Ruby sees !=, it simply uses the == operator and then inverts the result. This means that a class only needs to define the == operator to define its own notion of equality. Ruby gives you the != operator for free. In Ruby 1.9, however, classes can explicitly define their own != operators.

3.8.5.3 The eql? method

The eql? method is defined by Object as a synonym for equal?. Classes that override it typically use it as a strict version of == that does no type conversion. For example:

```
1 == 1.0     # true: Fixnum and Float objects can be ==
1.eql?(1.0) # false: but they are never eql!
```

The Hash class uses eql? to check whether two hash keys are equal. If two objects are eql?, their hash methods must also return the same value. Typically, if you create a class and define the == operator, you can simply write a hash method and define eql? to use ==.

3.8.5.4 The === operator

The === operator is commonly called the "case equality" operator and is used to test whether the target value of a case statement matches any of the when clauses of that statement. (The case statement is a multiway branch and is explained in Chapter 5.)

Object defines a default === operator so that it invokes the == operator. For many classes, therefore, case equality is the same as == equality. But certain key classes define ===

differently, and in these cases it is more of a membership or matching operator. Range defines === to test whether a value falls within the range. Regexp defines === to test whether a string matches the regular expression. And Class defines === to test whether an object is an instance of that class. In Ruby 1.9, Symbol defines === to return true if the righthand operand is the same symbol as the left or if it is a string holding the same text. Examples:

```
(1..10) === 5    # true: 5 is in the range 1..10
/\d+/ === "123"  # true: the string matches the regular expression
String === "s"   # true: "s" is an instance of the class String
:s === "s"       # true in Ruby 1.9
```

It is uncommon to see the === operator used explicitly like this. More commonly, its use is simply implicit in a case statement.

3.8.5.5 The =~ operator

The =~ operator is defined by String and Regexp (and Symbol in Ruby 1.9) to perform pattern matching, and it isn't really an equality operator at all. But it does have an equals sign in it, so it is listed here for completeness. Object defines a no-op version of =~ that always returns false. You can define this operator in your own class, if that class defines some kind of pattern-matching operation or has a notion of approximate equality, for example. !~ is defined as the inverse of =~. It is definable in Ruby 1.9 but not in Ruby 1.8.

3.8.6 Object Order

Practically every class can define a useful == method for testing its instances for equality. Some classes can also define an ordering. That is: for any two instances of such a class, the two instances must be equal, or one instance must be "less than" the other. Numbers are the most obvious classes for which such an ordering is defined. Strings are also ordered, according to the numeric ordering of the character codes that comprise the strings. (With the ASCII text, this is a rough kind of case-sensitive alphabetical order.) If a class defines an ordering, then instances of the class can be compared and sorted.

In Ruby, classes define an ordering by implementing the <=> operator. This operator should return -1 if its left operand is less than its right operand, 0 if the two operands are equal, and 1 if the left operand is greater than the right operand. If the two operands cannot be meaningfully compared (if the right operand is of a different class, for example), then the operator should return nil:

```
1 <=> 5    # -1
5 <=> 5    # 0
9 <=> 5    # 1
"1" <=> 5  # nil: integers and strings are not comparable
```

The <=> operator is all that is needed to compare values. But it isn't particularly intuitive. So classes that define this operator typically also include the Comparable module as a mixin. (Modules and mixins are covered in §7.5.2.) The `Comparable` mixin defines the following operators in terms of `<=>`:

`<`   Less than

`<=`   Less than or equal

`==`   Equal

`>=`   Greater than or equal

`>`   Greater than

`Comparable` does not define the `!=` operator; Ruby automatically defines that operator as the negation of the `==` operator. In addition to these comparison operators, `Comparable` also defines a useful comparison method named `between?`:

```
1.between?(0,10)  # true: 0 <= 1 <= 10
```

If the `<=>` operator returns `nil`, all the comparison operators derived from it return `false`. The special `Float` value `NaN` is an example:

```
nan = 0.0/0.0;     # zero divided by zero is not-a-number
nan < 0            # false: it is not less than zero
nan > 0            # false: it is not greater than zero
nan == 0           # false: it is not equal to zero
nan == nan         # false: it is not even equal to itself!
nan.equal?(nan)    # this is true, of course
```

Note that defining `<=>` and including the `Comparable` module defines a `==` operator for your class. Some classes define their own `==` operator, typically when they can implement this more efficiently than an equality test based on `<=>`. It is possible to define classes that implement different notions of equality in their `==` and `<=>` operators. A class might do case-sensitive string comparisons for the `==` operator, for example, but then do case-insensitive comparisons for `<=>`, so that instances of the class would sort more naturally. In general, though, it is best if `<=>` returns `0` if and only if `==` returns `true`.

3.8.7 Object Conversion

Many Ruby classes define methods that return a representation of the object as a value of a different class. The `to_s` method, for obtaining a `String` representation of an object, is probably the most commonly implemented and best known of these methods. The subsections that follow describe various categories of conversions.

3.8.7.1 Explicit conversions

Classes define explicit conversion methods for use by application code that needs to convert a value to another representation. The most common methods in this category are `to_s`, `to_i`, `to_f`, and `to_a` to convert to `String`, `Integer`, `Float`, and `Array`, respectively. Ruby 1.9 adds `to_c` and `to_r` methods to convert to `Complex` and `Rational`.

Built-in methods do not typically invoke these methods for you. If you invoke a method that expects a `String` and pass an object of some other kind, that method is not expected to convert the argument with `to_s`. (Values interpolated into double-quoted strings, however, are automatically converted with `to_s`.)

`to_s` is easily the most important of the conversion methods because string representations of objects are so commonly used in user interfaces. An important alternative to `to_s` is the `inspect` method. `to_s` is generally intended to return a human-readable representation of the object, suitable for end users. `inspect`, on the other hand, is intended for debugging use, and should return a representation that is helpful to Ruby developers. The default `inspect` method, inherited from `Object`, simply calls `to_s`.

3.8.7.2 Implicit conversions

Sometimes a class has strong characteristics of some other class. The Ruby `Exception` class represents an error or unexpected condition in a program and encapsulates an error message. In Ruby 1.8, `Exception` objects are not merely convertible to strings; they are string-like objects and can be treated as if they were strings in many contexts.[*] For example:

```
# Ruby 1.8 only
e = Exception.new("not really an exception")
msg = "Error: " + e  # String concatenation with an Exception
```

Because `Exception` objects are string-like, they can be used with the string concatenation operator. This does not work with most other Ruby classes. The reason that `Exception` objects can behave like `String` objects is that, in Ruby 1.8, `Exception` implements the implicit conversion method `to_str`, and the + operator defined by `String` invokes this method on its righthand operand.

Other implicit conversion methods are `to_int` for objects that want to be integer-like, `to_ary` for objects that want to be array-like, and `to_hash` for objects that want to be hash-like. Unfortunately, the circumstances under which these implicit conversion methods are called are not well documented. Among the built-in classes, these implicit conversion methods are not commonly implemented, either.

We noted earlier in passing that the == operator can perform a weak kind of type conversion when testing for equality. The == operators defined by `String`, `Array`, and `Hash` check to see if the righthand operand is of the same class as the lefthand operand. If so, they compare them. If not, they check to see if the righthand operand has a `to_str`, `to_ary`, or `to_hash` method. They don't invoke this method, but if it exists, they invoke the == method of the righthand operand and allow it to decide whether it is equal to the lefthand operand.

---

[*] Doing so is discouraged, however, and Ruby 1.9 no longer allows the implicit conversion of `Exception` to `String`.

In Ruby 1.9, the built-in classes String, Array, Hash, Regexp, and IO all define a class method named try_convert. These methods convert their argument if it defines an appropriate implicit conversion method, or they return nil otherwise. Array.try_convert(o) returns o.to_ary if o defines that method; otherwise, it returns nil. These try_convert methods are convenient if you want to write methods that allow implicit conversions on their arguments.

3.8.7.3 Conversion functions

The Kernel module defines four conversion methods that behave as global conversion functions. These functions—Array, Float, Integer, and String—have the same names as the classes that they convert to, and they are unusual in that they begin with a capital letter.

The Array function attempts to convert its argument to an array by calling to_ary. If that method is not defined or returns nil, it tries the to_a method. If to_a is not defined or returns nil, the Array function simply returns a new array containing the argument as its single element.

The Float function converts Numeric arguments to Float objects directly. For any non-Numeric value, it calls the to_f method.

The Integer function converts its argument to a Fixnum or Bignum. If the argument is a Numeric value, it is converted directly. Floating-point values are truncated rather than rounded. If the argument is a string, it looks for a radix indicator (a leading 0 for octal, 0x for hexadecimal, or 0b for binary) and converts the string accordingly. Unlike String.to_i it does not allow nonnumeric trailing characters. For any other kind of argument, the Integer function first attempts conversion with to_int and then with to_i.

Finally, the String function converts its argument to a string simply by calling its to_s method.

3.8.7.4 Arithmetic operator type coercions

Numeric types define a conversion method named coerce. The intent of this method is to convert the argument to the same type as the numeric object on which the method is invoked, or to convert both objects to some more general compatible type. The coerce method always returns an array that holds two numeric values of the same type. The first element of the array is the converted value of the argument to coerce. The second element of the returned array is the value (converted, if necessary) on which coerce was invoked:

```
1.1.coerce(1)       # [1.0, 1.1]: coerce Fixnum to Float
require "rational"  # Use Rational numbers
r = Rational(1,3)   # One third as a Rational number
r.coerce(2)         # [Rational(2,1), Rational(1,3)]: Fixnum to Rational
```

The coerce method is used by the arithmetic operators. The + operator defined by Fixnum doesn't know about Rational numbers, for example, and if its righthand operand is a Rational value, it doesn't know how to add it. coerce provides the solution. Numeric operators are written so that if they don't know the type of the righthand operand, they invoke the coerce method of the righthand operand, passing the lefthand operand as an argument. Returning to our example of adding a Fixnum and a Rational, the coerce method of Rational returns an array of two Rational values. Now the + operator defined by Fixnum can simply invoke + on the values in the array.

3.8.7.5 Boolean type conversions

Boolean values deserve a special mention in the context of type conversion. Ruby is very strict with its Boolean values: true and false have to_s methods, which return "true" and "false" but define no other conversion methods. And there is no to_b method to convert other values to Booleans.

In some languages, false is the same thing as 0, or can be converted to and from 0. In Ruby, the values true and false are their own distinct objects, and there are no implicit conversions that convert other values to true or false. This is only half the story, however. Ruby's Boolean operators and its conditional and looping constructs that use Boolean expressions can work with values other than true and false. The rule is simple: in Boolean expressions, any value other than false or nil behaves like (but is not converted to) true. nil, on the other hand behaves like false.

Suppose you want to test whether the variable x is nil or not. In some languages, you must explicitly write a comparison expression that evaluates to true or false:

```
if x != nil   # Expression "x != nil" returns true or false to the if
  puts x      # Print x if it is defined
end
```

This code works in Ruby, but it is more common simply to take advantage of the fact that all values other than nil and false behave like true:

```
if x        # If x is non-nil
  puts x    # Then print it
end
```

It is important to remember that values like 0, 0.0, and the empty string "" behave like true in Ruby, which is surprising if you are used to languages like C or JavaScript.

3.8.8 Copying Objects

The Object class defines two closely related methods for copying objects. Both clone and dup return a shallow copy of the object on which they are invoked. If the copied object includes internal state that refers to other objects, only the object references are copied, not the referenced objects themselves.

If the object being copied defines an `initialize_copy` method, then `clone` and `dup` simply allocate a new, empty instance of the class and invoke the `initialize_copy` method on this empty instance. The object to be copied is passed as an argument, and this "copy constructor" can initialize the copy however it desires. For example, the `initialize_copy` method could recursively copy the internal data of an object so that the resulting object is not a simple shallow copy of the original.

Classes can also override the `clone` and `dup` methods directly to produce any kind of copy they desire.

There are two important differences between the `clone` and `dup` methods defined by `Object`. First, `clone` copies both the frozen and tainted state (defined shortly) of an object, whereas `dup` only copies the tainted state; calling `dup` on a frozen object returns an unfrozen copy. Second, `clone` copies any singleton methods of the object, whereas `dup` does not.

3.8.9 Marshaling Objects

You can save the state of an object by passing it to the class method `Marshal.dump`.[*] If you pass an I/O stream object as the second argument, `Marshal.dump` writes the state of the object (and, recursively, any objects it references) to that stream. Otherwise, it simply returns the encoded state as a binary string.

To restore a marshaled object, pass a string or an I/O stream containing the object to `Marshal.load`.

Marshaling an object is a very simple way to save its state for later use, and these methods can be used to provide an automatic file format for Ruby programs. Note, however, that the binary format used by `Marshal.dump` and `Marshal.load` is version-dependent, and newer versions of Ruby are not guaranteed to be able to read marshaled objects written by older versions of Ruby.

Another use for `Marshal.dump` and `Marshal.load` is to create deep copies of objects:

```
def deepcopy(o)
  Marshal.load(Marshal.dump(o))
end
```

Note that files and I/O streams, as well as `Method` and `Binding` objects, are too dynamic to be marshaled; there would be no reliable way to restore their state.

YAML ("YAML Ain't Markup Language") is a commonly used alternative to the `Marshal` module that dumps objects to (and loads objects from) a human-readable text format. It is in the standard library, and you must `require 'yaml'` to use it.

---

[*] The word "marshal" and its variants are sometimes spelled with two ls: marshall, marshalled, etc. If you spell the word this way, you'll need to remember that the name of the Ruby class has only a single l.

3.8.10 Freezing Objects

Any object may be *frozen* by calling its `freeze` method. A frozen object becomes immutable—none of its internal state may be changed, and an attempt to call any of its mutator methods fails:

```
s = "ice"      # Strings are mutable objects
s.freeze       # Make this string immutable
s.frozen?      # true: it has been frozen
s.upcase!      # TypeError: can't modify frozen string
s[0] = "ni"    # TypeError: can't modify frozen string
```

Freezing a class object prevents the addition of any methods to that class.

You can check whether an object is frozen with the `frozen?` method. Once frozen, there is no way to "thaw" an object. If you copy a frozen object with `clone`, the copy will also be frozen. If you copy a frozen object with `dup`, however, the copy will not be frozen.

3.8.11 Tainting Objects

Web applications must often keep track of data derived from untrusted user input to avoid SQL injection attacks and similar security risks. Ruby provides a simple solution to this problem: any object may be marked as tainted by calling its `taint` method. Once an object is tainted, any objects derived from it will also be tainted. The taint of an object can be tested with the `tainted?` method:

```
s = "untrusted"    # Objects are normally untainted
s.taint            # Mark this untrusted object as tainted
s.tainted?         # true: it is tainted
s.upcase.tainted?  # true: derived objects are tainted
s[3,4].tainted?    # true: substrings are tainted
```

User input—such as command-line arguments, environment variables, and strings read with `gets`—are automatically tainted.

Copies of tainted objects made with `clone` and `dup` remain tainted. A tainted object may be untainted with the `untaint` method. You should only do this, of course, if you have examined the object and are convinced that it presents no security risks.

The object tainting mechanism of Ruby is most powerful when used with the global variable `$SAFE`. When this variable is set to a value greater than zero, Ruby restricts various built-in methods so that they will not work with tainted data. See Chapter 10 for further details on the `$SAFE` variable.

CHAPTER 4
Expressions and Operators

An *expression* is a chunk of Ruby code that the Ruby interpreter can evaluate to produce a value. Here are some sample expressions:

```
2                      # A numeric literal
x                      # A local variable reference
Math.sqrt(2)           # A method invocation
x = Math.sqrt(2)       # Assignment
x*x                    # Multiplication with the * operator
```

As you can see, primary expressions—such as literals, variable references, and method invocations—can be combined into larger expressions with *operators*, such as the assignment operator and the multiplication operator.

Many programming languages distinguish between low-level expressions and higher-level *statements*, such as conditionals and loops. In these languages, statements control the flow of a program, but they do not have values. They are executed, rather than evaluated. In Ruby, there is no clear distinction between statements and expressions; everything in Ruby, including class and method definitions, can be evaluated as an expression and will return a value. It is still useful, however, to distinguish syntax typically used as expressions from syntax typically used as statements. Ruby expressions that affect flow-of-control are documented in Chapter 5. Ruby expressions that define methods and classes are covered in Chapters 6 and 7.

This chapter covers the simpler, more traditional sort of expressions. The simplest expressions are literal values, which we already documented in Chapter 3. This chapter explains variable and constant references, method invocations, assignment, and compound expressions created by combining smaller expressions with operators.

4.1 Literals and Keyword Literals

Literals are values such as `1.0`, `'hello world'`, and `[]` that are embedded directly into your program text. We introduced them in Chapter 2 and documented them in detail in Chapter 3.

It is worth noting that many literals, such as numbers, are primary expressions—the simplest possible expressions not composed of simpler expressions. Other literals, such as array and hash literals and double-quoted strings that use interpolation, include subexpressions and are therefore not primary expressions.

Certain Ruby keywords are primary expressions and can be considered *keyword literals* or specialized forms of variable reference:

nil	Evaluates to the nil value, of class NilClass.
true	Evaluates to the singleton instance of class TrueClass, an object that represents the Boolean value true.
false	Evaluates to the singleton instance of class FalseClass, an object that represents the Boolean value false.
self	Evaluates to the current object. (See Chapter 7 for more about self.)

`__FILE__`	Evaluates to a string that names the file that the Ruby interpreter is executing. This can be useful in error messages.
`__LINE__`	Evaluates to an integer that specifies the line number within `__FILE__` of the current line of code.
`__ENCODING__`	Evaluates to an `Encoding` object that specifies the encoding of the current file. (Ruby 1.9 only.)

4.2 Variable References

A *variable* is simply a name for a value. Variables are created and values assigned to them by assignment expressions, which are covered later in this chapter. When the name of a variable appears in a program anywhere other than the lefthand side of an assignment, it is a variable reference expression and evaluates to the value of the variable:

```
one = 1.0      # This is an assignment expression
one            # This variable reference expression evaluates to 1.0
```

As explained in Chapter 2, there are four kinds of variables in Ruby, and lexical rules govern their names. Variables that begin with $ are global variables, visible throughout a Ruby program. Variables that begin with @ and @@ are instance variables and class variables, used in object-oriented programming and explained in Chapter 7. And variables whose names begin with an underscore or a lowercase letter are local variables, defined only within the current method or block. (See §5.4.3 for more about the scope of local variables.)

Variables always have simple, unqualified names. If a . or :: appears in an expression, then that expression is either a reference to a constant or a method invocation. For example, `Math::PI` is a reference to a constant, and the expression `item.price` is an invocation of the method named `price` on the value held by the variable `item`.

The Ruby interpreter predefines a number of global variables when it starts up. See Chapter 10 for a list of these variables.

4.2.1 Uninitialized Variables

In general, you should always assign a value to, or *initialize*, your variables before using them in expressions. In some circumstances, however, Ruby will allow you to use variables that have not yet been initialized. The rules are different for different kinds of variables:

Class variables
    Class variables must always have a value assigned to them before they are used. Ruby raises a `NameError` if you refer to a class variable to which no value has been assigned.

Instance variables

> If you refer to an uninitialized instance variable, Ruby returns `nil`. It is considered bad programming to rely on this behavior, however. Ruby will issue a warning about the uninitialized variable if you run it with the `-w` option.

Global variables

> Uninitialized global variables are like uninitialized instance variables: they evaluate to `nil`, but cause a warning when Ruby is run with the `-w` flag.

Local variables

> This case is more complicated than the others because local variables don't have a punctuation character as a prefix. This means that local variable references look just like method invocation expressions. If the Ruby interpreter has seen an assignment to a local variable, it knows it is a variable and not a method, and it can return the value of the variable. If there has been no assignment, then Ruby treats the expression as a method invocation. If no method by that name exists, Ruby raises a `NameError`.

> In general, therefore, attempting to use a local variable before it has been initialized results in an error. There is one quirk—a variable comes into existence when the Ruby interpreter sees an assignment expression for that variable. This is the case even if that assignment is not actually executed. A variable that exists but has not been assigned a value is given the default value `nil`. For example:

```
a = 0.0 if false    # This assignment is never executed
print a             # Prints nil: the variable exists but is not assigned
print b             # NameError: no variable or method named b exists
```

4.3 Constant References

A constant in Ruby is like a variable, except that its value is supposed to remain constant for the duration of a program. The Ruby interpreter does not actually enforce the constancy of constants, but it does issue a warning if a program changes the value of a constant. Lexically, the names of constants look like the names of local variables, except that they begin with a capital letter. By convention, most constants are written in all uppercase with underscores to separate words, `LIKE_THIS`. Ruby class and module names are also constants, but they are conventionally written using initial capital letters and camel case, `LikeThis`.

Although constants look like local variables with capital letters, they have the visibility of global variables: they can be used anywhere in a Ruby program without regard to scope. Unlike global variables, however, constants can be defined by classes and modules and can therefore have qualified names.

A constant reference is an expression that evaluates to the value of the named constant. The simplest constant references are primary expressions—they consist simply of the name of the constant:

```
CM_PER_INCH = 2.54  # Define a constant.
CM_PER_INCH         # Refer to the constant. Evaluates to 2.54.
```

In addition to simple references like this one, constant references can also be compound expressions. In this case, `::` is used to separate the name of the constant from the class or module in which it is defined. The lefthand side of the `::` may be an arbitrary expression that evaluates to a class or module object. (Usually, however, this expression is a simple constant reference that just names the class or module.) The righthand side of the `::` is the name of a constant defined by the class or module. For example:

```
Conversions::CM_PER_INCH # Constant defined in the Conversions module
modules[0]::NAME         # Constant defined by an element of an array
```

Modules may be nested, which means that constants may be defined in nested namespaces like this:

```
Conversions::Area::HECTARES_PER_ACRE
```

The lefthand side of the `::` may be omitted, in which case the constant is looked up in the global scope:

```
::ARGV      # The global constant ARGV
```

Note that there is not actually a "global scope" for constants. Like global functions, global constants are defined (and looked up) within the `Object` class. The expression `::ARGV`, therefore, is simply shorthand for `Object::ARGV`.

When a constant reference expression is qualified with a `::`, Ruby knows exactly where to look up the specified constant. When there is no qualifying `::`, however, the Ruby interpreter must search for an appropriate definition of the constant. It searches the lexically enclosing scope as well as the inheritance hierarchy of the enclosing class or module. Complete details are in §7.9.

When Ruby evaluates a constant reference expression, it returns the value of the constant, or it raises a `NameError` exception if no constant by that name could be found. Note that constants do not exist until a value is actually assigned to them. This is unlike variables that can come into existence when the interpreter sees, but does not execute, an assignment.

The Ruby interpreter predefines some constants when it starts up. See Chapter 10 for a list.

4.4 Method Invocations

A method invocation expression has four parts:

- An arbitrary expression whose value is the object on which the method is invoked. This expression is followed by `.` or `::` to separate it from the method name that follows. The expression and separator are optional; if omitted, the method is invoked on `self`.

- The name of the method being invoked. This is the only required piece of a method invocation expression.

- The argument values being passed to the method. The list of arguments may be enclosed in parentheses, but these are usually optional. (Optional and required parentheses are discussed in detail in §6.3.) If there is more than one argument, they are separated from each other with commas. The number and type of arguments required depend on the method definition. Some methods expect no arguments.

- An optional block of code delimited by curly braces or by a do/end pair. The method may invoke this code using the yield keyword. This ability to associate arbitrary code with any method invocation is the basis for Ruby's powerful iterator methods. We'll learn much more about blocks associated with method invocations in §5.3 and §5.4.

A method name is usually separated from the object on which it is invoked with a .. :: is also allowed, but it is rarely used because it can make method invocations look more like constant reference expressions.

When the Ruby interpreter has the name of a method and an object on which it is to be invoked, it finds the appropriate definition of that named method using a process known as "method lookup" or "method name resolution." The details are not important here, but they are explained thoroughly in §7.8.

The value of a method invocation expression is the value of the last evaluated expression in the body of the method. We'll have more to say about method definitions, method invocations, and method return values in Chapter 6. Here, however, are some examples of method invocations:

```
puts "hello world"   # "puts" invoked on self, with one string arg
Math.sqrt(2)         # "sqrt" invoked on object Math with one arg
message.length       # "length" invoked on object message; no args
a.each {|x| p x }    # "each" invoked on object a, with an associated block
```

Invoking Global Functions

Look again at this method invocation shown earlier:

```
puts "hello world"
```

This is an invocation of the Kernel method puts. Methods defined by Kernel are global functions, as are any methods defined at the top-level, outside of any classes. Global functions are defined as private methods of the Object class. We'll learn about private methods in Chapter 7. For now, you just need to know that private methods are not allowed to be explicitly invoked on a receiver object—they are always implicitly invoked on self. self is always defined, and no matter what its value is, that value is an Object. Because global functions are methods of Object, these methods can always be invoked (implicitly) in any context, regardless of the value of self.

One of the method invocation examples shown earlier was `message.length`. You may be tempted to think of it as a variable reference expression, evaluating to the value of the variable `length` in the object `message`. This is not the case, however. Ruby has a very pure object-oriented programming model: Ruby objects may encapsulate any number of internal instance variables, but they expose only methods to the outside world. Because the `length` method expects no arguments and is invoked without optional parentheses, it looks like a variable reference. In fact, this is intentional. Methods like these are called attribute accessor methods, and we say that the `message` object has a `length` attribute.[*] As we'll see, it is possible for the `message` object to define a method named `length=`. If this method expects a single argument, then it is an attribute setter method and Ruby invokes it in response to assignment. If such a method is defined, then these two lines of code would both invoke the same method:

```
message.length=(3)    # Traditional method invocation
message.length = 3    # Method invocation masquerading as assignment
```

Now consider the following line of code, assuming that the variable `a` holds an array:

```
a[0]
```

You might again think that this is a special kind of variable reference expression, where the variable in question is actually an array element. Again, however, this is method invocation. The Ruby interpreter converts the array access into this:

```
a.[](0)
```

The array access becomes an invocation of the method named [ ] on the array, with the array index as its argument. This array access syntax is not limited to arrays. Any object is allowed to define a method named [ ]. When the object is "indexed" with square brackets, any values within the brackets will be passed to the method. If the [ ] method is written to expect three arguments, then you should put three comma-separated expressions within the square brackets.

Assignment to arrays is also done via method invocation. If the object o defines a method named [ ]=, then the expression o[x]=y becomes o.[]=(x,y), and the expression o[x,y]=z becomes o.[]=(x,y,z).

We'll see later in this chapter that many of Ruby's operators are defined as methods, and expressions like x+y are evaluated as x.+(y), where the method name is +. The fact that many of Ruby's operators are defined as methods means that you can redefine these operators in your own classes.

Now let's consider this very simple expression:

```
x
```

---

[*] This is not to say that every no-argument method is an attribute accessor. The **sort** method of an array, for example, has no arguments, but it cannot be said to return an attribute value.

If a variable named x exists (that is, if the Ruby interpreter has seen an assignment to x), then this is a variable reference expression. If no such variable exists, then this is an invocation of the method x, with no arguments, on self.

The Ruby-reserved word super is a special kind of method invocation expression. This keyword is used when creating a subclass of another class. By itself, super passes the arguments of the current method to the method with the same name in the superclass. It can also be used as if it were actually the name of a method and can be followed by an arbitrary argument list. The super keyword is covered in detail in §7.3.3.

4.5 Assignments

An assignment expression specifies one or more values for one or more lvalues. *lvalue* is the term for something that can appear on the lefthand side of an assignment operator. (Values on the righthand side of an assignment operator are sometimes called *rvalues* by contrast.) Variables, constants, attributes, and array elements are lvalues in Ruby. The rules for and the meaning of assignment expressions are somewhat different for different kinds of lvalues, and each kind is described in detail in this section.

There are three different forms of assignment expressions in Ruby. Simple assignment involves one lvalue, the = operator, and one rvalue. For example:

```
x = 1     # Set the lvalue x to the value 1
```

Abbreviated assignment is a shorthand expression that updates the value of a variable by applying some other operation (such as addition) to the current value of the variable. Abbreviated assignment uses assignment operators like += and *= that combine binary operators with an equals sign:

```
x += 1    # Set the lvalue x to the value x + 1
```

Finally, parallel assignment is any assignment expression that has more than one lvalue or more than one rvalue. Here is a simple example:

```
x,y,z = 1,2,3   # Set x to 1, y to 2 and z to 3
```

Parallel assignment is more complicated when the number of lvalues is not the same as the number of rvalues or when there is an array on the right. Complete details follow.

The value of an assignment expression is the value (or an array of the values) assigned. Also, the assignment operator is "right-associative"—if multiple assignments appear in a single expression, they are evaluated from right to left. This means that the assignment can be chained to assign the same value to multiple variables:

```
x = y = 0   # Set x and y to 0
```

Note that this is not a case of parallel assignment—it is two simple assignments, chained together: y is assigned the value 0, and then x is assigned the value (also 0) of that first assignment.

Assignment and Side Effects

More important than the value of an assignment expression is the fact that assignments set the value of a variable (or other lvalue) and thereby affect program state. This effect on program state is called a *side effect* of the assignment.

Many expressions have no side effects and do not affect program state. They are *idempotent*. This means that the expression may be evaluated over and over again and will return the same value each time. And it means that evaluating the expression has no effect on the value of other expressions. Here are some expressions without side effects:

```
x + y
Math.sqrt(2)
```

It is important to understand that assignments are not idempotent:

```
x = 1       # Affects the value of other expressions that use x
x += 1      # Returns a different value each time it is evaluated
```

Some methods, such as `Math.sqrt`, are idempotent: they can be invoked without side effects. Other methods are not, and this largely depends on whether those methods perform assignments to nonlocal variables.

4.5.1 Assigning to Variables

When we think of assignment, we usually think of variables, and indeed, these are the most common lvalues in assignment expressions. Recall that Ruby has four kinds of variables: local variables, global variables, instance variables, and class variables. These are distinguished from each other by the first character in the variable name. Assignment works the same for all four kinds of variables, so we do not need to distinguish between the types of variables here.

Keep in mind that the instance variables of Ruby's objects are never visible outside of the object, and variable names are never qualified with an object name. Consider this assignment:

```
point.x, point.y = 1, 2
```

The lvalues in this expression are not variables; they are attributes, and are explained shortly.

Assignment to a variable works as you would expect: the variable is simply set to the specified value. The only wrinkle has to do with variable declaration and an ambiguity between local variable names and method names. Ruby has no syntax to explicitly declare a variable: variables simply come into existence when they are assigned. Also, local variable names and method names look the same—there is no prefix like $ to distinguish them. Thus, a simple expression such as x could refer to a local variable named x or a method of `self` named x. To resolve this ambiguity, Ruby treats an identifier as a local variable if it has seen any previous assignment to the variable. It does this even if that assignment was never executed. The following code demonstrates:

```
class Ambiguous
  def x; 1; end # A method named "x". Always returns 1

  def test
    puts x       # No variable has been seen; refers to method above: prints 1

    # The line below is never evaluated, because of the "if false" clause. But
    # the parser sees it and treats x as a variable for the rest of the method.
    x = 0 if false

    puts x      # x is a variable, but has never been assigned to: prints nil

    x = 2       # This assignment does get evaluated
    puts x      # So now this line prints 2
  end
end
```

4.5.2 Assigning to Constants

Constants are different from variables in an obvious way: their values are intended to remain constant throughout the execution of a program. Therefore, there are some special rules for assignment to constants:

- Assignment to a constant that already exists causes Ruby to issue a warning. Ruby does execute the assignment, however, which means that constants are not really constant.

- Assignment to constants is not allowed within the body of a method. Ruby assumes that methods are intended to be invoked more than once; if you could assign to a constant in a method, that method would issue warnings on every invocation after the first. So, this is simply not allowed.

Unlike variables, constants do not come into existence until the Ruby interpreter actually executes the assignment expression. A nonevaluated expression like the following does *not* create a constant:

```
N = 100 if false
```

Note that this means a constant is never in an uninitialized state. If a constant exists, then it has a value assigned to it. A constant will only have the value nil if that is actually the value it was given.

4.5.3 Assigning to Attributes and Array Elements

Assignment to an attribute or array element is actually Ruby shorthand for method invocation. Suppose an object o has a method named m=: the method name has an equals sign as its last character. Then o.m can be used as an lvalue in an assignment expression. Suppose, furthermore, that the value v is assigned:

```
o.m = v
```

The Ruby interpreter converts this assignment to the following method invocation:

```
o.m=(v)  # If we omit the parens and add a space, this looks like assignment!
```

That is, it passes the value v to the method m=. That method can do whatever it wants with the value. Typically, it will check that the value is of the desired type and within the desired range, and it will then store it in an instance variable of the object. Methods like m= are usually accompanied by a method m, which simply returns the value most recently passed to m=. We say that m= is a *setter* method and m is a *getter* method. When an object has this pair of methods, we say that it has an attribute m. Attributes are sometimes called "properties" in other languages. We'll learn more about attributes in Ruby in §7.1.5.

Assigning values to array elements is also done by method invocation. If an object o defines a method named [ ]= (the method name is just those three punctuation characters) that expects two arguments, then the expression o[x] = y is actually executed as:

```
o.[]=(x,y)
```

If an object has a [ ]= method that expects three arguments, then it can be indexed with two values between the square brackets. The following two expressions are equivalent in this case:

```
o[x,y] = z
o.[]=(x,y,z)
```

4.5.4 Abbreviated Assignment

Abbreviated assignment is a form of assignment that combines assignment with some other operation. It is used most commonly to increment variables:

```
x += 1
```

+= is not a real Ruby operator, and the expression above is simply an abbreviation for:

```
x = x + 1
```

Abbreviated assignment cannot be combined with parallel assignment: it only works when there is a single lvalue on the left and a single value on the right. It should not be used when the lvalue is a constant because it will reassign the constant and cause a warning. Abbreviated assignment can, however, be used when the lvalue is an attribute. The following two expressions are equivalent:

```
o.m += 1
o.m=(o.m()+1)
```

Abbreviated assignment even works when the lvalue is an array element. These two expressions are equivalent:

```
o[x] -= 2
o.[]=(x, o.[](x) - 2)
```

Note that this code uses -= instead of +=. As you might expect, the -= pseudooperator subtracts its rvalue from its lvalue.

In addition to += and -=, there are 11 other pseudooperators that can be used for abbreviated assignment. They are listed in Table 4-1. Note that these are not true operators themselves, they are simply shorthand for expressions that use other operators. The meanings of those other operators are described in detail later in this chapter. Also, as we'll see later, many of these other operators are defined as methods. If a class defines a method named +, for example, then that changes the meaning of abbreviated assignment with += for all instances of that class.

Table 4-1. Abbreviated assignment pseudooperators

Assignment	Expansion
x += y	x = x + y
x -= y	x = x - y
x *= y	x = x * y
x /= y	x = x / y
x %= y	x = x % y
x **= y	x = x ** y
x &&= y	x = x && y
x ||= y	x = x || y
x &= y	x = x & y
x |= y	x = x	y
x ^= y	x = x ^ y
x <<= y	x = x << y
x >>= y	x = x >> y

The ||= Idiom

As noted at the beginning of this section, the most common use of abbreviated assignment is to increment a variable with +=. Variables are also commonly decremented with -=. The other pseudooperators are much less commonly used. One idiom is worth knowing about, however. Suppose you are writing a method that computes some values, appends them to an array, and returns the array. You want to allow the user to specify the array that the results should be appended to. But if the user does not specify the array, you want to create a new, empty array. You might use this line:

```
results ||= []
```

Think about this for a moment. It expands to:

```
results = results || []
```

If you know the || operator from other languages, or if you've read ahead to learn about || in Ruby, then you know that the righthand side of this assignment evaluates to the value of `results`, unless that is `nil` or `false`. In that case, it evaluates to a new, empty array. This means that the abbreviated assignment shown here leaves `results` unchanged, unless it is `nil` or `false`, in which case it assigns a new array.

The abbreviated assignment operator ||= actually behaves slightly differently than the expansion shown here. If the lvalue of ||= is not `nil` or `false`, no assignment is actually performed. If the lvalue is an attribute or array element, the setter method that performs assignment is not invoked.

4.5.5 Parallel Assignment

Parallel assignment is any assignment expression that has more than one lvalue, more than one rvalue, or both. Multiple lvalues and multiple rvalues are separated from each other with commas. lvalues and rvalues may be prefixed with *, which is sometimes called the *splat operator*, though it is not a true operator. The meaning of * is explained later in this section.

Most parallel assignment expressions are straightforward, and it is obvious what they mean. There are some complicated cases, however, and the following subsections explain all the possibilities.

4.5.5.1 Same number of lvalues and rvalues

Parallel assignment is at its simplest when there are the same number of lvalues and rvalues:

```
x, y, z = 1, 2, 3    # x=1; y=2; z=3
```

In this case, the first rvalue is assigned to the first lvalue; the second rvalue is assigned to the second lvalue; and so on.

These assignments are effectively performed in parallel, not sequentially. For example, the following two lines are not the same:

```
x,y = y,x      # Parallel: swap the value of two variables
x = y; y = x  # Sequential: both variables have same value
```

4.5.5.2 One lvalue, multiple rvalues

When there is a single lvalue and more than one rvalue, Ruby creates an array to hold the rvalues and assigns that array to the lvalue:

```
x = 1, 2, 3      # x = [1,2,3]
```

You can place an * before the lvalue without changing the meaning or the return value of this assignment.

If you want to prevent the multiple rvalues from being combined into a single array, follow the lvalue with a comma. Even with no lvalue after that comma, this makes Ruby behave as if there were multiple lvalues:

```
x, = 1, 2, 3    # x = 1; other values are discarded
```

4.5.5.3 Multiple lvalues, single array rvalue

When there are multiple lvalues and only a single rvalue, Ruby attempts to expand the rvalue into a list of values to assign. If the rvalue is an array, Ruby expands the array so that each element becomes its own rvalue. If the rvalue is not an array but implements a to_ary method, Ruby invokes that method and then expands the array it returns:

```
x, y, z = [1, 2, 3]  # Same as x,y,z = 1,2,3
```

The parallel assignment has been transformed so that there are multiple lvalues and zero (if the expanded array was empty) or more rvalues. If the number of lvalues and rvalues are the same, then assignment occurs as described earlier in §4.5.5.1. If the numbers are different, then assignment occurs as described next in §4.5.5.4.

We can use the trailing-comma trick described above to transform an ordinary non-parallel assignment into a parallel assignment that automatically unpacks an array on the right:

```
x = [1,2]    # x becomes [1,2]: this is not parallel assignment
x, = [1,2]   # x becomes 1: the trailing comma makes it parallel
```

4.5.5.4 Different numbers of lvalues and rvalues

If there are more lvalues than rvalues, and no splat operator is involved, then the first rvalue is assigned to the first lvalue, the second rvalue is assigned to the second lvalue, and so on, until all the rvalues have been assigned. Next, each of the remaining lvalues is assigned nil, overwriting any existing value for that lvalue:

```
x, y, z = 1, 2  # x=1; y=2; z=nil
```

If there are more rvalues than lvalues, and no splat operator is involved, then rvalues are assigned—in order—to each of the lvalues, and the remaining rvalues are discarded:

```
x, y = 1, 2, 3 # x=1; y=2; 3 is not assigned anywhere
```

4.5.5.5 The splat operator

When an rvalue is preceded by an asterisk, it means that that value is an array (or an array-like object) and that its elements should each be rvalues. The array elements replace the array in the original rvalue list, and assignment proceeds as described above:

```
x, y, z = 1, *[2,3]  # Same as x,y,z = 1,2,3
```

In Ruby 1.8, a splat may only appear before the last rvalue in an assignment. In Ruby 1.9, the list of rvalues in a parallel assignment may have any number of splats, and they may appear at any position in the list. It is not legal, however, in either version of the language, to attempt a "double splat" on a nested array:

```
x,y = **[[1,2]]   # SyntaxError!
```

Array, range and hash rvalues can be splatted. In general, any rvalue that defines a to_a method can be prefixed with a splat. Any Enumerable object, including enumerators (see §5.3.4) can be splatted, for example. When a splat is applied to an object that does not define a to_a method, no expansion is performed and the splat evaluates to the object itself.

When an lvalue is preceded by an asterisk, it means that all extra rvalues should be placed into an array and assigned to this lvalue. The value assigned to that lvalue is always an array, and it may have zero, one, or more elements:

```
x,*y = 1, 2, 3 # x=1; y=[2,3]
x,*y = 1, 2     # x=1; y=[2]
x,*y = 1        # x=1; y=[]
```

In Ruby 1.8, a splat may only precede the last lvalue in the list. In Ruby 1.9, the lefthand side of a parallel assignment may include one splat operator, but it may appear at any position in the list:

```
# Ruby 1.9 only
*x,y = 1, 2, 3 # x=[1,2]; y=3
*x,y = 1, 2     # x=[1]; y=2
*x,y = 1        # x=[]; y=1
```

Note that splats may appear on both sides of a parallel assignment expression:

```
x, y, *z = 1, *[2,3,4]  # x=1; y=2; z=[3,4].
```

Finally, recall that earlier we described two simple cases of parallel assignment in which there is a single lvalue or a single rvalue. Note that both of these cases behave as if there is a splat before the single lvalue or rvalue. Explicitly including a splat in these cases has no additional effect.

4.5.5.6 Parentheses in parallel assignment

One of the least-understood features of parallel assignment is that the lefthand side can use parentheses for "subassignment." If a group of two or more lvalues is enclosed in parentheses, then it is initially treated as a single lvalue. Once the corresponding rvalue has been determined, the rules of parallel assignment are applied recursively—that rvalue is assigned to the group of lvalues that was in parentheses. Consider the following assignment:

```
x,(y,z) = a, b
```

This is effectively two assignments executed at the same time:

```
x = a
y,z = b
```

But note that the second assignment is itself a parallel assignment. Because we used parentheses on the lefthand side, a recursive parallel assignment is performed. In order for it to work, b must be a splattable object such as an array or enumerator.

Here are some concrete examples that should make this clearer. Note that parentheses on the left act to "unpack" one level of nested array on the right:

```
x,y,z = 1,[2,3]         # No parens: x=1;y=[2,3];z=nil
x,(y,z) = 1,[2,3]       # Parens: x=1;y=2;z=3

a,b,c,d = [1,[2,[3,4]]]       # No parens: a=1;b=[2,[3,4]];c=d=nil
a,(b,(c,d)) = [1,[2,[3,4]]]   # Parens: a=1;b=2;c=3;d=4
```

4.5.5.7 The value of parallel assignment

The return value of a parallel assignment expression is the array of rvalues (after being augmented by any splat operators).

Parallel Assignment and Method Invocation

As an aside, note that if a parallel assignment is prefixed with the name of a method, the Ruby interpreter will interpret the commas as method argument separators rather than as lvalue and rvalue separators. If you want to test the return value of a parallel assignment, you might write the following code to print it out:

```
puts x,y=1,2
```

This doesn't do what you want, however; Ruby thinks you're invoking the puts method with three arguments: x, y=1, and 2. Next, you might try putting the parallel assignment within parentheses for grouping:

```
puts (x,y=1,2)
```

This doesn't work, either; the parentheses are interpreted as part of the method invocation (though Ruby complains about the space between the method name and the opening parenthesis). To actually accomplish what you want, you must use nested parentheses:

```
puts((x,y=1,2))
```

This is one of those strange corner cases in the Ruby grammar that comes as part of the expressiveness of the grammar. Fortunately, the need for syntax like this rarely arises.

4.6 Operators

An *operator* is a token in the Ruby language that represents an operation (such as addition or comparison) to be performed on one or more operands. The operands are expressions, and operators allow us to combine these operand expressions into larger expressions. The numeric literal 2 and the operator +, for example, can be combined into the expression 2+2. And the following expression combines a numeric literal, a method invocation expression, and a variable reference expression with the multiplication operator and the less-than operator:

```
2 * Math.sqrt(2) < limit
```

Table 4-2 later in this section summarizes each of Ruby's operators, and the sections that follow describe each one in detail. To fully understand operators, however, you need to understand operator arity, precedence, and associativity.

The *arity* of an operator is the number of operands it operates on. Unary operators expect a single operand. Binary operators expect two operands. Ternary operators (there is only one of these) expect three operands. The arity of each operator is listed in column N of Table 4-2. Note that the operators + and – have both unary and binary forms.

The *precedence* of an operator specifies how "tightly" an operator is bound to its operands, and affects the order of evaluation of an expression. Consider this expression, for example:

```
1 + 2 * 3     # => 7
```

The multiplication operator has higher precedence than the addition operator, so the multiplication is performed first and the expression evaluates to 7. Table 4-2 is arranged in order from high-precedence operators to low-precedence operators. Note that there are both high- and low-precedence operators for Boolean AND, OR, and NOT operations.

Operator precedence only specifies the default order of evaluation for an expression. You can always use parentheses to group subexpressions and specify your own order of evaluation. For example:

```
(1 + 2) * 3    # => 9
```

The *associativity* of an operator specifies the order of evaluation when the same operator (or operators with the same precedence) appear sequentially in an expression. Column A of Table 4-2 specifies the associativity of each operator. The value "L" means that expressions are evaluated from left to right. The value "R" means that expressions are evaluated from right to left. And the value "N" means that the operator is *nonassociative* and cannot be used multiple times in an expression without parentheses to specify the evaluation order.

Most arithmetic operators are left-associative, which means that 10-5-2 is evaluated as (10-5)-2 instead of 10-(5-2). Exponentiation, on the other hand, is right-associative, so 2**3**4 is evaluated as 2**(3**4). Assignment is another right-associative operator. In the expression a=b=0, the value 0 is first assigned to the variable b. Then the value of that expression (also 0) is assigned to the variable a.

Ruby implements a number of its operators as methods, allowing classes to define new meanings for those operators. Column M of Table 4-2 specifies which operators are methods. Operators marked with a "Y" are implemented with methods and may be redefined, and operators marked with an "N" may not. In general, classes may define their own arithmetic, ordering, and equality operators, but they may not redefine the various Boolean operators. We categorize operators in this chapter according to their most common purpose for the standard Ruby classes. Other classes may define different meanings for the operators. The + operator, for example, performs numeric addition and is categorized as an arithmetic operator. But it is also used to concatenate strings and arrays. A method-based operator is invoked as a method of its lefthand operand (or its only operand, in the case of unary operators). The righthand operand is passed as an argument to the method. You can look up a class's definition of any method-based operator as you would look up any other method of a class. For example, use *ri* to look up the definition of the * operator for strings:

```
ri 'String.*'
```

To define unary + and unary – operators, use method names +@ and -@ to avoid ambiguity with the binary operators that use the same symbols. The != and !~ operators are defined as the negation of the == and =~ operators. In Ruby 1.9, you can redefine != and !~. In earlier versions of the language, you cannot. Ruby 1.9 also allows the unary ! operator to be redefined.

Table 4-2. Ruby operators, by precedence (high to low), with arity (N), associativity (A), and definability (M)

Operator(s)	N	A	M	Operation
! ~ +	1	R	Y	Boolean NOT, bitwise complement, unary plus[a]
**	2	R	Y	Exponentiation
-	1	R	Y	Unary minus (define with -@)
* / %	2	L	Y	Multiplication, division, modulo (remainder)
+ -	2	L	Y	Addition (or concatenation), subtraction
<< >>	2	L	Y	Bitwise shift-left (or append), bitwise shift-right
&	2	L	Y	Bitwise AND
| ^	2	L	Y	Bitwise OR, bitwise XOR
< <= >= >	2	L	Y	Ordering
== === != =~ !~ <=>	2	N	Y	Equality, pattern matching, comparison[b]
&&	2	L	N	Boolean AND
||	2	L	N	Boolean OR
.. ...	2	N	N	Range creation and Boolean flip-flops
?:	3	R	N	Conditional
rescue	2	L	N	Exception-handling modifier
= **= *= /= %= += -= <<= >>= &&= &= ||= |= ^=	2	R	N	Assignment

Operator(s)	N	A	M	Operation
defined?	1	N	N	Test variable definition and type
not	1	R	N	Boolean NOT (low precedence)
and or	2	L	N	Boolean AND, Boolean OR (low precedence)
if unless while until	2	N	N	Conditional and loop modifiers

[a] ! may not be redefined prior to Ruby 1.9. Define unary plus with +@.

[b] != and !~ may not be redefined prior to Ruby 1.9.

4.6.1 Unary + and −

The unary minus operator changes the sign of its numeric argument. The unary plus is allowed, but it has no effect on numeric operands—it simply returns the value of its operand. It is provided for symmetry with unary minus, and can, of course, be redefined. Note that unary minus has slightly lower precedence than unary plus; this is described in the next section on the ** operator.

The names of these unary operators as methods are -@ and +@. Use these names when redefining the operators, invoking the operators as methods, or looking up documentation for the operators. These special names are necessary to disambiguate the unary plus and minus operators from binary plus and minus.

4.6.2 Exponentiation: **

** performs exponentiation, raising its first argument to the power of the second. Note that you can compute roots of a number by using a fractional number as the second operand. For example, the cube root of x is x**(1.0/3.0). Similarly, x**-y is the same as 1/(x**y). The ** operator is right-associative, so x**y**z is the same thing as x**(y**z). Finally, note that ** has higher precedence than the unary minus operator, so -1**0.5 is the same thing as -(1**0.5). If you really want to take the square root of -1, you must use parentheses: (-1)**0.5. (The imaginary result is not-a-number, and the expression evaluates to NaN.)

4.6.3 Arithmetic: +, −, *, /, and %

The operators +, -, *, and / perform addition, subtraction, multiplication, and division on all Numeric classes. Integer division returns an integer result and discards any remainder. The remainder can be computed with the modulo operator %. Integer division by zero raises ZeroDivisionError. Floating-point division by zero returns plus or minus Infinity. Floating-point division of zero by zero returns NaN. See §3.1.3 for further details on Ruby's integer and floating-point arithmetic.

The String class uses the + operator for string concatenation, the * operator for string repetition, and the % operator for sprintf argument substitution into a string.

The Array class uses + for array concatenation and – for array subtraction. Array uses the * operator in different ways, depending on the class of the second operand. When an array is "multiplied" by a number, the result is a new array that repeats the contents of the operand array the specified number of times. But when an array is multiplied by a string, the result is the same as calling the join method of the array and passing that string as the argument.

4.6.4 Shift and Append: << and >>

The Fixnum and Bignum classes define the << and >> operators to shift the bits of the lefthand argument to the left and to the right. The righthand argument is the number of positions to shift the bits, and negative values result in a shift in the opposite direction: a left-shift of –2 is the same as a right-shift of 2. High-order bits are never "shifted off" when a Fixnum is shifted left. If the result of a shift does not fit in a Fixnum, a Bignum value is returned. Right shifts, however, always discard the low-order bits of the argument.

Shifting a number left by 1 bit is the same as multiplication by 2. Shifting a number right by 1 bit is the same as integer division by 2. Here are some examples that express numbers in binary notation and then convert their results back to binary form:

```
(0b1011 << 1).to_s(2)   # => "10110"    11 << 1 => 22
(0b10110 >> 2).to_s(2)  # => "101"      22 >> 2 => 5
```

The << operator is also used as an append operator, and it's probably more common in this form. The String, Array, and IO classes define it in this way, as do a number of other "appendable" classes from the standard library, such as Queue and Logger:

```
message = "hello"        # A string
messages = []            # An empty array
message << " world"      # Append to the string
messages << message      # Append message to the array
STDOUT << message        # Print the message to standard output stream
```

4.6.5 Complement, Union, Intersection: ~, &, |, and ^

Fixnum and Bignum define these operators to perform bitwise NOT, AND, OR, and XOR operations. ~ is a high-precedence unary operator, and the others are medium-precedence binary operators.

~ changes each 0 bit of its integer operand to a 1, and each 1 bit to a 0, producing the binary 1s-complement of a number. For any integer x, ~x is the same as -x-1.

& is the bitwise AND operator for two numbers. The bits of the result are set to 1 only if the corresponding bit in each operand is set to 1. For example:

```
(0b1010 & 0b1100).to_s(2)  # => "1000"
```

| is the bitwise OR operator for two integers. A bit in the result is 1 if either corresponding bit in the operands is 1. For example:

```
(0b1010 | 0b1100).to_s(2)   # => "1110"
```

^ is the bitwise XOR (exclusive-OR) for integers. A bit in the result is 1 if one (but not both) of the corresponding bits in the operands is 1. For example:

```
(0b1010 ^ 0b1100).to_s(2)   # => "110"
```

Other classes use these operators as well, usually in ways that are compatible with their logical AND, OR, and NOT meanings. Arrays use & and | for set intersection and union operations. When & is applied to two arrays, it returns a new array that contains only those elements that appear in the lefthand array AND the righthand array. When | is applied to two arrays, it returns a new array that contains any elements that appear in either the lefthand array OR the righthand array. See §9.5.2.7 for details and examples.

TrueClass, FalseClass, and NilClass define &, |, and ^ (but not ~), so that they can be used as Boolean operators. Note, however, that this is rarely the correct thing to do. The Boolean operators && and || (described later in §4.6.8) are intended for Boolean operands, and are more efficient because they do not evaluate their righthand operand unless its value will affect the result of the operation.

4.6.6 Comparison: <, <=, >, >=, and <=>

Some classes define a natural order for their values. Numbers are ordered by magnitude; strings are ordered alphabetically; dates are ordered chronologically. The less-than (<), less-than-or-equal-to (<=), greater-than-or-equal-to (>=), and greater-than (>) operators make assertions about the relative order of two values. They evaluate to true if the assertion is true, and they evaluate to false otherwise. (And they typically raise an exception if their arguments are of incomparable types.)

Classes may define the comparison operators individually. It is easier and more common, however, for a class to define the single <=> operator. This is a general-purpose comparison operator, and its return value indicates the relative order of the two operands. If the lefthand operand is less than the righthand operand, then <=> returns –1. If the lefthand operand is greater, it returns +1. If the two operands are equal, the operator returns 0. And if the two operands are not comparable, it returns nil.[*] Once the <=> operator is defined, a class may simply include the module Comparable, which defines the other comparison operators (including the == operator) in terms of <=>.

The Module class deserves special mention: it implements the comparison operators to indicate subclass relationships (Module is the superclass of Class). For classes A and B, A < B is true if A is a subclass or descendant of B. In this case, "less than" means "is

---

[*] Some implementations of this operator may return any value less than 0 or any value greater than 0, instead of –1 and +1. If you implement <=>, your implementation should return –1, 0, or +1. But if you use <=>, you should test for values less than or greater than zero, rather than assuming that the result will always be –1, 0, or +1.

more specialized than" or "is a narrower type than." As a mnemonic, note that (as we'll learn in Chapter 7) the < character is also used when declaring a subclass:

```
# Declare class A as a subclass of B
class A < B
end
```

`Module` defines `>` to work like `<` with its operands reversed. And it defines `<=` and `>=` so that they also return `true` if the two operands are the same class. The most interesting things about these `Module` comparison operators is that `Module` only defines a partial ordering on its values. Consider the classes `String` and `Numeric`. Both are subclasses of `Object`, and neither one is a subclass of the other. In this case, when the two operands are unrelated, the comparison operators return `nil` instead of `true` or `false`:

```
String < Object      # true: String is more specialized than Object
Object > Numeric     # true: Object is more general than Numeric
Numeric < Integer    # false: Numeric is not more specialized than Integer
String < Numeric     # nil: String and Numeric are not related
```

If a class defines a total ordering on its values, and `a < b` is not true, then you can be sure that `a >= b` *is* true. But when a class, like `Module`, defines only a partial ordering, you must not make this assumption.

4.6.7 Equality: ==, !=, =~, !~, and ===

`==` is the equality operator. It determines whether two values are equal, according to the lefthand operand's definition of "equal." The `!=` operator is simply the inverse of `==`: it calls `==` and then returns the opposite. You can redefine `!=` in Ruby 1.9 but not in Ruby 1.8. See §3.8.5 for a more detailed discussion of object equality in Ruby.

`=~` is the pattern-matching operator. `Object` defines this operator so that it always returns `false`. String redefines it so that it expects a `Regexp` as its righthand argument. And `Regexp` redefines the operator so that it expects a `String` as its righthand argument. Both of these operators return `nil` if the string does not match the pattern. If the string does match the pattern, the operators return the integer index at which the match begins. (Note that in Boolean expressions, `nil` works like `false` and any integer works like `true`.)

The `!~` operator is the inverse of `=~`: it calls `=~` and returns `true` if `=~` returned `nil` or `false` if `=~` returned an integer. You can redefine `!~` in Ruby 1.9 but not in Ruby 1.8.

The `===` operator is the case-equality operator. It is used implicitly by `case` statements (see Chapter 5). Its explicit use is much less common than `==`. `Range`, `Class`, and `Regexp` define this operator as a kind of membership or pattern-matching operator. Other classes inherit `Object`'s definition, which simply invokes the `==` operator instead. See §3.8.5. Note that there is no `!==` operator; if you want to negate `===`, you must do it yourself.

4.6.8 Boolean Operators: &&, ||, !, and, or, not

Ruby's Boolean operators are built into the language and are not based on methods: classes, for example, cannot define their own && method. The reason for this is that Boolean operators can be applied to any value and must behave consistently for any kind of operand. Ruby defines special true and false values but does not have a Boolean type. For the purposes of all Boolean operators, the values false and nil are considered false. And every other value, including true, 0, NaN, "", [], and {}, is considered true. Note that ! is an exception; you can redefine this operator in Ruby 1.9 (but not in Ruby 1.8). Note also that you can define methods named and, or, and not, but these methods are ordinary methods and do not alter the behavior of the operators with the same name.

Another reason that Ruby's Boolean operators are a core part of the language rather than redefinable methods is that the binary operators are "short-circuiting." If the value of the operation is completely determined by the lefthand operand, then the righthand operand is ignored and is never even evaluated. If the righthand operand is an expression with side effects (such as assignment, or an invocation of a method with side effects), then that side effect may or may not occur, based on the value of the lefthand operand.

&& is a Boolean AND operator. It returns a true value if both its left operand AND its right operand are true values. Otherwise, it returns a false value. Note that this description says "a true value" and "a false value" instead of "the true value" and "the false value." && is often used in conjunction with comparison operators, such as == and <, in expressions like this:

```
x == 0 && y > 1
```

The comparison and equality operators actually evaluate to the values true and false, and in this case, the && operator is operating on actual Boolean values. But this is not always the case. The operator can also be used like this:

```
x && y
```

In this case, x and y can be anything. The value of the expression is either the value of x or it is the value of y. If both x and y are true values, then the value of the expression is the value of y. If x is a false value, then the value of the expression is x. Otherwise, y must be a false value, and the value of the expression is y.

Here's how the && operator actually works. First, it evaluates its lefthand operand. If this operand is nil or false, then it returns that value and skips the righthand operand altogether. Otherwise, the lefthand operand is a true value and the overall value of the && operator depends on the value of the righthand operand. In this case, the operator evaluates its righthand operand and returns that value.

The fact that && may skip its righthand operand can be used to advantage in your code. Consider this expression:

```
x && print(x.to_s)
```

This code prints the value of x as a string, but only if x is not nil or false.[*]

The || operator returns the Boolean OR of its operands. It returns a true value if either of its operands is a true value. If both operands are false values, then it returns a false value. Like &&, the || operator ignores its righthand operand if its value has no impact on the value of the operation. The || operator works like this: first, it evaluates its lefthand operand. If this is any value other than nil or false, it simply returns that value. Otherwise, it evaluates its righthand operand and returns that value.

|| can be used as a conjunction to join multiple comparison or equality expressions:

```
x < 0 || y < 0 || z < 0    # Are any of the coordinates negative?
```

In this case, the operands to || will be actual true or false values, and the result will also be true or false. But || is not restricted to working with true and false. One idiomatic use of || is to return the first non-nil value in a series of alternatives:

```
# If the argument x is nil, then get its value from a hash of user preferences
# or from a constant default value.
x = x || preferences[:x] || Defaults::X
```

Note that && has higher precedence than ||. Consider this expression:

```
1 || 2 && nil    # => 1
```

The && is performed first, and the value of this expression is 1. If the || was performed first, however, the value would be nil:

```
(1 || 2) && nil    # => nil
```

The ! operator performs a unary Boolean NOT. If the operand is nil or false, then the ! operator returns true. Otherwise, ! returns false.

The ! operator is at the highest precedence. This means that if you want to compute the logical inverse of an expression that itself uses operators, you must use parentheses:

```
!(a && b)
```

Incidentally, one of the principles of Boolean logic allows the expression above to be rewritten as:

```
!a || !b
```

The and, or, and not operators are low-precedence versions of &&, ||, and !. One reason to use these variants is simply that their names are English and this can make your code easier to read. Try reading this line of code, for example:

```
if x > 0 and y > 0 and not defined? d then d = Math.sqrt(x*x + y*y) end
```

Another reason for these alternate versions of the Boolean operators is the fact that they have lower precedence than the assignment operator. This means that you can write a

---

[*] Just because an expression can be written this way doesn't mean that it should be. In Chapter 5, we'll see that this expression is better written as:

```
print(x.to_s) if x
```

Boolean expression such as the following that assigns values to variables until it encounters a false value:

```
if a = f(x) and b = f(y) and c = f(z) then d = g(a,b,c) end
```

This expression simply would not work if written with **&&** instead of **and**.

You should note that **and** and **or** have the same precedence (and **not** is just slightly higher). Because **and** and **or** have the same precedence, and **&&** and **||** have different precedences, the following two expressions compute different values:

```
x || y && nil      # && is performed first   => x
x or y and nil     # evaluated left-to-right => nil
```

4.6.9 Ranges and Flip-Flops: .. and ...

We've seen **..** and **...** before in §3.5 where they were described as part of the **Range** literal syntax. When the start and end points of a range are themselves integer literals, as in **1..10**, the Ruby interpreter creates a literal **Range** object while parsing. But if the start and end point expressions are anything more complicated than integer literals, as in **x..2*x**, then it is not really accurate to call this a **Range** literal. Instead, it is a range creation expression. It follows, therefore, that **..** and **...** are operators rather than just range literal syntax.

The **..** and **...** operators are not method-based and cannot be redefined. They have relatively low precedence, which means that they can usually be used without putting parentheses around the left or right operands:

```
x+1..x*x
```

The value of these operators is a **Range** object. **x..y** is the same as:

```
Range.new(x,y)
```

And **x...y** is the same as:

```
Range.new(x,y,true)
```

4.6.9.1 Boolean flip-flops

When the **..** and **...** operators are used in a conditional, such as an **if** statement, or in a loop, such as a **while** loop (see Chapter 5 for more about conditionals and loops), they do not create **Range** objects. Instead, they create a special kind of Boolean expression called a *flip-flop*. A flip-flop expression evaluates to **true** or **false**, just as comparison and equality expressions do. The extraordinarily unusual thing about a flip-flop expression, however, is that its value depends on the value of previous evaluations. This means that a flip-flop expression has state associated with it; it must remember information about previous evaluations. Because it has state, you would expect a flip-flop to be an object of some sort. But it isn't—it's a Ruby expression, and the Ruby interpreter stores the state (just a single Boolean value) it requires in its internal parsed representation of the expression.

With that background in mind, consider the flip-flop in the following code. Note that the first `..` in the code creates a `Range` object. The second one creates the flip-flop expression:

```
(1..10).each {|x| print x if x==3..x==5 }
```

The flip-flop consists of two Boolean expressions joined with the `..` operator, in the context of a conditional or loop. A flip-flop expression is `false` unless and until the lefthand expression evaluates to `true`. Once that expression has become `true`, the expression "flips" into a persistent `true` state. It remains in that state, and subsequent evaluations return `true` until the righthand expression evaluates to `true`. When that happens, the flip-flop "flops" back to a persistent `false` state. Subsequent evaluations of the expression return `false` until the lefthand expression becomes `true` again.

In the code example, the flip-flop is evaluated repeatedly, for values of x from 1 to 10. It starts off in the `false` state, and evaluates to `false` when x is 1 and 2. When x==3, the flip-flop flips to `true` and returns `true`. It continues to return `true` when x is 4 and 5. When x==5, however, the flip-flop flops back to `false`, and returns `false` for the remaining values of x. The result is that this code prints 345.

Flip-flops can be written with either `..` or `....`. The difference is that when a `..` flip-flop flips to `true`, it returns `true` but also tests its righthand expression to see if it should flop its internal state back to `false`. The `...` form waits for its next evaluation before testing the righthand expression. Consider these two lines:

```
# Prints "3". Flips and flops back when x==3
(1..10).each {|x| print x if x==3..x>=3 }
# Prints "34". Flips when x == 3 and flops when x==4
(1..10).each {|x| print x if x==3...x>=3 } # Prints "34"
```

Flip-flops are a fairly obscure feature of Ruby and are probably best avoided in your code. They are not unique to Ruby, however. Ruby inherits this feature from Perl, which in turn inherits them from the Unix text-processing tools *sed* and *awk*.[*] Flip-flops were originally intended for matching the lines of a text file between a start pattern and an end pattern. This continues to be a useful way to use them. The following simple Ruby program demonstrates a flip-flop. It reads a text file line-by-line and prints any line that contains the text "TODO". It then continues printing lines until it reads a blank line:

```
ARGF.each do |line|   # For each line of standard in or of named files
  print line if line=~/TODO/..line=~/^$/ # Print lines when flip-flop is true
end
```

It is difficult to formally describe the precise behavior of a flip-flop. It is easier to understand flip-flops by studying code that behaves in an equivalent way. The following function behaves like the flip-flop x==3..x==5. It hardcodes the lefthand and righthand conditions into the function itself, and it uses a global variable to store the state of the flip-flop:

---

[*] `..` creates an *awk*-style flip-flop, and `...` creates a *sed*-style flip-flop.

```
$state = false              # Global storage for flip-flop state
def flipflop(x)             # Test value of x against flip-flop
  if !$state                # If saved state is false
    result = (x == 3)       # Result is value of lefthand operand
    if result              # If that result is true
      $state = !(x == 5)    # Then saved state is not of the righthand operand
    end
    result                  # Return result
  else                      # Otherwise, if saved state is true
    $state = !(x == 5)      # Then save the inverse of the righthand operand
    true                    # And return true without testing lefthand
  end
end
```

With this flip-flop function defined, we can write the following code, which prints 345 just like our earlier example:

```
(1..10).each {|x| print x if flipflop(x) }
```

The following function simulates the behavior of the three-dot flip-flop x==3...x>=3:

```
$state2 = false
def flipflop2(x)
  if !$state2
    $state2 = (x == 3)
  else
    $state2 = !(x >= 3)
    true
  end
end

# Now try it out
(1..10).each {|x| print x if x==3...x>=3 }  # Prints "34"
(1..10).each {|x| print x if flipflop2(x) } # Prints "34"
```

4.6.10 Conditional: ?:

The ?: operator is known as the conditional operator. It is the only ternary operator (three operands) in Ruby. The first operand appears before the question mark. The second operand appears between the question mark and the colon. And the third operand appears after the colon.

The ?: operator always evaluates its first operand. If the first operand is anything other than false or nil, the value of the expression is the value of the second operand. Otherwise, if the first operand is false or nil, then the value of the expression is the value of the third operand. In either case, one of the operands is never evaluated (which matters if it includes side effects like assignment). Here is an example use of this operator:

```
"You have #{n} #{n==1 ? 'message' : 'messages'}"
```

As you can see, the ?: operator acts like a compact if/then/else statement. (Ruby's if conditional is described in Chapter 5.) The first operand is the condition that is being tested, like the expression after the `if`. The second operand is like the code that follows the `then`. And the third operand is like the code that follows the `else`. The difference between the `?:` operator and the `if` statement, of course, is that the `if` statement allows arbitrary amounts of code in its `then` and `else` clauses, whereas the `?:` operator allows only single expressions.

The `?:` operator has fairly low precedence, which means that it is usually not necessary to put parentheses around the operands. If the first operand uses the `defined?` operator, or if the second and third operands perform assignments, then parentheses are necessary. Remember that Ruby allows method names to end with a question mark. If the first operand of the `?:` operator ends with an identifier, you must put parentheses around the first operand or include a disambiguating space between that operand and the question mark. If you don't do this, the Ruby interpreter thinks that the question mark of the operator is part of the previous identifier. For example:

```
x==3?y:z       # This is legal
3==x?y:z       # Syntax error: x? is interpreted as a method name
(3==x)?y:z     # Okay: parentheses fix the problem
3==x ?y:z      # Spaces also resolve the problem
```

The question mark must appear on the same line as the first argument. In Ruby 1.8, the colon must appear on the same line as the second argument. In Ruby 1.9, however, a newline is allowed before the colon. You must follow the colon by a space in this case, however, so it doesn't appear to introduce a symbol literal.

Table 4-2 (earlier in this chapter) says that the `?:` operator is right-associative. If the operator is used twice in the same expression, the rightmost one is grouped:

```
a ? b : c ? d : e    # This expression...
a ? b : (c ? d : e)  # is evaluated like this..
(a ? b : c) ? d : e  # NOT like this
```

This kind of ambiguity is actually fairly rare with the `?:` operator. The following expression uses three conditional operators to compute the maximum value of three variables. No parentheses are required (although spaces are required before the question marks), as there is only one possible way to parse the statement:

```
max = x>y ? x>z ? x : z : y>z ? y : z
max = x>y ? (x>z ? x : z) : (y>z ? y : z)  # With explicit parentheses
```

4.6.11 Assignment Operators

You've already read about assignment expressions in §4.5. It is worth noting here a few points about the assignment operators used in those expressions. First, the value of an assignment expression is the value (or an array of the values) that appears on the righthand side of the assignment operator. Second, assignment operators are right-associative. Points one and two together are what make expressions like this one work:

```
x = y = z = 0      # Assign zero to variables x, y, and z
x = (y = (z = 0))  # This equivalent expression shows order of evaluation
```

Third, note that assignment has very low precedence. Precedence rules mean that just about anything that follows an assignment operator will be evaluated before the assignment is performed. The main exceptions are the **and**, **or**, and **not** operators.

Finally, note that although assignment operators cannot be defined as methods, the compound assignment operators like += use redefinable operators like +. Redefining the + operator does not affect the assignment performed by the += operator, but it does affect the addition performed by that operator.

4.6.12 The defined? Operator

defined? is a unary operator that tests whether its operand is defined or not. Normally, using an undefined variable or method raises an exception. When the expression on the right of the **defined?** operator uses an undefined variable or method (including operators defined as methods), **defined?** simply returns nil. Similarly, **defined?** returns nil if the operand is an expression that uses **yield** or **super** in an inappropriate context (i.e., when there is no block to yield to, or no superclass method to invoke). It is important to understand that the expression that is the operand to **defined?** is not actually evaluated; it is simply checked to see whether it *could be* evaluated without error. Here is a typical use of the **defined?** operator:

```
# Compute f(x), but only if f and x are both defined
y = f(x) if defined? f(x)
```

If the operand is defined, the **defined?** operator returns a string. The content of this returned string is usually unimportant; what matters is that it is a true value—neither nil nor **false**. It is possible, however, to inspect the value returned by this operator to learn something about the type of the expression on the righthand side. Table 4-3 lists the possible return values of this operator.

Table 4-3. Return values of the defined? operator

Operand expression type	Return value
Reference to defined local variable	"local-variable"
Reference to defined block local variable (Ruby 1.8 only)	"local-variable(in-block)"
Reference to defined global variable	"global-variable"
Special regular expression global variables, $&, $+, $`, $', and $1 to $9, when defined following a successful match (Ruby 1.8 only)	Name of variable, as a string
Reference to defined constant	"constant"
Reference to defined instance variable	"instance-variable"
Reference to defined class variable	"class variable" (note no hyphen)
nil	"nil" (note this is a string)
true, false	"true", "false"

Operand expression type	Return value
self	"self"
yield when there is a block to yield to (see also Kernel method block_given?)	"yield"
super when in context where it is allowed	"super"
Assignment (assignment is not actually performed)	"assignment"
Method invocation, including operators defined as methods (method is not actually invoked and need not have correct number of arguments; see also Object.respond_to?)	"method"
Any other valid expression, including literals and built-in operators	"expression"
Any expression that uses an undefined variable or method name, or that uses yield or super where they are not allowed	nil

The defined? operator has very low precedence. If you want to test whether two variables are defined, use and instead of &&:

```
defined? a and defined? b    # This works
defined? a && defined? b     # Evaluated as: defined?((a && defined? b))
```

4.6.13 Statement Modifiers

rescue, if, unless, while, and until are conditional, looping, and exception-handling statements that affect the flow-of-control of a Ruby program. They can also be used as statement modifiers, in code like this:

```
print x if x
```

In this modifier form, they can be considered operators in which the value of the right-hand expression affects the execution of the lefthand expression. (Or, in the case of the rescue modifier, the exception status of the lefthand expression affects the execution of the righthand operand.)

It is not particularly useful to describe these keywords as operfators. They are documented, in both their statement and expression modifier form, in Chapter 5. The keywords are listed in Table 4-2 simply to show their precedence relative to other operators. Note that they all have very low precedence, but that the rescue statement modifier has higher precedence than assignment.

4.6.14 Nonoperators

Most of Ruby's operators are written using punctuation characters. Ruby's grammar also uses a number of punctuation characters that are not operators. Although we've seen (or will see) much of this nonoperator punctuation elsewhere in this book, let's review it here:

()

Parentheses are an optional part of method definition and invocation syntax. It is better to think of method invocation as a special kind of expression than to think of () as a method-invocation operator. Parentheses are also used for grouping to affect the order of evaluation of subexpressions.

[]

Square brackets are used in array literals and for querying and setting array and hash values. In that context, they are syntactic sugar for method invocation and behave somewhat like redefinable operators with arbitrary arity. See §4.4 and §4.5.3.

{}

Curly braces are an alternative to do/end in blocks, and are also used in hash literals. In neither case do they act as operators.

. and ::

. and :: are used in qualified names, separating the name of a method from the object on which it is invoked, or the name of a constant from the module in which it is defined. These are not operators because the righthand side is not a value but an identifier.

;, ,, and =>

These punctuation characters are separators rather than operators. The semicolon (;) is used to separate statements on the same line; the comma (,) is used to separate method arguments and the elements of array and hash literals; and the arrow (=>) is used to separate hash keys from hash values in hash literals.

:

A colon is used to prefix symbol literals and is also used in Ruby 1.9 hash syntax.

*, &, and <

These punctuation characters are operators in some contexts, but they are also used in ways that are not operators. Putting * before an array in an assignment or method invocation expression expands or unpacks the array into its individual elements. Although it is sometimes known as the splat operator, it is not really an operator; *a cannot stand alone as an expression.

& can be used in a method declaration before the name of the last method argument, and this causes any block passed to the method to be assigned to that argument. (See Chapter 6.) It can also be used in method invocation to pass a proc to a method as if it were a block.

< is used in class definitions to specify the superclass of class.

## CHAPTER 5

Statements and Control Structures

Consider the following Ruby program. It adds two numbers passed to it on the command line and prints the sum:

```ruby
x = ARGV[0].to_f  # Convert first argument to a number
y = ARGV[1].to_f  # Convert second argument to a number
sum = x + y       # Add the arguments
puts sum          # Print the sum
```

This is a simple program that consists primarily of variable assignment and method invocations. What makes it particularly simple is its purely sequential execution. The four lines of code are executed one after the other without branching or repetition. It is a rare program that can be this simple. This chapter introduces Ruby's control structures, which alter the sequential execution, or *flow-of-control*, of a program. We cover:

- Conditionals
- Loops
- Iterators and blocks
- Flow-altering statements like return and break
- Exceptions
- The special-case BEGIN and END statements
- The esoteric control structures known as *fibers* and *continuations*

5.1 Conditionals

The most common control structure, in any programming language, is the conditional. This is a way of telling the computer to conditionally execute some code: to execute it only if some condition is satisfied. The condition is an expression—if it evaluates to any value other than false or nil, then the condition is satisfied.

Ruby has a rich vocabulary for expressing conditionals. The syntax choices are described in the subsections that follow. When writing Ruby code, you can choose the one that seems most elegant for the task at hand.

5.1.1 if

The most straightforward of the conditionals is if. In its simplest form, it looks like this:

```ruby
if expression
  code
end
```

The *code* between if and end is executed if (and only if) the *expression* evaluates to something other than false or nil. The *code* must be separated from the *expression* with a newline or semicolon or the keyword then.* Here are two ways to write the same simple conditional:

```
# If x is less than 10, increment it
if x < 10                    # newline separator
  x += 1
end
if x < 10 then x += 1 end    # then separator
```

You can also use then as the separator token, and follow it with a newline. Doing so makes your code robust; it will work even if the newline is subsequently removed:

```
if x < 10 then
  x += 1
end
```

Programmers who are used to C, or languages whose syntax is derived from C, should note two important things about Ruby's if statement:

- Parentheses are not required (and typically not used) around the conditional expression. The newline, semicolon, or then keyword serves to delimit the expression instead.

- The end keyword is required, even when the code to be conditionally executed consists of a single statement. The modifier form of if, described below, provides a way to write simple conditionals without the end keyword.

5.1.1.1 else

An if statement may include an else clause to specify code to be executed if the condition is not true:

```
if expression
  code
else
  code
end
```

The *code* between the if and else is executed if *expression* evaluates to anything other than false or nil. Otherwise (if *expression* is false or nil), the *code* between the else and end is executed. As in the simple form of if, the *expression* must be separated from the *code* that follows it by a newline, a semicolon, or the keyword then. The else and end keywords fully delimit the second chunk of *code*, and no newlines or additional delimiters are required.

Here is an example of a conditional that includes an else clause:

```
if data         # If the array exists
  data << x      #   then append a value to it.
else            # Otherwise...
```

---

* Ruby 1.8 also allows a colon, but this syntax is no longer legal in 1.9.

```
    data = [x]      #   create a new array that holds the value.
    end             # This is the end of the conditional.
```

5.1.1.2 elsif

If you want to test more than one condition within a conditional, you can add one or more elsif clauses between an if and an else. elsif is a shortened form of "else if." Note that there is only one *e* in elsif. A conditional using elsif looks like this:

```
if expression1
  code1
elsif expression2
  code2
    .
    .
    .
elsif expressionN
  codeN
else
  code
end
```

If *expression1* evaluates to anything other than false or nil, then *code1* is executed. Otherwise, *expression2* is evaluated. If it is anything other than false or nil, then *code2* is executed. This process continues until an expression evaluates to something other than false or nil, or until all elsif clauses have been tested. If the expression associated with the last elsif clause is false or nil, and the elsif clause is followed by an else clause, then the code between else and end is executed. If no else clause is present, then no code is executed at all.

elsif is like if: the expression must be separated from the code by a newline, a semi-colon, or a then keyword. Here is an example of a multiway conditional using elsif:

```
if x == 1
  name = "one"
elsif x == 2
  name = "two"
elsif x == 3 then name = "three"
elsif x == 4; name = "four"
else
  name = "many"
end
```

5.1.1.3 Return value

In most languages, the if conditional is a statement. In Ruby, however, everything is an expression, even the control structures that are commonly called statements. The return value of an if "statement" (i.e., the value that results from evaluating an if expression) is the value of the last expression in the code that was executed, or nil if no block of code was executed.

The fact that `if` statements return a value means that, for example, the multiway conditional shown previously can be elegantly rewritten as follows:

```
name = if    x == 1 then "one"
       elsif x == 2 then "two"
       elsif x == 3 then "three"
       elsif x == 4 then "four"
       else             "many"
       end
```

5.1.2 if As a Modifier

When `if` is used in its normal statement form, Ruby's grammar requires that it be terminated with the `end` keyword. For simple, single-line conditionals, this is somewhat awkward. This is just a parsing problem, and the solution is to use the `if` keyword itself as the delimiter that separates the code to be executed from the conditional expression. Instead of writing:

```
if expression then code end
```

we can simply write:

```
code if expression
```

When used in this form, `if` is known as a statement (or expression) *modifier*. If you're a Perl programmer, you may be accustomed to this syntax. If not, please note that the code to execute comes first, and the expression follows. For example:

```
puts message if message    # Output message, if it is defined
```

This syntax places more emphasis on the code to be executed, and less emphasis on the condition under which it will be executed. Using this syntax can make your code more readable when the condition is a trivial one or when the condition is almost always true.

Even though the condition is written last, it is evaluated first. If it evaluates to anything other than `false` or `nil`, then the code is evaluated, and its value is used as the return value of the modified expression. Otherwise, the code is not executed, and the return value of the modified expression is `nil`. Obviously, this syntax does not allow any kind of `else` clause.

To use `if` as a modifier, it must follow the modified statement or expression immediately, with no intervening line break. Inserting a newline into the previous example turns it into an unmodified method invocation followed by an incomplete `if` statement:

```
puts message       # Unconditional
if message         # Incomplete!
```

The `if` modifier has very low precedence and binds more loosely than the assignment operator. Be sure you know just what expression you are modifying when you use it. For example, the following two lines of code are different:

```
y = x.invert if x.respond_to? :invert
y = (x.invert if x.respond_to? :invert)
```

In the first line, the modifier applies to the assignment expression. If x does not have a method named `invert`, then nothing happens at all, and the value of y is not modified. In the second line, the if modifier applies only to the method call. If x does not have an `invert` method, then the modified expression evaluates to `nil`, and this is the value that is assigned to y.

An if modifier binds to the single nearest expression. If you want to modify more than one expression, you can use parentheses or a `begin` statement for grouping. But this approach is problematic because readers don't know that the code is part of a conditional until they reach the bottom. Also, using an if modifier in this way gives up the conciseness that is the primary benefit of this syntax. When more than one line of code is involved, you should typically use a traditional if statement rather than an if modifier. Compare the following three side-by-side alternatives:

```
if expression       begin              (
  line1               line1              line1
  line2               line2              line2
end                 end if expression  ) end if expression
```

Note that an expression modified with an if clause is itself an expression that can be modified. It is therefore possible to attach multiple if modifiers to an expression:

```
# Output message if message exists and the output method is defined
puts message if message if defined? puts
```

Repeating an if modifier like this is hard to read, however, and it makes more sense to combine the two conditions into a single expression:

```
puts message if message and defined? puts
```

5.1.3 unless

`unless`, as a statement or a modifier, is the opposite of `if`: it executes code only if an associated expression evaluates to `false` or `nil`. Its syntax is just like `if`, except that `elsif` clauses are not allowed:

```
# single-way unless statement
unless condition
  code
end

# two-way unless statement
unless condition
  code
else
  code
end

# unless modifier
code unless condition
```

The unless statement, like the if statement, requires that the condition and the code are separated by a newline, a semicolon, or the then keyword. Also like if, unless statements are expressions and return the value of the code they execute, or nil if they execute nothing:

```ruby
# Call the to_s method on object o, unless o is nil
s = unless o.nil?                        # newline separator
  o.to_s
end
s = unless o.nil? then o.to_s end        # then separator
```

For single-line conditionals like this, the modifier form of unless is usually clearer:

```ruby
s = o.to_s unless o.nil?
```

Ruby has no equivalent of the elsif clause for an unless conditional. You can still write a multiway unless statement, however, if you're willing to be a little more verbose:

```ruby
unless x == 0
  puts "x is not 0"
else
  unless y == 0
    puts "y is not 0"
  else
    unless z == 0
      puts "z is not 0"
    else
      puts "all are 0"
    end
  end
end
```

5.1.4 case

The case statement is a multiway conditional. There are two forms of this statement. The simple (and infrequently used) form is nothing more than an alternative syntax for if/elsif/else. These two side-by-side expressions are equivalent:

```ruby
name = case                    name = if    x == 1 then "one"
  when x == 1 then "one"              elsif x == 2 then "two"
  when x == 2 then "two"              elsif x == 3 then "three"
  when x == 3 then "three"            elsif x == 4 then "four"
  when x == 4 then "four"             else "many"
  else "many"                  end
end
```

As you can see from this code, the case statement returns a value, just as the if statement does. As with the if statement, the then keyword following the when clauses can be replaced with a newline or semicolon:[*]

---

[*] Ruby 1.8 also allows a colon in place of then, as it does for the if statement. But this syntax is no longer allowed in Ruby 1.9.

```
case
when x == 1
  "one"
when x == 2
  "two"
when x == 3
  "three"
end
```

The case statement tests each of its when expressions in the order they are written until it finds one that evaluates to true. If it finds one, it evaluates the statements that come between that when and the following when, else, or end. The last expression evaluated becomes the return value of the case statement. Once a when clause that evaluates to true has been found, no other when clauses are considered.

The else clause of a case statement is optional, but if it appears, it must come at the end of the statement, after all when clauses. If no when clause is true, and there is an else clause, then the code between else and end is executed. The value of the last expression evaluated in this code becomes the value of the case statement. If no when clause is true and there is no else clause, then no code is executed and the value of the case statement is nil.

A when clause within a case statement may have more than one (comma-separated) expression associated with it. If any one of these expressions evaluates to true, then the code associated with that when is executed. In this simple form of the case statement, the commas aren't particularly useful and act just like the || operator:

```
case
when x == 1, y == 0 then  "x is one or y is zero"  # Obscure syntax
when x == 2 || y == 1 then "x is two or y is one"  # Easier to understand
end
```

All the case examples we've seen so far demonstrate the simpler, less common form of the statement. case is really more powerful than this. Notice that in most of the examples, the left side of each when clause expression is the same. In the common form of case, we factor this repeated lefthand expression of the when clause and associate it with the case itself:

```
name = case x
       when 1                 # Just the value to compare to x
         "one"
       when 2 then "two"    # Then keyword instead of newline
       when 3; "three"      # Semicolon instead of newline
       else "many"          # Optional else clause at end
       end
```

In this form of the case statement, the expression associated with the case is evaluated once, and then it's compared to the values obtained by evaluating the when expression. The comparisons are performed in the order in which the when clauses are written, and the code associated with the first matching when is executed. If no match is found, the code associated with the else clause (if there is one) is executed. The return value of this form of the case statement is the same as the return value of the simpler form: the value of the last expression evaluated, or `nil` if no `when` or `else` matches.

The important thing to understand about the `case` statement is how the values of the `when` clauses are compared to the expression that follows the `case` keyword. This comparison is done using the `===` operator. This operator is invoked on the value of the `when` expression and is passed the value of the `case` expression. Therefore, the `case` statement above is equivalent to the following (except that x is only evaluated once in the code above):

```ruby
name = case
       when 1 === x then "one"
       when 2 === x then "two"
       when 3 === x then "three"
       else "many"
       end
```

`===` is the *case equality operator*. For many classes, such as the `Fixnum` class used earlier, the `===` operator behaves just the same as `==`. But certain classes define this operator in interesting ways. The `Class` class defines `===` so that it tests whether the righthand operand is an instance of the class named by the lefthand operand. `Range` defines this operator to test whether the value on the right falls within the range on the left. `Regexp` defines it so that it tests whether the text on the right matches the pattern on the left. In Ruby 1.9, `Symbol` defines `===` so that it tests for symbol or string equality. With these definitions of case equality, we are able to write interesting `case` statements like the following:

```ruby
# Take different actions depending on the class of x
puts case x
     when String then "string"
     when Numeric then "number"
     when TrueClass, FalseClass then "boolean"
     else "other"
     end

# Compute 2006 U.S. income tax using case and Range objects
tax = case income
      when 0..7550
        income * 0.1
      when 7550..30650
        755 + (income-7550)*0.15
      when 30650..74200
        4220 + (income-30655)*0.25
      when 74200..154800
        15107.5 + (income-74201)*0.28
      when 154800..336550
        37675.5 + (income-154800)*0.33
      else
        97653 + (income-336550)*0.35
      end

# Get user's input and process it, ignoring comments and exiting
```

```
                             # when the user enters the word "quit"
while line=gets.chomp do     # Loop, asking the user for input each time
  case line
  when /^\s*#/               # If input looks like a comment...
    next                     #   skip to the next line.
  when /^quit$/i             # If input is "quit" (case insensitive)...
    break                    #   exit the loop.
  else                       # Otherwise...
    puts line.reverse        #   reverse the user's input and print it.
  end
end
```

A when clause can have more than one expression associated with it. Multiple expressions are separated by commas, and the === operator is invoked on each one. That is, it is possible to trigger the same block of code with more than one value:

```
def hasValue?(x)            # Define a method named hasValue?
  case x                    # Multiway conditional based on value of x
  when nil, [], "", 0       # if nil===x || []===x || ""===x || 0===x then
    false                   #   method return value is false
  else                      # Otherwise
    true                    #   method return value is true
  end
end
```

---

case versus switch

Java programmers and others accustomed to C-derived language syntax are familiar with a multiway conditional switch statement, which is similar to Ruby's case statement. There are, however, a number of important differences:

- In Java and related languages, the name of the statement is switch and its clauses are labeled with case and default. Ruby uses case as the name of the statement, and when and else for the clauses.

- The switch statement of other languages simply transfers control to the start of the appropriate case. From there, control continues and can "fall through" to other cases, until it reaches the end of the switch statement or encounters a break or return statement. This fall-through behavior allows multiple case clauses to refer to the same block of code. In Ruby, this same purpose is served by allowing multiple comma-separated expressions to be associated with each when clause. Ruby's case statement never allows fall-through.

- In Java and most compiled languages with C-like syntax, the expressions associated with each case label must be compile-time constants rather than arbitrary runtime expressions. This often allows the compiler to implement the switch statement using a very fast lookup table. There is no such restriction on Ruby's case statement, and its performance is equivalent to using an if statement with repeated elsif clauses.

5.1.5 The ?: Operator

The conditional operator ?:, described earlier in §4.6.10, behaves much like an if statement, with ? replacing then and : replacing else. It provides a succinct way to express conditionals:

```
def how_many_messages(n) # Handle singular/plural
  "You have " + n.to_s + (n==1 ? " message." : " messages.")
end
```

5.2 Loops

This section documents Ruby's simple looping statements: while, until, and for. Ruby also includes the ability to define custom looping constructs known as *iterators*. Iterators (see §5.3) are probably more commonly used than Ruby's built-in looping statements; they are documented later in this chapter.

5.2.1 while and until

Ruby's basic looping statements are while and until. They execute a chunk of code *while* a certain condition is true, or *until* the condition becomes true. For example:

```
x = 10                  # Initialize a loop counter variable
while x >= 0 do         # Loop while x is greater than or equal to 0
  puts x                #   Print out the value of x
  x = x - 1             #   Subtract 1 from x
end                     # The loop ends here

# Count back up to 10 using an until loop
x = 0                   # Start at 0 (instead of -1)
until x > 10 do         # Loop until x is greater than 10
  puts x
  x = x + 1
end                     # Loop ends here
```

The loop condition is the Boolean expression that appears between the while or until and do keywords. The loop body is the Ruby code that appears between the do and the end keyword. The while loop evaluates its condition. If the value is anything other than false or nil, it executes its body, and then loops to evaluate its condition again. In this way, the body is executed repeatedly, zero or more times, while the condition remains true (or, more strictly, non-false and non-nil).

The until loop is the reverse. The condition is tested and the body is executed if the condition evaluates to false or nil. This means that the body is executed zero or more times while the condition is false or nil. Note that any until loop can be converted to a while simply by negating the condition. Most programmers are familiar with while loops, but many have not used until loops before. For this reason, you may want to use while loops except when until truly improves the clarity of your code.

The do keyword in a `while` or `until` loop is like the `then` keyword in an `if` statement: it may be omitted altogether as long as a newline (or semicolon) appears between the loop condition and the loop body.[*]

5.2.2 while and until As Modifiers

If the body of a loop is a single Ruby expression, you can express that loop in a particularly compact form by using `while` or `until` as a modifier after the expression. For example:

```
x = 0                      # Initialize loop variable
puts x = x + 1 while x < 10   # Output and increment in a single expression
```

This modifier syntax uses the `while` keyword itself to separate the loop body from the loop condition, and avoids the need for the `do` (or newline) and `end` keywords. Contrast this code with the more traditional `while` loop written on a single line:

```
x = 0
while x < 10 do puts x = x + 1 end
```

`until` can be used as a modifier just as `while` can be:

```
a = [1,2,3]                # Initialize an array
puts a.pop until a.empty?   # Pop elements from array until empty
```

Note that when `while` and `until` are used as modifiers, they must appear on the same line as the loop body that they modify. If there is a newline between the loop body and the `while` or `until` keyword, the Ruby interpreter will treat the loop body as an unmodified expression and the `while` or `until` as the beginning of a regular loop.

When `while` and `until` are used as modifiers for a single Ruby expression, the loop condition is tested first, even though it is written after the loop body. The loop body is executed zero or more times, just as if it were formatted as a regular `while` or `until` loop.

There is a special-case exception to this rule. When the expression being evaluated is a compound expression delimited by `begin` and `end` keywords, then the body is executed first before the condition is tested:

```
x = 10              # Initialize loop variable
begin               # Start a compound expression: executed at least once
  puts x            #    output x
  x = x - 1         #    decrement x
end until x == 0    # End compound expression and modify it with a loop
```

This results in a construct much like the `do/while` loop of C, C++, and Java. Despite its similarity to the `do/while` loop of other languages, this special-case behavior of loop modifiers with the `begin` statement is counterintuitive and its use is discouraged. Future releases of Ruby may forbid the use of `while` and `until` modifiers with `begin/end`.

---

[*] In Ruby 1.8, a colon may be used in place of the `do` keyword. This is no longer allowed in Ruby 1.9.

Note that if you group multiple statements with parentheses and apply an until modifier to that grouped expression, you do not get this special case behavior:

```
x = 0           # Initialize loop variable
(               # Start a compound expression: may be executed 0 times
  puts x        #    output x
  x = x - 1     #    decrement x
) until x == 0  # End compound expression and modify it with a loop
```

5.2.3 The for/in Loop

The for loop, or for/in loop, iterates through the elements of an enumerable object (such as an array). On each iteration, it assigns an element to a specified loop variable and then executes the body of the loop. A for loop looks like this:

```
for var in collection do
  body
end
```

var is a variable or a comma-separated list of variables. *collection* is any object that has an each iterator method. Arrays and hashes define the each method, and many other Ruby objects do, too. The for/in loop calls the each method of the specified object. As that iterator yields values, the for loop assigns each value (or each set of values) to the specified variable (or variables) and then executes the code in *body*. As with the while and until loops, the do keyword is optional and may be replaced with a newline or semicolon.

Here are some sample for loops:

```
# Print the elements in an array
array = [1,2,3,4,5]
for element in array
  puts element
end

# Print the keys and values in a hash
hash = {:a=>1, :b=>2, :c=>3}
for key,value in hash
  puts "#{key} => #{value}"
end
```

The loop variable or variables of a for loop are not local to the loop; they remain defined even after the loop exits. Similarly, new variables defined within the body of the loop continue to exist after the loop exits.

The fact that the for loop depends on the each iterator method implies that for loops are much like iterators. For example, the for loop shown above for enumerating the keys and values of a hash could also be written with an explicit use of the each iterator:

```
hash = {:a=>1, :b=>2, :c=>3}
hash.each do |key,value|
  puts "#{key} => #{value}"
end
```

The only difference between the for version of the loop and the each version is that the block of code that follows an iterator does define a new variable scope. Details are in the discussion of iterators later in this chapter.

5.3 Iterators and Enumerable Objects

Although while, until, and for loops are a core part of the Ruby language, it is probably more common to write loops using special methods known as *iterators*. Iterators are one of the most noteworthy features of Ruby, and examples such as the following are common in introductory Ruby tutorials:

```
3.times { puts "thank you!" }   # Express gratitude three times
data.each {|x| puts x }         # Print each element x of data
[1,2,3].map {|x| x*x }          # Compute squares of array elements
factorial = 1                   # Compute the factorial of n
2.upto(n) {|x| factorial *= x }
```

The times, each, map, and upto methods are all iterators, and they interact with the *block* of code that follows them. The complex control structure behind this is yield. The yield statement temporarily returns control from the iterator method to the method that invoked the iterator. Specifically, control flow goes from the iterator to the block of code associated with the invocation of the iterator. When the end of the block is reached, the iterator method regains control and execution resumes at the first statement following the yield. In order to implement some kind of looping construct, an iterator method will typically invoke the yield statement multiple times. Figure 5-1 illustrates this complex flow of control. Blocks and yield are described in detail in §5.4 below; for now, we focus on the iteration itself rather than the control structure that enables it.

As you can see from the previous examples, blocks may be parameterized. Vertical bars at the start of a block are like parentheses in a method definition—they hold a list of parameter names. The yield statement is like a method invocation; it is followed by zero or more expressions whose values are assigned to the block parameters.

Iterators that Don't Iterate

We use the term *iterator* in this book to mean any method that uses the yield statement. They do not actually have to serve an iteration or looping function.[*] The tap method defined (in Ruby 1.9 and 1.8.7) by the Object class is an example. It invokes the associated block once, passing the receiver as the only argument. Then it returns the receiver. It is handy for "tapping into" a method chain, as in the following code which uses tap to output debugging messages:

---

[*] Within the Japanese Ruby community, the term "iterator" has fallen out of use because it implies an iteration that is not actually required. A phrase like "method that expects an associated block" is verbose but more precise.

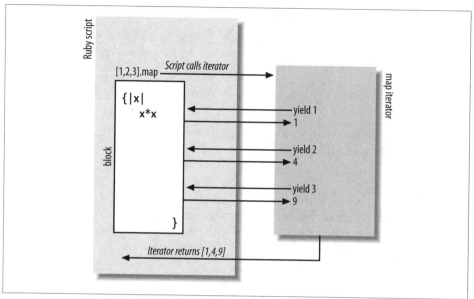

Figure 5-1. An iterator yielding to its invoking method

```
chars = "hello world".tap {|x| puts "original object: #{x.inspect}"}
  .each_char          .tap {|x| puts "each_char returns: #{x.inspect}"}
  .to_a               .tap {|x| puts "to_a returns: #{x.inspect}"}
  .map {|c| c.succ }  .tap {|x| puts "map returns: #{x.inspect}" }
  .sort               .tap {|x| puts "sort returns: #{x.inspect}"}
```

Another common function for iterators is automatic resource deallocation. The `File.open` method can be used as an iterator, for example. It opens the named file, creating a `File` object to represent it. If no block is associated with the invocation, it simply returns the `File` object and leaves the responsibility for closing the file with the calling code. If there is a block associated with the `File.open` call, however, it passes the new `File` object to that block and then automatically closes the file when the block returns. This ensures that files will always be closed and frees programmers from this housekeeping detail. In this case, when a block is associated with the call to `File.open`, the return value of method is not a `File` object but whatever value the block returned.

5.3.1 Numeric Iterators

The core Ruby API provides a number of standard iterators. The `Kernel` method `loop` behaves like an infinite loop, running its associated block repeatedly until the block executes a `return`, `break`, or other statement that exits from the loop.

The Integer class defines three commonly used iterators. The `upto` method invokes its associated block once for each integer between the integer on which it is invoked and the integer which is passed as an argument. For example:

```
4.upto(6) {|x| print x}   # => prints "456"
```

As you can see, upto yields each integer to the associated block, and it includes both the starting point and the end point in the iteration. In general, n.upto(m) runs its block m-n+1 times.

The downto method is just like upto but iterates from a larger number down to a smaller number.

When the Integer.times method is invoked on the integer n, it invokes its block n times, passing values 0 through n-1 on successive iterations. For example:

```
3.times {|x| print x }    # => prints "012"
```

In general, n.times is equivalent to 0.upto(n-1).

If you want to do a numeric iteration using floating-point numbers, you can use the more complex step method defined by the Numeric class. The following iterator, for example, starts at 0 and iterates in steps of 0.1 until it reaches Math::PI:

```
0.step(Math::PI, 0.1) {|x| puts Math.sin(x) }
```

5.3.2 Enumerable Objects

Array, Hash, Range, and a number of other classes define an each iterator that passes each element of the collection to the associated block. This is perhaps the most commonly used iterator in Ruby; as we saw earlier, the for loop only works for iterating over objects that have each methods. Examples of each iterators:

```
[1,2,3].each {|x| print x }   # => prints "123"
(1..3).each  {|x| print x }   # => prints "123" Same as 1.upto(3)
```

The each iterator is not only for traditional "data structure" classes. Ruby's IO class defines an each iterator that yields lines of text read from the Input/Output object. Thus, you can process the lines of a file in Ruby with code like this:

```
File.open(filename) do |f|     # Open named file, pass as f
  f.each {|line| print line }  # Print each line in f
end                            # End block and close file
```

Most classes that define an each method also include the Enumerable module, which defines a number of more specialized iterators that are implemented on top of the each method. One such useful iterator is each_with_index, which allows us to add line numbering to the previous example:

```
File.open(filename) do |f|
  f.each_with_index do |line,number|
    print "#{number}: #{line}"
  end
end
```

Some of the most commonly used Enumerable iterators are the rhyming methods collect, select, reject, and inject. The collect method (also known as map) executes its associated block for each element of the enumerable object, and collects the return values of the blocks into an array:

```
squares = [1,2,3].collect {|x| x*x}   # => [1,4,9]
```

The `select` method invokes the associated block for each element in the enumerable object, and returns an array of elements for which the block returns a value other than `false` or `nil`. For example:

```
evens = (1..10).select {|x| x%2 == 0} # => [2,4,6,8,10]
```

The `reject` method is simply the opposite of `select`; it returns an array of elements for which the block returns `nil` or `false`. For example:

```
odds = (1..10).reject {|x| x%2 == 0}  # => [1,3,5,7,9]
```

The `inject` method is a little more complicated than the others. It invokes the associated block with two arguments. The first argument is an accumulated value of some sort from previous iterations. The second argument is the next element of the enumerable object. The return value of the block becomes the first block argument for the next iteration, or becomes the return value of the iterator after the last iteration. The initial value of the accumulator variable is either the argument to `inject`, if there is one, or the first element of the enumerable object. (In this case, the block is invoked just once for the first two elements.) Examples make `inject` more clear:

```
data = [2, 5, 3, 4]
sum = data.inject {|sum, x| sum + x }     # => 14     (2+5+3+4)
floatprod = data.inject(1.0) {|p,x| p*x } # => 120.0 (1.0*2*5*3*4)
max = data.inject {|m,x| m>x ? m : x }    # => 5      (largest element)
```

See §9.5.1 for further details on the `Enumerable` module and its iterators.

5.3.3 Writing Custom Iterators

The defining feature of an iterator method is that it invokes a block of code associated with the method invocation. You do this with the `yield` statement. The following method is a trivial iterator that just invokes its block twice:

```
def twice
  yield
  yield
end
```

To pass argument values to the block, follow the `yield` statement with a comma-separated list of expressions. As with method invocation, the argument values may optionally be enclosed in parentheses. The following simple iterator shows a use of `yield`:

```
# This method expects a block. It generates n values of the form
# m*i + c, for i from 0..n-1, and yields them, one at a time,
# to the associated block.
def sequence(n, m, c)
```

```
    i = 0
    while(i < n)        # Loop n times
      yield m*i + c     # Invoke the block, and pass a value to it
      i += 1            # Increment i each time
    end
  end

  # Here is an invocation of that method, with a block.
  # It prints the values 1, 6, and 11
  sequence(3, 5, 1) {|y| puts y }
```

Nomenclature: yield and Iterators

Depending on your programming background, you may find the terms "yield" and "iterator" confusing. The sequence method shown earlier is a fairly clear example of why yield has the name it does. After computing each number in the sequence, the method yields control (and yields the computed number) to the block, so that the block can work with it. It is not always this clear, however; in some code it may seem as if it is the block that is yielding a result back to the method that invoked it.

A method such as sequence that expects a block and invokes it multiple times is called an *iterator* because it looks and behaves like a loop. This may be confusing if you are used to languages like Java in which iterators are objects. In Java, the client code that uses the iterator is in control and "pulls" values from the iterator when it needs them. In Ruby, the iterator method is in control and "pushes" values to the block that wants them.

This nomenclature issue is related to the distinction between "internal iterators" and "external iterators," which is discussed later in this section.

Here is another example of a Ruby iterator; it passes two arguments to its block. It is worth noticing that the implementation of this iterator uses another iterator internally:

```
  # Generate n points evenly spaced around the circumference of a
  # circle of radius r centered at (0,0). Yield the x and y coordinates
  # of each point to the associated block.
  def circle(r,n)
    n.times do |i|     # Notice that this method is implemented with a block
      angle = Math::PI * 2 * i / n
      yield r*Math.cos(angle), r*Math.sin(angle)
    end
  end

  # This invocation of the iterator prints:
  # (1.00, 0.00) (0.00, 1.00) (-1.00, 0.00) (-0.00, -1.00)
  circle(1,4) {|x,y| printf "(%.2f, %.2f) ", x, y }
```

Using the yield keyword really is a lot like invoking a method. (See Chapter 6 for complete details on method invocation.) Parentheses around the arguments are optional. You can use * to expand an array into individual arguments. yield even allows you to pass a hash literal without the curly braces around it. Unlike a method invocation, however, a `yield` expression may not be followed by a block. You cannot pass a block to a block.

If a method is invoked without a block, it is an error for that method to `yield`, because there is nothing to yield to. Sometimes you want to write a method that yields to a block if one is provided but takes some default action (other than raising an error) if invoked with no block. To do this, use `block_given?` to determine whether there is a block associated with the invocation. `block_given?`, and its synonym `iterator?`, are `Kernel` methods, so they act like global functions. Here is an example:

```
# Return an array with n elements of the form m*i+c
# If a block is given, also yield each element to the block
def sequence(n, m, c)
  i, s = 0, []                 # Initialize variables
  while(i < n)                 # Loop n times
    y = m*i + c                # Compute value
    yield y if block_given?    # Yield, if block
    s << y                     # Store the value
    i += 1
  end
  s                            # Return the array of values
end
```

5.3.4 Enumerators

An *enumerator* is an `Enumerable` object whose purpose is to enumerate some other object. To use enumerators in Ruby 1.8, you must `require 'enumerator'`. In Ruby 1.9 (and also 1.8.7), enumerators are built-in and no `require` is necessary. (As we'll see later, the built-in enumerators have substantially more functionality than that provided by the `enumerator` library.)

Enumerators are of class `Enumerable::Enumerator`. Although this class can be instantiated directly with `new`, this is not how enumerators are typically created. Instead, use `to_enum` or its synonym `enum_for`, which are methods of `Object`. With no arguments, `to_enum` returns an enumerator whose **each** method simply calls the **each** method of the target object. Suppose you have an array and a method that expects an enumerable object. You don't want to pass the array object itself, because it is mutable, and you don't trust the method not to modify it. Instead of making a defensive deep copy of the array, just call `to_enum` on it, and pass the resulting enumerator instead of the array itself. In effect, you're creating an enumerable but immutable proxy object for your array:

```
# Call this method with an Enumerator instead of a mutable array.
# This is a useful defensive strategy to avoid bugs.
process(data.to_enum)  # Instead of just process(data)
```

You can also pass arguments to `to_enum`, although the `enum_for` synonym seems more natural in this case. The first argument should be a symbol that identifies an iterator method. The **each** method of the resulting `Enumerator` will invoke the named method of the original object. Any remaining arguments to enum_for will be passed to that named method. In Ruby 1.9, the String class is not Enumerable, but it defines three iterator methods: each_char, each_byte, and each_line. Suppose we want to use an Enumerable method, such as map, and we want it to be based on the each_char iterator. We do this by creating an enumerator:

```
s = "hello"
s.enum_for(:each_char).map {|c| c.succ }  # => ["i", "f", "m", "m", "p"]
```

In Ruby 1.9 (and 1.8.7), it is usually not even necessary to use to_enum or enum_for explicitly as we did in the previous examples. This is because the built-in iterator methods of Ruby 1.9 (which include the numeric iterators times, upto, downto, and step, as well as each and related methods of Enumerable) automatically return an enumerator when invoked with no block. So, to pass an array enumerator to a method rather than the array itself, you can simply call the each method:

```
process(data.each_char)  # Instead of just process(data)
```

This syntax is even more natural if we use the chars alias in place of each_char. To map the characters of a string to an array of characters, for example, just use .chars.map:

```
"hello".chars.map {|c| c.succ }  # => ["i", "f", "m", "m", "p"]
```

Here are some other examples that rely on enumerator objects returned by iterator methods. Note that it is not just iterator methods defined by Enumerable that can return enumerator objects; numeric iterators like times and upto do the same:

```
enumerator = 3.times           # An enumerator object
enumerator.each {|x| print x }  # Prints "012"

# downto returns an enumerator with a select method
10.downto(1).select {|x| x%2==0}  # => [10,8,6,4,2]

# each_byte iterator returns an enumerator with a to_a method
"hello".each_byte.to_a         # => [104, 101, 108, 108, 111]
```

You can duplicate this behavior in your own iterator methods by returning self.to_enum when no block is supplied. Here, for example, is a version of the twice iterator shown earlier that can return an enumerator if no block is provided:

```
def twice
  if block_given?
    yield
    yield
  else
    self.to_enum(:twice)
  end
end
```

In Ruby 1.9, enumerator objects define a with_index method that is not available in the Ruby 1.8 enumerator module. with_index simply returns a new enumerator that adds an index parameter to the iteration. For example, the following returns an enumerator that yields the characters of a string and their index within the string:

```
enumerator = s.each_char.with_index
```

Finally, keep in mind that enumerators, in both Ruby 1.8 and 1.9, are `Enumerable` objects that can be used with the `for` loop. For example:

```
for line, number in text.each_line.with_index
  print "#{number+1}: #{line}"
end
```

5.3.5 External Iterators

Our discussion of enumerators has focused on their use as `Enumerable` proxy objects. In Ruby 1.9, (and 1.8.7, though the implementation is not as efficient) however, enumerators have another very important use: they are *external iterators*. You can use an enumerator to loop through the elements of a collection by repeatedly calling the `next` method. When there are no more elements, this method raises a `StopIteration` exception:

```
iterator = 9.downto(1)              # An enumerator as external iterator
begin                               # So we can use rescue below
  print iterator.next while true    # Call the next method repeatedly
rescue StopIteration                # When there are no more values
  puts "...blastoff!"               # An expected, nonexceptional condition
end
```

Internal versus External Iterators

The "gang of four" define and contrast internal and external iterators quite clearly in their design patterns book:[*]

> A fundamental issue is deciding which party controls the iteration, the iterator or the client that uses the iterator. When the client controls the iteration, the iterator is called an **external iterator**, and when the iterator controls it, the iterator is an **internal iterator**. Clients that use an external iterator must advance the traversal and request the next element explicitly from the iterator. In contrast, the client hands an internal iterator an operation to perform, and the iterator applies that operation to every element....

> External iterators are more flexible than internal iterators. It's easy to compare two collections for equality with an external iterator, for example, but it's practically impossible with internal iterators.... But on the other hand, internal iterators are easier to use, because they define the iteration logic for you.

In Ruby, iterator methods like `each` are internal iterators; they control the iteration and "push" values to the block of code associated with the method invocation. Enumerators have an `each` method for internal iteration, but in Ruby 1.9 and later, they also work as external iterators—client code can sequentially "pull" values from an enumerator with `next`.

---

[*] *Design Patterns: Elements of Reusable Object-Oriented Software*, by Gamma, Helm, Johnson, and Vlissides (Addison-Wesley).

External iterators are quite simple to use: just call next each time you want another element. When there are no more elements left, next will raise a StopIteration exception. This may seem unusual—an exception is raised for an expected termination condition rather than an unexpected and exceptional event. (StopIteration is a descendant of StandardError and IndexError; note that it is one of the only exception classes that does not have the word "error" in its name.) Ruby follows Python in this external iteration technique. By treating loop termination as an exception, it makes your looping logic extremely simple; there is no need to check the return value of next for a special end-of-iteration value, and there is no need to call some kind of next? predicate before calling next.

To simplify looping with external iterators, the Kernel.loop method includes (in Ruby 1.9) an implicit rescue clause and exits cleanly when StopIteration is raised. Thus, the countdown code shown earlier could more easily be written like this:

```
iterator = 9.downto(1)
loop do                   # Loop until StopIteration is raised
  print iterator.next    # Print next item
end
puts "...blastoff!"
```

Many external iterators can be restarted by calling the rewind method. Note, however, that rewind is not effective for all enumerators. If an enumerator is based on an object like a File which reads lines sequentially, calling rewind will not restart the iteration from the beginning. In general, if new invocations of each on the underlying Enumerable object do not restart the iteration from the beginning, then calling rewind will not restart it either.

Once an external iteration has started (i.e., after next has been called for the first time), an enumerator cannot be cloned or duplicated. It is typically possible to clone an enumerator before next is called, or after StopIteration has been raised or rewind is called.

Normally, enumerators with next methods are created from Enumerable objects that have an each method. If, for some reason, you define a class that provides a next method for external iteration instead of an each method for internal iteration, you can easily implement each in terms of next. In fact, turning an externally iterable class that implements next into an Enumerable class is as simple as mixing in (with include—see §7.5) a module like this:

```
module Iterable
  include Enumerable      # Define iterators on top of each
  def each                # And define each on top of next
    loop { yield self.next }
  end
end
```

Another way to use an external iterator is to pass it to an internal iterator method like this one:

```
def iterate(iterator)
  loop { yield iterator.next }
```

```
end

    iterate(9.downto(1)) {|x| print x }
```

The earlier quote from *Design Patterns* alluded to one of the key features of external iterators: they solve the parallel iteration problem. Suppose you have two Enumerable collections and need to iterate their elements in pairs: the first elements of each collection, then the second elements, and so on. Without an external iterator, you must convert one of the collections to an array (with the to_a method defined by Enumerable) so that you can access its elements while iterating the other collection with each.

Example 5-1 shows the implementation of three iterator methods. All three accept an arbitrary number of Enumerable objects and iterate them in different ways. One is a simple sequential iteration using only internal iterators; the other two are parallel iterations and can only be done using the external iteration features of Ruby 1.9.

Example 5-1. Parallel iteration with external iterators

```
# Call the each method of each collection in turn.
# This is not a parallel iteration and does not require enumerators.
def sequence(*enumerables, &block)
  enumerables.each do |enumerable|
    enumerable.each(&block)
  end
end

# Iterate the specified collections, interleaving their elements.
# This can't be done efficiently without external iterators.
# Note the use of the uncommon else clause in begin/rescue.
def interleave(*enumerables)
  # Convert enumerable collections to an array of enumerators.
  enumerators = enumerables.map {|e| e.to_enum }
  # Loop until we don't have any more enumerators.
  until enumerators.empty?
    begin
      e = enumerators.shift    # Take the first enumerator
      yield e.next             # Get its next and pass to the block
    rescue StopIteration       # If no more elements, do nothing
    else                       # If no exception occurred
      enumerators << e         # Put the enumerator back
    end
  end
end

# Iterate the specified collections, yielding tuples of values,
# one value from each of the collections. See also Enumerable.zip.
def bundle(*enumerables)
  enumerators = enumerables.map {|e| e.to_enum }
  loop { yield enumerators.map {|e| e.next} }
end

# Examples of how these iterator methods work
a,b,c = [1,2,3], 4..6, 'a'..'e'
```

```
sequence(a,b,c) {|x| print x}   # prints "123456abcde"
interleave(a,b,c) {|x| print x} # prints "14a25b36cde"
bundle(a,b,c) {|x| print x}     # '[1, 4, "a"][2, 5, "b"][3, 6, "c"]'
```

The `bundle` method of Example 5-1 is similar to the `Enumerable.zip` method. In Ruby
1.8, `zip` must first convert its `Enumerable` arguments to arrays and then use those arrays
while iterating through the Enumerable object it is called on. In Ruby 1.9, however,
the `zip` method can use external iterators. This makes it (typically) more efficient in
space and time, and also allows it to work with unbounded collections that could not
be converted into an array of finite size.

5.3.6 Iteration and Concurrent Modification

In general, Ruby's core collection of classes iterate over live objects rather than private
copies or "snapshots" of those objects, and they make no attempt to detect or prevent
concurrent modification to the collection while it is being iterated. If you call the
`each` method of an array, for example, and the block associated with that invocation
calls the `shift` method of the same array, the results of the iteration may be surprising:

```
a = [1,2,3,4,5]
a.each {|x| puts "#{x},#{a.shift}" }  # prints "1,1\n3,2\n5,3"
```

You may see similarly surprising behavior if one thread modifies a collection while
another thread is iterating it. One way to avoid this is to make a defensive copy of the
collection before iterating it. The following code, for example, adds a method
`each_in_snapshot` to the `Enumerable` module:

```
module Enumerable
  def each_in_snapshot &block
    snapshot = self.dup    # Make a private copy of the Enumerable object
    snapshot.each &block   # And iterate on the copy
  end
end
```

5.4 Blocks

The use of blocks is fundamental to the use of iterators. In the previous section, we
focused on iterators as a kind of looping construct. Blocks were implicit to our discussion but were not the subject of it. Now we turn our attention to the block themselves.
The subsections that follow explain:

- The syntax for associating a block with a method invocation
- The "return value" of a block
- The scope of variables in blocks
- The difference between block parameters and method parameters

---

5.4.1 Block Syntax

Blocks may not stand alone; they are only legal following a method invocation. You can, however, place a block after any method invocation; if the method is not an iterator and never invokes the block with yield, the block will be silently ignored. Blocks are delimited with curly braces or with do and end keywords. The opening curly brace or the do keyword must be on the same line as the method invocation, or else Ruby interprets the line terminator as a statement terminator and invokes the method without the block:

```
# Print the numbers 1 to 10
1.upto(10) {|x| puts x }    # Invocation and block on one line with braces
1.upto(10) do |x|           # Block delimited with do/end
  puts x
end
1.upto(10)                  # No block specified
  {|x| puts x }             # Syntax error: block not after an invocation
```

One common convention is to use curly braces when a block fits on a single line, and to use do and end when the block extends over multiple lines. This is not completely a matter of convention, however; the Ruby parser binds { tightly to the token that precedes it. If you omit the parentheses around method arguments and use curly brace delimiters for a block, then the block will be associated with the last method argument rather than the method itself, which is probably not what you want. To avoid this case, put parentheses around the arguments or delimit the block with do and end:

```
1.upto(3) {|x| puts x }    # Parens and curly braces work
1.upto 3 do |x| puts x end # No parens, block delimited with do/end
1.upto 3 {|x| puts x }     # Syntax Error: trying to pass a block to 3!
```

Blocks can be parameterized, just as methods can. Block parameters are separated with commas and delimited with a pair of vertical bar (|) characters, but they are otherwise much like method parameters:

```
# The Hash.each iterator passes two arguments to its block
hash.each do |key, value|   # For each (key,value) pair in the hash
  puts "#{key}: #{value}"   # Print the key and the value
end                         # End of the block
```

It is a common convention to write the block parameters on the same line as the method invocation and the opening brace or do keyword, but this is not required by the syntax.

5.4.2 The Value of a Block

In the iterator examples shown so far in this chapter, the iterator method has yielded values to its associated block but has ignored the value returned by the block. This is not always the case, however. Consider the Array.sort method. If you associate a block with an invocation of this method, it will yield pairs of elements to the block, and it is the block's job to sort them. The block's return value (-1, 0, or 1) indicates the ordering of the two arguments. The "return value" of the block is available to the iterator method as the value of the `yield` statement.

The "return value" of a block is simply the value of the last expression evaluated in the block. So, to sort an array of words from longest to shortest, we could write:

```
# The block takes two words and "returns" their relative order
words.sort! {|x,y| y.length <=> x.length}
```

We've been placing the phrase "return value" in quotes for a very important reason: you should not normally use the `return` keyword to return from a block. A `return` inside a block causes the containing method (not the iterator method that yields to the block, but the method that the block is part of) to return. There are, of course, times when this is exactly what you want to do. But don't use `return` if you just want to return from a block to the method that called `yield`. If you need to force a block to return to the invoking method before it reaches the last expression, or if you want to return more than one value, you can use `next` instead of `return`. (`return`, `next`, and the related statement `break` are explained in detail in §5.5.) Here is an example that uses `next` to return from the block:

```
array.collect do |x|
  next 0 if x == nil  # Return prematurely if x is nil
  next x, x*x         # Return two values
end
```

Note that it is not particularly common to use `next` in this way, and the code above is easily rewritten without it:

```
array.collect do |x|
  if x == nil
    0
  else
    [x, x*x]
  end
end
```

5.4.3 Blocks and Variable Scope

Blocks define a new variable scope: variables created within a block exist only within that block and are undefined outside of the block. Be cautious, however; the local variables in a method are available to any blocks within that method. So if a block assigns a value to a variable that is already defined outside of the block, this does not create a new block-local variable but instead assigns a new value to the already-existing variable. Sometimes, this is exactly the behavior we want:

```
total = 0
data.each {|x| total += x }  # Sum the elements of the data array
puts total                   # Print out that sum
```

Sometimes, however, we do not want to alter variables in the enclosing scope, but we do so inadvertently. This problem is a particular concern for block parameters in Ruby

1.8. In Ruby 1.8, if a block parameter shares the name of an existing variable, then invocations of the block simply assign a value to that existing variable rather than creating a new block-local variable. The following code, for example, is problematic because it uses the same identifier i as the block parameter for two nested blocks:

```
1.upto(10) do |i|        # 10 rows
  1.upto(10) do |i|      # Each has 10 columns
    print "#{i} "        # Print column number
  end
  print " ==> Row #{i}\n" # Try to print row number, but get column number
end
```

Ruby 1.9 is different: block parameters are always local to their block, and invocations of the block never assign values to existing variables. If Ruby 1.9 is invoked with the -w flag, it will warn you if a block parameter has the same name as an existing variable. This helps you avoid writing code that runs differently in 1.8 and 1.9.

Ruby 1.9 is different in another important way, too. Block syntax has been extended to allow you to declare block-local variables that are guaranteed to be local, even if a variable by the same name already exists in the enclosing scope. To do this, follow the list of block parameters with a semicolon and a comma-separated list of block local variables. Here is an example:

```
x = y = 0             # local variables
1.upto(4) do |x;y|    # x and y are local to block
                      # x and y "shadow" the outer variables
  y = x + 1           # Use y as a scratch variable
  puts y*y            # Prints 4, 9, 16, 25
end
[x,y]                 # => [0,0]: block does not alter these
```

In this code, x is a block parameter: it gets a value when the block is invoked with yield. y is a block-local variable. It does not receive any value from a yield invocation, but it has the value nil until the block actually assigns some other value to it. The point of declaring these block-local variables is to guarantee that you will not inadvertently clobber the value of some existing variable. (This might happen if a block is cut-and-pasted from one method to another, for example.) If you invoke Ruby 1.9 with the -w option, it will warn you if a block-local variable shadows an existing variable.

Blocks can have more than one parameter and more than one local variable, of course. Here is a block with two parameters and three local variables:

```
hash.each {|key,value; i,j,k| ... }
```

5.4.4 Passing Arguments to a Block

We've said previously that the parameters to a block are much like the parameters to a method. They are not strictly the same, however. The argument values that follow a yield keyword are assigned to block parameters following rules that are closer to the rules for variable assignment than to the rules for method invocation. Thus, when an iterator executes yield k,v to invoke a block declared with parameters |key, value|, it is equivalent to this assignment statement:

```
key,value = k,v
```

The Hash.each_pair iterator yields a key/value pair like this:[*]

```
{:one=>1}.each_pair {|key,value| ... } # key=:one, value=1
```

In Ruby 1.8, it is even more clear that block invocation uses variable assignment. Recall that in Ruby 1.8 parameters are only local to the block if they are not already in use as local variables of the containing method. If they are already local variables, then they are simply assigned to. In fact, Ruby 1.8 allows any kind of variable to be used as a block parameter, including global variables and instance variables:

```
{:one=>1}.each_pair {|$key, @value| ... } # No longer works in Ruby 1.9
```

This iterator sets the global variable $key to :one and sets the instance variable @value to 1. As already noted, Ruby 1.9 makes block parameters local to the block. This also means that block parameters can no longer be global or instance variables.

The Hash.each iterator yields key/value pairs as two elements of a single array. It is very common, however, to see code like this:

```
hash.each {|k,v| ... }  # key and value assigned to params k and v
```

This also works by parallel assignment. The yielded value, a two-element array, is assigned to the variables k and v:

```
k,v = [key, value]
```

By the rules of parallel assignment (see §4.5.5), a single array on the right is expanded to and its elements assigned to the multiple variables on the left.

Block invocation does not work exactly like parallel assignment. Imagine an iterator that passes two values to its block. By the rules of parallel assignment, we might expect to be able to declare a block with a single parameter and have the two values automatically filled into an array for us. But it does not work that way:

```
def two; yield 1,2; end  # An iterator that yields two values
two {|x| p x }      # Ruby 1.8: warns and prints [1,2],
two {|x| p x }      # Ruby 1.9: prints 1, no warning
two {|*x| p x }     # Either version: prints [1,2]; no warning
two {|x,| p x }     # Either version: prints 1; no warning
```

In Ruby 1.8, multiple arguments are packed into an array when there is a single block parameter, but this is deprecated and generates a warning message. In Ruby 1.9, the first value yielded is assigned to the block parameter and the second value is silently discarded. If we want multiple yielded values to be packed into an array and assigned

---

[*] The Ruby 1.8 each_pair yields two separate values to the block. In Ruby 1.9, the each_pair iterator is a synonym for each and passes a single array argument, as will be explained shortly. The code shown here, however, works correctly in both versions.

to a single block parameter, we must explicitly indicate this by prefixing the parameter with an *, exactly as we'd do in a method declaration. (See Chapter 6 for a thorough discussion of method parameters and method declaration.) Also note that we can explicitly discard the second yielded value by declaring a block parameter list that ends with a comma, as if to say: "There is another parameter, but it is unused and I can't be bothered to pick a name for it."

Although block invocation does not behave like parallel assignment in this case, it does not behave like method invocation, either. If we declare a method with one argument and then pass two arguments to it, Ruby doesn't just print a warning, it raises an error.

In Ruby 1.8, only the last block parameter may have an * prefix. Ruby 1.9 lifts this restriction and allows any one block parameter, regardless of its position in the list, to have an * prefix:

```ruby
def five; yield 1,2,3,4,5; end    # Yield 5 values
five do |head, *body, tail|       # Extra values go into body array
  print head, body, tail          # Prints "1[2,3,4]5"
end
```

The yield statement allows bare hashes as the last argument value, just as method invocations (see §6.4.4) do. That is, if the last argument to yield is a hash literal, you may omit the curly braces. Because it is not common for iterators to yield hashes, we have to contrive an example to demonstrate this:

```ruby
def hashiter; yield :a=>1, :b=>2; end  # Note no curly braces
hashiter {|hash| puts hash[:a] }        # Prints 1
```

In Ruby 1.9, the final block parameter may be prefixed with & to indicate that it is to receive any block associated with the invocation of the block. Recall, however, that a yield invocation may not have a block associated with it. We'll learn in Chapter 6 that a block can be converted into a Proc, and blocks *can* be associated with Proc invocations. The following code example should make sense once you have read Chapter 6:

```ruby
# This Proc expects a block
printer = lambda {|&b| puts b.call } # Print value returned by b
printer.call { "hi" }                # Pass a block to the block!
```

An important difference between block parameters and method parameters is that block parameters are not allowed to have default values assigned as method parameters are. That is, it is *not* legal to write this:

```ruby
[1,2,3].each {|x,y=10| print x*y }     # SyntaxError!
```

Ruby 1.9 defines a new syntax for creating Proc objects and this new syntax does allow argument defaults. Details will have to wait until you've read about Proc objects in Chapter 6, but this code can be rewritten as follows:

```ruby
[1,2,3].each &->(x,y=10) { print x*y }  # Prints "102030"
```

5.5 Altering Control Flow

In addition to conditionals, loops, and iterators, Ruby supports a number of statements that alter the flow-of-control in a Ruby program. These statements are:

return
> Causes a method to exit and return a value to its caller.

break
> Causes a loop (or iterator) to exit.

next
> Causes a loop (or iterator) to skip the rest of the current iteration and move on to the next iteration.

redo
> Restarts a loop or iterator from the beginning.

retry
> Restarts an iterator, reevaluating the entire expression. The retry keyword can also be used in exception handling, as we'll see later in the chapter.

throw/catch
> A very general control structure that is named like and works like an exception propagation and handling mechanism. throw and catch are not Ruby's primary exception mechanism (that would be raise and rescue, described later in this chapter). Instead, they are used as a kind of multilevel or labeled break.

The subsections that follow describe each of these statements in detail.

5.5.1 return

The return statement causes the enclosing method to return to its caller. If you know C, Java, or a related language, you probably already have an intuitive understanding of the return statement. Don't skip this section, however, because the behavior of return within a block may not be intuitive to you.

return may optionally be followed by an expression, or a comma-separated list of expressions. If there is no expression, then the return value of the method is nil. If there is one expression, then the value of that expression becomes the return value of the method. If there is more than one expression after the return keyword, then the return value of the method is an array containing the values of those expressions.

Note that most methods do not require the return statement. When flow-of-control reaches the end of a method, the method automatically returns to its caller. The return value in this case is the value of the last expression in the method. Most Ruby programmers omit return when it is not necessary. Instead of writing return x as the last line of a method, they would simply write x.

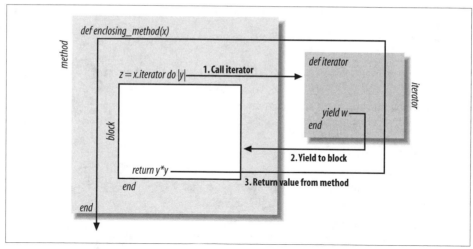

Figure 5-2. The return statement in a block

`return` is useful if you want to return from a method prematurely, or if you want to return more than one value. For example:

```
# Return two copies of x, if x is not nil
def double(x)
  return nil if x == nil    # Return prematurely
  return x, x.dup           # Return multiple values
end
```

When first learning about Ruby blocks, it is natural to think of them as some kind of nested function or mini-method. And if you think of them this way, you might expect `return` simply to cause the block to return to the iterator that yielded to it. But blocks are not methods, and the `return` keyword does not work this way. In fact, `return` is remarkably consistent; it always causes the enclosing method to return, regardless of how deeply nested within blocks it is.[*]

Note that the enclosing method is not the same thing as the invoking method. When the `return` statement is used in a block, it does not just cause the block to return. And it does not just cause the iterator that invokes the block to return. `return` always causes the enclosing method to return. The enclosing method, also called the *lexically enclosing* method, is the method that the block appears inside of when you look at the source code. Figure 5-2 illustrates the behavior of the `return` statement in a block.

The following code defines a method that uses `return` to return from inside a block:

```
# Return the index of the first occurrence of target within array or nil
# Note that this code just duplicates the Array.index method
def find(array, target)
  array.each_with_index do |element,index|
```

---

[*] We'll see an exception when we consider lambdas in §6.5.5.1. A lambda is a kind of function created from a block, and the behavior of `return` within a lambda is different from its behavior in an ordinary block.

```
    return index if (element == target)  # return from find
  end
  nil  # If we didn't find the element, return nil
end
```

The `return` statement in this code does not just cause the block to return to the iterator that invoked it. And it does not just cause the `each_with_index` iterator to return. It causes the `find` method to return a value to its caller.

5.5.2 break

When used within a loop, the `break` statement transfers control out of the loop to the first expression following the loop. Readers who know C, Java, or a similar language will already be familiar with the use of `break` in a loop:

```
while(line = gets.chop)     # A loop starts here
  break if line == "quit"   # If this break statement is executed...
  puts eval(line)
end
puts "Good bye"             # ...then control is transferred here
```

When used in a block, `break` transfers control out of the block, out of the iterator that invoked the block, and to the first expression following the invocation of the iterator. For example:

```
f.each do |line|            # Iterate over the lines in file f
  break if line == "quit\n" # If this break statement is executed...
  puts eval(line)
end
puts "Good bye"             # ...then control is transferred here
```

As you can see, using `break` inside a block is lexically the same as using it inside a loop. If you consider the call stack, however, `break` in a block is more complicated because it forces the iterator method that the block is associated with to return. Figure 5-3 illustrates this.

Note that unlike `return`, `break` never causes the lexically enclosing method to return. `break` can only appear within a lexically enclosing loop or within a block. Using it in any other context causes a `LocalJumpError`.

5.5.2.1 break with a value

Recall that all syntactic constructs in Ruby are expressions, and all can have a value. The `break` statement can specify a value for the loop or iterator it is breaking out of. The `break` keyword may be followed by an expression or a comma-separated list of expressions. If `break` is used with no expression, then the value of the loop expression, or the return value of the iterator method, is `nil`. If `break` is used with a single expression, then the value of that expression becomes the value of the loop expression or the return value of the iterator. And if `break` is used with multiple expressions, then the values of

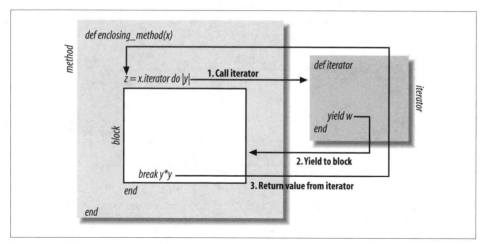

Figure 5-3. The break statement in a block

those expressions are placed into an array, and that array becomes the value of the loop expression or the return value of the iterator.

By contrast, a while loop that terminates normally with no **break** always has a value of nil. The return value of an iterator that terminates normally is defined by the iterator method. Many iterators, such as **times** and **each**, simply return the object on which they were invoked.

5.5.3 next

The **next** statement causes a loop or iterator to end the current iteration and begin the next. C and Java programmers know this control structure by the name **continue**. Here is **next** in a loop:

```
while(line = gets.chop)     # A loop starts here
  next if line[0,1] == "#"  # If this line is a comment, go on to the next
  puts eval(line)
  # Control goes here when the next statement is executed
end
```

When **next** is used within a block, it causes the block to exit immediately, returning control to the iterator method, which may then begin a new iteration by invoking the block again:

```
f.each do |line|            # Iterate over the lines in file f
  next if line[0,1] == "#"  # If this line is a comment, go to the next
  puts eval(line)
  # Control goes here when the next statement is executed
end
```

Using **next** in a block is lexically the same as using it in a **while**, **until**, or **for/in** loop. When you consider the calling sequence, however, the block case is more complicated, as Figure 5-4 illustrates.

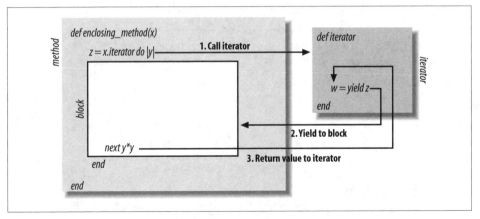

Figure 5-4. The next statement in a block

next, break, and return

It is instructive to contrast Figure 5-4 with Figures 5-2 and 5-3. The next statement causes a block to return to the iterator method that invoked it. The break statement causes the block to return to its iterator and the iterator to return to the enclosing method. And the return statement causes the block to return to the iterator, the iterator to return to the enclosing method, and the enclosing method to return to its caller.

next may only be used within a loop or a block; it raises a `LocalJumpError` when used in any other context.

5.5.3.1 next and block value

Like the return and break keywords, next may be used alone, or it may be followed by an expression or a comma-separated list of expressions. When next is used in a loop, any values following next are ignored. In a block, however, the expression or expressions become the "return value" of the yield statement that invoked the block. If next is not followed by an expression, then the value of the yield is nil. If next is followed by one expression, then the value of that expression becomes the value of the yield. And if next is followed by a list of expressions, then the value of the yield is an array of the value of those expressions.

In our earlier discussion of the return statement, we were careful to explain that blocks are not functions, and that the return statement does not make a block return to the iterator that invoked it. As you can see, this is exactly what the next statement does. Here is code where you might use it in this way:

```
squareroots = data.collect do |x|
  next 0 if x < 0  # Return 0 for negative values
```

```
    Math.sqrt(x)
  end
```

Normally, the value of a `yield` expression is the value of the last expression in the block. As with the `return` statement, it is not often necessary to explicitly use `next` to specify a value. This code could also have been written like this, for example:

```
squareroots = data.collect do |x|
  if (x < 0) then 0 else Math.sqrt(x) end
end
```

5.5.4 redo

The `redo` statement restarts the current iteration of a loop or iterator. This is not the same thing as `next`. `next` transfers control to the end of a loop or block so that the next iteration can begin, whereas `redo` transfers control back to the top of the loop or block so that the iteration can start over. If you come to Ruby from C-like languages, then `redo` is probably a new control structure for you.

`redo` transfers control to the first expression in the body of the loop or in a block. It does not retest the loop condition, and it does not fetch the next element from an iterator. The following `while` loop would normally terminate after three iterations, but a `redo` statement makes it iterate four times:

```
i = 0
while(i < 3)    # Prints "0123" instead of "012"
  # Control returns here when redo is executed
  print i
  i += 1
  redo if i == 3
end
```

`redo` is not a commonly used statement, and many examples, like this one, are contrived. One use, however, is to recover from input errors when prompting a user for input. The following code uses `redo` within a block for this purpose:

```
puts "Please enter the first word you think of"
words = %w(apple banana cherry)    # shorthand for ["apple", "banana", "cherry"]
response = words.collect do |word|
  # Control returns here when redo is executed
  print word + "> "               # Prompt the user
  response = gets.chop            # Get a response
  if response.size == 0          # If user entered nothing
    word.upcase!                 # Emphasize the prompt with uppercase
    redo                         # And skip to the top of the block
  end
  response                       # Return the response
end
```

5.5.5 retry

The `retry` statement is normally used in a `rescue` clause to reexecute a block of code that raised an exception. This is described in §5.6.3.5. In Ruby 1.8, however, `retry` has another use: it restarts an iterator-based iteration (or any method invocation) from the beginning. This use of the `retry` statement is extremely rare, and it has been removed from the language in Ruby 1.9. It should, therefore, be considered a deprecated language feature and should not be used in new code.

In a block, the `retry` statement does not just redo the current invocation of the block; it causes the block and the iterator method to exit and then reevaluates the iterator expression to restart the iteration. Consider the following code:

```
n = 10
n.times do |x|    # Iterate n times from 0 to n-1
  print x         # Print iteration number
  if x == 9       # If we've reached 9
    n -= 1        # Decrement n (we won't reach 9 the next time!)
    retry         # Restart the iteration
  end
end
```

The code uses `retry` to restart the iterator, but it is careful to avoid an infinite loop. On the first invocation, it prints the numbers 0123456789 and then restarts. On the second invocation, it prints the numbers 012345678 and does not restart.

The magic of the `retry` statement is that it does not retry the iterator in exactly the same way each time. It completely reevaluates the iterator expression, which means that the arguments to the iterator (and even the object on which it is invoked) may be different each time the iterator is retried. If you are not used to highly dynamic languages like Ruby, this reevaluation may seem counterintuitive to you.

The `retry` statement is not restricted to use in blocks; it always just reevaluates the nearest containing method invocation. This means that it can be used (prior to Ruby 1.9) to write iterators like the following that works like a `while` loop:

```
# This method behaves like a while loop: if x is non-nil and non-false,
# invoke the block and then retry to restart the loop and test the
# condition again. This method is slightly different than a true while loop:
# you can use C-style curly braces to delimit the loop body. And
# variables used only within the body of the loop remain local to the block.
def repeat_while(x)
  if x      # If the condition was not nil or false
    yield   # Run the body of the loop
    retry   # Retry and re-evaluate loop condition
  end
end
```

5.5.6 throw and catch

throw and catch are Kernel methods that define a control structure that can be thought of as a multilevel break. throw doesn't just break out of the current loop or block but can actually transfer out any number of levels, causing the block defined with a catch to exit. The catch need not even be in the same method as the throw. It can be in the calling method, or somewhere even further up the call stack.

Languages like Java and JavaScript allow loops to be named or labeled with an arbitrary prefix. When this is done, a control structure known as a "labeled break" causes the named loop to exit. Ruby's catch method defines a labeled block of code, and Ruby's throw method causes that block to exit. But throw and catch are much more general than a labeled break. For one, it can be used with any kind of statement and is not restricted to loops. More profoundly, a throw can propagate up the call stack to cause a block in an invoking method to exit.

If you are familiar with languages like Java and JavaScript, then you probably recognize throw and catch as the keywords those languages use for raising and handling exceptions. Ruby does exceptions differently, using raise and rescue, which we'll learn about later in this chapter. But the parallel to exceptions is intentional. Calling throw is very much like raising an exception. And the way a throw propagates out through the lexical scope and then up the call stack is very much the same as the way an exception propagates out and up. (We'll see much more about exception propagation later in the chapter.) Despite the similarity to exceptions, it is best to consider throw and catch as a general-purpose (if perhaps infrequently used) control structure rather than an exception mechanism. If you want to signal an error or exceptional condition, use raise instead of throw.

The following code demonstrates how throw and catch can be used to "break out" of nested loops:

```
for matrix in data do          # Process a deeply nested data structure.
  catch :missing_data do       # Label this statement so we can break out.
    for row in matrix do
      for value in row do
        throw :missing_data unless value # Break out of two loops at once.
        # Otherwise, do some actual data processing here.
      end
    end
  end
  # We end up here after the nested loops finish processing each matrix.
  # We also get here if :missing_data is thrown.
end
```

Note that the catch method takes a symbol argument and a block. It executes the block and returns when the block exits or when the specified symbol is thrown. throw also expects a symbol as its argument and causes the corresponding catch invocation to return. If no catch call matches the symbol passed to throw, then a NameError exception is raised. Both catch and throw can be invoked with string arguments instead of symbols. These are converted internally to symbols.

One of the features of throw and catch is that they work even when the throw and catch are in different methods. We could refactor this code to put the innermost loop into a separate method, and the control flow would still work correctly.

If throw is never called, a catch invocation returns the value of the last expression in its block. If throw is called, then the return value of the corresponding catch is, by default, nil. You can, however, specify an arbitrary return value for catch by passing a second argument to throw. The return value of catch can help you distinguish normal completion of the block from abnormal completion with throw, and this allows you to write code that does any special processing necessary to respond to the throw.

throw and catch are not commonly used in practice. If you find yourself using catch and throw within the same method, consider refactoring the catch into a separate method definition and replacing the throw with a return.

5.6 Exceptions and Exception Handling

An *exception* is an object that represents some kind of exceptional condition; it indicates that something has gone wrong. This could be a programming error—attempting to divide by zero, attempting to invoke a method on an object that does not define the method, or passing an invalid argument to a method. Or it could be the result from some kind of external condition—making a network request when the network is down, or trying to create an object when the system is out of memory.

When one of these errors or conditions occurs, an exception is *raised* (or *thrown*). By default, Ruby programs terminate when an exception occurs. But it is possible to declare exception handlers. An exception handler is a block of code that is executed if an exception occurs during the execution of some other block of code. In this sense, exceptions are a kind of control statement. Raising an exception transfers the flow-of-control to exception handling code. This is like using the break statement to exit from a loop. As we'll see, though, exceptions are quite different from the break statement; they may transfer control out of many enclosing blocks and even up the call stack in order to reach the exception handler.

Ruby uses the Kernel method raise to raise exceptions, and uses a rescue clause to handle exceptions. Exceptions raised by raise are instances of the Exception class or one of its many subclasses. The throw and catch methods described earlier in this chapter are not intended to signal and handle exceptions, but a symbol thrown by throw propagates in the same way that an exception raised by raise does. Exception objects, exception propagation, the raise method, and the rescue clause are described in detail in the subsections that follow.

5.6.1 Exception Classes and Exception Objects

Exception objects are instances of the Exception class or one of its subclasses. Numerous subclasses exist. These subclasses do not typically define new methods or new behavior, but they allow exceptions to be categorized by type. The class hierarchy is illustrated in Figure 5-5.

```
Object
  +--Exception
      +--NoMemoryError
      +--ScriptError
      |   +--LoadError
      |   +--NotImplementedError
      |   +--SyntaxError
      +--SecurityError        # Was a StandardError in 1.8
      +--SignalException
      |   +--Interrupt
      +--SystemExit
      +--SystemStackError     # Was a StandardError in 1.8
      +--StandardError
          +--ArgumentError
          +--FiberError       # New in 1.9
          +--IOError
          |   +--EOFError
          +--IndexError
          |   +--KeyError     # New in 1.9
          |   +--StopIteration # New in 1.9
          +--LocalJumpError
          +--NameError
          |   +--NoMethodError
          +--RangeError
          |   +--FloatDomainError
          +--RegexpError
          +--RuntimeError
          +--SystemCallError
          +--ThreadError
          +--TypeError
          +--ZeroDivisionError
```

Figure 5-5. The Ruby Exception Class Hierarchy

You don't need to be familiar with each of these exception subclasses. Their names tell you what they are used for. It is important to note that most of these subclasses extend a class known as StandardError. These are the "normal" exceptions that typical Ruby programs try to handle. The other exceptions represent lower-level, more serious, or less recoverable conditions, and normal Ruby programs do not typically attempt to handle them.

If you use *ri* to find documentation for these exception classes, you'll find that most of them are undocumented. This is in part because most of them add no new methods to those defined by the base `Exception` class. The important thing to know about a given exception class is when it can be raised. This is typically documented by the methods that raise the exception rather than by the exception class itself.

5.6.1.1 The methods of exception objects

The `Exception` class defines two methods that return details about the exception. The `message` method returns a string that may provide human-readable details about what went wrong. If a Ruby program exits with an unhandled exception, this message will typically be displayed to the end user, but the primary purpose of this message is to aid a programmer in diagnosing the problem.

The other important method of exception objects is `backtrace`. This method returns an array of strings that represents the call stack at the point that the exception was raised. Each element of the array is a string of the form:

```
filename : linenumber in methodname
```

The first element of the array specifies the position at which the exception was raised; the second element specifies the position at which the method that raised the exception was called; the third element specifies the position at which that method was called; and so on. (The `Kernel` method `caller` returns a stack trace in this same format; you can try it out in *irb*.) Exception objects are typically created by the `raise` method. When this is done, the `raise` method sets the stack trace of the exception appropriately. If you create your own exception object, you can set the stack trace to whatever you want with the `set_backtrace` method.

5.6.1.2 Creating exception objects

Exception objects are typically created by the `raise` method, as we'll see below. However, you can create your own objects with the normal `new` method, or with another class method named `exception`. Both accept a single optional string argument. If specified, the string becomes the value of the `message` method.

5.6.1.3 Defining new exception classes

If you are defining a module of Ruby code, it is often appropriate to define your own subclass of `StandardError` for exceptions that are specific to your module. This may be a trivial, one-line subclass:

```
class MyError < StandardError; end
```

5.6.2 Raising Exceptions with raise

The `Kernel` method `raise` raises an exception. `fail` is a synonym that is sometimes used when the expectation is that the exception will cause the program to exit. There are several ways to invoke `raise`:

- If raise is called with no arguments, it creates a new RuntimeError object (with no message) and raises it. Or, if raise is used with no arguments inside a rescue clause, it simply re-raises the exception that was being handled.
- If raise is called with a single Exception object as its argument, it raises that exception. Despite its simplicity, this is not actually a common way to use raise.
- If raise is called with a single string argument, it creates a new RuntimeError exception object, with the specified string as its message, and raises that exception. This is a very common way to use raise.
- If the first argument to raise is an object that has an exception method, then raise invokes that method and raises the Exception object that it returns. The Exception class defines an exception method, so you can specify the class object for any kind of exception as the first argument to raise.

  raise accepts a string as its optional second argument. If a string is specified, it is passed to the exception method of the first argument. This string is intended for use as the exception message.

  raise also accepts an optional third argument. An array of strings may be specified here, and they will be used as the backtrace for the exception object. If this third argument is not specified, raise sets the backtrace of the exception itself (using the Kernel method caller).

The following code defines a simple method that raises an exception if invoked with a parameter whose value is invalid:

```
def factorial(n)                  # Define a factorial method with argument n
  raise "bad argument" if n < 1   # Raise an exception for bad n
  return 1 if n == 1              # factorial(1) is 1
  n * factorial(n-1)              # Compute other factorials recursively
end
```

This method invokes raise with a single string argument. These are some equivalent ways to raise the same exception:

```
raise RuntimeError, "bad argument" if n < 1
raise RuntimeError.new("bad argument") if n < 1
raise RuntimeError.exception("bad argument") if n < 1
```

In this example, an exception of class ArgumentError is probably more appropriate than RuntimeError:

```
raise ArgumentError if n < 1
```

And a more detailed error message would be helpful:

```
raise ArgumentError, "Expected argument >= 1. Got #{n}" if n < 1
```

The intent of the exception we're raising here is to point out a problem with the invocation of the factorial method, not with the code inside the method. The exception raised by the code here will have a backtrace whose first element identifies where raise was called. The second element of the array will actually identify the code that called `factorial` with the bad argument. If we want to point directly to the problem code, we can provide a custom stack trace as the third argument to **raise** with the Kernel method `caller`:

```
if n < 1
  raise ArgumentError, "Expected argument >= 1. Got #{n}", caller
end
```

Note that the `factorial` method checks whether its argument is in the correct range, but it does not check whether it is of the right type. We might add more careful error-checking by adding the following as the first line of the method:

```
raise TypeError, "Integer argument expected" if not n.is_a? Integer
```

On the other hand, notice what happens if we pass a string argument to the `factorial` method as it is written above. Ruby compares the argument n to the integer 1 with the < operator. If the argument is a string, the comparison makes no sense, and it fails by raising a `TypeError`. If the argument is an instance of some class that does not define the < operator, then we get a `NoMethodError` instead.

The point here is that exceptions can occur even if we do not call **raise** in our own code. It is important, therefore, to know how to handle exceptions, even if we never raise them ourselves. Handling exceptions is covered in the next section.

5.6.3 Handling Exceptions with rescue

raise is a Kernel method. A **rescue** clause, by contrast, is a fundamental part of the Ruby language. **rescue** is not a statement in its own right, but rather a clause that can be attached to other Ruby statements. Most commonly, a **rescue** clause is attached to a **begin** statement. The **begin** statement exists simply to delimit the block of code within which exceptions are to be handled. A **begin** statement with a **rescue** clause looks like this:

```
begin
  # Any number of Ruby statements go here.
  # Usually, they are executed without exceptions and
  # execution continues after the end statement.
rescue
  # This is the rescue clause; exception-handling code goes here.
  # If an exception is raised by the code above, or propagates up
  # from one of the methods called above, then execution jumps here.
end
```

5.6.3.1 Naming the exception object

In a **rescue** clause, the global variable $! refers to the Exception object that is being handled. The exclamation mark is a mnemonic: an exception is kind of like an exclamation. If your program includes the line:

```
require 'English'
```

then you can use the global variable $ERROR_INFO instead.

A better alternative to $! or $ERROR_INFO is to specify a variable name for the exception object in the rescue clause itself:

```
rescue => ex
```

The statements of this rescue clause can now use the variable ex to refer to the Exception object that describes the exception. For example:

```
begin                                  # Handle exceptions in this block
  x = factorial(-1)                    # Note illegal argument
rescue => ex                           # Store exception in variable ex
  puts "#{ex.class}: #{ex.message}"    # Handle exception by printing message
end                                    # End the begin/rescue block
```

Note that a rescue clause does not define a new variable scope, and a variable named in the rescue clause is visible even after the end of the rescue clause. If you use a variable in a rescue clause, then an exception object may be visible after the rescue is complete, even when $! is no longer set.

5.6.3.2 Handling exceptions by type

The rescue clauses shown here handle any exception that is a StandardError (or subclass) and ignore any Exception object that is not a StandardError. If you want to handle nonstandard exceptions outside the StandardError hierarchy, or if you want to handle only specific types of exceptions, you must include one or more exception classes in the rescue clause. Here's how you would write a rescue clause that would handle any kind of exception:

```
rescue Exception
```

Here's how you would write a rescue clause to handle an ArgumentError and assign the exception object to the variable e:

```
rescue ArgumentError => e
```

Recall that the factorial method we defined earlier can raise ArgumentError or TypeError. Here's how we would write a rescue clause to handle exceptions of either of these types and assign the exception object to the variable error:

```
rescue ArgumentError, TypeError => error
```

Here, finally, we see the syntax of the rescue clause at its most general. The rescue keyword is followed by zero or more comma-separated expressions, each of which must evaluate to a class object that represents the Exception class or a subclass. These expressions are optionally followed by => and a variable name.

Now suppose we want to handle both ArgumentError and TypeError, but we want to handle these two exceptions in different ways. We might use a case statement to run different code based on the class of the exception object. It is more elegant, however, to simply use multiple rescue clauses. A begin statement can have zero or more of them:

```
begin
  x = factorial(1)
rescue ArgumentError => ex
  puts "Try again with a value >= 1"
rescue TypeError => ex
  puts "Try again with an integer"
end
```

Note that the Ruby interpreter attempts to match exceptions to `rescue` clauses in the order they are written. Therefore, you should list your most specific exception sub-classes first and follow these with more general types. If you want to handle `EOFError` differently than `IOError`, for example, be sure to put the `rescue` clause for `EOFError` first or the `IOError` code will handle it. If you want a "catch-all" `rescue` clause that handles any exception not handled by previous clauses, use `rescue Exception` as the last `rescue` clause.

5.6.3.3 Propagation of exceptions

Now that we've introduced `rescue` clauses, we can explain in more detail the propagation of exceptions. When an exception is raised, control is immediately transferred outward and upward until a suitable `rescue` clause is found to handle the exception. When the `raise` method executes, the Ruby interpreter looks to see whether the containing block has a `rescue` clause associated with it. If not (or if the `rescue` clause is not declared to handle that kind of exception), then the interpreter looks at the containing block of the containing block. If there is no suitable `rescue` clause anywhere in the method that called `raise`, then the method itself exits.

When a method exits because of an exception, it is not the same thing as a normal return. The method does not have a return value, and the exception object continues propagating from the site of the method invocation. The exception propagates outward through the enclosing blocks, looking for a `rescue` clause declared to handle it. And if no such clause is found, then this method returns to *its* caller. This continues up the call stack. If no exception handler is ever located, then the Ruby interpreter prints the exception message and backtrace and exits. For a concrete example, consider the following code:

```
def explode         # This method raises a RuntimeError 10% of the time
  raise "bam!" if rand(10) == 0
end

def risky
  begin             # This block
    10.times do     # contains another block
      explode       # that might raise an exception.
    end             # No rescue clause here, so propagate out.
  rescue TypeError  # This rescue clause cannot handle a RuntimeError..
    puts $!         # so skip it and propagate out.
  end
  "hello"           # This is the normal return value, if no exception occurs.
end                 # No rescue clause here, so propagate up to caller.
```

```
def defuse
  begin                    # The following code may fail with an exception.
    puts risky             # Try to invoke and print the return value.
  rescue RuntimeError => e  # If we get an exception
    puts e.message         # print the error message instead.
  end
end

defuse
```

An exception is raised in the method explode. That method has no rescue clause, so the exception propagates out to its caller, a method named risky. risky has a rescue clause, but it is only declared to handle TypeError exceptions, not RuntimeError exceptions. The exception propagates out through the lexical blocks of risky and then propagates up to the caller, a method named defuse. defuse has a rescue clause for RuntimeError exceptions, so control is transferred to this rescue clause and the exception stops propagating.

Note that this code includes the use of an iterator (the Integer.times method) with an associated block. For simplicity, we said that the exception simply propagated outward through this lexical block. The truth is that blocks behave more like method invocations for the purposes of exception propagation. The exception propagates from the block up to the iterator that invoked the block. Predefined looping iterators like Integer.times do no exception handling of their own, so the exception propagates up the call stack from the times iterator to the risky method that invoked it.

5.6.3.4 Exceptions during exception handling

If an exception occurs during the execution of a rescue clause, the exception that was originally being handled is discarded, and the new exception propagates from the point at which it was raised. Note that this new exception cannot be handled by rescue clauses that follow the one in which it occurred.

5.6.3.5 retry in a rescue clause

When the retry statement is used within a rescue clause, it reruns the block of code to which the rescue is attached. When an exception is caused by a transient failure, such as an overloaded server, it might make sense to handle the exception by simply trying again. Many other exceptions, however, reflect programming errors (TypeError, ZeroDivisionError) or nontransient failures (EOFError or NoMemoryError). retry is not a suitable handling technique for these exceptions.

Here is a simple example that uses retry in an attempt to wait for a network failure to be resolved. It tries to read the contents of a URL, and retries upon failure. It never tries more than four times in all, and it uses "exponential backoff" to increase the wait time between attempts:

```
require 'open-uri'

tries = 0        # How many times have we tried to read the URL
begin            # This is where a retry begins
  tries += 1     # Try to print out the contents of a URL
  open('http://www.example.com/') {|f| puts f.readlines }
rescue OpenURI::HTTPError => e  # If we get an HTTP error
  puts e.message                # Print the error message
  if (tries < 4)                # If we haven't tried 4 times yet...
    sleep(2**tries)             # Wait for 2, 4, or 8 seconds
    retry                       # And then try again!
  end
end
```

5.6.4 The else Clause

A begin statement may include an else clause after its rescue clauses. You might guess that the else clause is a catch-all rescue: that it handles any exception that does not match a previous rescue clause. This is not what else is for. The else clause is an alternative to the rescue clauses; it is used if none of the rescue clauses are needed. That is, the code in an else clause is executed if the code in the body of the begin statement runs to completion without exceptions.

Putting code in an else clause is a lot like simply tacking it on to the end of the begin clause. The only difference is that when you use an else clause, any exceptions raised by that clause are not handled by the rescue statements.

The use of an else clause is not particularly common in Ruby, but they can be stylistically useful to emphasize the difference between normal completion of a block of code and exceptional completion of a block of code.

Note that it does not make sense to use an else clause without one or more rescue clauses. The Ruby interpreter allows it but issues a warning. No rescue clause may appear after an else clause.

Finally, note that the code in an else clause is only executed if the code in the begin clause runs to completion and "falls off" the end. If an exception occurs, then the else clause will obviously not be executed. But break, return, next, and similar statements in the begin clause may also prevent the execution of the else clause.

5.6.5 The ensure Clause

A begin statement may have one final clause. The optional ensure clause, if it appears, must come after all rescue and else clauses. It may also be used by itself without any rescue or else clauses.

The ensure clause contains code that always runs, no matter what happens with the code following begin:

- If that code runs to completion, then control jumps to the else clause—if there is one—and then to the ensure clause.
- If the code executes a return statement, then the execution skips the else clause and jumps directly to the ensure clause before returning.
- If the code following begin raises an exception, then control jumps to the appropriate rescue clause, and then to the ensure clause.
- If there is no rescue clause, or if no rescue clause can handle the exception, then control jumps directly to the ensure clause. The code in the ensure clause is executed before the exception propagates out to containing blocks or up the call stack.

The purpose of the ensure clause is to ensure that housekeeping details such as closing files, disconnecting database connections, and committing or aborting transactions get taken care of. It is a powerful control structure, and you should use it whenever you allocate a resource (such as a file handle or database connection) to ensure that proper deallocation or cleanup occurs.

Note that ensure clauses complicate the propagation of exceptions. In our earlier explanation, we omitted any discussion of ensure clauses. When an exception propagates, it does not simply jump magically from the point where it is raised to the point where it is handled. There really is a propagation process. The Ruby interpreter searches out through containing blocks and up through the call stack. At each begin statement, it looks for a rescue clause that can handle the exception. And it looks for associated ensure clauses, and executes all of them that it passes through.

An ensure clause can cancel the propagation of an exception by initiating some other transfer of control. If an ensure clause raises a new exception, then that new exception propagates in place of the original. If an ensure clause includes a return statement, then exception propagation stops, and the containing method returns. Control statements such as break and next have similar effects: exception propagation is abandoned, and the specified control transfer takes place.

An ensure clause also complicates the idea of a method return value. Although ensure clauses are usually used to ensure that code will run even if an exception occurs, they also work to ensure that code will be run before a method returns. If the body of a begin statement includes a return statement, the code in the ensure clause will be run before the method can actually return to its caller. Furthermore, if an ensure clause contains a return statement of its own, it will change the return value of the method. The following code, for example, returns the value 2:

```
begin
  return 1      # Skip to the ensure clause before returning to caller
ensure
  return 2      # Replace the return value with this new value
end
```

Note that an ensure clause does not alter the return value of a method unless it explicitly uses a return statement. The following method, for example, returns 1, not 2:

```
def test
  begin return 1 ensure 2 end
end
```

If a begin statement does not propagate an exception, then the value of the statement is the value of the last expression evaluated in the begin, rescue, or else clauses. The code in the ensure clause is guaranteed to run, but it does not affect the value of the begin statement.

5.6.6 rescue with Method, Class, and Module Definitions

Throughout this discussion of exception handling, we have described the rescue, else, and ensure keywords as clauses of a begin statement. In fact, they can also be used as clauses of the def statement (defines a method), the class statement (defines a class), and the module statement (defines a module). Method definitions are covered in Chapter 6; class and module definitions are covered in Chapter 7.

The following code is a sketch of a method definition with rescue, else, and ensure clauses:

```
def method_name(x)
  # The body of the method goes here.
  # Usually, the method body runs to completion without exceptions
  # and returns to its caller normally.
rescue
  # Exception-handling code goes here.
  # If an exception is raised within the body of the method, or if
  # one of the methods it calls raises an exception, then control
  # jumps to this block.
else
  # If no exceptions occur in the body of the method
  # then the code in this clause is executed.
ensure
  # The code in this clause is executed no matter what happens in the
  # body of the method. It is run if the method runs to completion, if
  # it throws an exception, or if it executes a return statement.
end
```

5.6.7 rescue As a Statement Modifier

In addition to its use as a clause, rescue can also be used as a statement modifier. Any statement can be followed by the keyword rescue and another statement. If the first statement raises an exception, the second statement is executed instead. For example:

```
# Compute factorial of x, or use 0 if the method raises an exception
y = factorial(x) rescue 0
```

This is equivalent to:

```
y = begin
      factorial(x)
    rescue
```

```
    0
  end
```

The advantage of the statement modifier syntax is that the begin and end keywords are not required. When used in this way, rescue must be used alone, with no exception class names and no variable name. A rescue modifier handles any StandardError exception but does not handle exceptions of other types. Unlike if and while modifiers, the rescue modifier has higher precedence (see Table 4-2 in the previous chapter) than assignment operators. This means that it applies only to the righthand side of an assignment (like the example above) rather than to the assignment expression as a whole.

5.7 BEGIN and END

BEGIN and END are reserved words in Ruby that declare code to be executed at the very beginning and very end of a Ruby program. (Note that BEGIN and END in capital letters are completely different from begin and end in lowercase.) If there is more than one BEGIN statement in a program, they are executed in the order in which the interpreter encounters them. If there is more than one END statement, they are executed in the reverse of the order in which they are encountered—that is, the first one is executed last. These statements are not commonly used in Ruby. They are inherited from Perl, which in turn inherited them from the awk text-processing language.

BEGIN and END must be followed by an open curly brace, any amount of Ruby code, and a close curly brace. The curly braces are required; do and end are not allowed here. For example:

```
BEGIN {
  # Global initialization code goes here
}

END {
  # Global shutdown code goes here
}
```

The BEGIN and END statements are different from each other in subtle ways. BEGIN statements are executed before anything else, including any surrounding code. This means that they define a local variable scope that is completely separate from the surrounding code. It only really makes sense to put BEGIN statements in top-level code; a BEGIN within a conditional or loop will be executed without regard for the conditions that surround it. Consider this code:

```
if (false)
  BEGIN {
    puts "if";           # This will be printed
    a = 4;               # This variable only defined here
  }
else
  BEGIN { puts "else" }  # Also printed
end
```

```
10.times {BEGIN { puts "loop" }} # Only printed once
```

The code associated with all three BEGIN statements will be executed once, and only once, regardless of the context in which it appears. Variables defined within BEGIN blocks will not be visible outside the block, and no variables outside the block will have been defined yet.

END statements are different. They are executed during normal program execution, so they share local variables with the surrounding code. If an END statement is within a conditional that is not executed, then the code associated with it is never registered for execution at program termination. If an END statement is within a loop and is executed more than once, then the code associated with it is still only registered once:

```
a = 4;
if (true)
  END {                         # This END is executed
    puts "if";                  # This code is registered
    puts a                      # The variable is visible; prints "4"
  }
else
  END { puts "else" }           # This is not executed
end
10.times {END { puts "loop" }} # Only executed once
```

The Kernel method at_exit provides an alternative to the END statement; it registers a block of code to be executed just before the interpreter exits. As with END blocks, the code associated with the first at_exit call will be executed last. If the at_exit method is called multiple times within a loop, then the block associated with it will be executed multiple times when the interpreter exits.

5.8 Threads, Fibers, and Continuations

This section introduces threads, which are Ruby's control structure for concurrent execution, and also two more esoteric control structures, called fibers and continuations.

5.8.1 Threads for Concurrency

A *thread of execution* is a sequence of Ruby statements that run (or appear to run) in parallel with the main sequence of statements that the interpreter is running. Threads are represented by Thread objects, but they can also be thought of as control structures for concurrency. Concurrent programming in Ruby is covered in detail in §9.9. This section is just a simple overview that shows how to create threads.

Ruby's use of blocks makes it very easy to create new threads. Simply call Thread.new and associate a block with it. A new thread of execution will be created and will start running the code in the block. Meanwhile, the original thread will return from the

`Thread.new` call and will continue with the following statement. The newly created thread will exit when the block exits. The return value of the block becomes available through the `value` method of the `Thread` object. (If you call this method before the thread has completed, the caller will block until the thread returns a value.)

The following code shows how you might use threads to read the contents of multiple files in parallel:

```
# This method expects an array of filenames.
# It returns an array of strings holding the content of the named files.
# The method creates one thread for each named file.
def readfiles(filenames)
  # Create an array of threads from the array of filenames.
  # Each thread starts reading a file.
  threads = filenames.map do |f|
    Thread.new { File.read(f) }
  end

  # Now create an array of file contents by calling the value
  # method of each thread. This method blocks, if necessary,
  # until the thread exits with a value.
  threads.map {|t| t.value }
end
```

See §9.9 for much more about threads and concurrency in Ruby.

5.8.2 Fibers for Coroutines

Ruby 1.9 introduces a control structure known as a *fiber* and represented by an object of class `Fiber`. The name "fiber" has been used elsewhere for a kind of lightweight thread, but Ruby's fibers are better described as *coroutines* or, more accurately, *semi-coroutines*. The most common use for coroutines is to implement *generators*: objects that can compute a partial result, yield the result back to the caller, and save the state of the computation so that the caller can resume that computation to obtain the next result. In Ruby, the `Fiber` class is used to enable the automatic conversion of internal iterators, such as the `each` method, into enumerators or external iterators.

Note that fibers are an advanced and relatively obscure control structure; the majority of Ruby programmers will never need to use the `Fiber` class directly. If you have never programed with coroutines or generators before, you may find them difficult to understand at first. If so, study the examples carefully and try out some examples of your own.

A fiber has a body of code like a thread does. Create a fiber with `Fiber.new`, and associate a block with it to specify the code that the fiber is to run. Unlike a thread, the body of a fiber does not start executing right away. To run a fiber, call the `resume` method of the `Fiber` object that represents it. The first time `resume` is called on a fiber, control is transferred to the beginning of the fiber body. That fiber then runs until it reaches the end of the body, or until it executes the class method `Fiber.yield`. The `Fiber.yield` method transfers control back to the caller and makes the call to resume return. It also saves the state of the fiber, so that the next call to resume makes the fiber pick up where it left off. Here is a simple example:

```
f = Fiber.new {                    # Line  1: Create a new fiber
  puts "Fiber says Hello"          # Line  2:
  Fiber.yield                      # Line  3: goto line 9
  puts "Fiber says Goodbye"        # Line  4:
}                                  # Line  5: goto line 11
                                   # Line  6:
puts "Caller says Hello"           # Line  7:
f.resume                           # Line  8: goto line 2
puts "Caller says Goodbye"         # Line  9:
f.resume                           # Line 10: goto line 4
                                   # Line 11:
```

The body of the fiber does not run when it is first created, so this code creates a fiber but does not produce any output until it reaches line 7. The resume and Fiber.yield calls then transfer control back and forth so that the messages from the fiber and the caller are interleaved. The code produces the following output:

```
Caller says Hello
Fiber says Hello
Caller says Goodbye
Fiber says Goodbye
```

It is worth noting here that the "yielding" performed by Fiber.yield is completely different than the yielding performed by the yield statement. Fiber.yield yields control from the current fiber back to the caller that invoked it. The yield statement, on the other hand, yields control from an iterator method to the block associated with the method.

5.8.2.1 Fiber arguments and return values

Fibers and their callers can exchange data through the arguments and return values of resume and yield. The arguments to the first call to resume are passed to the block associated with the fiber: they become the values of the block parameters. On subsequent calls, the arguments to resume become the return value of Fiber.yield. Conversely, any arguments to Fiber.yield become the return value of resume. And when the block exits, the value of the last expression evaluated also becomes the return value of resume. The following code demonstrates this:

```
f = Fiber.new do |message|
  puts "Caller said: #{message}"
  message2 = Fiber.yield("Hello")   # "Hello" returned by first resume
  puts "Caller said: #{message2}"
  "Fine"                            # "Fine" returned by second resume
end

response = f.resume("Hello")        # "Hello" passed to block
puts "Fiber said: #{response}"
```

```
response2 = f.resume("How are you?") # "How are you?" returned by Fiber.yield
puts "Fiber said: #{response2}"
```

The caller passes two messages to the fiber, and the fiber returns two responses to the caller. It prints:

```
Caller said: Hello
Fiber said: Hello
Caller said: How are you?
Fiber said: Fine
```

In the caller's code, the messages are always arguments to `resume`, and the responses are always the return value of that method. In the body of the fiber, all messages but the first are received as the return value of `Fiber.yield`, and all responses but the last are passed as arguments to `Fiber.yield`. The first message is received through block parameters, and the last response is the return value of the block itself.

5.8.2.2 Implementing generators with fibers

The fiber examples shown so far have not been terribly realistic. Here we demonstrate some more typical uses. First, we write a Fibonacci number generator—a `Fiber` object that returns successive members of the Fibonacci sequence on each call to `resume`:

```
# Return a Fiber to compute Fibonacci numbers
def fibonacci_generator(x0,y0)    # Base the sequence on x0,y0
  Fiber.new do
    x,y = x0, y0                  # Initialize x and y
    loop do                       # This fiber runs forever
      Fiber.yield y               # Yield the next number in the sequence
      x,y = y,x+y                 # Update x and y
    end
  end
end

g = fibonacci_generator(0,1)      # Create a generator
10.times { print g.resume, " " }  # And use it
```

The code above prints the first 10 Fibonacci numbers:

```
1 1 2 3 5 8 13 21 34 55
```

Because `Fiber` is a confusing control structure, we might prefer to hide its API when writing generators. Here is another version of a Fibonacci number generator. It defines its own class and implements the same `next` and `rewind` API that enumerators do:

```
class FibonacciGenerator
  def initialize
    @x,@y = 0,1
    @fiber = Fiber.new do
      loop do
        @x,@y = @y, @x+@y
        Fiber.yield @x
      end
    end
  end
```

```
  def next              # Return the next Fibonacci number
    @fiber.resume
  end

  def rewind            # Restart the sequence
    @x,@y = 0,1
  end
end

g = FibonacciGenerator.new      # Create a generator
10.times { print g.next, " " }  # Print first 10 numbers
g.rewind; puts                  # Start over, on a new line
10.times { print g.next, " " }  # Print the first 10 again
```

Note that we can make this FibonacciGenerator class Enumerable by including the Enumerable module and adding the following each method (which we first used in §5.3.5):

```
def each
  loop { yield self.next }
end
```

Conversely, suppose we have an Enumerable object and want to make an enumerator-style generator out of it. We can use this class:

```
class Generator
  def initialize(enumerable)
    @enumerable = enumerable  # Remember the enumerable object
    create_fiber             # Create a fiber to enumerate it
  end

  def next                   # Return the next element
    @fiber.resume            # by resuming the fiber
  end

  def rewind                 # Start the enumeration over
    create_fiber             # by creating a new fiber
  end

  private
  def create_fiber           # Create the fiber that does the enumeration
    @fiber = Fiber.new do    # Create a new fiber
      @enumerable.each do |x| # Use the each method
        Fiber.yield(x)       # But pause during enumeration to return values
      end
      raise StopIteration    # Raise this when we're out of values
    end
  end
end

g = Generator.new(1..10)  # Create a generator from an Enumerable like this
loop { print g.next }     # And use it like an enumerator like this
g.rewind                  # Start over like this
g = (1..10).to_enum       # The to_enum method does the same thing
loop { print g.next }
```

Although it is useful to study the implementation of this Generator class, the class itself doesn't provide any functionality over that provided by the to_enum method.

5.8.2.3 Advanced fiber features

The fiber module in the standard library enables additional, more powerful features of the fibers. To use these features, you must:

```
require 'fiber'
```

However, you should avoid using these additional features wherever possible, because:

- They are not supported by all implementations. JRuby, for example, cannot support them on current Java VMs.
- They are so powerful that misusing them can crash the Ruby VM.

The core features of the Fiber class implement semicoroutines. These are not true co-routines because there is a fundamental asymmetry between the caller and the fiber: the caller uses resume and the fiber uses yield. If you require the fiber library, however, the Fiber class gets a transfer method that allows any fiber to transfer control to any other fiber. Here is an example in which two fibers use the transfer method to pass control (and values) back and forth:

```
require 'fiber'

f = g = nil

f = Fiber.new {|x|       # 1:
  puts "f1: #{x}"        # 2: print "f1: 1"
  x = g.transfer(x+1)    # 3: pass 2 to line 8
  puts "f2: #{x}"        # 4: print "f2: 3"
  x = g.transfer(x+1)    # 5: return 4 to line 10
  puts "f3: #{x}"        # 6: print "f3: 5"
  x + 1                  # 7: return 6 to line 13
}
g = Fiber.new {|x|       # 8:
  puts "g1: #{x}"        # 9: print "g1: 2"
  x = f.transfer(x+1)    #10: return 3 to line 3
  puts "g2: #{x}"        #11: print "g2: 4"
  x = f.transfer(x+1)    #12: return 5 to line 5
}
puts f.transfer(1)       #13: pass 1 to line 1
```

This code produces the following output:

```
f1: 1
g1: 2
f2: 3
g2: 4
f3: 5
6
```

You will probably never need to use this transfer method, but its existence helps explain the name "fiber." Fibers can be thought of as independent paths of execution within a single thread of execution. Unlike threads, however, there is no scheduler to transfer control among fibers; fibers must explicitly schedule themselves with `transfer`.

In addition to the `transfer` method, the `fiber` library also defines an instance method `alive?`, to determine if the body of a fiber is still running, and a class method `current`, to return the `Fiber` object that currently has control.

5.8.3 Continuations

A *continuation* is another complex and obscure control structure that most programmers will never need to use. A continuation takes the form of the `Kernel` method `callcc` and the `Continuation` object. Continuations are part of the core platform in Ruby 1.8, but they have been replaced by fibers and moved to the standard library in Ruby 1.9. To use them in Ruby 1.9, you must explicitly require them with:

```
require 'continuation'
```

Implementation difficulties prevent other implementations of Ruby (such as JRuby, the Java-based implementation) from supporting continuations. Because they are no longer well supported, continuations should be considered a curiosity, and new Ruby code should not use them. If you have Ruby 1.8 code that relies on continuations, you may be able to convert it to use fibers in Ruby 1.9.

The `Kernel` method `callcc` executes its block, passing a newly created `Continuation` object as the only argument. The `Continuation` object has a `call` method, which makes the `callcc` invocation return to its caller. The value passed to `call` becomes the return value of the `callcc` invocation. In this sense, `callcc` is like `catch`, and the `call` method of the `Continuation` object is like `throw`.

Continuations are different, however, because the `Continuation` object can be saved into a variable outside of the `callcc` block. The `call` method of this object may be called repeatedly, and causes control to jump to the first statement following the `callcc` invocation.

The following code demonstrates how continuations can be used to define a method that works like the `goto` statement in the BASIC programming language:

```
# Global hash for mapping line numbers (or symbols) to continuations
$lines = {}

# Create a continuation and map it to the specified line number
def line(symbol)
  callcc {|c| $lines[symbol] = c }
end

# Look up the continuation associated with the number, and jump there
def goto(symbol)
  $lines[symbol].call
end

# Now we can pretend we're programming in BASIC
```

```
i = 0
line 10              # Declare this spot to be line 10
puts i += 1
goto 10 if i < 5     # Jump back to line 10 if the condition is met

line 20              # Declare this spot to be line 20
puts i -= 1
goto 20 if i > 0
```

Methods, Procs, Lambdas, and Closures

A *method* is a named block of parameterized code associated with one or more objects. A method *invocation* specifies the method name, the object on which it is to be invoked (sometimes called the *receiver*), and zero or more argument values that are assigned to the named method parameters. The value of the last expression evaluated in the method becomes the value of the method invocation expression.

Many languages distinguish between functions, which have no associated object, and methods, which are invoked on a receiver object. Because Ruby is a purely object-oriented language, all methods are true methods and are associated with at least one object. We have not covered class definitions in Ruby yet, so the example methods defined in this chapter look like global functions with no associated object. In fact, Ruby implicitly defines and invokes them as private methods of the `Object` class.

Methods are a fundamental part of Ruby's syntax, but they are not values that Ruby programs can operate on. That is, Ruby's methods are not objects in the way that strings, numbers, and arrays are. It is possible, however, to obtain a `Method` object that represents a given method, and we can invoke methods indirectly through `Method` objects.

Methods are not Ruby's only form of parameterized executable code. Blocks, which we introduced in §5.4, are executable chunks of code and may have parameters. Unlike methods, blocks do not have names, and they can only be invoked indirectly through an iterator method.

Blocks, like methods, are not objects that Ruby can manipulate. But it's possible to create an object that represents a block, and this is actually done with some frequency in Ruby programs. A `Proc` object represents a block. Like a `Method` object, we can execute the code of a block through the `Proc` that represents it. There are two varieties of `Proc` objects, called *procs* and *lambdas*, which have slightly different behavior. Both procs and lambdas are functions rather than methods invoked on an object. An important feature of procs and lambdas is that they are *closures*: they retain access to the local variables that were in scope when they were defined, even when the proc or lambda is invoked from a different scope.

Methods have a rich and fairly complex syntax in Ruby, and the first four sections of this chapter are dedicated to them. We begin by explaining how to define simple methods, and then follow this introductory section with three more advanced sections covering methods names, method parentheses, and method parameters. Note that method invocation is a kind of expression, covered earlier in §4.4. Further details on method invocation are provided throughout the first four sections of this chapter.

After covering methods, we turn our attention to procs and lambdas, explaining how to create and invoke them, and also detailing the somewhat subtle differences between them. A separate section covers the use of procs and lambdas as closures. This is followed by a section on the `Method` object, which actually behaves much like a lambda. The chapter ends with an advanced exploration of functional programming in Ruby.

6.1 Defining Simple Methods

You've seen many method invocations in examples throughout this book, and method invocation syntax was described in detail in §4.4. Now we turn to the syntax for defining methods. This section explains method definition basics. It is followed by three more sections that cover method names, method parentheses, and method arguments in more detail. These additional sections explain more advanced material and are relevant to both method definition and method invocation.

Methods are defined with the def keyword. This is followed by the method name and an optional list of parameter names in parentheses. The Ruby code that constitutes the method body follows the parameter list, and the end of the method is marked with the end keyword. Parameter names can be used as variables within the method body, and the values of these named parameters come from the arguments to a method invocation. Here is an example method:

```
# Define a method named 'factorial' with a single parameter 'n'
def factorial(n)
  if n < 1                   # Test the argument value for validity
    raise "argument must be > 0"
  elsif n == 1               # If the argument is 1
    1                        # then the value of the method invocation is 1
  else                       # Otherwise, the factorial of n is n times
    n * factorial(n-1)       # the factorial of n-1
  end
end
```

This code defines a method named factorial. The method has a single parameter named n. The identifier n is used as a variable within the body of the method. This is a recursive method, so the body of the method includes an invocation of the method. The invocation is simply the name of the method followed by the argument value in parentheses.

6.1.1 Method Return Value

Methods may terminate normally or abnormally. Abnormal termination occurs when the method raises an exception. The factorial method shown earlier terminates abnormally if we pass it an argument less than 1. If a method terminates normally, then the value of the method invocation expression is the value of the last expression evaluated within the method body. In the factorial method, that last expression will either be 1 or n*factorial(n-1).

The return keyword is used to force a return prior to the end of the method. If an expression follows the return keyword, then the value of that expression is returned. If no expression follows, then the return value is nil. In the following variant of the factorial method, the return keyword is required:

```
def factorial(n)
  raise "bad argument" if n < 1
```

```
    return 1 if n == 1
    n * factorial(n-1)
  end
```

We could also use **return** on the last line of this method body to emphasize that this expression is the method's return value. In common practice, however, **return** is omitted where it is not required.

Ruby methods may return more than one value. To do this, use an explicit **return** statement, and separate the values to be returned with commas:

```
# Convert the Cartesian point (x,y) to polar (magnitude, angle) coordinates
def polar(x,y)
  return Math.hypot(y,x), Math.atan2(y,x)
end
```

When there is more than one return value, the values are collected into an array, and the array becomes the single return value of the method. Instead of using the **return** statement with multiple values, we can simply create an array of values ourselves:

```
# Convert polar coordinates to Cartesian coordinates
def cartesian(magnitude, angle)
  [magnitude*Math.cos(angle), magnitude*Math.sin(angle)]
end
```

Methods of this form are typically intended for use with parallel assignment (see §4.5.5) so that each return value is assigned to a separate variable:

```
distance, theta = polar(x,y)
x,y = cartesian(distance,theta)
```

6.1.2 Methods and Exception Handling

A **def** statement that defines a method may include exception-handling code in the form of **rescue**, **else**, and **ensure** clauses, just as a **begin** statement can. These exception-handling clauses go after the end of the method body but before the **end** of the **def** statement. In short methods, it can be particularly tidy to associate your **rescue** clauses with the **def** statement. This also means you don't have to use a **begin** statement and the extra level of indentation that comes with it. See §5.6.6 for further details.

6.1.3 Invoking a Method on an Object

Methods are always invoked on an object. (This object is sometimes called the receiver in a reference to an object-oriented paradigm in which methods are called "messages" and are "sent to" receiver objects.) Within the body of a method, the keyword **self** refers to the object on which the method was invoked. If we don't specify an object when invoking a method, then the method is implicitly invoked on **self**.

You'll learn how to define methods for classes of objects in Chapter 7. Notice, however, that you've already seen examples of invoking methods on objects, in code like this:

```
first = text.index(pattern)
```

Like most object-oriented languages, Ruby uses . to separate the object from the method to be invoked on it. This code passes the value of the variable `pattern` to the method named `index` of the object stored in the variable `text`, and stores the return value in the variable `first`.

6.1.4 Defining Singleton Methods

The methods we've defined so far are all global methods. If we place a `def` statement like the ones shown earlier inside a `class` statement, then the methods that are defined are instance methods of the class; these methods are defined on all objects that are instances of the class. (Classes and instance methods are explained in Chapter 7.)

It is also possible, however, to use the `def` statement to define a method on a single specified object. Simply follow the `def` keyword with an expression that evaluates to an object. This expression should be followed by a period and the name of the method to be defined. The resulting method is known as a *singleton method* because it is available only on a single object:

```
o = "message"      # A string is an object
def o.printme      # Define a singleton method for this object
  puts self
end
o.printme          # Invoke the singleton
```

Class methods (covered in Chapter 7) such as `Math.sin` and `File.delete` are actually singleton methods. `Math` is a constant that refers to a `Module` object, and `File` is a constant that refers to a `Class` object. These two objects have singleton methods named `sin` and `delete`, respectively.

Ruby implementations typically treat `Fixnum` and `Symbol` values as immediate values rather than as true object references. (See §3.8.1.1.) For this reason, singleton methods may not be defined on `Fixnum` and `Symbol` objects. For consistency, singletons are also prohibited on other `Numeric` objects.

6.1.5 Undefining Methods

Methods are defined with the `def` statement and may be undefined with the `undef` statement:

```
def sum(x,y); x+y; end    # Define a method
puts sum(1,2)             # Use it
undef sum                 # And undefine it
```

In this code, the `def` statement defines a global method, and `undef` undefines it. `undef` also works within classes (which are the subject of Chapter 7) to undefine the instance methods of the class. Interestingly, `undef` can be used to undefine inherited methods, without affecting the definition of the method in the class from which it is inherited. Suppose class `A` defines a method `m`, and class `B` is a subclass of `A` and therefore inherits `m`. (Subclasses and inheritance are also explained in Chapter 7.) If you don't want to allow instances of class B to be able to invoke m, you can use undef m within the body of the subclass.

undef is not a commonly used statement. In practice, it is much more common to redefine a method with a new def statement than it is to *undefine* or delete the method.

Note that the undef statement must be followed by a single identifier that specifies the method name. It cannot be used to undefine a singleton method in the way that def can be used to define such a method.

Within a class or module, you can also use undef_method (a private method of Module) to undefine methods. Pass a symbol representing the name of the method to be undefined.

6.2 Method Names

By convention, method names begin with a lowercase letter. (Method names can begin with a capital letter, but that makes them look like constants.) When a method name is longer than one word, the usual convention is to separate the words with underscores like_this rather than using mixed case likeThis.

Method Name Resolution

This section describes the names you give to methods when you define them. A related topic is method name resolution: how does the Ruby interpreter find the definition of the method named in a method invocation expression? The answer to that question must wait until we've discussed classes in Ruby. It is covered in §7.8.

Method names may (but are not required to) end with an equals sign, a question mark, or an exclamation point. An equals sign suffix signifies that the method is a *setter* that can be invoked using assignment syntax. Setter methods are described in §4.5.3 and additional examples are provided in §7.1.5. The question mark and exclamation point suffixes have no special meaning to the Ruby interpreter, but they are allowed because they enable two extraordinarily useful naming conventions.

The first convention is that any method whose name ends with a question mark returns a value that answers the question posed by the method invocation. The empty? method of an array, for example, returns true if the array has no elements. Methods like these are called *predicates* and. Predicates typically return one of the Boolean values true or false, but this is not required, as any value other than false or nil works like true when a Boolean value is required. (The Numeric method nonzero?, for example, returns nil if the number it is invoked on is zero, and just returns the number otherwise.)

The second convention is that any method whose name ends with an exclamation mark should be used with caution. The Array object, for example, has a sort method that makes a copy of the array, and then sorts that copy. It also has a sort! method that sorts the array in place. The exclamation mark indicates that you need to be more careful when using that version of the method.

Often, methods that end with an exclamation mark are *mutators*, which alter the internal state of an object. But this is not always the case; there are many mutators that do not end with an exclamation mark, and a number of nonmutators that do. Mutating methods (such as `Array.fill`) that do not have a nonmutating variant do not typically have an exclamation point.

Consider the global function `exit`: it makes the Ruby program stop running in a controlled way. There is also a variant named `exit!` that aborts the program immediately without running any `END` blocks or shutdown hooks registered with `at_exit`. `exit!` isn't a mutator; it's the "dangerous" variant of the `exit` method and is flagged with ! to remind a programmer using it to be careful.

6.2.1 Operator Methods

Many of Ruby's operators, such as +, *, and even the array index operator [ ], are implemented with methods that you can define in your own classes. You define an operator by defining a method with the same "name" as the operator. (The only exceptions are the unary plus and minus operators, which use method names +@ and -@.) Ruby allows you to do this even though the method name is all punctuation. You might end up with a method definition like this:

```
def +(other)              # Define binary plus operator: x+y is x.+(y)
    self.concatenate(other)
end
```

Table 4-2 in Chapter 4 specifies which of Ruby's operators are defined as methods. These operators are the only punctuation-based method names that you can use: you can't invent new operators or define methods whose names consist of other sequences of punctuation characters. There are additional examples of defining method-based operators in §7.1.6.

Methods that define a unary operator are passed no arguments. Methods that define binary operators are passed one argument and should operate on `self` and the argument. The array access operators [] and []= are special because they can be invoked with any number of arguments. For []=, the last argument is always the value being assigned.

6.2.2 Method Aliases

It is not uncommon for methods in Ruby to have more than one name. The language has a keyword `alias` that serves to define a new name for an existing method. Use it like this:

```
alias aka also_known_as   # alias new_name existing_name
```

After executing this statement, the identifier `aka` will refer to the same method thats `also_known_as` does.

Method aliasing is one of the things that makes Ruby an expressive and natural language. When there are multiple names for a method, you can choose the one that seems most natural in your code. The Range class, for example, defines a method for testing whether a value falls within the range. You can call this method with the name `include?` or with the name `member?`. If you are treating a range as a kind of set, the name `member?` may be the most natural choice.

A more practical reason for aliasing methods is to insert new functionality into a method. The following is a common idiom for augmenting existing methods:

```ruby
def hello                       # A nice simple method
  puts "Hello World"            # Suppose we want to augment it...
end

alias original_hello hello      # Give the method a backup name

def hello                       # Now we define a new method with the old name
  puts "Your attention please"  # That does some stuff
  original_hello                # Then calls the original method
  puts "This has been a test"   # Then does some more stuff
end
```

In this code, we're working on global methods. It is more common to use `alias` with the instance methods of a class. (We'll learn about this in Chapter 7.) In this situation, `alias` must be used within the `class` whose method is to be renamed. Classes in Ruby can be "reopened" (again, this is discussed in Chapter 7)—which means that your code can take an existing class, 'open' it with a `class` statement, and then use `alias` as shown in the example to augment or alter the existing methods of that class. This is called "alias chaining" and is covered in detail in §8.11.

Aliasing Is Not Overloading

A Ruby method may have two names, but two methods cannot share a single name. In statically typed languages, methods can be distinguished by the number and type of their arguments, and two or more methods may share the same name as long as they expect different numbers or types of arguments. This kind of overloading is not possible in Ruby.

On the other hand, method overloading is not really necessary in Ruby. Methods can accept arguments of any class and can be written to do different things based on the type of the arguments they are passed. Also (as we'll see later), Ruby's method arguments can be declared with default values, and these arguments may be omitted form method invocations. This allows a single method to be invoked with differing numbers of arguments.

6.3 Methods and Parentheses

Ruby allows parentheses to be omitted from most method invocations. In simple cases, this results in clean-looking code. In complex cases, however, it causes syntactic ambiguities and confusing corner cases. We'll consider these in the sections that follow.

6.3.1 Optional Parentheses

Parentheses are omitted from method invocations in many common Ruby idioms. The following two lines of code, for example, are equivalent:

```
puts "Hello World"
puts("Hello World")
```

In the first line, `puts` looks like a keyword, statement, or command built in to the language. The equivalent second line demonstrates that it is simply the invocation of a global method, with the parentheses omitted. Although the second form is clearer, the first form is more concise, more commonly used, and arguably more natural.

Next, consider this code:

```
greeting = "Hello"
size = greeting.length
```

If you are accustomed to other object-oriented languages, you may think that `length` is a property, field, or variable of string objects. Ruby is strongly object oriented, however, and its objects are fully encapsulated; the only way to interact with them is by invoking their methods. In this code, `greeting.length` is a method invocation. The `length` method expects no arguments and is invoked without parentheses. The following code is equivalent:

```
size = greeting.length()
```

Including the optional parentheses emphasizes that a method invocation is occurring. Omitting the parentheses in method invocations with no arguments gives the illusion of property access, and is a very common practice.

Parentheses are very commonly omitted when there are zero or one arguments to the invoked method. Although it is less common, the parentheses may be omitted even when there are multiple arguments, as in the following code:

```
x = 3            # x is a number
x.between? 1,5   # same as x.between?(1,5)
```

Parentheses may also be omitted around the parameter list in method definitions, though it is hard to argue that this makes your code clearer or more readable. The following code, for example, defines a method that returns the sum of its arguments:

```
def sum x, y
  x+y
end
```

6.3.2 Required Parentheses

Some code is ambiguous if the parentheses are omitted, and here Ruby requires that you include them. The most common case is nested method invocations of the form `f g x, y`. In Ruby, invocations of that form mean `f(g(x,y))`. Ruby 1.8 issues a warning, however, because the code could also be interpreted as `f(g(x),y)`. The warning has been removed in Ruby 1.9. The following code, using the `sum` method defined above, prints 4, but issues a warning in Ruby 1.8:

```
puts sum 2, 2
```

To remove the warning, rewrite the code with parentheses around the arguments:

```
puts sum(2,2)
```

Note that using parentheses around the outer method invocation does not resolve the ambiguity:

```
puts(sum 2,2)    # Does this mean puts(sum(2,2)) or puts(sum(2), 2)?
```

An expression involving nested function calls is only ambiguous when there is more than one argument. The Ruby interpreter can only interpret the following code in one way:

```
puts factorial x    # This can only mean puts(factorial(x))
```

Despite the lack of ambiguity here, Ruby 1.8 still issues a warning if you omit the parentheses around the `x`.

Sometimes omitting parentheses is a true syntax error rather than a simple warning. The following expressions, for example, are completely ambiguous without parentheses, and Ruby doesn't even attempt to guess what you mean:

```
puts 4, sum 2,2    # Error: does the second comma go with the 1st or 2nd method?
[sum 2,2]          # Error: two array elements or one?
```

There is another wrinkle that arises from the fact that parentheses are optional. When you *do* use parentheses in a method invocation, the opening parenthesis *must* immediately follow the method name, with no intervening space. This is because parentheses do double-duty: they can be used around an argument list in a method invocation, and they can be used for grouping expressions. Consider the following two expressions, which differ only by a single space:

```
square(2+2)*2    # square(4)*2 = 16*2 = 32
square (2+2)*2   # square(4*2) = square(8) = 64
```

In the first expression, the parentheses represent method invocation. In the second, they represent expression grouping. To reduce the potential for confusion, you should always use parentheses around a method invocation if any of the arguments use parentheses. The second expression would be written more clearly as:

```
square((2+2)*2)
```

We'll end this discussion of parentheses with one final twist. Recall that the following expression is ambiguous and causes a warning:

```
puts(sum 2,2)    # Does this mean puts(sum(2,2)) or puts(sum(2), 2)?
```

The best way to resolve this ambiguity is to put parentheses around the arguments to the sum method. Another way is to add a space between puts and the opening parenthesis:

```
puts (sum 2,2)
```

Adding the space converts the method invocation parentheses into expression grouping parentheses. Because these parentheses group a subexpression, the comma can no longer be interpreted as an argument delimiter for the puts invocation.

6.4 Method Arguments

Simple method declarations include a comma-separated list of argument names (in optional parentheses) after the method name. But there is much more to Ruby's method arguments. The subsections that follow explain:

- How to declare an argument that has a default value, so that the argument can be omitted when the method is invoked
- How to declare a method that accepts any number of arguments
- How to simulate named method arguments with special syntax for passing a hash to a method
- How to declare a method so that the block associated with an invocation of the method is treated as a method argument

6.4.1 Parameter Defaults

When you define a method, you can specify default values for some or all of the parameters. If you do this, then your method may be invoked with fewer argument values than the declared number of parameters. If arguments are omitted, then the default value of the parameter is used in its place. Specify a default value by following the parameter name with an equals sign and a value:

```
def prefix(s, len=1)
  s[0,len]
end
```

This method declares two parameters, but the second one has a default. This means that we can invoke it with either one argument or two:

```
prefix("Ruby", 3)    # => "Rub"
prefix("Ruby")       # => "R"
```

Argument defaults need not be constants: they may be arbitrary expressions, and can refer to instance variables and to previous parameters in the parameter list. For example:

```ruby
# Return the last character of s or the substring from index to the end
def suffix(s, index=s.size-1)
  s[index, s.size-index]
end
```

Parameter defaults are evaluated when a method is invoked rather than when it is parsed. In the following method, the default value [] produces a new empty array on each invocation, rather than reusing a single array created when the method is defined:

```ruby
# Append the value x to the array a, return a.
# If no array is specified, start with an empty one.
def append(x, a=[])
  a << x
end
```

In Ruby 1.8, method parameters with default values must appear after all ordinary parameters in the parameter list. Ruby 1.9 relaxes this restriction and allows ordinary parameters to appear after parameters with defaults. It still requires all parameters with defaults to be adjacent in the parameter list—you can't declare two parameters with default values with an ordinary parameter between them, for example. When a method has more than one parameter with a default value, and you invoke the method with an argument for some, but not all, of these parameters, they are filled in from left to right. Suppose a method has two parameters, and both of those parameters have defaults. You can invoke this method with zero, one, or two arguments. If you specify one argument, it is assigned to the first parameter and the second parameter uses its default value. There is no way, however, to specify a value for the second parameter and use the default value of the first parameter.

6.4.2 Variable-Length Argument Lists and Arrays

Sometimes we want to write methods that can accept an arbitrary number of arguments. To do this, we put an * before one of the method's parameters. Within the body of the method, this parameter will refer to an array that contains the zero or more arguments passed at that position. For example:

```ruby
# Return the largest of the one or more arguments passed
def max(first, *rest)
  # Assume that the required first argument is the largest
  max = first
  # Now loop through each of the optional arguments looking for bigger ones
  rest.each {|x| max = x if x > max }
  # Return the largest one we found
  max
end
```

The `max` method requires at least one argument, but it may accept any number of additional arguments. The first argument is available through the `first` parameter. Any additional arguments are stored in the `rest` array. We can invoke `max` like this:

```
max(1)     # first=1, rest=[]
max(1,2)   # first=1, rest=[2]
max(1,2,3) # first=1, rest=[2,3]
```

Note that in Ruby, all `Enumerable` objects automatically have a `max` method, so the method defined here is not particularly useful.

No more than one parameter may be prefixed with an *. In Ruby 1.8, this parameter must appear after all ordinary parameters and after all parameters with defaults specified. It should be the last parameter of the method, unless the method also has a parameter with an & prefix (see below). In Ruby 1.9, a parameter with an * prefix must still appear after any parameters with defaults specified, but it may be followed by additional ordinary parameters. It must also still appear before any &-prefixed parameter.

6.4.2.1 Passing arrays to methods

We've seen how * can be used in a method declaration to cause multiple arguments to be gathered or coalesced into a single array. It can also be used in a method invocation to scatter, expand, or explode the elements of an array (or range or enumerator) so that each element becomes a separate method argument. The * is sometimes called the splat operator, although it is not a true operator. We've seen it used before in the discussion of parallel assignment in §4.5.5.

Suppose we wanted to find the maximum value in an array (and that we didn't know that Ruby arrays have a built-in `max` method!). We could pass the elements of the array to the `max` method (defined earlier) like this:

```
data = [3, 2, 1]
m = max(*data)   # first = 3, rest=[2,1] => 3
```

Consider what happens without the *:

```
m = max(data)    # first = [3,2,1], rest=[] => [3,2,1]
```

In this case, we're passing an array as the first and only argument, and our `max` method returns that first argument without performing any comparisons on it.

The * can also be used with methods that return arrays to expand those arrays for use in another method invocation. Consider the `polar` and `cartesian` methods defined earlier in this chapter:

```
# Convert the point (x,y) to Polar coordinates, then back to Cartesian
x,y = cartesian(*polar(x, y))
```

In Ruby 1.9, enumerators are splattable objects. To find the largest letter in a string, for example, we could write:

```
max(*"hello world".each_char)  # => 'w'
```

6.4.3 Mapping Arguments to Parameters

When a method definition includes parameters with default values or a parameter prefixed with an *, the assignment of argument values to parameters during method invocation gets a little bit tricky.

In Ruby 1.8, the position of the special parameters is restricted so that argument values are assigned to parameters from left to right. The first arguments are assigned to the ordinary parameters. If there are any remaining arguments, they are assigned to the parameters that have defaults. And if there are still more arguments, they are assigned to the array argument.

Ruby 1.9 has to be more clever about the way it maps arguments to parameters because the order of the parameters is no longer constrained. Suppose we have a method that is declared with o ordinary parameters, d parameters with default values, and one array parameter prefixed with *, and that these parameters appear in some arbitrary order. Now assume that we invoke this method with a arguments.

If a is less than o, an `ArgumentError` is raised; we have not supplied the minimum required number of arguments.

If a is greater than or equal to o and less than or equal to o+d, then the leftmost a-o parameters with defaults will have arguments assigned to them. The remaining (to the right) o+d-a parameters with defaults will not have arguments assigned to them, and will just use their default values.

If a is greater than o+d, then the array parameter whose name is prefixed with an * will have a-o-d arguments stored in it; otherwise, it will be empty.

Once these calculations are performed, the arguments are mapped to parameters from left to right, assigning the appropriate number of arguments to each parameter.

6.4.4 Hashes for Named Arguments

When a method requires more than two or three arguments, it can be difficult for the programmer invoking the method to remember the proper order for those arguments. Some languages allow you to write method invocations that explicitly specify a parameter name for each argument that is passed. Ruby does not support this method invocation syntax, but it can be approximated if you write a method that expects a hash as its argument or as one of its arguments:

```
# This method returns an array a of n numbers. For any index i, 0 <= i < n,
# the value of element a[i] is m*i+c. Arguments n, m, and c are passed
# as keys in a hash, so that it is not necessary to remember their order.
def sequence(args)
  # Extract the arguments from the hash.
  # Note the use of the || operator to specify defaults used
  # if the hash does not define a key that we are interested in.
  n = args[:n] || 0
  m = args[:m] || 1
```

```
  c = args[:c] || 0

  a = []                    # Start with an empty array
  n.times {|i| a << m*i+c }  # Calculate the value of each array element
  a                         # Return the array
end
```

You might invoke this method with a hash literal argument like this:

```
sequence({:n=>3, :m=>5})      # => [0, 5, 10]
```

In order to better support this style of programming, Ruby allows you to omit the curly braces around the hash literal if it is the last argument to the method (or if the only argument that follows it is a block argument, prefixed with &). A hash without braces is sometimes called a *bare hash*, and when we use one it looks like we are passing separate named arguments, which we can reorder however we like:

```
sequence(:m=>3, :n=>5)        # => [0, 3, 6, 9, 12]
```

As with other ruby methods, we can omit the parentheses, too:

```
# Ruby 1.9 hash syntax
sequence c:1, m:3, n:5        # => [1, 4, 7, 10, 13]
```

If you omit the parentheses, then you *must* omit the curly braces. If curly braces follow the method name outside of parentheses, Ruby thinks you're passing a block to the method:

```
sequence {:m=>3, :n=>5}       # Syntax error!
```

6.4.5 Block Arguments

Recall from §5.3 that a block is a chunk of Ruby code associated with a method invocation, and that an iterator is a method that expects a block. Any method invocation may be followed by a block, and any method that has a block associated with it may invoke the code in that block with the `yield` statement. To refresh your memory, the following code is a block-oriented variant on the `sequence` method developed earlier in the chapter:

```
# Generate a sequence of n numbers m*i + c and pass them to the block
def sequence2(n, m, c)
  i = 0
  while(i < n)          # loop n times
    yield i*m + c       # pass next element of the sequence to the block
    i += 1
  end
end

# Here is how you might use this version of the method
sequence2(5, 2, 2) {|x| puts x }  # Print numbers 2, 4, 6, 8, 10
```

One of the features of blocks is their anonymity. They are not passed to the method in a traditional sense, they have no name, and they are invoked with a keyword rather than with a method. If you prefer more explicit control over a block (so that you can pass it on to some other method, for example), add a final argument to your method, and prefix the argument name with an ampersand.* If you do this, then that argument will refer to the block—if any—that is passed to the method. The value of the argument will be a `Proc` object, and instead of using `yield`, you invoke the `call` method of the `Proc`:

```
def sequence3(n, m, c, &b) # Explicit argument to get block as a Proc
  i = 0
  while(i < n)
    b.call(i*m + c)        # Invoke the Proc with its call method
    i += 1
  end
end

# Note that the block is still passed outside of the parentheses
sequence3(5, 2, 2) {|x| puts x }
```

Notice that using the ampersand in this way changes only the method definition. The method invocation remains the same. We end up with the block argument being declared inside the parentheses of the method definition, but the block itself is still specified outside the parentheses of the method invocation.

Passing Proc Objects Explicitly

If you create your own `Proc` object (we'll see how to do this later in the chapter) and want to pass it explicitly to a method, you can do this as you would pass any other value—a `Proc` is an object like any other. In this case, you should not use an ampersand in the method definition:

```
# This version expects an explicitly-created Proc object, not a block
def sequence4(n, m, c, b)  # No ampersand used for argument b
  i = 0
  while(i < n)
    b.call(i*m + c)        # Proc is called explicitly
    i += 1
  end
end

p = Proc.new {|x| puts x } # Explicitly create a Proc object
sequence4(5, 2, 2, p)      # And pass it as an ordinary argument
```

Twice before in this chapter, we've said that a special kind of parameter must be the last one in the parameter list. Block arguments prefixed with ampersands must *really* be the last one. Because blocks are passed unusually in method invocations, named block arguments are different and do not interfere with array or hash parameters in which the brackets and braces have been omitted. The following two methods are legal, for example:

---

* We use the term "block argument" instead of "block parameter" for method parameters prefixed with &.
  This is because the phrase "block parameter" refers to the parameter list (such as |x|) of the block itself.

```
def sequence5(args, &b) # Pass arguments as a hash and follow with a block
  n, m, c = args[:n], args[:m], args[:c]
  i = 0
  while(i < n)
    b.call(i*m + c)
    i += 1
  end
end

# Expects one or more arguments, followed by a block
def max(first, *rest, &block)
  max = first
  rest.each {|x| max = x if x > max }
  block.call(max)
  max
end
```

These methods work fine, but notice that you can avoid the complexity of these cases by simply leaving your blocks anonymous and calling them with `yield`.

It is also worth noting that the `yield` statement still works in a method defined with an `&` parameter. Even if the block has been converted to a `Proc` object and passed as an argument, it can still be invoked as an anonymous block, as if the block argument was not there.

6.4.5.1 Using & in method invocation

We saw earlier that you can use `*` in a method definition to specify that multiple arguments should be packed into an array, and that you can use `*` in a method invocation to specify that an array should be unpacked so that its elements become separate arguments. `&` can also be used in definitions and invocations. We've just seen that `&` in a method definition allows an ordinary block associated with a method invocation to be used as a named `Proc` object inside the method. When `&` is used before a `Proc` object in a method invocation, it treats the `Proc` as if it was an ordinary block following the invocation.

Consider the following code which sums the contents of two arrays:

```
a, b = [1,2,3], [4,5]                    # Start with some data.
sum = a.inject(0) {|total,x| total+x }   # => 6. Sum elements of a.
sum = b.inject(sum) {|total,x| total+x } # => 15. Add the elements of b in.
```

We described the `inject` iterator earlier in §5.3.2. If you don't remember, you can look up its documentation with `ri Enumerable.inject`. The important thing to notice about this example is that the two blocks are identical. Rather than having the Ruby interpreter parse the same block twice, we can create a `Proc` to represent the block, and use the single `Proc` object twice:

```
a, b = [1,2,3], [4,5]                     # Start with some data.
summation = Proc.new {|total,x| total+x } # A Proc object for summations.
sum = a.inject(0, &summation)             # => 6
sum = b.inject(sum, &summation)           # => 15
```

If you use & in a method invocation, it must appear before the last argument in the invocation. Blocks can be associated with any method call, even when the method is not expecting a block, and never uses yield. In the same way, any method invocation may have an & argument as its last argument.

In a method invocation an & typically appears before a Proc object. But it is actually allowed before any object with a to_proc method. The Method class (covered later in this chapter) has such a method, so Method objects can be passed to iterators just as Proc objects can.

In Ruby 1.9, the Symbol class defines a to_proc method, allowing symbols to be prefixed with & and passed to iterators. When a symbol is passed like this, it is assumed to be the name of a method. The Proc object returned by the to_proc method invokes the named method of its first argument, passing any remaining arguments to that named method. The canonical case is this: given an array of strings, create a new array of those strings, converted to uppercase. Symbol.to_proc allows us to accomplish this elegantly as follows:

```ruby
words = ['and', 'but', 'car']     # An array of words
uppercase = words.map &:upcase     # Convert to uppercase with String.upcase
upper = words.map {|w| w.upcase }  # This is the equivalent code with a block
```

6.5 Procs and Lambdas

Blocks are syntactic structures in Ruby; they are not objects, and cannot be manipulated as objects. It is possible, however, to create an object that represents a block. Depending on how the object is created, it is called a *proc* or a *lambda*. Procs have block-like behavior and lambdas have method-like behavior. Both, however, are instances of class Proc.

The subsections that follow explain:

- How to create Proc objects in both proc and lambda forms
- How to invoke Proc objects
- How to determine how many arguments a Proc expects
- How to determine if two Proc objects are the same
- How procs and lambdas differ from each other

6.5.1 Creating Procs

We've already seen one way to create a Proc object: by associating a block with a method that is defined with an ampersand-prefixed block argument. There is nothing preventing such a method from returning the Proc object for use outside the method:

```ruby
# This method creates a proc from a block
def makeproc(&p)  # Convert associated block to a Proc and store in p
```

```
    p                    # Return the Proc object
  end
```

With a `makeproc` method like this defined, we can create a `Proc` object for ourselves:

```
adder = makeproc {|x,y| x+y }
```

The variable `adder` now refers to a `Proc` object. `Proc` objects created in this way are procs, not lambdas. All `Proc` objects have a `call` method that, when invoked, runs the code contained by the block from which the proc was created. For example:

```
sum = adder.call(2,2)  # => 4
```

In addition to being invoked, `Proc` objects can be passed to methods, stored in data structures and otherwise manipulated like any other Ruby object.

As well as creating procs by method invocation, there are three methods that create `Proc` objects (both procs and lambdas) in Ruby. These methods are commonly used, and it is not actually necessary to define a `makeproc` method like the one shown earlier. In addition to these `Proc`-creation methods, Ruby 1.9 also supports a new literal syntax for defining lambdas. The subsections that follow discuss the methods `Proc.new`, `lambda`, and `proc`, and also explain the Ruby 1.9 lambda literal syntax.

6.5.1.1 Proc.new

We've already seen `Proc.new` used in some of the previous examples in this chapter. This is the normal `new` method that most classes support, and it's the most obvious way to create a new instance of the `Proc` class. `Proc.new` expects no arguments, and returns a `Proc` object that is a proc (not a lambda). When you invoke `Proc.new` with an associated block, it returns a proc that represents the block. For example:

```
p = Proc.new {|x,y| x+y }
```

If `Proc.new` is invoked without a block from within a method that does have an associated block, then it returns a proc representing the block associated with the containing method. Using `Proc.new` in this way provides an alternative to using an ampersand-prefixed block argument in a method definition. The following two methods are equivalent, for example:

```
def invoke(&b)      def invoke
  b.call              Proc.new.call
end                 end
```

6.5.1.2 Kernel.lambda

Another technique for creating `Proc` objects is with the `lambda` method. `lambda` is a method of the `Kernel` module, so it behaves like a global function. As its name suggests, the `Proc` object returned by this method is a lambda rather than a proc. `lambda` expects no arguments, but there must be a block associated with the invocation:

```
is_positive = lambda {|x| x > 0 }
```

Lambda History

Lambdas and the `lambda` method are so named in reference to *lambda calculus*, a branch of mathematical logic that has been applied to functional programming languages. Lisp also uses the term "lambda" to refer to functions that can be manipulated as objects.

6.5.1.3 Kernel.proc

In Ruby 1.8, the global `proc` method is a synonym for `lambda`. Despite its name, it returns a lambda, not a proc. Ruby 1.9 fixes this; in that version of the language, `proc` is a synonym for `Proc.new`.

Because of this ambiguity, you should never use `proc` in Ruby 1.8 code. The behavior of your code might change if the interpreter was upgraded to a newer version. If you are using Ruby 1.9 code and are confident that it will never be run with a Ruby 1.8 interpreter, you can safely use `proc` as a more elegant shorthand for `Proc.new`.

6.5.1.4 Lambda Literals

Ruby 1.9 supports an entirely new syntax for defining lambdas as literals. We'll begin with a Ruby 1.8 lambda, created with the `lambda` method:

```ruby
succ = lambda {|x| x+1}
```

In Ruby 1.9, we can convert this to a literal as follows:

- Replace the method name `lambda` with the punctuation `->`.
- Move the list of arguments outside of and just before the curly braces.
- Change the argument list delimiters from `||` to `()`.

With these changes, we get a Ruby 1.9 lambda literal:

```ruby
succ = ->(x){ x+1 }
```

`succ` now holds a `Proc` object, which we can use just like any other:

```ruby
succ.call(2)    # => 3
```

The introduction of this syntax into Ruby was controversial, and it takes some getting used to. Note that the arrow characters `->` are different from those used in hash literals. A lambda literal uses an arrow made with a hyphen, whereas a hash literal uses an arrow made with an equals sign.

As with blocks in Ruby 1.9, the argument list of a lambda literal may include the declaration of block-local variables that are guaranteed not to overwrite variables with the same name in the enclosing scope. Simply follow the parameter list with a semicolon and a list of local variables:

```ruby
# This lambda takes 2 args and declares 3 local vars
f = ->(x,y; i,j,k) { ... }
```

One benefit of this new lambda syntax over the traditional block-based lambda creation methods is that the Ruby 1.9 syntax allows lambdas to be declared with argument defaults, just as methods can be:

```
zoom = ->(x,y,factor=2) { [x*factor, y*factor] }
```

As with method declarations, the parentheses in lambda literals are optional, because the parameter list and local variable lists are completely delimited by the ->, ;, and {. We could rewrite the three lambdas above like this:

```
succ = ->x { x+1 }
f = -> x,y; i,j,k { ... }
zoom = ->x,y,factor=2 { [x*factor, y*factor] }
```

Lambda parameters and local variables are optional, of course, and a lambda literal can omit this altogether. The minimal lambda, which takes no arguments and returns nil, is the following:

```
->{}
```

One benefit of this new syntax is its succinctness. It can be helpful when you want to pass a lambda as an argument to a method or to another lambda:

```
def compose(f,g)            # Compose 2 lambdas
  ->(x) { f.call(g.call(x)) }
end
succOfSquare = compose(->x{x+1}, ->x{x*x})
succOfSquare.call(4)        # => 17: Computes (4*4)+1
```

Lambda literals create `Proc` objects and are not the same thing as blocks. If you want to pass a lambda literal to a method that expects a block, prefix the literal with &, just as you would with any other `Proc` object. Here is how we might sort an array of numbers into descending order using both a block and a lambda literal:

```
data.sort {|a,b| b-a }   # The block version
data.sort &->(a,b){ b-a } # The lambda literal version
```

In this case, as you can see, regular block syntax is simpler.

6.5.2 Invoking Procs and Lambdas

Procs and lambdas are objects, not methods, and they cannot be invoked in the same way that methods are. If p refers to a `Proc` object, you cannot invoke p as a method. But because p is an object, you can invoke a method of p. We've already mentioned that the `Proc` class defines a method named `call`. Invoking this method executes the code in the original block. The arguments you pass to the `call` method become arguments to the block, and the return value of the block becomes the return value of the `call` method:

```
f = Proc.new {|x,y| 1.0/(1.0/x + 1.0/y) }
z = f.call(x,y)
```

The Proc class also defines the array access operator to work the same way as call. This means that you can invoke a proc or lambda using a syntax that is like method invocation, where parentheses have been replaced with square brackets. The proc invocation above, for example, could be replaced with this code:

```
z = f[x,y]
```

Ruby 1.9 offers an additional way to invoke a Proc object; as an alternative to square brackets, you can use parentheses prefixed with a period:

```
z = f.(x,y)
```

.() looks like a method invocation missing the method name. This is not an operator that can be defined, but rather is syntactic-sugar that invokes the call method. It can be used with any object that defines a call method and is not limited to Proc objects.

Ruby 1.9 adds a curry method to the Proc class. Calling this method returns a curried version of a proc or lambda. When a curried proc or lambda is invoked with insufficient arguments it returns a new Proc object (also curried) with the given arguments applied. Currying is a common technique in the functional programming paradigm:

```
product = ->(x,y){ x*y }  # Define a lambda
triple = product.curry[3] # Curry it, then specify the first argument
[triple[10],triple[20]]   # => [30,60]:
lambda {|w,x,y,z| w+x+y+z}.curry[1][2,3][4] # => 10
```

6.5.3 The Arity of a Proc

The *arity* of a proc or lambda is the number of arguments it expects. (The word is derived from the "ary" suffix of unary, binary, ternary, etc.) Proc objects have an arity method that returns the number of arguments they expect. For example:

```
lambda{||}.arity       # => 0. No arguments expected
lambda{|x| x}.arity    # => 1. One argument expected
lambda{|x,y| x+y}.arity # => 2. Two arguments expected
```

The notion of arity gets confusing when a Proc accepts an arbitrary number of arguments in an *-prefixed final argument. When a Proc allows optional arguments, the arity method returns a negative number of the form -n-1. A return value of this form indicates that the Proc requires n arguments, but it may optionally take additional arguments as well. -n-1 is known as the one's-complement of n, and you can invert it with the ~ operator. So if arity returns a negative number m, then ~m (or -m-1) gives you the number of required arguments:

```
lambda {|*args|}.arity       # => -1.  ~-1 = -(-1)-1 = 0 arguments required
lambda {|first, *rest|}.arity # => -2.  ~-2 = -(-2)-1 = 1 argument required
```

There is one final wrinkle to the arity method. In Ruby 1.8, a Proc declared without any argument clause at all (that is, without any || characters) may be invoked with any number of arguments (and these arguments are ignored). The arity method returns -1 to indicate that there are no required arguments. This has changed in Ruby 1.9: a

`Proc` declared like this has an arity of 0. If it is a lambda, then it is an error to invoke it with any arguments:

```
puts lambda {}.arity  # -1 in Ruby 1.8; 0 in Ruby 1.9
```

6.5.4 Proc Equality

The `Proc` class defines an `==` method to determine whether two `Proc` objects are equal. It is important to understand, however, that merely having the same source code is not enough to make two procs or lambdas equal to each other:

```
lambda {|x| x*x } == lambda {|x| x*x }  # => false
```

The `==` method only returns `true` if one `Proc` is a clone or duplicate of the other:

```
p = lambda {|x| x*x }
q = p.dup
p == q                      # => true: the two procs are equal
p.object_id == q.object_id  # => false: they are not the same object
```

6.5.5 How Lambdas Differ from Procs

A proc is the object form of a block, and it behaves like a block. A lambda has slightly modified behavior and behaves more like a method than a block. Calling a proc is like yielding to a block, whereas calling a lambda is like invoking a method. In Ruby 1.9, you can determine whether a `Proc` object is a proc or a lambda with the instance method `lambda?`. This predicate returns `true` for lambdas and `false` for procs. The subsections that follow explain the differences between procs and lambdas in detail.

6.5.5.1 Return in blocks, procs, and lambdas

Recall from Chapter 5 that the `return` statement returns from the lexically enclosing method, even when the statement is contained within a block. The `return` statement in a block does not just return from the block to the invoking iterator, it returns from the method that invoked the iterator. For example:

```
def test
  puts "entering method"
  1.times { puts "entering block"; return }  # Makes test method return
  puts "exiting method"  # This line is never executed
end
test
```

A proc is like a block, so if you call a proc that executes a `return` statement, it attempts to return from the method that encloses the block that was converted to the proc. For example:

```
def test
  puts "entering method"
  p = Proc.new { puts "entering proc"; return }
  p.call                     # Invoking the proc makes method return
  puts "exiting method"  # This line is never executed
```

```
  end
test
```

Using a `return` statement in a proc is tricky, however, because procs are often passed around between methods. By the time a proc is invoked, the lexically enclosing method may already have returned:

```
def procBuilder(message)          # Create and return a proc
  Proc.new { puts message; return } # return returns from procBuilder
  # but procBuilder has already returned here!
end

def test
  puts "entering method"
  p = procBuilder("entering proc")
  p.call                  # Prints "entering proc" and raises LocalJumpError!
  puts "exiting method"  # This line is never executed
end
test
```

By converting a block into an object, we are able to pass that object around and use it "out of context." If we do this, we run the risk of returning from a method that has already returned, as was the case here. When this happens, Ruby raises a `LocalJumpError`.

The fix for this contrived example is to remove the unnecessary `return` statement, of course. But a `return` statement is not always unnecessary, and another fix is to use a lambda instead of a proc. As we said earlier, lambdas work more like methods than blocks. A `return` statement in a lambda, therefore, returns from the lambda itself, not from the method that surrounds the creation site of the lambda:

```
def test
  puts "entering method"
  p = lambda { puts "entering lambda"; return }
  p.call                  # Invoking the lambda does not make the method return
  puts "exiting method"  # This line *is* executed now
end
test
```

The fact that `return` in a lambda only returns from the lambda itself means that we never have to worry about `LocalJumpError`:

```
def lambdaBuilder(message)        # Create and return a lambda
  lambda { puts message; return } # return returns from the lambda
end

def test
  puts "entering method"
  l = lambdaBuilder("entering lambda")
  l.call                  # Prints "entering lambda"
  puts "exiting method"  # This line is executed
end
test
```

6.5.5.2 Break in blocks, procs and lambdas

Figure 5-3 illustrated the behavior of the break statement in a block; it causes the block to return to its iterator and the iterator to return to the method that invoked it. Because procs work like blocks, we expect break to do the same thing in a proc. We can't easily test this, however. When we create a proc with Proc.new, Proc.new is the iterator that break would return from. And by the time we can invoke the proc object, the iterator has already returned. So it never makes sense to have a top-level break statement in a proc created with Proc.new:

```
def test
  puts "entering test method"
  proc = Proc.new { puts "entering proc"; break }
  proc.call                    # LocalJumpError: iterator has already returned
  puts "exiting test method"
end
test
```

If we create a proc object with an & argument to the iterator method, then we can invoke it and make the iterator return:

```
def iterator(&proc)
  puts "entering iterator"
  proc.call  # invoke the proc
  puts "exiting iterator"   # Never executed if the proc breaks
end

def test
  iterator { puts "entering proc"; break }
end
test
```

Lambdas are method-like, so putting a break statement at the top-level of a lambda, without an enclosing loop or iteration to break out of, doesn't actually make any sense! We might expect the following code to fail because there is nothing to break out of in the lambda. In fact, the top-level break just acts like a return:

```
def test
  puts "entering test method"
  lambda = lambda { puts "entering lambda"; break; puts "exiting lambda" }
  lambda.call
  puts "exiting test method"
end
test
```

6.5.5.3 Other control-flow statements

A top-level next statement works the same in a block, proc, or lambda: it causes the yield statement or call method that invoked the block, proc, or lambda to return. If next is followed by an expression, then the value of that expression becomes the *return value* of the block, proc, or lambda.

redo also works the same in procs and lambdas: it transfers control back to the beginning of the proc or lambda.

retry is never allowed in procs or lambdas: using it always results in a LocalJumpError.

raise behaves the same in blocks, procs, and lambdas. Exceptions always propagate up the call stack. If a block, proc, or lambda raises an exception and there is no local rescue clause, the exception first propagates to the method that invoked the block with yield or that invoked the proc or lambda with call.

6.5.5.4 Argument passing to procs and lambdas

Invoking a block with yield is similar to, but not the same as, invoking a method. There are differences in the way argument values in the invocation are assigned to the argument variables declared in the block or method. The yield statement uses *yield semantics*, whereas method invocation uses *invocation semantics*. Yield semantics are similar to parallel assignment and are described in §5.4.4. As you might expect, invoking a proc uses yield semantics and invoking a lambda uses invocation semantics:

```
p = Proc.new {|x,y| print x,y }
p.call(1)       # x,y=1:     nil used for missing rvalue:  Prints 1nil
p.call(1,2)     # x,y=1,2:   2 lvalues, 2 rvalues:         Prints 12
p.call(1,2,3)   # x,y=1,2,3: extra rvalue discarded:       Prints 12
p.call([1,2])   # x,y=[1,2]: array automatically unpacked: Prints 12
```

This code demonstrates that the call method of a proc handles the arguments it receives flexibly: silently discarding extras, silently adding nil for omitted arguments, and even unpacking arrays. (Or, not demonstrated here, packing multiple arguments into a single array when the proc expects only a single argument.)

Lambdas are not flexible in this way; like methods, they must be invoked with precisely the number of arguments they are declared with:

```
l = lambda {|x,y| print x,y }
l.call(1,2)     # This works
l.call(1)       # Wrong number of arguments
l.call(1,2,3)   # Wrong number of arguments
l.call([1,2])   # Wrong number of arguments
l.call(*[1,2])  # Works: explicit splat to unpack the array
```

6.6 Closures

In Ruby, procs and lambdas are *closures*. The term "closure" comes from the early days of computer science; it refers to an object that is both an invocable function and a variable binding for that function. When you create a proc or a lambda, the resulting Proc object holds not just the executable block but also bindings for all the variables used by the block.

You already know that blocks can use local variables and method arguments that are defined outside the block. In the following code, for example, the block associated with the `collect` iterator uses the method argument n:

```
# multiply each element of the data array by n
def multiply(data, n)
  data.collect {|x| x*n }
end

puts multiply([1,2,3], 2)   # Prints 2,4,6
```

What is more interesting, and possibly even surprising, is that if the block were turned into a proc or lambda, it could access n even after the method to which it is an argument had returned. The following code demonstrates:

```
# Return a lambda that retains or "closes over" the argument n
def multiplier(n)
  lambda {|data| data.collect{|x| x*n } }
end
doubler = multiplier(2)     # Get a lambda that knows how to double
puts doubler.call([1,2,3])  # Prints 2,4,6
```

The `multiplier` method returns a lambda. Because this lambda is used outside of the scope in which it is defined, we call it a closure; it encapsulates or "closes over" (or just retains) the binding for the method argument n.

6.6.1 Closures and Shared Variables

It is important to understand that a closure does not just retain the value of the variables it refers to—it retains the actual variables and extends their lifetime. Another way to say this is that the variables used in a lambda or proc are not statically bound when the lambda or proc is created. Instead, the bindings are dynamic, and the values of the variables are looked up when the lambda or proc is executed.

As an example, the following code defines a method that returns two lambdas. Because the lambdas are defined in the same scope, they share access to the variables in that scope. When one lambda alters the value of a shared variable, the new value is available to the other lambda:

```
# Return a pair of lambdas that share access to a local variable.
def accessor_pair(initialValue=nil)
  value = initialValue  # A local variable shared by the returned lambdas.
  getter = lambda { value }        # Return value of local variable.
  setter = lambda {|x| value = x } # Change value of local variable.
  return getter,setter             # Return pair of lambdas to caller.
end

getX, setX = accessor_pair(0) # Create accessor lambdas for initial value 0.
puts getX[]       # Prints 0. Note square brackets instead of call.
setX[10]          # Change the value through one closure.
puts getX[]       # Prints 10. The change is visible through the other.
```

The fact that lambdas created in the same scope share access to variables can be a feature or a source of bugs. Any time you have a method that returns more than one closure, you should pay particular attention to the variables they use. Consider the following code:

```
# Return an array of lambdas that multiply by the arguments
def multipliers(*args)
  x = nil
  args.map {|x| lambda {|y| x*y }}
end

double,triple = multipliers(2,3)
puts double.call(2)    # Prints 6 in Ruby 1.8
```

This `multipliers` method uses the `map` iterator and a block to return an array of lambdas (created inside the block). In Ruby 1.8, block arguments are not always local to the block (see §5.4.3), and so all of the lambdas that are created end up sharing access to x, which is a local variable of the `multipliers` method. As noted above, closures don't capture the current value of the variable: they capture the variable itself. Each of the lambdas created here share the variable x. That variable has only one value, and all of the returned lambdas use that same value. That is why the lambda we name `double` ends up tripling its argument instead of doubling it.

In this particular code, the issue goes away in Ruby 1.9 because block arguments are always block-local in that version of the language. Still, you can get yourself in trouble any time you create lambdas within a loop and use loop variables (such as an array index) within the lambda.

6.6.2 Closures and Bindings

The `Proc` class defines a method named `binding`. Calling this method on a proc or lambda returns a `Binding` object that represents the bindings in effect for that closure.

More About Bindings

We've been discussing the bindings of a closure as if they were simply a mapping from variable names to variable values. In fact, bindings involve more than just variables. They hold all the information necessary to execute a method, such as the value of `self`, and the block, if any, that would be invoked by a `yield`.

A `Binding` object doesn't have interesting methods of its own, but it can be used as the second argument to the global `eval` function (see §8.2), providing a context in which to evaluate a string of Ruby code. In Ruby 1.9, `Binding` has its own `eval` method, which you may prefer to use. (Use `ri` to learn more about `Kernel.eval` and `Binding.eval`.)

The use of a `Binding` object and the `eval` method gives us a back door through which we can manipulate the behavior of a closure. Take another look at this code from earlier:

```
# Return a lambda that retains or "closes over" the argument n
def multiplier(n)
  lambda {|data| data.collect{|x| x*n } }
end
doubler = multiplier(2)    # Get a lambda that knows how to double
puts doubler.call([1,2,3]) # Prints 2,4,6
```

Now suppose we want to alter the behavior of doubler:

```
eval("n=3", doubler.binding) # Or doubler.binding.eval("n=3") in Ruby 1.9
puts doubler.call([1,2,3])    # Now this prints 3,6,9!
```

As a shortcut, the eval method allows you to pass a Proc object directly instead of passing the Binding object of the Proc. So we could replace the eval invocation above with:

```
eval("n=3", doubler)
```

Bindings are not only a feature of closures. The Kernel.binding method returns a Binding object that represents the bindings in effect at whatever point you happen to call it.

6.7 Method Objects

Ruby's methods and blocks are executable language constructs, but they are not objects. Procs and lambdas are object versions of blocks; they can be executed and also manipulated as data. Ruby has powerful metaprogramming (or *reflection*) capabilities, and methods can actually be represented as instances of the Method class. (Metaprogramming is covered in Chapter 8, but Method objects are introduced here.) You should note that invoking a method through a Method object is less efficient than invoking it directly. Method objects are not typically used as often as lambdas and procs.

The Object class defines a method named method. Pass it a method name, as a string or a symbol, and it returns a Method object representing the named method of the receiver (or throws a NameError if there is no such method). For example:

```
m = 0.method(:succ)  # A Method representing the succ method of Fixnum 0
```

In Ruby 1.9, you can also use public_method to obtain a Method object. It works like method does but ignores protected and private methods (see §7.2).

The Method class is not a subclass of Proc, but it behaves much like it. Method objects are invoked with the call method (or the [] operator), just as Proc objects are. And Method defines an arity method just like the arity method of Proc. To invoke the Method m:

```
puts m.call    # Same as puts 0.succ. Or use puts m[].
```

Invoking a method through a Method object does not change the invocation semantics, nor does it alter the meaning of control-flow statements such as return and break. The call method of a `Method` object uses method-invocation semantics, not yield semantics. `Method` objects, therefore, behave more like lambdas than like procs.

`Method` objects work very much like `Proc` objects and can usually be used in place of them. When a true `Proc` is required, you can use `Method.to_proc` to convert a `Method` to a `Proc`. This is why `Method` objects can be prefixed with an ampersand and passed to a method in place of a block. For example:

```
def square(x); x*x; end
puts (1..10).map(&method(:square))
```

Defining Methods with Procs

In addition to obtaining a `Method` object that represents a method and converting it to a `Proc`, we can also go in the other direction. The `define_method` method (of `Module`) expects a `Symbol` as an argument, and creates a method with that name using the associated block as the method body. Instead of using a block, you can also pass a `Proc` or a `Method` object as the second argument.

One important difference between `Method` objects and `Proc` objects is that `Method` objects are not closures. Ruby's methods are intended to be completely self-contained, and they never have access to local variables outside of their own scope. The only binding retained by a `Method` object, therefore, is the value of `self`—the object on which the method is to be invoked.

In Ruby 1.9, the `Method` class defines three methods that are not available in 1.8: `name` returns the name of the method as a string; `owner` returns the class in which the method was defined; and `receiver` returns the object to which the method is bound. For any method object `m`, `m.receiver.class` must be equal to or a subclass of `m.owner`.

6.7.1 Unbound Method Objects

In addition to the `Method` class, Ruby also defines an `UnboundMethod` class. As its name suggests, an `UnboundMethod` object represents a method, without a binding to the object on which it is to be invoked. Because an `UnboundMethod` is unbound, it cannot be invoked, and the `UnboundMethod` class does not define a `call` or `[]` method.

To obtain an `UnboundMethod` object, use the `instance_method` method of any class or module:

```
unbound_plus = Fixnum.instance_method("+")
```

In Ruby 1.9, you can also use `public_instance_method` to obtain an `UnboundMethod` object. It works like `instance_method` does, but it ignores protected and private methods (see §7.2).

In order to invoke an unbound method, you must first bind it to an object using the `bind` method:

```
plus_2 = unbound_plus.bind(2)    # Bind the method to the object 2
```

The bind method returns a Method object, which can be invoked with its call method:

```
sum = plus_2.call(2)    # => 4
```

Another way to obtain an UnboundMethod object is with the unbind method of the Method class:

```
plus_3 = plus_2.unbind.bind(3)
```

In Ruby 1.9, UnboundMethod has name and owner methods that work just as they do for the Method class.

6.8 Functional Programming

Ruby is not a functional programming language in the way that languages like Lisp and Haskell are, but Ruby's blocks, procs, and lambdas lend themselves nicely to a functional programming style. Any time you use a block with an Enumerable iterator like map or inject, you're programming in a functional style. Here are examples using the map and inject iterators:

```
# Compute the average and standard deviation of an array of numbers
mean = a.inject {|x,y| x+y } / a.size
sumOfSquares = a.map{|x| (x-mean)**2 }.inject{|x,y| x+y }
standardDeviation = Math.sqrt(sumOfSquares/(a.size-1))
```

If the functional programming style is attractive to you, it is easy to add features to Ruby's built-in classes to facilitate functional programming. The rest of this chapter explores some possibilities for working with functions. The code in this section is dense and is presented as a mind-expanding exploration, not as a prescription for good programming style. In particular, redefining operators as heavily as the code in the next section does is likely to result in programs that are difficult for others to read and maintain!

This is advanced material and the code that follows assumes familiarity with Chapter 7. You may, therefore, want to skip the rest of this chapter the first time through the book.

6.8.1 Applying a Function to an Enumerable

mapand inject are two of the most important iterators defined by Enumerable. Each expects a block. If we are to write programs in a function-centric way, we might like methods on our functions that allow us to apply those functions to a specified Enumerable object:

```
# This module defines methods and operators for functional programming.
module Functional

  # Apply this function to each element of the specified Enumerable,
  # returning an array of results. This is the reverse of Enumerable.map.
```

```
# Use | as an operator alias. Read "|" as "over" or "applied over".
#
# Example:
#   a = [[1,2],[3,4]]
#   sum = lambda {|x,y| x+y}
#   sums = sum|a    # => [3,7]
def apply(enum)
  enum.map &self
end
alias | apply

# Use this function to "reduce" an enumerable to a single quantity.
# This is the inverse of Enumerable.inject.
# Use <= as an operator alias.
# Mnemonic: <= looks like a needle for injections
# Example:
#   data = [1,2,3,4]
#   sum = lambda {|x,y| x+y}
#   total = sum<=data    # => 10
def reduce(enum)
  enum.inject &self
end
alias <= reduce
end

# Add these functional programming methods to Proc and Method classes.
class Proc; include Functional; end
class Method; include Functional; end
```

Notice that we define methods in a module named Functional, and then we include this module into both the Proc and Method classes. In this way, apply and reduce work for both proc and method objects. Most of the methods that follow also define methods in this Functional module, so that they work for both Proc and Method.

With apply and reduce defined as above, we could refactor our statistical computations as follows:

```
sum = lambda {|x,y| x+y }        # A function to add two numbers
mean = (sum<=a)/a.size           # Or sum.reduce(a) or a.inject(&sum)
deviation = lambda {|x| x-mean } # Function to compute difference from mean
square = lambda {|x| x*x }       # Function to square a number
standardDeviation = Math.sqrt((sum<=square|(deviation|a))/(a.size-1))
```

Notice that the last line is succinct but that all the nonstandard operators make it hard to read. Also notice that the | operator is left-associative, even when we define it ourselves. The syntax, therefore, for applying multiple functions to an Enumerable requires parentheses. That is, we must write square|(deviation|a) instead of square|deviation|a.

6.8.2 Composing Functions

If we have two functions f and g, we sometimes want to define a new function h which is f(g()), or *f composed with g*. We can write a method that performs function composition automatically, as follows:

```ruby
module Functional
  # Return a new lambda that computes self[f[args]].
  # Use * as an operator alias for compose.
  # Examples, using the * alias for this method.
  #
  # f = lambda {|x| x*x }
  # g = lambda {|x| x+1 }
  # (f*g)[2]    # => 9
  # (g*f)[2]    # => 5
  #
  # def polar(x,y)
  #   [Math.hypot(y,x), Math.atan2(y,x)]
  # end
  # def cartesian(magnitude, angle)
  #   [magnitude*Math.cos(angle), magnitude*Math.sin(angle)]
  # end
  # p,c = method :polar, method :cartesian
  # (c*p)[3,4]  # => [3,4]
  #
  def compose(f)
    if self.respond_to?(:arity) && self.arity == 1
      lambda {|*args| self[f[*args]] }
    else
      lambda {|*args| self[*f[*args]] }
    end
  end

  # * is the natural operator for function composition.
  alias * compose
end
```

The example code in the comment demonstrates the use of compose with Method objects as well as lambdas. We can use this new * function composition operator to slightly simplify our computation of standard deviation. Using the same definitions of the lambdas sum, square, and deviation, the computation becomes:

```ruby
standardDeviation = Math.sqrt((sum<=square*deviation|a)/(a.size-1))
```

The difference is that we compose square and deviation into a single function before applying it to the array a.

6.8.3 Partially Applying Functions

In functional programming, *partial application* is the process of taking a function and a partial set of argument values and producing a new function that is equivalent to the original function with the specified arguments fixed. This is similar to, but not quite the same as currying with the Proc.curry method. For example:

```
product = lambda {|x, y| x*y }      # A function of two arguments
double = lambda {|x| product(2,x) } # Apply one argument
```

Partial application can be simplified with appropriate methods (and operators) in our
Functional module:

```
module Functional
  #
  # Return a lambda equivalent to this one with one or more initial
  # arguments applied. When only a single argument
  # is being specified, the >> alias may be simpler to use.
  # Example:
  #   product = lambda {|x,y| x*y}
  #   doubler = lambda >> 2
  #
  def apply_head(*first)
    lambda {|*rest| self[*first.concat(rest)]}
  end


  #
  # Return a lambda equivalent to this one with one or more final arguments
  # applied. When only a single argument is being specified,
  # the << alias may be simpler.
  # Example:
  #   difference = lambda {|x,y| x-y }
  #   decrement = difference << 1
  #
  def apply_tail(*last)
    lambda {|*rest| self[*rest.concat(last)]}
  end

  # Here are operator alternatives for these methods. The angle brackets
  # point to the side on which the argument is shifted in.
  alias >> apply_head    # g = f >> 2 -- set first arg to 2
  alias << apply_tail    # g = f << 2 -- set last arg to 2
end
```

Using these methods and operators, we can define our double function simply as
product>>2. We can use partial application to make our standard deviation computation somewhat more abstract, by building our deviation function from a more general-
purpose difference function:

```
difference = lambda {|x,y| x-y }  # Compute difference of two numbers
deviation = difference<<mean      # Apply second argument
```

6.8.4 Memoizing Functions

Memoization is a functional programming term for caching the results of a function
invocation. If a function always returns the same value when passed the same arguments, if there is reason to believe that the same arguments will be used repeatedly,
and if the computation it performs is somewhat expensive, then memoization may be
a useful optimization. We can automate memoization for Proc and Method objects with
the following method:

```
module Functional
  #
  # Return a new lambda that caches the results of this function and
  # only calls the function when new arguments are supplied.
  #
  def memoize
    cache = {}  # An empty cache. The lambda captures this in its closure.
    lambda {|*args|
      # notice that the hash key is the entire array of arguments!
      unless cache.has_key?(args)  # If no cached result for these args
        cache[args] = self[*args]  # Compute and cache the result
      end
      cache[args]                  # Return result from cache
    }
  end
  # A (probably unnecessary) unary + operator for memoization
  # Mnemonic: the + operator means "improved"
  alias +@ memoize        # cached_f = +f
end
```

Here's how we might use the `memoize` method or the unary + operator:

```
# A memoized recursive factorial function
factorial = lambda {|x| return 1 if x==0; x*factorial[x-1]; }.memoize
# Or, using the unary operator syntax
factorial = +lambda {|x| return 1 if x==0; x*factorial[x-1]; }
```

Note that the `factorial` function here is a recursive function. It calls the memoized version of itself, which produces optimal caching. It would not work as well if you defined a recursive nonmemoized version of the function and then defined a distinct memoized version of that:

```
factorial = lambda {|x| return 1 if x==0; x*factorial[x-1]; }
cached_factorial = +factorial # Recursive calls aren't cached!
```

6.8.5 Symbols, Methods, and Procs

There is a close relationship between the `Symbol`, `Method`, and `Proc` classes. We've already seen the `method` method, which takes a `Symbol` argument and returns a `Method` object.

Ruby 1.9 adds a useful `to_proc` method to the `Symbol` class. This method allows a symbol to be prefixed with & and passed as a block to an iterator. The symbol is assumed to name a method. When the `Proc` created with this `to_proc` method is invoked, it calls the named method of its first argument, passing any remaining arguments to that named method. Here's how you might use it:

```
# Increment an array of integers with the Fixnum.succ method
[1,2,3].map(&:succ)  # => [2,3,4]
```

Without `Symbol.to_proc`, we'd have to be slightly more verbose:

```
[1,2,3].map {|n| n.succ }
```

`Symbol.to_proc` was originally devised as an extension for Ruby 1.8, and it is typically implemented like this:

```
class Symbol
  def to_proc
    lambda {|receiver, *args| receiver.send(self, *args)}
  end
end
```

This implementation uses the **send** method (see §8.4.3) to invoke a method named by a symbol. We could also do it like this:

```
class Symbol
  def to_proc
    lambda {|receiver, *args| receiver.method(self)[*args]}
  end
end
```

In addition to **to_proc**, we can define some related and possibly useful utilities. Let's start with the **Module** class:

```
class Module
  # Access instance methods with array notation. Returns UnboundMethod,
  alias [] instance_method
end
```

Here, we're simply defining a shorthand for the `instance_method` method of the **Module** class. Recall that that method returns an **UnboundMethod** object, that cannot be invoked until bound to a particular instance of its class. Here's an example using this new notation (notice the appeal of indexing a class with the names of its methods!):

```
String[:reverse].bind("hello").call   # => "olleh"
```

Binding an unbound method can also be made simpler with a bit of the same syntactic sugar:

```
class UnboundMethod
  # Allow [] as an alternative to bind.
  alias [] bind
end
```

With this alias in place, and using the existing [] alias for calling a method, this code becomes:

```
String[:reverse]["hello"][]   # => "olleh"
```

The first pair of brackets indexes the method, the second pair binds it, and the third pair calls it.

Next, if we're going to use the [] operator for looking up the instance methods of a class, how about using []= for defining instance methods:

```
class Module
  # Define a instance method with name sym and body f.
  # Example: String[:backwards] = lambda { reverse }
  def []=(sym, f)
```

```
      self.instance_eval { define_method(sym, f) }
    end
  end
```

The definition of this []= operator may be confusing—this is advanced Ruby. define_method is a private method of Module. We use instance_eval (a public method of Object) to run a block (including the invocation of a private method) as if it were inside the module on which the method is being defined. We'll see instance_eval and define_method again in Chapter 8.

Let's use this new []= operator to define a new Enumerable.average method:

```
Enumerable[:average] = lambda do
  sum, n = 0.0, 0
  self.each {|x| sum += x; n += 1 }
  if n == 0
    nil
  else
    sum/n
  end
end
```

We've used the [] and []= operators here to get and set instance methods of a class or module. We can do something similar for the singleton methods of an object (which include the class methods of a class or module). Any object can have a singleton method, but it doesn't make sense to define an [] operator on the Object class, as so many subclasses define that operator. For singleton methods, therefore, we could take the opposite approach and define operators on the Symbol class:

```
#
# Add [] and []= operators to the Symbol class for accessing and setting
# singleton methods of objects. Read : as "method" and [] as "of".
# So :m[o] reads "method m of o".
#
class Symbol
  # Return the Method of obj named by this symbol. This may be a singleton
  # method of obj (such as a class method) or an instance method defined
  # by obj.class or inherited from a superclass.
  # Examples:
  #   creator = :new[Object]  # Class method Object.new
  #   doubler = :*[2]         # * method of Fixnum 2
  #
  def [](obj)
    obj.method(self)
  end

  # Define a singleton method on object o, using Proc or Method f as its body.
  # This symbol is used as the name of the method.
  # Examples:
  #
  #   :singleton[o] = lambda { puts "this is a singleton method of o" }
  #   :class_method[String] = lambda { puts "this is a class method" }
  #
  # Note that you can't create instance methods this way. See Module.[]=
```

```
  #
  def []=(o,f)
    # We can't use self in the block below, as it is evaluated in the
    # context of a different object. So we have to assign self to a variable.
    sym = self
    # This is the object we define singleton methods on.
    eigenclass = (class << o; self end)
    # define_method is private, so we have to use instance_eval to execute it.
    eigenclass.instance_eval { define_method(sym, f) }
  end
end
```

With this `Symbol.[]` method defined, along with the `Functional` module described previously, we can write clever (and unreadable) code like this:

```
dashes = :*['-']       # Method * of '-'
puts dashes[10]        # Prints "----------"

y = (:+[1]*:*[2])[x]   # Another way to write y = 2*x + 1
```

The definition of `[]=` for `Symbol` is like that of `[]=` for `Module`, in that it uses `instance_eval` to invoke the `define_method` method. The difference is that singleton methods are not defined within a class, as instance methods are, but in the *eigenclass* of the object. We'll encounter the eigenclass again in Chapter 7.

## CHAPTER 7

Classes and Modules

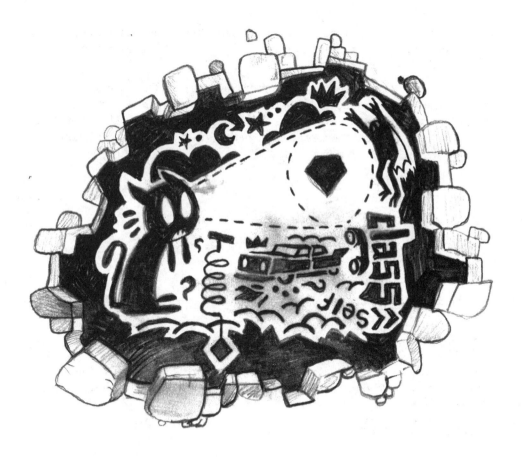

Ruby is an object-oriented language in a very pure sense: every value in Ruby is (or at least behaves like) an object. Every object is an instance of a class. A class defines a set of methods that an object responds to. Classes may extend or subclass other classes, and inherit or override the methods of their superclass. Classes can also include—or inherit methods from—modules.

Ruby's objects are strictly encapsulated: their state can be accessed only through the methods they define. The instance variables manipulated by those methods cannot be directly accessed from outside of the object. It is possible to define getter and setter accessor methods that appear to access object state directly. These pairs of accessor methods are known as *attributes* and are distinct from instance variables. The methods defined by a class may have "public," "protected," or "private" visibility, which affects how and where they may be invoked.

In contrast to the strict encapsulation of object state, Ruby's classes are very open. Any Ruby program can add methods to existing classes, and it is even possible to add "singleton methods" to individual objects.

Much of Ruby's OO architecture is part of the core language. Other parts, such as the creation of attributes and the declaration of method visibility, are done with methods rather than true language keywords. This chapter begins with an extended tutorial that demonstrates how to define a class and add methods to it. This tutorial is followed by sections on more advanced topics, including:

- Method visibility
- Subclassing and inheritance
- Object creation and initialization
- Modules, both as namespaces and as includable "mixins"
- Singleton methods and the eigenclass
- The method name resolution algorithm
- The constant name resolution algorithm

7.1 Defining a Simple Class

We begin our coverage of classes with an extended tutorial that develops a class named Point to represent a geometric point with X and Y coordinates. The subsections that follow demonstrate how to:

- Define a new class
- Create instances of that class
- Write an initializer method for the class
- Add attribute accessor methods to the class
- Define operators for the class

- Define an iterator method and make the class `Enumerable`
- Override important `Object` methods such as `to_s`, `==`, `hash`, and `<=>`
- Define class methods, class variables, class instance variables, and constants

7.1.1 Creating the Class

Classes are created in Ruby with the `class` keyword:

```
class Point
end
```

Like most Ruby constructs, a class definition is delimited with an `end`. In addition to defining a new class, the `class` keyword creates a new constant to refer to the class. The class name and the constant name are the same, so all class names must begin with a capital letter.

Within the body of a `class`, but outside of any instance methods defined by the class, the `self` keyword refers to the class being defined.

Like most statements in Ruby, `class` is an expression. The value of a `class` expression is the value of the last expression within the `class` body. Typically, the last expression within a class is a `def` statement that defines a method. The value of a `def` statement is always `nil`.

7.1.2 Instantiating a Point

Even though we haven't put anything in our `Point` class yet, we can still instantiate it:

```
p = Point.new
```

The constant `Point` holds a class object that represents our new class. All class objects have a method named `new` that creates a new instance.

We can't do anything very interesting with the newly created `Point` object we've stored in the local variable p, because we haven't yet defined any methods for the class. We can, however, ask the new object what kind of object it is:

```
p.class        # => Point
p.is_a? Point # => true
```

7.1.3 Initializing a Point

When we create new `Point` objects, we want to initialize them with two numbers that represent their X and Y coordinates. In many object-oriented languages, this is done with a "constructor." In Ruby, it is done with an `initialize` method:

```
class Point
  def initialize(x,y)
    @x, @y = x, y
```

```
    end
  end
```

This is only three new lines of code, but there are a couple of important things to point out here. We explained the def keyword in detail in Chapter 6. But that chapter focused on defining global functions that could be used from anywhere. When def is used like this with an unqualified method name inside of a class definition, it defines an *instance method* for the class. An instance method is a method that is invoked on an instance of the class. When an instance method is called, the value of self is an instance of the class in which the method is defined.

The next point to understand is that the initialize method has a special purpose in Ruby. The new method of the class object creates a new instance object, and then it automatically invokes the initialize method on that instance. Whatever arguments you passed to new are passed on to initialize. Because our initialize method expects two arguments, we must now supply two values when we invoke Point.new:

```
    p = Point.new(0,0)
```

In addition to being automatically invoked by Point.new, the initialize method is automatically made private. An object can call initialize on itself, but you cannot explicitly call initialize on p to reinitialize its state.

Now, let's look at the body of the initialize method. It takes the two values we've passed it, stored in local variables x and y, and assigns them to instance variables @x and @y. Instance variables always begin with @, and they always "belong to" whatever object self refers to. Each instance of our Point class has its own copy of these two variables, which hold its own X and Y coordinates.

Instance Variable Encapsulation

The instance variables of an object can only be accessed by the instance methods of that object. Code that is not inside an instance method cannot read or set the value of an instance variable (unless it uses one of the reflective techniques that are described in Chapter 8).

Finally, a caution for programmers who are used to Java and related languages. In statically typed languages, you must declare your variables, including instance variables. You know that Ruby variables don't need to be declared, but you might still feel that you have to write something like this:

```
# Incorrect code!
class Point
  @x = 0   # Create instance variable @x and assign a default. WRONG!
  @y = 0   # Create instance variable @y and assign a default. WRONG!

  def initialize(x,y)
    @x, @y = x, y   # Now initialize previously created @x and @y.
  end
end
```

This code does not do at all what a Java programmer expects. Instance variables are always resolved in the context of `self`. When the `initialize` method is invoked, `self` holds an instance of the `Point` class. But the code outside of that method is executed as part of the definition of the `Point` class. When those first two assignments are executed, `self` refers to the `Point` class itself, not to an instance of the class. The `@x` and `@y` variables inside the `initialize` method are completely different from those outside it.

7.1.4 Defining a to_s Method

Just about any class you define should have a `to_s` instance method to return a string representation of the object. This ability proves invaluable when debugging. Here's how we might do this for `Point`:

```
class Point
  def initialize(x,y)
    @x, @y = x, y
  end

  def to_s        # Return a String that represents this point
    "(#@x,#@y)"   # Just interpolate the instance variables into a string
  end
end
```

With this new method defined, we can create points and print them out:

```
p = new Point(1,2)   # Create a new Point object
puts p               # Displays "(1,2)"
```

7.1.5 Accessors and Attributes

Our `Point` class uses two instance variables. As we've noted, however, the value of these variables are only accessible to other instance methods. If we want users of the `Point` class to be able to use the X and Y coordinates of a point, we've got to provide accessor methods that return the value of the variables:

```
class Point
  def initialize(x,y)
    @x, @y = x, y
  end

  def x           # The accessor (or getter) method for @x
    @x
  end

  def y           # The accessor method for @y
    @y
  end
end
```

With these methods defined, we can write code like this:

```
p = Point.new(1,2)
q = Point.new(p.x*2, p.y*3)
```

The expressions `p.x` and `p.y` may look like variable references, but they are, in fact, method invocations without parentheses.

If we wanted our `Point` class to be mutable (which is probably not a good idea), we would also add setter methods to set the value of the instance variables:

```
class MutablePoint
  def initialize(x,y); @x, @y = x, y; end

  def x; @x; end        # The getter method for @x
  def y; @y; end        # The getter method for @y

  def x=(value)         # The setter method for @x
    @x = value
  end

  def y=(value)         # The setter method for @y
    @y = value
  end
end
```

Recall that assignment expressions can be used to invoke setter methods like these. So with these methods defined, we can write:

```
p = Point.new(1,1)
p.x = 0
p.y = 0
```

Using Setters Inside a Class

Once you've defined a setter method like `x=` for your class, you might be tempted to use it within other instance methods of your class. That is, instead of writing `@x=2`, you might write `x=2`, intending to invoke `x=(2)` implicitly on `self`. It doesn't work, of course; `x=2` simply creates a new local variable.

This is a not-uncommon mistake for novices who are just learning about setter methods and assignment in Ruby. The rule is that assignment expressions will only invoke a setter method when invoked through an object. If you want to use a setter from within the class that defines it, invoke it explicitly through `self`. For example: `self.x=2`.

This combination of instance variable with trivial getter and setter methods is so common that Ruby provides a way to automate it. The `attr_reader` and `attr_accessor` methods are defined by the `Module` class. All classes are modules, (the `Class` class is a subclass of `Module`) so you can invoke these methods inside any class definition. Both methods take any number of symbols naming attributes. `attr_reader` creates trivial getter methods for the instance variables with the same name. `attr_accessor` creates getter and setter methods. (The infrequently used `attr_writer` creates setter methods only.) Thus, if we were defining a mutable `Point` class, we could write:

```
class Point
  attr_accessor :x, :y # Define accessor methods for our instance variables
end
```

And if we were defining an immutable version of the class, we'd write:

```
class Point
  attr_reader :x, :y  # Define reader methods for our instance variables
end
```

Each of these methods can accept an attribute name or names as a string rather than as a symbol. The accepted style is to use symbols, but we can also write code like this:

```
attr_reader "x", "y"
```

attr is a similar method with a shorter name but with behavior that differs in Ruby 1.8 and Ruby 1.9. In 1.8, attr can define only a single attribute at a time. With a single symbol argument, it defines a getter method. If the symbol is followed by the value true, then it defines a setter method as well:

```
attr :x        # Define a trivial getter method x for @x
attr :y, true  # Define getter and setter methods for @y
```

In Ruby 1.9, attr can be used as it is in 1.8, or it can be used as a synonym for attr_reader.

The attr, attr_reader, and attr_accessor methods create instance methods for us. This is an example of *metaprogramming*, and the ability to do it is a powerful feature of Ruby. There are more examples of metaprogramming in Chapter 8. Note that attr and its related methods are invoked within a class definition but outside of any method definitions. They are only executed once, when the class is being defined. There are no efficiency concerns here: the getter and setter methods they create are just as fast as handcoded ones. Remember that these methods are only able to create trivial getters and setters that map directly to the value of an instance variable with the same name. If you need more complicated accessors, such as setters that set a differently named variable, or getters that return a value computed from two different variables, then you'll have to define those yourself.

7.1.6 Defining Operators

We'd like the + operator to perform vector addition of two Point objects, the * operator to multiply a Point by a scalar, and the unary - operator to do the equivalent of multiplying by -1. Method-based operators such as + are simply methods with punctuation for names. Because there are unary and binary forms of the - operator, Ruby uses the method name -@ for unary minus. Here is a version of the Point class with mathematical operators defined:

```
class Point
  attr_reader :x, :y   # Define accessor methods for our instance variables

  def initialize(x,y)
```

```
      @x,@y = x, y
    end

  def +(other)           # Define + to do vector addition
    Point.new(@x + other.x, @y + other.y)
  end

  def -@                 # Define unary minus to negate both coordinates
    Point.new(-@x, -@y)
  end

  def *(scalar)          # Define * to perform scalar multiplication
    Point.new(@x*scalar, @y*scalar)
  end
end
```

Take a look at the body of the + method. It is able to use the @x instance variable of self
—the object that the method is invoked on. But it cannot access @x in the other Point
object. Ruby simply does not have a syntax for this; all instance variable references
implicitly use self. Our + method, therefore, is dependent on the x and y getter methods. (We'll see later that it is possible to restrict the visibility of methods so that objects
of the same class can use each other's methods, but code outside the class cannot use
them.)

Type Checking and Duck Typing

Our + method does not do any type checking; it simply assumes that it has been passed
a suitable object. It is fairly common in Ruby programming to be loose about the definition of "suitable." In the case of our + method, any object that has methods named
x and y will do, as long as those methods expect no arguments and return a number of
some sort. We don't care if the argument actually *is* a point, as long as it looks and
behaves like a point. This approach is sometimes called "duck typing," after the adage
"if it walks like a duck and quacks like a duck, it must be a duck."

If we pass an object to + that is not suitable, Ruby will raise an exception. Attempting
to add 3 to a point, for example, results in this error message:

```
NoMethodError: undefined method `x' for 3:Fixnum
        from ./point.rb:37:in `+'
```

Translated, this tells us that the Fixnum 3 does not have a method named x, and that
this error arose in the + method of the Point class. This is all the information we need
to figure out the source of the problem, but it is somewhat obscure. Checking the class
of method arguments may make it easier to debug code that uses that method. Here is
a version of the method with class verification:

```
def +(other)
  raise TypeError, "Point argument expected" unless other.is_a? Point
  Point.new(@x + other.x, @y + other.y)
end
```

Here is a looser version of type checking that provides improved error messages but
still allows duck typing:

```
def +(other)
  raise TypeError, "Point-like argument expected" unless
    other.respond_to? :x and other.respond_to? :y
  Point.new(@x + other.x, @y + other.y)
end
```

Note that this version of the method still assumes that the x and y methods return numbers. We'd get an obscure error message if one of these methods returned a string, for example.

Another approach to type checking occurs after the fact. We can simply handle any exceptions that occur during execution of the method and raise a more appropriate exception of our own:

```
def +(other)         # Assume that other looks like a Point
  Point.new(@x + other.x, @y + other.y)
rescue               # If anything goes wrong above
  raise TypeError,   # Then raise our own exception
    "Point addition with an argument that does not quack like a Point!"
end
```

Note that our * method expects a numeric operand, not a Point. If p is point, then we can write p*2. As our class is written, however, we cannot write 2*p. That second expression invokes the * method of the Integer class, which doesn't know how to work with Point objects. Because the Integer class doesn't know how to multiply by a Point, it asks the point for help by calling its coerce method. (See §3.8.7.4 for more details.) If we want the expression 2*p to return the same result as p*2, we can define a coerce method:

```
# If we try passing a Point to the * method of an Integer, it will call
# this method on the Point and then will try to multiply the elements of
# the array. Instead of doing type conversion, we switch the order of
# the operands, so that we invoke the * method defined above.
def coerce(other)
  [self, other]
end
```

7.1.7 Array and Hash Access with [ ]

Ruby uses square brackets for array and hash access, and allows any class to define a [ ] method and use these brackets itself. Let's define a [ ] method for our class to allow Point objects to be treated as read-only arrays of length 2, or as read-only hashes with keys :x and :y:

```
# Define [] method to allow a Point to look like an array or
# a hash with keys :x and :y
def [](index)
  case index
  when 0, -2: @x      # Index 0 (or -2) is the X coordinate
  when 1, -1: @y      # Index 1 (or -1) is the Y coordinate
  when :x, "x": @x    # Hash keys as symbol or string for X
  when :y, "y": @y    # Hash keys as symbol or string for Y
```

```
    else nil          # Arrays and hashes just return nil on bad indexes
    end
end
```

7.1.8 Enumerating Coordinates

If a Point object can behave like an array with two elements, then perhaps we ought to be able to iterate through those elements as we can with a true array. Here is a definition of the each iterator for our Point class. Because a Point always has exactly two elements, our iterator doesn't have to loop; it can simply call yield twice:

```
# This iterator passes the X coordinate to the associated block, and then
# passes the Y coordinate, and then returns. It allows us to enumerate
# a point as if it were an array with two elements. This each method is
# required by the Enumerable module.
def each
  yield @x
  yield @y
end
```

With this iterator defined, we can write code like this:

```
p = Point.new(1,2)
p.each {|x| print x }   # Prints "12"
```

More importantly, defining the each iterator allows us to mix in the methods of the Enumerable module, all of which are defined in terms of each. Our class gains over 20 iterators by adding a single line:

```
include Enumerable
```

If we do this, then we can write interesting code like this:

```
# Is the point P at the origin?
p.all? {|x| x == 0 } # True if the block is true for all elements
```

7.1.9 Point Equality

As our class is currently defined, two distinct Point instances are never equal to each other, even if their X and Y coordinates are the same. To remedy this, we must provide an implementation of the == operator. (You may want to reread §3.8.5 in Chapter 3 to refresh your memory about Ruby's various notions of equality.)

Here is an == method for Point:

```
def ==(o)                # Is self == o?
  if o.is_a? Point       # If o is a Point object
    @x==o.x && @y==o.y   # then compare the fields.
  else                   # If o is not a Point
    false                # then, by definition, self != o.
  end
end
```

Recall from §3.8.5 that Ruby objects also define an `eql?` method for testing equality. By default, the `eql?` method, like the == operator, tests object identity rather than equality of object content. Often, we want `eql?` to work just like the == operator, and we can accomplish this with an alias:

```
class Point
  alias eql? ==
end
```

On the other hand, there are two reasons we might want `eql?` to be different from ==. First, some classes define `eql?` to perform a stricter comparison than ==. In `Numeric` and its subclasses, for example, == allows type conversion and `eql?` does not. If we believe that the users of our `Point` class might want to be able to compare instances in two different ways, then we might follow this example. Because points are just two numbers, it would make sense to follow the example set by `Numeric` here. Our `eql?` method would look much like the == method, but it would use `eql?` to compare point coordinates instead of ==:

```
def eql?(o)
  if o.instance_of? Point
    @x.eql?(o.x) && @y.eql?(o.y)
  else
    false
```

```
      end
   end
```

As an aside, note that this is the right approach for any classes that implement collections (sets, lists, trees) of arbitrary objects. The == operator should compare the
members of the collection using their == operators, and the eql? method should
compare the members using their eql? methods.

The second reason to implement an eql? method that is different from the == operator
is if you want instances of your class to behave specially when used as a hash key. The
Hash class uses eql? to compare hash keys (but not values). If you leave eql? undefined,
then hashes will compare instances of your class by object identity. This means that if
you associate a value with a key p, you will only be able to retrieve that value with the
exact same object p. An object q won't work, even if p == q. Mutable objects do not
work well as hash keys, but leaving eql? undefined neatly sidesteps the problem. (See
§3.4.2 for more on hashes and mutable keys.)

Because eql? is used for hashes, you must never implement this method by itself. If you
define an eql? method, you must also define a hash method to compute a hashcode for
your object. If two objects are equal according to eql?, then their hash methods *must*
return the same value. (Two unequal objects may return the same hashcode, but you
should avoid this to the extent possible.)

Implementing optimal hash methods can be very tricky. Fortunately, there is a simple
way to compute perfectly adequate hashcodes for just about any class: simply combine
the hashcodes of all the objects referenced by your class. (More precisely: combine the
hashcodes of all the objects compared by your eql? method.) The trick is to combine
the hashcodes in the proper way. The following hash method is *not* a good one:

```
def hash
   @x.hash + @y.hash
end
```

The problem with this method is that it returns the same hashcode for the point
(1,0) as it does for the point (0,1). This is legal, but it leads to poor performance when
points are used as hash keys. Instead, we should mix things up a bit:

```
def hash
   code = 17
   code = 37*code + @x.hash
   code = 37*code + @y.hash
   # Add lines like this for each significant instance variable
   code  # Return the resulting code
end
```

This general-purpose hashcode recipe should be suitable for most Ruby classes. It, and
its constants 17 and 37, are adapted from the book *Effective Java* by Joshua Bloch
(Prentice Hall).

7.1.10 Ordering Points

Suppose we wish to define an ordering for Point objects so that we can compare them and sort them. There are a number of ways to order points, but we'll chose to arrange them based on their distance from the origin. This distance (or magnitude) is computed by the Pythagorean theorem: the square root of the sum of the squares of the X and Y coordinates.

To define this ordering for Point objects, we need only define the <=> operator (see §4.6.6) and include the Comparable module. Doing this mixes in implementations of the equality and relational operators that are based on our implementation of the general <=> operator we defined. The <=> operator should compare self to the object it is passed. If self is less than that object (closer to the origin, in this case), it should return -1. If the two objects are equal, it should return 0. And if self is greater than the argument object, the method should return 1. (The method should return nil if the argument object and self are of incomparable types.) The following code is our implementation of <=>. There are two things to note about it. First, it doesn't bother with the Math.sqrt method and instead simply compares the sum of the squares of the coordinates. Second, after computing the sums of the squares, it simply delegates to the <=> operator of the Float class:

```
include Comparable    # Mix in methods from the Comparable module.

# Define an ordering for points based on their distance from the origin.
# This method is required by the Comparable module.
def <=>(other)
  return nil unless other.instance_of? Point
  @x**2 + @y**2 <=> other.x**2 + other.y**2
end
```

Note that the Comparable module defines an == method that uses our definition of <=>. Our distance-based comparison operator results in an == method that considers the points (1,0) and (0,1) to be equal. Because our Point class explicitly defines its own == method, however, the == method of Comparable is never invoked. Ideally, the == and <=> operators should have consistent definitions of equality. This was not possible in our Point class, and we end up with operators that allow the following:

```
p,q = Point.new(1,0), Point.new(0,1)
p == q        # => false: p is not equal to q
p < q         # => false: p is not less than q
p > q         # => false: p is not greater than q
```

Finally, It is worth noting here that the Enumerable module defines several methods, such as sort, min, and max, that only work if the objects being enumerated define the <=> operator.

7.1.11 A Mutable Point

The Point class we've been developing is *immutable*: once a point object has been created, there is no public API to change the X and Y coordinates of that point. This is probably as it should be. But let's detour and investigate some methods we might add if we wanted points to be mutable.

First of all, we'd need x= and y= setter methods to allow the X and Y coordinates to be set directly. We could define these methods explicitly, or simply change our attr_reader line to attr_accessor:

```
attr_accessor :x, :y
```

Next, we'd like an alternative to the + operator for when we want to add the coordinates of point q to the coordinates of point p, and modify point p rather than creating and returning a new Point object. We'll call this method add!, with the exclamation mark indicating that it alters the internal state of the object on which it is invoked:

```
def add!(p)          # Add p to self, return modified self
  @x += p.x
  @y += p.y
  self
end
```

When defining a mutator method, we normally only add an exclamation mark to the name if there is a nonmutating version of the same method. In this case, the name add! makes sense if we also define an add method that returns a new object, rather than altering its receiver. A nonmutating version of a mutator method is often written simply by creating a copy of self and invoking the mutator on the copied object:

```
def add(p)            # A nonmutating version of add!
  q = self.dup        # Make a copy of self
  q.add!(p)           # Invoke the mutating method on the copy
end
```

In this trivial example, our add method works just like the + operator we've already defined, and it's not really necessary. So if we don't define a nonmutating add, we should consider dropping the exclamation mark from add! and allowing the name of the method itself ("add" instead of "plus") to indicate that it is a mutator.

7.1.12 Quick and Easy Mutable Classes

If you want a mutable Point class, one way to create it is with Struct. Struct is a core Ruby class that generates other classes. These generated classes have accessor methods for the named fields you specify. There are two ways to create a new class with Struct.new:

```
Struct.new("Point", :x, :y)  # Creates new class Struct::Point
Point = Struct.new(:x, :y)   # Creates new class, assigns to Point
```

Once a class has been created with `Struct.new`, you can use it like any other class. Its new method will expect values for each of the named fields you specify, and its instance methods provide read and write accessors for those fields:

```
p = Point.new(1,2)   # => #<struct Point x=1, y=2>
p.x                  # => 1
p.y                  # => 2
p.x = 3              # => 3
p.x                  # => 3
```

Structs also define the [ ] and [ ]= operators for array and hash-style indexing, and even provide each and each_pair iterators for looping through the values held in an instance of the struct:

```
p[:x] = 4            # => 4: same as p.x =
p[:x]                # => 4: same as p.x
p[1]                 # => 2: same as p.y
p.each {|c| print c} # prints "42"
p.each_pair {|n,c| print n,c }   # prints "x4y2"
```

Struct-based classes have a working == operator, can be used as hash keys (though caution is necessary because they are mutable), and even define a helpful to_s method:

```
q = Point.new(4,2)
q == p         # => true
h = {q => 1}   # Create a hash using q as a key
h[p]           # => 1: extract value using p as key
q.to_s         # => "#<struct Point x=4, y=2>"
```

A `Point` class defined as a struct does not have point-specific methods like `add!` or the `<=>` operator defined earlier in this chapter. There is no reason we can't add them, though. Ruby class definitions are not static. Any class (including classes defined with `Struct.new`) can be "opened" and have methods added to it. Here's a `Point` class initially defined as a `Struct`, with point-specific methods added:

```
Point = Struct.new(:x, :y)   # Create new class, assign to Point
class Point                  # Open Point class for new methods
  def add!(other)            # Define an add! method
    self.x += other.x
    self.y += other.y
    self
  end
```

```
  include Comparable       # Include a module for the class
  def <=>(other)           # Define the <=> operator
    return nil unless other.instance_of? Point
    self.x**2 + self.y**2 <=> other.x**2 + other.y**2
  end
end
```

As noted at the beginning of this section, the Struct class is designed to create mutable classes. With just a bit of work, however, we can make a Struct-based class immutable:

```
Point = Struct.new(:x, :y)   # Define mutable class
class Point                  # Open the class
  undef x=,y=,[]=            # Undefine mutator methods
end
```

7.1.13 A Class Method

Let's take another approach to adding Point objects together. Instead of invoking an instance method of one point and passing another point to that method, let's write a method named sum that takes any number of Point objects, adds them together, and returns a new Point. This method is not an instance method invoked on a Point object. Rather, it is a *class method*, invoked through the Point class itself. We might invoke the sum method like this:

```
total = Point.sum(p1, p2, p3)   # p1, p2 and p3 are Point objects
```

Keep in mind that the expression Point refers to a Class object that represents our point class. To define a class method for the Point class, what we are really doing is defining a singleton method of the Point object. (We covered singleton methods in §6.1.4.) To define a singleton method, use the def statement as usual, but specify the object on which the method is to be defined as well as the name of the method. Our class method sum is defined like this:

```
class Point
  attr_reader :x, :y     # Define accessor methods for our instance variables

  def Point.sum(*points) # Return the sum of an arbitrary number of points
    x = y = 0
    points.each {|p| x += p.x; y += p.y }
    Point.new(x,y)
  end

  # ...the rest of class omitted here...
end
```

This definition of the class method names the class explicitly, and mirrors the syntax used to invoke the method. Class methods can also be defined using self instead of the class name. Thus, this method could also be written like this:

```
def self.sum(*points)  # Return the sum of an arbitrary number of points
  x = y = 0
  points.each {|p| x += p.x; y += p.y }
```

```
    Point.new(x,y)
  end
```

Using `self` instead of `Point` makes the code slightly less clear, but it's an application of the DRY (Don't Repeat Yourself) principle. If you use `self` instead of the class name, you can change the name of a class without having to edit the definition of its class methods.

There is yet another technique for defining class methods. Though it is less clear than the previously shown technique, it can be handy when defining multiple class methods, and you are likely to see it used in existing code:

```
# Open up the Point object so we can add methods to it
class << Point      # Syntax for adding methods to a single object
  def sum(*points)  # This is the class method Point.sum
    x = y = 0
    points.each {|p| x += p.x; y += p.y }
    Point.new(x,y)
  end

  # Other class methods can be defined here
end
```

This technique can also be used inside the class definition, where we can use `self` instead of repeating the class name:

```
class Point
  # Instance methods go here

  class << self
    # Class methods go here
  end
end
```

We'll learn more about this syntax in §7.7.

7.1.14 Constants

Many classes can benefit from the definition of some associated constants. Here are some constants that might be useful for our `Point` class:

```
class Point
  def initialize(x,y)  # Initialize method
    @x,@y = x, y
  end

  ORIGIN = Point.new(0,0)
  UNIT_X = Point.new(1,0)
  UNIT_Y = Point.new(0,1)

  # Rest of class definition goes here
end
```

Inside the class definition, these constants can be referred to by their unqualified names. Outside the definition, they must be prefixed by the name of the class, of course:

```
Point::UNIT_X + Point::UNIT_Y   # => (1,1)
```

Note that because our constants in this example refer to instances of the class, we cannot define the constants until after we've defined the `initialize` method of the class. Also, keep in mind that it is perfectly legal to define constants in the `Point` class from outside the class:

```
Point::NEGATIVE_UNIT_X = Point.new(-1,0)
```

7.1.15 Class Variables

Class variables are visible to, and shared by, the class methods and the instance methods of a class, and also by the class definition itself. Like instance variables, class variables are encapsulated; they can be used by the implementation of a class, but they are not visible to the users of a class. Class variables have names that begin with @@.

There is no real need to use class variables in our `Point` class, but for the purposes of this tutorial, let's suppose that we want to collect data about the number of `Point` objects that are created and their average coordinates. Here's how we might write the code:

```
class Point
  # Initialize our class variables in the class definition itself
  @@n = 0               # How many points have been created
  @@totalX = 0          # The sum of all X coordinates
  @@totalY = 0          # The sum of all Y coordinates

  def initialize(x,y)   # Initialize method
    @x,@y = x, y        # Sets initial values for instance variables

    # Use the class variables in this instance method to collect data
    @@n += 1            # Keep track of how many Points have been created
    @@totalX += x       # Add these coordinates to the totals
    @@totalY += y
  end

  # A class method to report the data we collected
  def self.report
    # Here we use the class variables in a class method
    puts "Number of points created: #@@n"
    puts "Average X coordinate: #{@@totalX.to_f/@@n}"
    puts "Average Y coordinate: #{@@totalY.to_f/@@n}"
  end
end
```

The thing to notice about this code is that class variables are used in instance methods, class methods, and in the class definition itself, outside of any method. Class variables are fundamentally different than instance variables. We've seen that instance variables are always evaluated in reference to `self`. That is why an instance variable reference in a class definition or class method is completely different from an instance variable reference in an instance method. Class variables, on the other hand, are always evaluated in reference to the class object created by the enclosing `class` definition statement.

7.1.16 Class Instance Variables

Classes are objects and can have instance variables just as other objects can. The instance variables of a class—often called class instance variables—are not the same as class variables. But they are similar enough that they can often be used instead of class variables.

An instance variable used inside a `class` definition but outside an instance method definition is a class instance variable. Like class variables, class instance variables are associated with the class rather than with any particular instance of the class. A disadvantage of class instance variables is that they cannot be used within instance methods as class variables can. Another disadvantage is the potential for confusing them with ordinary instance variables. Without the distinctive punctuation prefixes, it may be more difficult to remember whether a variable is associated with instances or with the class object.

One of the most important advantages of class instance variables over class variables has to do with the confusing behavior of class variables when subclassing an existing class. We'll return to this point later in the chapter.

Let's port our statistics-gathering version of the `Point` class to use class instance variables instead of class variables. The only difficulty is that because class instance variables cannot be used from instance methods, we must move the statistics gathering code out of the `initialize` method (which is an instance method) and into the new class method used to create points:

```
class Point
  # Initialize our class instance variables in the class definition itself
  @n = 0               # How many points have been created
  @totalX = 0          # The sum of all X coordinates
  @totalY = 0          # The sum of all Y coordinates

  def initialize(x,y) # Initialize method
    @x,@y = x, y       # Sets initial values for instance variables
  end

  def self.new(x,y)    # Class method to create new Point objects
    # Use the class instance variables in this class method to collect data
    @n += 1            # Keep track of how many Points have been created
    @totalX += x       # Add these coordinates to the totals
    @totalY += y

    super              # Invoke the real definition of new to create a Point
                       # More about super later in the chapter
  end
```

```
    # A class method to report the data we collected
    def self.report
      # Here we use the class instance variables in a class method
      puts "Number of points created: #@n"
      puts "Average X coordinate: #{@totalX.to_f/@n}"
      puts "Average Y coordinate: #{@totalY.to_f/@n}"
    end
  end
```

Because class instance variables are just instance variables of class objects, we can use `attr`, `attr_reader`, and `attr_accessor` to create accessor methods for them. The trick, however, is to invoke these metaprogramming methods in the right context. Recall that one way to define class methods uses the syntax `class << self`. This same syntax allows us to define attribute accessor methods for class instance variables:

```
class << self
  attr_accessor :n, :totalX, :totalY
end
```

With these accessors defined, we can refer to our raw data as `Point.n`, `Point.totalX`, and `Point.totalY`.

7.2 Method Visibility: Public, Protected, Private

Instance methods may be *public*, *private*, or *protected*. If you've programmed with other object-oriented languages, you may already be familiar with these terms. Pay attention anyway, because these words have a somewhat different meaning in Ruby than they do in other languages.

Methods are normally public unless they are explicitly declared to be private or protected. One exception is the `initialize` method, which is always implicitly private. Another exception is any "global" method declared outside of a class definition—those methods are defined as private instance methods of `Object`. A public method can be invoked from anywhere—there are no restrictions on its use.

A private method is internal to the implementation of a class, and it can only be called by other instance methods of the class (or, as we'll see later, its subclasses). Private methods are implicitly invoked on `self`, and may not be explicitly invoked on an object. If `m` is a private method, then you must invoke it in *functional style* as `m`. You cannot write `o.m` or even `self.m`.

A protected method is like a private method in that it can only be invoked from within the implementation of a class or its subclasses. It differs from a private method in that it may be explicitly invoked on any instance of the class, and it is not restricted to implicit invocation on `self`. A protected method can be used, for example, to define an accessor that allows instances of a class to share internal state with each other, but does not allow users of the class to access that state.

Protected methods are the least commonly defined and also the most difficult to understand. The rule about when a protected method can be invoked can be more formally described as follows: a protected method defined by a class C may be invoked on an object o by a method in an object p if and only if the classes of o and p are both subclasses of, or equal to, the class C.

Method visibility is declared with three methods named `public`, `private`, and `protected`. These are instance methods of the `Module` class. All classes are modules, and inside a class definition (but outside method definitions), `self` refers to the class being defined. Thus, `public`, `private`, and `protected` may be used bare as if they were keywords of the language. In fact, however, they are method invocations on `self`. There are two ways to invoke these methods. With no arguments, they specify that all subsequent method definitions will have the specified visibility. A class might use them like this:

```
class Point
  # public methods go here

  # The following methods are protected
  protected

  # protected methods go here

  # The following methods are private
  private

  # private methods go here
end
```

The methods may also be invoked with the names of one or more methods (as symbols or strings) as arguments. When invoked like this, they alter the visibility of the named methods. In this usage, the visibility declaration must come after the definition of the method. One approach is to declare all private and protected methods at once, at the end of a class. Another approach is to declare the visibility of each private or protected method immediately after it is defined. Here, for example, is a class with a private utility method and a protected accessor method:

```
class Widget
  def x              # Accessor method for @x
    @x
  end
  protected :x       # Make it protected

  def utility_method # Define a method
    nil
  end
  private :utility_method  # And make it private
end
```

Remember that `public`, `private`, and `protected` apply only to methods in Ruby. Instance and class variables are encapsulated and effectively private, and constants are effectively public. There is no way to make an instance variable accessible from outside a class (except by defining an accessor method, of course). And there is no way to define a constant that is inaccessible to outside use.

Occasionally, it is useful to specify that a class method should be private. If your class defines factory methods, for example, you might want to make the new method private. To do this, use the `private_class_method` method, specifying one or more method names as symbols:

```
private_class_method :new
```

You can make a private class method public again with `public_class_method`. Neither method can be invoked without arguments in the way that `public`, `protected`, and `private` can be.

Ruby is, by design, a very open language. The ability to specify that some methods are private and protected encourages good programming style, and prevents inadvertent use of methods that are not part of the public API of a class. It is important to understand, however, that Ruby's metaprogramming capabilities make it trivial to invoke private and protected methods and even to access encapsulated instance variables. To invoke the private utility method defined in the previous code, you can use the `send` method, or you can use `instance_eval` to evaluate a block in the context of the object:

```
w = Widget.new                       # Create a Widget
w.send :utility_method               # Invoke private method!
w.instance_eval { utility_method }   # Another way to invoke it
w.instance_eval { @x }               # Read instance variable of w
```

If you want to invoke a method by name, but you don't want to inadvertently invoke a private method that you don't know about, you can (in Ruby 1.9) use `public_send` instead of `send`. It works like `send`, but does not invoke private methods when called with an explicit receiver. `public_send` is covered in Chapter 8, as are `send` and `instance_eval`.

7.3 Subclassing and Inheritance

Most object-oriented programming languages, including Ruby, provide a *subclassing* mechanism that allows us to create new classes whose behavior is based on, but modified from, the behavior of an existing class. We'll begin this discussion of subclassing with definitions of basic terminology. If you've programmed in Java, C++, or a similar language, you are probably already familiar with these terms.

When we define a class, we may specify that it *extends*—or *inherits from*—another class, known as the *superclass*. If we define a class Ruby that extends a class Gem, we say that Ruby is a *subclass* of Gem, and that Gem is the *superclass* of Ruby. If you do not specify a superclass when you define a class, then your class implicitly extends Object. A class may have any number of subclasses, and every class has a single superclass except Object, which has none.

The fact that classes may have multiple subclasses but only a single superclass means that they can be arranged in a tree structure, which we call the Ruby *class hierarchy*. The Object class is the root of this hierarchy, and every class inherits directly or indirectly from it. The *descendants* of a class are the subclasses of the class plus the subclasses of the subclasses, and so on recursively. The *ancestors* of a class are the superclass, plus the superclass of the superclass, and so on up to Object. Figure 5-5 in Chapter 5 illustrates the portion of the Ruby class hierarchy that includes Exception and all of its descendants. In that figure, you can see that the ancestors of EOFError are IOError, StandardError, Exception, and Object.

BasicObject in Ruby 1.9

In Ruby 1.9, Object is no longer the root of the class hierarchy. A new class named BasicObject serves that purpose, and Object is a subclass of BasicObject. BasicObject is a very simple class, with almost no methods of its own, and it is useful as the superclass of delegating wrapper classes (like the one shown in Example 8-5 in Chapter 8).

When you create a class in Ruby 1.9, you still extend Object unless you explicitly specify the superclass, and most programmers will never need to use or extend BasicObject. Methods such as ==, equal?, instance_eval, and __send__ are normally considered to be Object methods even though they are actually defined by BasicObject.

The syntax for extending a class is simple. Just add a < character and the name of the superclass to your **class** statement. For example:

```
class Point3D < Point    # Define class Point3D as a subclass of Point
end
```

We'll flesh out this three-dimensional Point class in the subsections that follow, showing how methods are inherited from the superclass, and how to override or augment the inherited methods to define new behavior for the subclass.

Subclassing a Struct

Earlier in this chapter, we saw how to use Struct.new to automatically generate simple classes. It is also possible to subclass a struct-based class, so that methods other than the automatically generated ones can be added:

```
class Point3D < Struct.new("Point3D", :x, :y, :z)
  # Superclass struct gives us accessor methods, ==, to_s, etc.
  # Add point-specific methods here
end
```

7.3.1 Inheriting Methods

The Point3D class we have defined is a trivial subclass of Point. It declares itself an extension of Point, but there is no class body, so it adds nothing to that class. A

Point3D object is effectively the same thing as a Point object. One of the only observable differences is in the value returned by the class method:

```
p2 = Point.new(1,2)
p3 = Point3D.new(1,2)
print p2.to_s, p2.class    # prints "(1,2)Point"
print p3.to_s, p3.class    # prints "(1,2)Point3D"
```

The value returned by the class method is different, but what's more striking about this example is what is the same. Our Point3D object has inherited the to_s method defined by Point. It has also inherited the initialize method—this is what allows us to create a Point3D object with the same new call that we use to create a Point object.[*] There is another example of method inheritance in this code: both Point and Point3D inherit the class method from Object.

7.3.2 Overriding Methods

When we define a new class, we add new behavior to it by defining new methods. Just as importantly, however, we can customize the inherited behavior of the class by redefining inherited methods.

For example, the Object class defines a to_s method to convert an object to a string in a very generic way:

```
o = Object.new
puts o.to_s      # Prints something like "#<Object:0xb7f7fce4>"
```

When we defined a to_s method in the Point class, we were *overriding* the to_s method inherited from Object.

One of the important things to understand about object-oriented programming and subclassing is that when methods are invoked, they are looked up dynamically so that the appropriate definition or redefinition of the method is found. That is, method invocations are not bound statically at the time they are parsed, but rather, are looked up at the time they are executed. Here is an example to demonstrate this important point:

```
# Greet the World
class WorldGreeter
  def greet                    # Display a greeting
    puts "#{greeting} #{who}"
  end

  def greeting                 # What greeting to use
    "Hello"
  end
end
```

---

[*] If you're a Java programmer, this may be surprising to you. Java classes define special constructor methods for initialization, and those methods are not inherited. In Ruby, initialize is an ordinary method and is inherited like any other.

```ruby
  def who                        # Who to greet
    "World"
  end
end

# Greet the world in Spanish
class SpanishWorldGreeter < WorldGreeter
  def greeting                   # Override the greeting
    "Hola"
  end
end

# We call a method defined in WorldGreeter, which calls the overridden
# version of greeting in SpanishWorldGreeter, and prints "Hola World"
SpanishWorldGreeter.new.greet
```

If you've done object-oriented programming before, the behavior of this program is probably obvious and trivial to you. But if you're new to it, it may be profound. We call the `greet` method inherited from `WorldGreeter`. This `greet` method calls the `greeting` method. At the time that `greet` was defined, the `greeting` method returned "Hello". But we've subclassed `WorldGreeter`, and the object we're calling `greet` on has a new definition of `greeting`. When we invoke `greeting`, Ruby looks up the appropriate definition of that method for the object it is being invoked on, and we end up with a proper Spanish greeting rather than an English one. This runtime lookup of the appropriate definition of a method is called *method name resolution*, and is described in detail in §7.8 at the end of this chapter.

Notice that it is also perfectly reasonable to define an *abstract* class that invokes certain undefined "abstract" methods, which are left for subclasses to define. The opposite of abstract is *concrete*. A class that extends an abstract class is concrete if it defines all of the abstract methods of its ancestors. For example:

```ruby
# This class is abstract; it doesn't define greeting or who
# No special syntax is required: any class that invokes methods that are
# intended for a subclass to implement is abstract.
class AbstractGreeter
  def greet
    puts "#{greeting} #{who}"
  end
end

# A concrete subclass
class WorldGreeter < AbstractGreeter
  def greeting; "Hello"; end
  def who; "World"; end
end

WorldGreeter.new.greet  # Displays "Hello World"
```

7.3.2.1 Overriding private methods

Private methods cannot be invoked from outside the class that defines them. But they are inherited by subclasses. This means that subclasses can invoke them and can override them.

Be careful when you subclass a class that you did not write yourself. Classes often use private methods as internal helper methods. They are not part of the public API of the class and are not intended to be visible. If you haven't read the source code of the class, you won't even know the names of the private methods it defines for its own use. If you happen to define a method (whatever its visibility) in your subclass that has the same name as a private method in the superclass, you will have inadvertently overridden the superclass's internal utility method, and this will almost certainly cause unintended behavior.

The upshot is that, in Ruby, you should only subclass when you are familiar with the implementation of the superclass. If you only want to depend on the public API of a class and not on its implementation, then you should extend the functionality of the class by encapsulating and delegating to it, not by inheriting from it.

7.3.3 Augmenting Behavior by Chaining

Sometimes when we override a method, we don't want to replace it altogether, we just want to augment its behavior by adding some new code. In order to do this, we need a way to invoke the overridden method from the overriding method. This is known as *chaining*, and it is accomplished with the keyword super.

super works like a special method invocation: it invokes a method with the same name as the current one, in the superclass of the current class. (Note that the superclass need not define that method itself—it can inherit it from one of its ancestors.) You may specify arguments for super just as you would for a normal method invocation. One common and important place for method chaining is the initialize method of a class. Here is how we might write the initialize method of our Point3D class:

```ruby
class Point3D < Point
  def initialize(x,y,z)
    # Pass our first two arguments along to the superclass initialize method
    super(x,y)
    # And deal with the third argument ourself
    @z = z;
  end
end
```

If you use super as a bare keyword—with no arguments and no parentheses—then all of the arguments that were passed to the current method are passed to the superclass method. Note, however, that it's the current values of the method parameters that are passed to the superclass method. If the method has modified the values in its parameter variables, then the modified values are passed to the invocation of the superclass method.

As with normal method invocations, the parentheses around super arguments are optional. Because a bare super has special meaning, however, you must explicitly use a pair of empty parentheses if you want to pass zero arguments from a method that itself has one or more arguments.

7.3.4 Inheritance of Class Methods

Class methods may be inherited and overridden just as instance methods can be. If our Point class defines a class method sum, then our Point3D subclass inherits that method. That is, if Point3D does not define its own class method named sum, then the expression Point3D.sum invokes the same method as the expression Point.sum.

As a stylistic matter, it is preferable to invoke class methods through the class object on which they are defined. A code maintainer seeing an expression Point3D.sum would go looking for a definition of the sum method in the Point3D class, and he might have a hard time finding it in the Point class. When invoking a class method with an explicit receiver, you should avoid relying on inheritance—always invoke the class method through the class that defines it.[*]

Within the body of a class method, you may invoke the other class methods of the class without an explicit receiver—they are invoked implicitly on self, and the value of self in a class method is the class on which it was invoked. It is here, inside the body of a class method, that the inheritance of class methods is useful: it allows you to implicitly invoke a class method even when that class method is defined by a superclass.

Finally, note that class methods can use super just as instance methods can to invoke the same-named method in the superclass.

7.3.5 Inheritance and Instance Variables

Instance variables often appear to be inherited in Ruby. Consider this code, for example:

```ruby
class Point3D < Point
  def initialize(x,y,z)
    super(x,y)
    @z = z;
  end

  def to_s
    "(#@x, #@y, #@z)"  # Variables @x and @y inherited?
  end
end
```

The to_s method in Point3D references the @x and @y variables from the superclass Point. This code works as you probably expect it to:

---

[*] The Class.new method is an exception—it is inherited by and invoked on just about every new class we define.

```
Point3D.new(1,2,3).to_s   # => "(1, 2, 3)"
```

Because this code behaves as expected, you may be tempted to say that these variables are inherited. That is not how Ruby works, though. All Ruby objects have a set of instance variables. These are not defined by the object's class—they are simply created when a value is assigned to them. Because instance variables are not defined by a class, they are unrelated to subclassing and the inheritance mechanism.

In this code, `Point3D` defines an `initialize` method that chains to the `initialize` method of its superclass. The chained method assigns values to the variables `@x` and `@y`, which makes those variables come into existence for a particular instance of `Point3D`.

Programmers coming from Java—or from other strongly typed languages in which a class defines a set of fields for its instances—may find that this takes some getting used to. Really, though, it is quite simple: Ruby's instance variables are not inherited and have nothing to do with the inheritance mechanism. The reason that they sometimes appear to be inherited is that instance variables are created by the methods that first assign values to them, and those *methods* are often inherited or chained.

There is an important corollary. Because instance variables have nothing to do with inheritance, it follows that an instance variable used by a subclass cannot "shadow" an instance variable in the superclass. If a subclass uses an instance variable with the same name as a variable used by one of its ancestors, it will overwrite the value of its ancestor's variable. This can be done intentionally, to alter the behavior of the ancestor, or it can be done inadvertently. In the latter case, it is almost certain to cause bugs. As with the inheritance of private methods described earlier, this is another reason why it is only safe to extend Ruby classes when you are familiar with (and in control of) the implementation of the superclass.

Finally, recall that class instance variables are simply instance variables of the `Class` object that represents a class. As such, they are not inherited. Furthermore, the `Point` and `Point3D` objects (we're talking about the `Class` objects themselves, not the classes they represent) are both just instances of `Class`. There is no relationship between them, and no way that one could inherit variables from the other.

7.3.6 Inheritance and Class Variables

Class variables are shared by a class and all of its subclasses. If a class A defines a variable `@@a`, then subclass B can use that variable. Although this may appear, superficially, to be inheritance, is it actually something different.

The difference becomes clear when we think about setting the value of a class variable. If a subclass assigns a value to a class variable already in use by a superclass, it does not create its own private copy of the class variable, but instead alters the value seen by the superclass. It also alters the shared value seen by all other subclasses of the superclass. Ruby 1.8 prints a warning about this if you run it with `-w`. Ruby 1.9 does not issue this warning.

If a class uses class variables, then any subclass can alter the behavior of the class and all its descendants by changing the value of the shared class variable. This is a strong argument for the use of class instance variables instead of class variables.

The following code demonstrates the sharing of class variables. It outputs 123:

```
class A
  @@value = 1                    # A class variable
  def A.value; @@value; end      # An accessor method for it
end
print A.value                    # Display value of A's class variable
class B < A; @@value = 2; end    # Subclass alters shared class variable
print A.value                    # Superclass sees altered value
class C < A; @@value = 3; end    # Another alters shared variable again
print B.value                    # 1st subclass sees value from 2nd subclass
```

7.3.7 Inheritance of Constants

Constants are inherited and can be overridden, much like instance methods can. There is, however, a very important difference between the inheritance of methods and the inheritance of constants.

Our Point3D class can use the ORIGIN constant defined by its Point superclass, for example. Although the clearest style is to qualify constants with their defining class, Point3D could also refer to this constant with an unqualified ORIGIN or even as Point3D::ORIGIN.

Where inheritance of constants becomes interesting is when a class like Point3D redefines a constant. A three-dimensional point class probably wants a constant named ORIGIN to refer to a three-dimensional point, so Point3D is likely to include a line like this:

```
ORIGIN = Point3D.new(0,0,0)
```

As you know, Ruby issues a warning when a constant is redefined. In this case, however, this is a newly created constant. We now have two constants Point::ORIGIN and Point3D::ORIGIN.

The important difference between constants and methods is that constants are looked up in the lexical scope of the place they are used before they are looked up in the inheritance hierarchy (§7.9 has details). This means that if Point3D inherits methods that use the constant ORIGIN, the behavior of those inherited methods will not change when Point3D defines its own version of ORIGIN.

7.4 Object Creation and Initialization

Objects are typically created in Ruby by calling the new method of their class. This section explains exactly how that works, and it also explains other mechanisms (such as cloning and unmarshaling) that create objects. Each subsection explains how you can customize the initialization of the newly created objects.

7.4.1 new, allocate, and initialize

Every class inherits the class method new. This method has two jobs: it must allocate a new object—actually bring the object into existence—and it must initialize the object. It delegates these two jobs to the allocate and initialize methods, respectively. If the new method were actually written in Ruby, it would look something like this:

```
def new(*args)
  o = self.allocate   # Create a new object of this class
  o.initialize(*args) # Call the object's initialize method with our args
  o                   # Return new object; ignore return value of initialize
end
```

allocate is an instance method of Class, and it is inherited by all class objects. Its purpose is to create a new instance of the class. You can call this method yourself to create uninitialized instances of a class. But don't try to override it; Ruby always invokes this method directly, ignoring any overriding versions you may have defined.

initialize is an instance method. Most classes need one, and every class that extends a class other than Object should use super to chain to the initialize method of the superclass. The usual job of the initialize method is to create instance variables for the object and set them to their initial values. Typically, the value of these instance variables are derived from the arguments that the client code passed to new and that new passed to initialize. initialize does not need to return the initialized object. In fact, the return value of initialize is ignored. Ruby implicitly makes the initialize method private, which means that you cannot explicitly invoke it on an object.

Class::new and Class#new

Class defines two methods named new. One, Class#new, is an instance method, and the other, Class::new, is a class method (we use the disambiguating naming convention of the *ri* tool here). The first is the instance method that we've been describing here; it is inherited by all class objects, becoming a class method of the class, and is used to create and initialize new instances.

The class method Class::new is the Class class' own version of the method, and it can be used to create new classes.

7.4.2 Factory Methods

It is often useful to allow instances of a class to be initialized in more than one way. You can often do this by providing parameter defaults on the initialize method. With an initialize method defined as follows, for example, you can invoke new with either two or three arguments:

```
class Point
  # Initialize a Point with two or three coordinates
  def initialize(x, y, z=nil)
```

```
    @x,@y,@z = x, y, z
  end
end
```

Sometimes, however, parameter defaults are not enough, and we need to write *factory methods* other than new for creating instances of our class. Suppose that we want to be able to initialize Point objects using either Cartesian or polar coordinates:

```
class Point
  # Define an initialize method as usual...
  def initialize(x,y)  # Expects Cartesian coordinates
    @x,@y = x,y
  end

  # But make the factory method new private
  private_class_method :new

  def Point.cartesian(x,y)  # Factory method for Cartesian coordinates
    new(x,y)  # We can still call new from other class methods
  end

  def Point.polar(r, theta) # Factory method for polar coordinates
    new(r*Math.cos(theta), r*Math.sin(theta))
  end
end
```

This code still relies on new and initialize, but it makes new private, so that users of the Point class can't call it directly. Instead, they must use one of the custom factory methods.

7.4.3 dup, clone, and initialize_copy

Another way that new objects come into existence is as a result of the dup and clone methods (see §3.8.8). These methods allocate a new instance of the class of the object on which they are invoked. They then copy all the instance variables and the taintedness of the receiver object to the newly allocated object. clone takes this copying a step further than dup—it also copies singleton methods of the receiver object and freezes the copy object if the original is frozen.

If a class defines a method named initialize_copy, then clone and dup will invoke that method on the copied object after copying the instance variables from the original. (clone calls initialize_copy before freezing the copy object, so that initialize_copy is still allowed to modify it.) The initialize_copy method is passed the original object as an argument and has the opportunity to make any changes it desires to the copied object. It cannot create its own copy object, however; the return value of initialize_copy is ignored. Like initialize, Ruby ensures that initialize_copy is always private.

When clone and dup copy instance variables from the original object to the copy, they copy references to the values of those variables; they do not copy the actual values. In other words, these methods perform a shallow copy. And this is one reason that many classes might want to alter the behavior of these methods. Here is code that defines an initialize_copy method to do a deeper copy of internal state:

```
class Point                 # A point in n-space
  def initialize(*coords)   # Accept an arbitrary # of coordinates
    @coords = coords        # Store the coordinates in an array
  end

  def initialize_copy(orig) # If someone copies this Point object
    @coords = @coords.dup   # Make a copy of the coordinates array, too
  end
end
```

The class shown here stores its internal state in an array. Without an initialize_copy method, if an object were copied using clone or dup, the copied object would refer to the same array of state that the original object did. Mutations performed on the copy would affect the state of the original. As this is not the behavior we want, we must define initialize_copy to create a copy of the array as well.

Some classes, such as those that define enumerated types, may want to strictly limit the number of instances that exist. Classes like these need to make their new method private and also probably want to prevent copies from being made. The following code demonstrates one way to do that:

```
class Season
  NAMES = %w{ Spring Summer Autumn Winter }  # Array of season names
  INSTANCES = []                             # Array of Season objects

  def initialize(n)  # The state of a season is just its
    @n = n           # index in the NAMES and INSTANCES arrays
  end

  def to_s           # Return the name of a season
    NAMES[@n]
  end

  # This code creates instances of this class to represent the seasons
  # and defines constants to refer to those instances.
  # Note that we must do this after initialize is defined.
  NAMES.each_with_index do |name,index|
    instance = new(index)          # Create a new instance
    INSTANCES[index] = instance    # Save it in an array of instances
    const_set name, instance       # Define a constant to refer to it
  end

  # Now that we have created all the instances we'll ever need, we must
  # prevent any other instances from being created
  private_class_method :new,:allocate  # Make the factory methods private
  private :dup, :clone                 # Make copying methods private
end
```

This code involves some metaprogramming techniques that will make more sense after you have read Chapter 8. The main point of the code is the line at the end that makes the dup and clone methods private.

Another technique to prevent copying of objects is to use undef to simply remove the clone and dup methods. Yet another approach is to redefine the clone and dup methods so that they raise an exception with an error message that specifically says that copies are not permitted. Such an error message might be helpful to programmers who are using your class.

7.4.4 marshal_dump and marshal_load

A third way that objects are created is when Marshal.load is called to re-create objects previously marshaled (or "serialized") with Marshal.dump. Marshal.dump saves the class of an object and recursively marshals the value of each of its instance variables. This works well—most objects can be saved and restored using these two methods.

Some classes need to alter the way marshaling (and unmarshaling) is done. One reason is to provide a more compact representation of an object's state. Another reason is to avoid saving volatile data, such as the contents of a cache that would just need to be cleared when the object was unmarshaled. You can customize the way an object is marshaled by defining a marshal_dump instance method in the class; it should return a different object (such as a string or an array of selected instance variable values) to be marshaled in place of the receiver object.

If you define a custom marshal_dump method, you must define a matching marshal_load method, of course. marshal_load will be invoked on a newly allocated (with allocate) but uninitialized instance of the class. It will be passed a reconstituted copy of the object returned by marshal_dump, and it must initialize the state of the receiver object based on the state of the object it is passed.

As an example, let's return to the multidimensional Point class we started earlier. If we add the constraint that all coordinates are integers, then we can shave a few bytes off the size of the marshaled object by packing the array of integer coordinates into a string (you may want to use *ri* to read about Array.pack to help you understand this code):

```
class Point                  # A point in n-space
  def initialize(*coords)    # Accept an arbitrary # of coordinates
    @coords = coords         # Store the coordinates in an array
  end

  def marshal_dump           # Pack coords into a string and marshal that
    @coords.pack("w*")
  end

  def marshal_load(s)        # Unpack coords from unmarshaled string
    @coords = s.unpack("w*") # and use them to initialize the object
  end
end
```

If you are writing a class—such as the Season class shown previously—for which you have disabled the clone and dup methods, you will also need to implement custom marshaling methods because dumping and loading an object is an easy way to create a copy of it. You can prevent marshaling completely by defining marshal_dump and marshal_load methods that raise an exception, but that is rather heavy-handed. A more elegant solution is to customize the unmarshaling so that Marshal.load returns an existing object rather than creating a copy.

To accomplish this, we must define a different pair of custom marshaling methods because the return value of marshal_load is ignored. _dump is an instance method that must return the state of the object as a string. The matching _load method is a class method that accepts the string returned by _dump and returns an object. _load is allowed to create a new object or return a reference to an existing one.

To allow marshaling, but prevent copying, of Season objects, we add these methods to the class:

```
class Season
  # We want to allow Season objects to be marshaled, but we don't
  # want new instances to be created when they are unmarshaled.
  def _dump(limit)         # Custom marshaling method
    @n.to_s                # Return index as a string
  end

  def self._load(s)        # Custom unmarshaling method
    INSTANCES[Integer(s)]  # Return an existing instance
  end
end
```

7.4.5 The Singleton Pattern

A *singleton* is a class that has only a single instance. Singletons can be used to store global program state within an object-oriented framework and can be useful alternatives to class methods and class variables.

Singleton Terminology

This section discusses the "Singleton Pattern," a well-known design pattern in object-oriented programming. In Ruby, we have to be careful with the term "singleton" because it is overloaded. A method added to a single object rather than to a class of objects is known as a *singleton method* (see §6.1.4). The implicit class object to which such singleton methods are added is sometimes called a *singleton class* (though this book uses the term *eigenclass* instead; see §7.7).

Properly implementing a singleton requires a number of the tricks shown earlier. The new and allocate methods must be made private, dup and clone must be prevented from making copies, and so on. Fortunately, the Singleton module in the standard library does this work for us; just require 'singleton' and then include Singleton into your

---

class. This defines a class method named `instance`, which takes no arguments and returns the single instance of the class. Define an `initialize` method to perform initialization of the single instance of the class. Note, however, that no arguments will be passed to this method.

As an example, let's return to the `Point` class with which we started this chapter and revisit the problem of collecting point creation statistics. Instead of storing those statistics in class variables of the `Point` class itself, we'll use a singleton instance of a `PointStats` class:

```
require 'singleton'          # Singleton module is not built-in

class PointStats             # Define a class
  include Singleton          # Make it a singleton

  def initialize             # A normal initialization method
    @n, @totalX, @totalY = 0, 0.0, 0.0
  end

  def record(point)          # Record a new point
    @n += 1
    @totalX += point.x
    @totalY += point.y
  end

  def report                 # Report point statistics
    puts "Number of points created: #@n"
    puts "Average X coordinate: #{@totalX/@n}"
    puts "Average Y coordinate: #{@totalY/@n}"
  end
end
```

With a class like this in place, we might write the `initialize` method for our `Point` class like this:

```
def initialize(x,y)
  @x,@y = x,y
  PointStats.instance.record(self)
end
```

The `Singleton` module automatically creates the `instance` class method for us, and we invoke the regular instance method `record` on that singleton instance. Similarly, when we want to query the point statistics, we write:

```
PointStats.instance.report
```

7.5 Modules

Like a class, a *module* is a named group of methods, constants, and class variables. Modules are defined much like classes are, but the `module` keyword is used in place of the `class` keyword. Unlike a class, however, a module cannot be instantiated, and it cannot be subclassed. Modules stand alone; there is no "module hierarchy" of inheritance.

Modules are used as namespaces and as mixins. The subsections that follow explain these two uses.

Just as a class object is an instance of the Class class, a module object is an instance of the Module class. Class is a subclass of Module. This means that all classes are modules, but not all modules are classes. Classes can be used as namespaces, just as modules can. Classes cannot, however, be used as mixins.

7.5.1 Modules as Namespaces

Modules are a good way to group related methods when object-oriented programming is not necessary. Suppose, for example, you were writing methods to encode and decode binary data to and from text using the Base64 encoding. There is no need for special encoder and decoder objects, so there is no reason to define a class here. All we need are two methods: one to encode and one to decode. We could define just two global methods:

```
def base64_encode
end

def base64_decode
end
```

To prevent namespace collisions with other encoding and decoding methods, we've given our method names the base64 prefix. This solution works, but most programmers prefer to avoid adding methods to the global namespace when possible. A better solution, therefore, is to define the two methods within a Base64 module:

```
module Base64
  def self.encode
  end

  def self.decode
  end
end
```

Note that we define our methods with a self. prefix, which makes them "class methods" of the module. We could also explicitly reuse the module name and define the methods like this:

```
module Base64
  def Base64.encode
  end

  def Base64.decode
  end
end
```

Defining the methods this way is more repetitive, but it more closely mirrors the invocation syntax of these methods:

```
# This is how we invoke the methods of the Base64 module
text = Base64.encode(data)
data = Base64.decode(text)
```

Note that module names must begin with a capital letter, just as class names do. Defining a module creates a constant with the same name as the module. The value of this constant is the `Module` object that represents the module.

Modules may also contain constants. Our Base64 implementation would likely use a constant to hold a string of the 64 characters used as digits in Base64:

```
module Base64
  DIGITS = 'ABCDEFGHIJKLMNOPQRSTUVWXYZ' \
           'abcdefghijklmnopqrstuvwxyz' \
           '0123456789+/'
end
```

Outside the `Base64` module, this constant can be referred to as `Base64::DIGITS`. Inside the module, our `encode` and `decode` methods can refer to it by its simple name `DIGITS`. If the two methods had some need to share nonconstant data, they could use a class variable (with a `@@` prefix), just as they could if they were defined in a class.

7.5.1.1 Nested namespaces

Modules, including classes, may be nested. This creates nested namespaces but has no other effect: a class or module nested within another has no special access to the class or module it is nested within. To continue with our Base64 example, let's suppose that we wanted to define special classes for encoding and decoding. Because the `Encoder` and `Decoder` classes are still related to each other, we'll nest them within a module:

```
module Base64
  DIGITS = 'ABCDEFGHIJKLMNOPQRSTUVWXYZabcdefghijklmnopqrstuvwxyz0123456789+/'

  class Encoder
    def encode
    end
  end

  class Decoder
    def decode
    end
  end

  # A utility function for use by both classes
  def Base64.helper
  end
end
```

By structuring our code this way, we've defined two new classes, `Base64::Encoder` and `Base64::Decoder`. Inside the `Base64` module, the two classes can refer to each other by their unqualified names, without the `Base64` prefix. And each of the classes can use the `DIGITS` constant without a prefix.

On the other hand, consider the `Base64.helper` utility function. The nested `Encoder` and `Decoder` classes have no special access to the methods of the containing module, and they must refer to this helper method by its fully qualified name: `Base64.helper`.

Because classes are modules, they too can be nested. Nesting one class within another only affects the namespace of the inner class; it does not give that class any special access to the methods or variables of the outer class. If your implementation of a class requires a helper class, a proxy class, or some other class that is not part of a public API, you may want to consider nesting that internal class within the class that uses it. This keeps the namespace tidy but does not actually make the nested class private in any way.

See §7.9 for an explanation of how constant names are resolved when modules are nested.

7.5.2 Modules As Mixins

The second use of modules is more powerful than the first. If a module defines instance methods instead of the class methods, those instance methods can be mixed in to other classes. `Enumerable` and `Comparable` are well-known examples of mixin modules. `Enumerable` defines useful iterators that are implemented in terms of an `each` iterator. `Enumerable` doesn't define the `each` method itself, but any class that defines it can mix in the `Enumerable` module to instantly add many useful iterators. `Comparable` is similar; it defines comparison operators in terms of the general-purpose comparator `<=>`. If your class defines `<=>`, you can mix in `Comparable` to get `<`, `<=`, `== >`, `>=`, and `between?` for free.

To mix a module into a class, use `include`. `include` is usually used as if it were a language keyword:

```
class Point
  include Comparable
end
```

In fact, it is a private instance method of `Module`, implicitly invoked on `self`—the class into which the module is being included. In method form, this code would be:

```
class Point
  include(Comparable)
end
```

Because `include` is a private method, it must be invoked as a function, and we cannot write `self.include(Comparable)`. The `include` method accepts any number of `Module` objects to mix in, so a class that defines `each` and `<=>` might include the line:

```
include Enumerable, Comparable
```

The inclusion of a module affects the type-checking method is_a? and the switch-equality operator ===. For example, `String` mixes in the `Comparable` module and, in Ruby 1.8, also mixes in the `Enumerable` module:

```
"text".is_a? Comparable       # => true
Enumerable === "text"          # => true in Ruby 1.8, false in 1.9
```

Note that `instance_of?` only checks the class of its receiver, not superclasses or modules, so the following is false:

```
"text".instance_of? Comparable  # => false
```

Although every class is a module, the `include` method does not allow a class to be included within another class. The arguments to `include` must be modules declared with `module`, not classes.

It is legal, however, to include one module into another. Doing this simply makes the instance methods of the included modules into instance methods of the including module. As an example, consider this code from Chapter 5:

```
module Iterable           # Classes that define next can include this module
  include Enumerable      # Define iterators on top of each
  def each                # And define each on top of next
    loop { yield self.next }
  end
end
```

The normal way to mix in a module is with the `Module.include` method. Another way is with `Object.extend`. This method makes the instance methods of the specified module or modules into singleton methods of the receiver object. (And if the receiver object is a `Class` instance, then the methods of the receiver become class methods of that class.) Here is an example:

```
countdown = Object.new      # A plain old object
def countdown.each          # The each iterator as a singleton method
  yield 3
  yield 2
  yield 1
end
countdown.extend(Enumerable) # Now the object has all Enumerable methods
print countdown.sort         # Prints "[1, 2, 3]"
```

7.5.3 Includable Namespace Modules

It is possible to define modules that define a namespace but still allow their methods to be mixed in. The `Math` module works like this:

```
Math.sin(0)    # => 0.0: Math is a namespace
include Math    # The Math namespace can be included
sin(0)          # => 0.0: Now we have easy access to the functions
```

The `Kernel` module also works like this: we can invoke its methods through the `Kernel` namespace, or as private methods of `Object`, into which it is included.

If you want to create a module like `Math` or `Kernel`, define your methods as instance methods of the module. Then use `module_function` to convert those methods to "module functions." `module_function` is a private instance method of `Module`, much like the `public`, `protected`, and `private` methods. It accepts any number of method names (as symbols or strings) as arguments. The primary effect of calling `module_function` is that it makes class method copies of the specified methods. A secondary effect is that it makes the instance methods private (we'll have more to say about this shortly).

Like the `public`, `protected`, and `private` methods, the `module_function` method can also be invoked with no arguments. When invoked in this way, any instance methods subsequently defined in the module will be module functions: they will become public class methods and private instance methods. Once you have invoked `module_function` with no arguments, it remains in effect for the rest of the module definition—so if you want to define methods that are not module functions, define those first.

It may seem surprising at first that `module_function` makes the instance methods of a module private. The reason to do this is not really for access control, as obviously the methods are also available publicly through the module's namespace. Instead, the methods are made private to restrict them to function-style invocation without an explicit receiver. (The reason that these are called module *functions* instead of module methods is that they must be invoked in functional style.) Forcing included module functions to be invoked without a receiver makes it less likely that they'll be mistaken for true instance methods. Suppose we're defining a class whose methods perform a lot of trigonometry. For our own convenience, we include the `Math` module. Then we can invoke the `sin` method as a function instead of calling `Math.sin`. The `sin` method is implicitly invoked on `self`, but we don't actually expect it to do anything to `self`.

When defining a module function, you should avoid using `self`, because the value of `self` will depend on how it is invoked. It is certainly possible to define a module function that behaves differently depending on how it is invoked. But if you are going to do that, then it makes more sense to simply define one class method and one instance method.

7.6 Loading and Requiring Modules

Ruby programs may be broken up into multiple files, and the most natural way to partition a program is to place each nontrivial class or module into a separate file. These separate files can then be reassembled into a single program (and, if well-designed, can be reused by other programs) using `require` or `load`. These are global functions defined in `Kernel`, but are used like language keywords. The same `require` method is also used for loading files from the standard library.

`load` and `require` serve similar purposes, though `require` is much more commonly used than `load`. Both functions can load and execute a specified file of Ruby source code. If the file to load is specified with an absolute path, or is relative to ~ (the user's home directory), then that specific file is loaded. Usually, however, the file is specified as a relative path, and `load` and `require` search for it relative to the directories of Ruby's load path (details on the load path appear below).

Ruby 1.9 also defines a `require_relative` method. It works like `require`, except that it ignores the load path and searches for the named file relative to the directory from which the invoking code was loaded.

Despite their overall similarities, there are important differences between `load` and `require`:

- In addition to loading source code, `require` can also load binary extensions to Ruby. Binary extensions are, of course, implementation-dependent, but in C-based implementations, they typically take the form of shared library files with extensions like *.so* or *.dll*.

- `load` expects a complete filename including an extension. `require` is usually passed a library name, with no extension, rather than a filename. In that case, it searches for a file that has the library name as its base name and an appropriate source or native library extension. If a directory contains both an *.rb* source file and a binary extension file, `require` will load the source file instead of the binary file.

- `load` can load the same file multiple times. `require` tries to prevent multiple loads of the same file. (`require` can be fooled, however, if you use two different, but equivalent, paths to the same library file. In Ruby 1.9, `require` expands relative paths to absolute paths, which makes it somewhat harder to fool.) `require` keeps track of the files that have been loaded by appending them to the global array `$"` (also known as `$LOADED_FEATURES`). `load` does not do this.

- `load` loads the specified file at the current `$SAFE` level. `require` loads the specified library with `$SAFE` set to `0`, even if the code that called `require` has a higher value for that variable. See §10.5 for more on `$SAFE` and Ruby's security system. (Note that if `$SAFE` is set to a value higher than `0`, `require` will refuse to load any file with a tainted filename or from a world-writable directory. In theory, therefore, it should be safe for `require` to load files with a reduced `$SAFE` level.)

The subsections that follow provide further details about the behavior of `load` and `require`.

7.6.1 The Load Path

Ruby's load path is an array that you can access using either of the global variables `$LOAD_PATH` or `$:`. (The mnemonic for this global is that colons are used as path separator characters on Unix-like operating systems.) Each element of the array is the name of a directory that Ruby will search for files to load. Directories at the start of the array are searched before directories at the end of the array. The elements of `$LOAD_PATH` must be strings in Ruby 1.8, but in Ruby 1.9, they may be strings or any object that has a `to_path` method that returns a string.

The default value of `$LOAD_PATH` depends on your implementation of Ruby, on the operating system it is running on, and even on where in your filesystem you installed it. Here is a typical value for Ruby 1.8, obtained with `ruby -e 'puts $:'`:

```
/usr/lib/site_ruby/1.8
/usr/lib/site_ruby/1.8/i386-linux
/usr/lib/site_ruby
/usr/lib/ruby/1.8
/usr/lib/ruby/1.8/i386-linux
.
```

The */usr/lib/ruby/1.8/* directory is where the Ruby standard library is installed. The */usr/lib/ruby/1.8/i386-linux/* directory holds Linux binary extensions for the standard library. The *site_ruby* directories in the path are for site-specific libraries that you have installed. Note that site-specific directories are searched first, which means that you can override the standard library with files installed here. The current working directory "." is at the end of the search path. This is the directory from which a user invokes your Ruby program; it is not the same as the directory in which your Ruby program is installed.

In Ruby 1.9, the default load path is more complicated. Here is a typical value:

```
/usr/local/lib/ruby/gems/1.9/gems/rake-0.7.3/lib
/usr/local/lib/ruby/gems/1.9/gems/rake-0.7.3/bin
/usr/local/lib/ruby/site_ruby/1.9
/usr/local/lib/ruby/site_ruby/1.9/i686-linux
/usr/local/lib/ruby/site_ruby
/usr/local/lib/ruby/vendor_ruby/1.9
/usr/local/lib/ruby/vendor_ruby/1.9/i686-linux
/usr/local/lib/ruby/vendor_ruby
/usr/local/lib/ruby/1.9
/usr/local/lib/ruby/1.9/i686-linux
.
```

One minor load path change in Ruby 1.9 is the inclusion of *vendor_ruby* directories that are searched after *site_ruby* and before the standard library. These are intended for customizations provided by operating system vendors.

The more significant load path change in Ruby 1.9 is the inclusion of RubyGems installation directories. In the path shown here, the first two directories searched are for the *rake* package installed with the *gem* command of the RubyGems package management system. There is only one gem installed in this example, but if you have many gems on your system, your default load path may become quite long. (When running programs that do not use gems, you may get a minor speed boost by invoking Ruby with the `--disable-gems` command-line option, which prevents these directories from being added to the load path.) If more than one version of a gem is installed, the version with the highest version number is included in the default load path. Use the `Kernel.gem` method to alter this default.

RubyGems is built into Ruby 1.9: the *gem* command is distributed with Ruby and can be used to install new packages whose installation directories are automatically added to the default load path. In Ruby 1.8, RubyGems must be installed separately (though some distributions of Ruby 1.8 may automatically bundle it), and gem installation directories are never added to the load path. Instead, Ruby 1.8 programs require the rubygems module. Doing this replaces the default require method with a new version that knows where to look for installed gems. See §1.2.5 for more on RubyGems.

You can add new directories to the start of Ruby's search path with the -I command-line option to the Ruby interpreter. Use multiple -I options to specify multiple directories, or use a single -I and separate multiple directories from each other with colons (or semicolons on Windows).

Ruby programs can also modify their own load path by altering the contents of the $LOAD_PATH array. Here are some examples:

```
# Remove the current directory from the load path
$:.pop if $:.last == '.'

# Add the installation directory for the current program to
# the beginning of the load path instead of using require_relative.
$LOAD_PATH.unshift File.expand_path($PROGRAM_NAME)

# Add the value of an environment variable to the end of the path
$LOAD_PATH << ENV['MY_LIBRARY_DIRECTORY']
```

Finally, keep in mind that you can bypass the load path entirely by passing absolute filenames (that begin with / or ~) to load or require.

7.6.2 Executing Loaded Code

loadandrequireexecute the code in the specified file immediately. Calling these methods is not, however, equivalent to simply replacing the call to load or require with the code contained by the file.*

Files loaded with load or require are executed in a new top-level scope that is different from the one in which load or require was invoked. The loaded file can see all global variables and constants that have been defined at the time it is loaded, but it does not have access to the local scope from which the load was initiated. The implications of this include the following:

- The local variables defined in the scope from which load or require is invoked are not visible to the loaded file.

- Any local variables created by the loaded file are discarded once the load is complete; they are never visible outside the file in which they are defined.

---

* To put this another way for C programmers: load and require are different from C's #include directive. Passing a file of loaded code to the global eval function is closer to including it directly in a file: eval(File.read(filename)). But even this is not the same, as eval does not set local variables.

- At the start of the loaded file, the value of `self` is always the main object, just as it is when the Ruby interpreter starts running. That is, invoking `load` or `require` within a method invocation does not propagate the receiver object to the loaded file.

- The current module nesting is ignored within the loaded file. You cannot, for example, open a class and then load a file of method definitions. The file will be processed in a top-level scope, not inside any class or module.

7.6.2.1 Wrapped loads

The `load` method has an infrequently used feature that we did not describe earlier. If called with a second argument that is anything other than `nil` or `false`, then it "wraps" the specified file and loads it into an anonymous module. This means that the loaded file cannot affect the global namespace; any constants (including classes and modules) it defines are trapped within the anonymous module. You can use wrapped loads as a security precaution (or as a way to minimize bugs caused by namespace collisions). We'll see in §10.5 that when Ruby is running untrusted code in a "sandbox," that code is not allowed to call `require` and can use `load` only for wrapped loads.

When a file is loaded into an anonymous module, it can still set global variables, and the variables it sets will be visible to the code that loaded it. Suppose you write a file *util.rb* that defines a `Util` module of useful utility methods. If you want those methods to be accessible even if your file is loaded wrapped, you might add the following line to the end of the file:

```ruby
$Util = Util   # Store a reference to this module in a global variable
```

Now, the code that loads *util.rb* into an anonymous namespace can access the utility functions through the global `$Util` instead of the constant `Util`.

In Ruby 1.8, it is even possible to pass the anonymous module itself back to the loading code:

```ruby
if Module.nesting.size > 0      # If we're loaded into a wrapper module
  $wrapper = Module.nesting[0]  # Pass the module back to the loading code
end
```

See §8.1.1 for more on `Module.nesting`.

7.6.3 Autoloading Modules

The `autoload` methods of `Kernel` and `Module` allow lazy loading of files on an as-needed basis. The global `autoload` function allows you to register the name of an undefined constant (typically a class or module name) and a name of the library that defines it. When that constant is first referenced, the named library is loaded using `require`. For example:

```ruby
# Require 'socket' if and when the TCPSocket is first used
autoload :TCPSocket, "socket"
```

The `Module` class defines its own version of `autoload` to work with constants nested within another module.

Use `autoload?` or `Module.autoload?` to test whether a reference to a constant will cause a file to be loaded. This method expects a symbol argument. If a file will be loaded when the constant named by the symbol is referenced, then `autoload?` returns the name of the file. Otherwise (if no autoload was requested, or if the file has already been loaded), `autoload?` returns `nil`.

7.7 Singleton Methods and the Eigenclass

We learned in Chapter 6 that it is possible to define singleton methods—methods that are defined for only a single object rather than a class of objects. To define a singleton method `sum` on an object `Point`, we'd write:

```
def Point.sum
  # Method body goes here
end
```

As noted earlier in this chapter, the class methods of a class are nothing more than singleton methods on the `Class` instance that represents that class.

The singleton methods of an object are not defined by the class of that object. But they are methods and they must be associated with a class of some sort. The singleton methods of an object are instance methods of the anonymous *eigenclass* associated with that object. "Eigen" is a German word meaning (roughly) "self," "own," "particular to," or "characteristic of." The eigenclass is also called the *singleton class* or (less commonly) the *metaclass*. The term "eigenclass" is not uniformly accepted within the Ruby community, but it is the term we'll use in this book.

Ruby defines a syntax for opening the eigenclass of an object and adding methods to it. This provides an alternative to defining singleton methods one by one; we can instead define any number of instance methods of the eigenclass. To open the eigenclass of the object `o`, use `class << o`. For example, we can define class methods of `Point` like this:

```
class << Point
  def class_method1      # This is an instance method of the eigenclass.
  end                    # It is also a class method of Point.

  def class_method2
  end
end
```

If you open the eigenclass of a class object within the definition of a class itself, then you can use `self` instead of repeating the name of the class. To repeat an example from earlier in this chapter:

```
class Point
  # instance methods go here

  class << self
```

```
        # class methods go here as instance methods of the eigenclass
    end
  end
```

Be careful with your syntax. Note that there is considerable difference between the following three lines:

```
class Point            # Create or open the class Point
class Point3D < Point  # Create a subclass of Point
class << Point         # Open the eigenclass of the object Point
```

In general, it is clearer to define class methods as individual singleton methods without explicitly opening the eigenclass.

When you open the eigenclass of an object, `self` refers to the eigenclass object. The idiom for obtaining the eigenclass of an object o is therefore:

```
eigenclass = class << o; self; end
```

We can formalize this into a method of `Object`, so that we can ask for the eigenclass of any object:

```
class Object
  def eigenclass
    class << self; self; end
  end
end
```

Unless you are doing sophisticated metaprogramming with Ruby, you are unlikely to really need an `eigenclass` utility function like the one shown here. It is worth understanding eigenclasses, however, because you'll occasionally see them used in existing code, and because they're an important part of Ruby's method name resolution algorithm, which we describe next.

7.8 Method Lookup

When Ruby evaluates a method invocation expression, it must first figure out which method is to be invoked. The process for doing this is called *method lookup* or *method name resolution*. For the method invocation expression o.m, Ruby performs name resolution with the following steps:

1. First, it checks the eigenclass of o for singleton methods named m.

2. If no method m is found in the eigenclass, Ruby searches the class of o for an instance method named m.

3. If no method m is found in the class, Ruby searches the instance methods of any modules included by the class of o. If that class includes more than one module, then they are searched in the reverse of the order in which they were included. That is, the most recently included module is searched first.

4. If no instance method m is found in the class of o or in its modules, then the search moves up the inheritance hierarchy to the superclass. Steps 2 and 3 are repeated

for each class in the inheritance hierarchy until each ancestor class and its included modules have been searched.

5. If no method named m is found after completing the search, then a method named method_missing is invoked instead. In order to find an appropriate definition of this method, the name resolution algorithm starts over at step 1. The Kernel module provides a default implementation of method_missing, so this second pass of name resolution is guaranteed to succeed. The method_missing method is covered in more detail in §8.4.5.

Let's consider a concrete example of this algorithm. Suppose we have the following code:

```
message = "hello"
message.world
```

We want to invoke a method named world on the String instance "hello". Name resolution proceeds as follows:

1. Check the eigenclass for singleton methods. There aren't any in this case.
2. Check the String class. There is no instance method named world.
3. Check the Comparable and Enumerable modules of the String class for an instance method named world. Neither module defines such a method.
4. Check the superclass of String, which is Object. The Object class does not define a method named world, either.
5. Check the Kernel module included by Object. The world method is not found here either, so we now switch to looking for a method named method_missing.
6. Look for method_missing in each of the spots above (the eigenclass of the String object, the String class, the Comparable and Enumerable modules, the Object class, and the Kernel module). The first definition of method_missing we find is in the Kernel module, so this is the method we invoke. What it does is raise an exception:

```
NoMethodError: undefined method `world' for "hello":String
```

This may seem like it requires Ruby to perform an exhaustive search every time it invokes a method. In typical implementations, however, successful method lookups will be cached so that subsequent lookups of the same name (with no intervening method definitions) will be very quick.

7.8.1 Class Method Lookup

The name resolution algorithm for class methods is exactly the same as it is for instance methods, but there is a twist. Let's start with a simple case, without the twist. Here is a class C that defines no class methods of its own:

```
class C
end
```

Remember that after we define a class like this, the constant C refers to an object that is an instance of Class. Any class methods we define are simply singleton methods of the object C.

Once we have defined a class C, we are likely to write a method invocation expression involving the class method new:

```
c = C.new
```

To resolve the method new, Ruby first looks for singleton methods in the eigenclass of the object C. Our class does not have any class methods, so nothing is found there. After searching the eigenclass, the name resolution algorithm searches the class object of C. The class of C is Class, so Ruby next looks for methods in Class, and it finds an instance method named new there.

You read that right. The method name resolution algorithm for the *class* method C.new ends up locating the *instance* method Class.new. The distinction between instance methods and class methods is a useful one to draw in the object-oriented programming paradigm, but the truth is that in Ruby—where classes are represented by objects—the distinction is somewhat artificial. Every method invocation, whether instance method or class method, has a receiver object and a method name. The name resolution algorithm finds the appropriate method definition for that object. Our object C is an instance of class Class, so we can of course invoke the instance methods of Class through C. Furthermore, Class inherits the instance methods of Module, Object, and Kernel, so those inherited methods are also available as methods of C. The only reason we call these "class methods" is that our object C happens to be a class.

Our class method C.new is found as an instance method of Class. If it had not been found there, however, the name resolution algorithm would have continued just as it would have for an instance method. After searching Class unsuccessfully, we would have looked at modules (Class doesn't include any) and then at the superclass Module. Next, we would search the modules of Module (there aren't any), and finally the superclass of Module, Object, and its module Kernel.

The twist mentioned at the beginning of this section has to do with the fact that class methods are inherited just like instance methods are. Let's define a class method Integer.parse to use as an example:

```
def Integer.parse(text)
  text.to_i
end
```

Because Fixnum is a subclass of Integer, we can invoke this method with an expression like this:

```
n = Fixnum.parse("1")
```

From the description of the method name resolution algorithm that we've seen previously, we know that Ruby would first search the eigenclass of Fixnum for singleton methods. Next, it would search for instance methods of Class, Module, Object, and

Kernel. So where does it find the `parse` method? A class method of `Integer` is just a singleton method of the `Integer` object, which means that it is defined by the eigenclass of `Integer`. So how does this eigenclass of `Integer` get involved in the name resolution algorithm?

Class objects are special: they have superclasses. The eigenclasses of class objects are also special: they have superclasses, too. The eigenclass of an ordinary object stands alone and has no superclass. Let's use the names `Fixnum'` and `Integer'` to refer to the eigenclasses of `Fixnum` and `Integer`. The superclass of `Fixnum'` is `Integer'`.

With that twist in mind, we can now more fully explain the method name resolution algorithm and say that when Ruby searches for singleton methods in the eigenclass of an object, it also searches the superclass (and all ancestors) of the eigenclass as well. So when looking for a class method of `Fixnum`, Ruby first checks the singleton methods of `Fixnum`, `Integer`, `Numeric`, and `Object`, and then checks the instance methods of `Class`, `Module`, `Object`, and `Kernel`.

7.9 Constant Lookup

When a constant is referenced without any qualifying namespace, the Ruby interpreter must find the appropriate definition of the constant. To do so, it uses a name resolution algorithm, just as it does to find method definitions. However, constants are resolved much differently than methods.

Ruby first attempts to resolve a constant reference in the lexical scope of the reference. This means that it first checks the class or module that encloses the constant reference to see if that class or module defines the constant. If not, it checks the next enclosing class or module. This continues until there are no more enclosing classes or modules. Note that top-level or "global" constants are not considered part of the lexical scope and are not considered during this part of constant lookup. The class method `Module.nesting` returns the list of classes and modules that are searched in this step, in the order they are searched.

If no constant definition is found in the lexically enclosing scope, Ruby next tries to resolve the constant in the inheritance hierarchy by checking the ancestors of the class or module that referred to the constant. The `ancestors` method of the containing class or module returns the list of classes and modules searched in this step.

If no constant definition is found in the inheritance hierarchy, then top-level constant definitions are checked.

If no definition can be found for the desired constant, then the `const_missing` method —if there is one—of the containing class or module is called and given the opportunity to provide a value for the constant. This `const_missing` hook is covered in Chapter 8, and Example 8-3 illustrates its use.

There are a few points about this constant lookup algorithm that are worth noting in more detail:

- Constants defined in enclosing modules are found in preference to constants defined in included modules.
- The modules included by a class are searched before the superclass of the class.
- The `Object` class is part of the inheritance hierarchy of all classes. Top-level constants, defined outside of any class or module, are like top-level methods: they are implicitly defined in `Object`. When a top-level constant is referenced from within a class, therefore, it is resolved during the search of the inheritance hierarchy. If the constant is referenced within a module definition, however, an explicit check of `Object` is needed after searching the ancestors of the module.
- The `Kernel` module is an ancestor of `Object`. This means that constants defined in `Kernel` behave like top-level constants but can be overridden by true top-level constants, that are defined in `Object`.

Example 7-1 defines and resolves constants in six different scopes and demonstrates the constant name lookup algorithm described previously.

Example 7-1. Constant name resolution
```
module Kernel
  # Constants defined in Kernel
  A = B = C = D = E = F = "defined in kernel"
end

# Top-level or "global" constants defined in Object
A = B = C = D = E = "defined at toplevel"

class Super
  # Constants defined in a superclass
  A = B = C = D = "defined in superclass"
end

module Included
  # Constants defined in an included module
  A = B = C = "defined in included module"
end

module Enclosing
  # Constants defined in an enclosing module
  A = B = "defined in enclosing module"

  class Local < Super
    include Included

    # Locally defined constant
    A = "defined locally"

    # The list of modules searched, in the order searched
    # [Enclosing::Local, Enclosing, Included, Super, Object, Kernel]
```

```
    search = (Module.nesting + self.ancestors + Object.ancestors).uniq

    puts A  # Prints "defined locally"
    puts B  # Prints "defined in enclosing module"
    puts C  # Prints "defined in included module"
    puts D  # Prints "defined in superclass"
    puts E  # Prints "defined at toplevel"
    puts F  # Prints "defined in kernel"
  end
end
```

## CHAPTER 8

Reflection and Metaprogramming

We've seen that Ruby is a very dynamic language; you can insert new methods into classes at runtime, create aliases for existing methods, and even define methods on individual objects. In addition, it has a rich API for *reflection*. Reflection, also called *introspection*, simply means that a program can examine its state and its structure. A Ruby program can, for example, obtain the list of methods defined by the Hash class, query the value of a named instance variable within a specified object, or iterate through all Regexp objects currently defined by the interpreter. The reflection API actually goes further and allows a program to alter its state and structure. A Ruby program can dynamically set named variables, invoke named methods, and even define new classes and new methods.

Ruby's reflection API—along with its generally dynamic nature, its blocks-and-iterators control structures, and its parentheses-optional syntax—makes it an ideal language for *metaprogramming*. Loosely defined, metaprogramming is writing programs (or frameworks) that help you write programs. To put it another way, metaprogramming is a set of techniques for extending Ruby's syntax in ways that make programming easier. Metaprogramming is closely tied to the idea of writing *domain-specific languages*, or DSLs. DSLs in Ruby typically use method invocations and blocks as if they were keywords in a task-specific extension to the language.

This chapter starts with several sections that introduce Ruby's reflection API. This API is surprisingly rich and consists of quite a few methods. These methods are defined, for the most part, by Kernel, Object, and Module.

As you read these introductory sections, keep in mind that reflection is not, by itself, metaprogramming. Metaprogramming typically extends the syntax or the behavior of Ruby in some way, and often involves more than one kind of reflection. After introducing Ruby's core reflection API, this chapter moves on to demonstrate, by example, common metaprogramming techniques that use that API.

Note that this chapter covers advanced topics. You can be a productive Ruby programmer without ever reading this chapter. You may find it helpful to read the remaining chapters of this book first, and then return to this chapter. Consider this chapter a kind of final exam: if you understand the examples (particularly the longer ones at the end), then you have mastered Ruby!

8.1 Types, Classes, and Modules

The most commonly used reflective methods are those for determining the type of an object—what class it is an instance of and what methods it responds to. We introduced most of these important methods early in this book in §3.8.4. To review:

o.class
    Returns the class of an object o.

c.superclass
    Returns the superclass of a class c.

o.instance_of? c
> Determines whether the object o.class == c.

o.is_a? c
> Determines whether o is an instance of c, or of any of its subclasses. If c is a module, this method tests whether o.class (or any of its ancestors) includes the module.

o.kind_of? c
> kind_of? is a synonym for is_a?.

c === o
> For any class or module c, determines if o.is_a?(c).

o.respond_to? name
> Determines whether the object o has a public or protected method with the specified name. Pass true as the second argument to check private methods as well.

8.1.1 Ancestry and Modules

In addition to these methods that you've already seen, there are a few related reflective methods for determining the ancestors of a class or module and for determining which modules are included by a class or module. These methods are easy to understand when demonstrated:

```
module A; end           # Empty module
module B; include A; end;   # Module B includes A
class C; include B; end;    # Class C includes module B

C < B                   # => true: C includes B
B < A                   # => true: B includes A
C < A                   # => true
Fixnum < Integer        # => true: all fixnums are integers
Integer < Comparable    # => true: integers are comparable
Integer < Fixnum        # => false: not all integers are fixnums
String < Numeric        # => nil: strings are not numbers

A.ancestors            # => [A]
B.ancestors            # => [B, A]
C.ancestors            # => [C, B, A, Object, Kernel]
String.ancestors       # => [String, Enumerable, Comparable, Object, Kernel]
                       # Note: in Ruby 1.9 String is no longer Enumerable

C.include?(B)          # => true
C.include?(A)          # => true
B.include?(A)          # => true
A.include?(A)          # => false
A.include?(B)          # => false

A.included_modules     # => []
B.included_modules     # => [A]
C.included_modules     # => [B, A, Kernel]
```

This code demonstrates `include?`, which is a public instance method defined by the `Module` class. But it also features two invocations of the `include` method (without the question mark), which is a private instance method of `Module`. As a private method, it can only be invoked implicitly on `self`, which restricts its usage to the body of a `class` or `module` definition. This use of the method `include` as if it were a keyword is a meta-programming example in Ruby's core syntax.

A method related to the private `include` method is the public `Object.extend`. This method extends an object by making the instance methods of each of the specified modules into singleton methods of the object:

```ruby
module Greeter; def hi; "hello"; end; end # A silly module
s = "string object"
s.extend(Greeter)      # Add hi as a singleton method to s
s.hi                   # => "hello"
String.extend(Greeter) # Add hi as a class method of String
String.hi              # => "hello"
```

The class method `Module.nesting` is not related to module inclusion or ancestry; instead, it returns an array that specifies the nesting of modules at the current location. `Module.nesting[0]` is the current class or module, `Module.nesting[1]` is the containing class or module, and so on:

```ruby
module M
  class C
    Module.nesting   # => [M::C, M]
  end
end
```

8.1.2 Defining Classes and Modules

Classes and modules are instances of the `Class` and `Module` classes. As such, you can create them dynamically:

```ruby
M = Module.new       # Define a new module M
C = Class.new        # Define a new class C
D = Class.new(C) {   # Define a subclass of C
  include M          # that includes module M
}
D.to_s               # => "D": class gets constant name by magic
```

One nice feature of Ruby is that when a dynamically created anonymous module or class is assigned to a constant, the name of that constant is used as the name of the module or class (and is returned by its `name` and `to_s` methods).

8.2 Evaluating Strings and Blocks

One of the most powerful and straightforward reflective features of Ruby is its `eval` method. If your Ruby program can generate a string of valid Ruby code, the `Kernel.eval` method can evaluate that code:

```
x = 1
eval "x + 1"  # => 2
```

eval is a very powerful function, but unless you are actually writing a shell program (like *irb*) that executes lines of Ruby code entered by a user you are unlikely to really need it. (And in a networked context, it is almost never safe to call eval on text received from a user, as it could contain malicious code.) Inexperienced programmers sometimes end up using eval as a crutch. If you find yourself using it in your code, see if there isn't a way to avoid it. Having said that, there are some more useful ways to use eval and eval-like methods.

8.2.1 Bindings and eval

A Binding object represents the state of Ruby's variable bindings at some moment. The Kernel.binding object returns the bindings in effect at the location of the call. You may pass a Binding object as the second argument to eval, and the string you specify will be evaluated in the context of those bindings. If, for example, we define an instance method that returns a Binding object that represents the variable bindings inside an object, then we can use those bindings to query and set the instance variables of that object. We might accomplish this as follows:

```
class Object      # Open Object to add a new method
  def bindings    # Note plural on this method
    binding       # This is the predefined Kernel method
  end
end

class Test        # A simple class with an instance variable
  def initialize(x); @x = x; end
end

t = Test.new(10)       # Create a test object
eval("@x", t.bindings) # => 10: We've peeked inside t
```

Note that it is not actually necessary to define an Object.bindings method of this sort to peek at the instance variables of an object. Several other methods described shortly offer easier ways to query (and set) the value of the instance variables of an object.

As described in §6.6.2, the Proc object defines a public binding method that returns a Binding object representing the variable bindings in effect for the body of that Proc. Furthermore, the eval method allows you to pass a Proc object instead of a Binding object as the second argument.

Ruby 1.9 defines an eval method on Binding objects, so instead of passing a Binding as the second argument to the global eval, you can instead invoke the eval method on a Binding. Which one you choose is purely a stylistic matter; the two techniques are equivalent.

8.2.2 instance_eval and class_eval

The `Object` class defines a method named `instance_eval`, and the `Module` class defines a method named `class_eval`. (`module_eval` is a synonym for `class_eval`.) Both of these methods evaluate Ruby code, like `eval` does, but there are two important differences. The first difference is that they evaluate the code in the context of the specified object or in the context of the specified module—the object or module is the value of `self` while the code is being evaluated. Here are some examples:

```
o.instance_eval("@x")  # Return the value of o's instance variable @x

# Define an instance method len of String to return string length
String.class_eval("def len; size; end")

# Here's another way to do that
# The quoted code behaves just as if it was inside "class String" and "end"
String.class_eval("alias len size")

# Use instance_eval to define class method String.empty
# Note that quotes within quotes get a little tricky...
String.instance_eval("def empty; ''; end")
```

Note the subtle but crucial difference between `instance_eval` and `class_eval` when the code being evaluated contains a method definition. `instance_eval` defines singleton methods of the object (and this results in class methods when it is called on a class object). `class_eval` defines regular instance methods.

The second important difference between these two methods and the global `eval` is that `instance_eval` and `class_eval` can accept a block of code to evaluate. When passed a block instead of a string, the code in the block is executed in the appropriate context. Here, therefore, are alternatives to the previously shown invocations:

```
o.instance_eval { @x }
String.class_eval {
  def len
    size
  end
}
String.class_eval { alias len size }
String.instance_eval { def empty; ""; end }
```

8.2.3 instance_exec and class_exec

Ruby 1.9 defines two more evaluation methods: `instance_exec` and `class_exec` (and its alias, `module_exec`). These methods evaluate a block (but not a string) of code in the context of the receiver object, as `instance_eval` and `class_eval` do. The difference is that the `exec` methods accept arguments and pass them to the block. Thus, the block of code is evaluated in the context of the specified object, with parameters whose values come from outside the object.

8.3 Variables and Constants

Kernel, Object, and Moduledefine reflective methods for listing the names (as strings) of all defined global variables, currently defined local variables, all instance variables of an object, all class variables of a class or module, and all constants of a class or module:

```ruby
global_variables   # => ["$DEBUG", "$SAFE", ...]
x = 1              # Define a local variable
local_variables    # => ["x"]

# Define a simple class
class Point
  def initialize(x,y); @x,@y = x,y; end # Define instance variables
  @@classvar = 1                        # Define a class variable
  ORIGIN = Point.new(0,0)               # Define a constant
end

Point::ORIGIN.instance_variables # => ["@y", "@x"]
Point.class_variables            # => ["@@classvar"]
Point.constants                  # => ["ORIGIN"]
```

The global_variables, local_variables, instance_variables, class_variables, and constants methods return arrays of strings in Ruby 1.8 and arrays of symbols in Ruby 1.9.

8.3.1 Querying, Setting, and Testing Variables

In addition to listing defined variables and constants, Ruby Object and Module also define reflective methods for querying, setting, and removing instance variables, class variables, and constants. There are no special purpose methods for querying or setting local variables or global variables, but you can use the eval method for this purpose:

```ruby
x = 1
varname = "x"
eval(varname)          # => 1
eval("varname = '$g'") # Set varname to "$g"
eval("#{varname} = x") # Set $g to 1
eval(varname)          # => 1
```

Note that eval evaluates its code in a temporary scope. eval can alter the value of instance variables that already exist. But any new instance variables it defines are local to the invocation of eval and cease to exist when it returns. (It is as if the evaluated code is run in the body of a block—variables local to a block do not exist outside the block.)

You can query, set, and test the existence of instance variables on any object and of class variables and constants on any class or module:

```ruby
o = Object.new
o.instance_variable_set(:@x, 0)   # Note required @ prefix
o.instance_variable_get(:@x)      # => 0
o.instance_variable_defined?(:@x) # => true
```

```
Object.class_variable_set(:@@x, 1)    # Private in Ruby 1.8
Object.class_variable_get(:@@x)       # Private in Ruby 1.8
Object.class_variable_defined?(:@@x) # => true; Ruby 1.9 and later

Math.const_set(:EPI, Math::E*Math::PI)
Math.const_get(:EPI)          # => 8.53973422267357
Math.const_defined? :EPI      # => true
```

In Ruby 1.9, you can pass `false` as the second argument to `const_get` and `const_defined?` to specify that these methods should only look at the current class or module and should not consider inherited constants.

The methods for querying and setting class variables are private in Ruby 1.8. In that version, you can invoke them with `class_eval`:

```
String.class_eval { class_variable_set(:@@x, 1) }  # Set @@x in String
String.class_eval { class_variable_get(:@@x) }     # => 1
```

`Object` and `Module` define private methods for undefining instance variables, class variables, and constants. They all return the value of the removed variable or constant. Because these methods are private, you can't invoke them directly on an object, class, or module, and you must use an `eval` method or the `send` method (described later in this chapter):

```
o.instance_eval { remove_instance_variable :@x }
String.class_eval { remove_class_variable(:@@x) }
Math.send :remove_const, :EPI  # Use send to invoke private method
```

The `const_missing` method of a module is invoked, if there is one, when a reference is made to an undefined constant. You can define this method to return the value of the named constant. (This feature can be used, for example, to implement an autoload facility in which classes or modules are loaded on demand.) Here is a simpler example:

```
def Symbol.const_missing(name)
  name # Return the constant name as a symbol
end
Symbol::Test   # => :Test: undefined constant evaluates to a Symbol
```

8.4 Methods

The `Object` and `Module` classes define a number of methods for listing, querying, invoking, and defining methods. We'll consider each category in turn.

8.4.1 Listing and Testing For Methods

`Object` defines methods for listing the names of methods defined on the object. These methods return arrays of methods names. Those name are strings in Ruby 1.8 and symbols in Ruby 1.9:

```
o = "a string"
o.methods                 # => [ names of all public methods ]
```

```
o.public_methods         # => the same thing
o.public_methods(false)  # Exclude inherited methods
o.protected_methods      # => []: there aren't any
o.private_methods        # => array of all private methods
o.private_methods(false) # Exclude inherited private methods
def o.single; 1; end     # Define a singleton method
o.singleton_methods      # => ["single"] (or [:single] in 1.9)
```

It is also possible to query a class for the methods it defines rather than querying an instance of the class. The following methods are defined by `Module`. Like the `Object` methods, they return arrays of strings in Ruby 1.8 and arrays of symbols in 1.9:

```
String.instance_methods == "s".public_methods        # => true
String.instance_methods(false) == "s".public_methods(false)  # => true
String.public_instance_methods == String.instance_methods    # => true
String.protected_instance_methods      # => []
String.private_instance_methods(false) # => ["initialize_copy",
                                       #     "initialize"]
```

Recall that the class methods of a class or module are singleton methods of the `Class` or `Module` object. So to list class methods, use `Object.singleton_methods`:

```
Math.singleton_methods  # => ["acos", "log10", "atan2", ... ]
```

In addition to these listing methods, the `Module` class defines some predicates for testing whether a specified class or module defines a named instance method:

```
String.public_method_defined? :reverse    # => true
String.protected_method_defined? :reverse # => false
String.private_method_defined? :initialize # => true
String.method_defined? :upcase!           # => true
```

`Module.method_defined?` checks whether the named method is defined as a public or protected method. It serves essentially the same purpose as `Object.respond_to?`. In Ruby 1.9, you can pass `false` as the second argument to specify that inherited methods should not be considered.

8.4.2 Obtaining Method Objects

To query a specific named method, call `method` on any object or `instance_method` on any module. The former returns a callable `Method` object bound to the receiver, and the latter returns an `UnboundMethod`. In Ruby 1.9, you can limit your search to public methods by calling `public_method` and `public_instance_method`. We covered these methods and the objects they return in §6.7:

```
"s".method(:reverse)             # => Method object
String.instance_method(:reverse) # => UnboundMethod object
```

8.4.3 Invoking Methods

As noted earlier, and in §6.7, you can use the `method` method of any object to obtain a `Method` object that represents a named method of that object. `Method` objects have a `call` method just like `Proc` objects do; you can use it to invoke the method.

Usually, it is simpler to invoke a named method of a specified object with `send`:

```
"hello".send :upcase        # => "HELLO": invoke an instance method
Math.send(:sin, Math::PI/2) # => 1.0: invoke a class method
```

`send` invokes on its receiver the method named by its first argument, passing any remaining arguments to that method. The name "send" derives from the object-oriented idiom in which invoking a method is called "sending a message" to an object.

`send` can invoke any named method of an object, including private and protected methods. We saw `send` used earlier to invoke the private method `remove_const` of a `Module` object. Because global functions are really private methods of `Object`, we can use `send` to invoke these methods on any object (though this is not anything that we'd ever actually want to do):

```
"hello".send :puts, "world"        # prints "world"
```

Ruby 1.9 defines `public_send` as an alternative to `send`. This method works like `send`, but will only invoke public methods, not private or protected methods:

```
"hello".public_send :puts, "world"  # raises NoMethodError
```

`send` is a very fundamental method of `Object`, but it has a common name that might be overridden in subclasses. Therefore, Ruby defines `__send__` as a synonym, and issues a warning if you attempt to delete or redefine `__send__`.

8.4.4 Defining, Undefining, and Aliasing Methods

If you want to define a new instance method of a class or module, use `define_method`. This instance method of `Module` takes the name of the new method (as a `Symbol`) as its first argument. The body of the method is provided either by a `Method` object passed as the second argument or by a block. It is important to understand that `define_method` is private. You must be inside the class or module you want to use it on in order to call it:

```
# Add an instance method named m to class c with body b
def add_method(c, m, &b)
  c.class_eval {
    define_method(m, &b)
  }
end

add_method(String, :greet) { "Hello, " + self }

"world".greet   # => "Hello, world"
```

To define a class method (or any singleton method) with `define_method`, invoke it on the eigenclass:

```ruby
def add_class_method(c, m, &b)
  eigenclass = class << c; self; end
  eigenclass.class_eval {
    define_method(m, &b)
  }
end

add_class_method(String, :greet) {|name| "Hello, " + name }

String.greet("world")  # => "Hello, world"
```

In Ruby 1.9, you can more easily use `define_singleton_method`, which is a method of `Object`:

```ruby
String.define_singleton_method(:greet) {|name| "Hello, " + name }
```

One shortcoming of `define_method` is that it does not allow you to specify a method body that expects a block. If you need to dynamically create a method that accepts a block, you will need to use the `def` statement with `class_eval`. And if the method you are creating is sufficiently dynamic, you may not be able to pass a block to `class_eval` and will instead have to specify the method definition as a string to be evaluated. We'll see examples of this later in the chapter.

To create a synonym or an alias for an existing method, you can normally use the `alias` statement:

```ruby
alias plus +        # Make "plus" a synonym for the + operator
```

When programming dynamically, however, you sometimes need to use `alias_method` instead. Like `define_method`, `alias_method` is a private method of `Module`. As a method, it can accept two arbitrary expressions as its arguments, rather than requiring two identifiers to be hardcoded in your source code. (As a method, it also requires a comma between its arguments.) `alias_method` is often used for *alias chaining* existing methods. Here is a simple example; we'll see more later in the chapter:

```ruby
# Create an alias for the method m in the class (or module) c
def backup(c, m, prefix="original")
  n = :"#{prefix}_#{m}"     # Compute the alias
  c.class_eval {            # Because alias_method is private
```

```
      alias_method n, m       # Make n an alias for m
  }
end

backup(String, :reverse)
"test".original_reverse # => "tset"
```

As we learned in §6.1.5, you can use the undef statement to undefine a method. This works only if you can express the name of a method as a hardcoded identifier in your program. If you need to dynamically delete a method whose name has been computed by your program, you have two choices: remove_method or undef_method. Both are private methods of Module. remove_method removes the definition of the method from the current class. If there is a version defined by a superclass, that version will now be inherited. undef_method is more severe; it prevents any invocation of the specified method through an instance of the class, even if there is an inherited version of that method.

If you define a class and want to prevent any dynamic alterations to it, simply invoke the freeze method of the class. Once frozen, a class cannot be altered.

8.4.5 Handling Undefined Methods

When the method name resolution algorithm (see §7.8) fails to find a method, it looks up a method named method_missing instead. When this method is invoked, the first argument is a symbol that names the method that could not be found. This symbol is followed by all the arguments that were to be passed to the original method. If there is a block associated with the method invocation, that block is passed to method_missing as well.

The default implementation of method_missing, in the Kernel module, simply raises a NoMethodError. This exception, if uncaught, causes the program to exit with an error message, which is what you would normally expect to happen when you try to invoke a method that does not exist.

Defining your own method_missing method for a class allows you an opportunity to handle any kind of invocation on instances of the class. The method_missing hook is one of the most powerful of Ruby's dynamic capabilities, and one of the most commonly used metaprogramming techniques. We'll see examples of its use later in this chapter. For now, the following example code adds a method_missing method to the Hash class. It allows us to query or set the value of any named key as if the key were the name of a method:

```
class Hash
  # Allow hash values to be queried and set as if they were attributes.
  # We simulate attribute getters and setters for any key.
  def method_missing(key, *args)
    text = key.to_s

    if text[-1,1] == "="              # If key ends with = set a value
```

```
      self[text.chop.to_sym] = args[0]  # Strip = from key
    else                               # Otherwise...
      self[key]                        # ...just return the key value
    end
  end
end


h = {}         # Create an empty hash object
h.one = 1      # Same as h[:one] = 1
puts h.one     # Prints 1. Same as puts h[:one]
```

8.4.6 Setting Method Visibility

§7.2 introduced public, protected, and private. These look like language keywords but are actually private instance methods defined by Module. These methods are usually used as a static part of a class definition. But, with class_eval, they can also be used dynamically:

```
String.class_eval { private :reverse }
"hello".reverse  # NoMethodError: private method 'reverse'
```

private_class_method and public_class_method are similar, except that they operate on class methods and are themselves public:

```
# Make all Math methods private
# Now we have to include Math in order to invoke its methods
Math.private_class_method *Math.singleton_methods
```

8.5 Hooks

Module, Class, and Objectimplement several callback methods, or *hooks*. These methods are not defined by default, but if you define them for a module, class, or object, then they will be invoked when certain events occur. This gives you an opportunity to extend Ruby's behavior when classes are subclassed, when modules are included, or when methods are defined. Hook methods (except for some deprecated ones not described here) have names that end in "ed."

When a new class is defined, Ruby invokes the class method inherited on the superclass of the new class, passing the new class object as the argument. This allows classes to add behavior to or enforce constraints on their descendants. Recall that class methods are inherited, so that the an inherited method will be invoked if it is defined by any of the ancestors of the new class. Define Object.inherited to receive notification of all new classes that are defined:

```
def Object.inherited(c)
  puts "class #{c} < #{self}"
end
```

When a module is included into a class or into another module, the included class method of the included module is invoked with the class or module object into which it was included as an argument. This gives the included module an opportunity to augment or alter the class in whatever way it wants—it effectively allows a module to define its own meaning for include. In addition to adding methods to the class into which it is included, a module with an included method might also alter the existing methods of that class, for example:

```
module Final            # A class that includes Final can't be subclassed
  def self.included(c)   # When included in class c
    c.instance_eval do   # Define a class method of c
      def inherited(sub) # To detect subclasses
        raise Exception, # And abort with an exception
              "Attempt to create subclass #{sub} of Final class #{self}"
      end
    end
  end
end
```

Similarly, if a module defines a class method named extended, that method will be invoked any time the module is used to extend an object (with Object.extend). The argument to the extended method will be the object that was extended, of course, and the extended method can take whatever actions it wants on that object.

In addition to hooks for tracking classes and the modules they include, there are also hooks for tracking the methods of classes and modules and the singleton methods of arbitrary objects. Define a class method named method_added for any class or module and it will be invoked when an instance method is defined for that class or module:

```
def String.method_added(name)
  puts "New instance method #{name} added to String"
end
```

Note that the method_added class method is inherited by subclasses of the class on which it is defined. But no class argument is passed to the hook, so there is no way to tell whether the named method was added to the class that defines method_added or whether it was added to a subclass of that class. A workaround for this problem is to define an inherited hook on any class that defines a method_added hook. The inherited method can then define a method_added method for each subclass.

When a singleton method is defined for any object, the method singleton_method_added is invoked on that object, passing the name of the new method. Remember that for classes, singleton methods are class methods:

```
def String.singleton_method_added(name)
  puts "New class method #{name} added to String"
end
```

Interestingly, Ruby invokes this singleton_method_added hook when the hook method itself is first defined. Here is another use of the hook. In this case, singleton_method_added is defined as an instance method of any class that includes a module. It is notified of any singleton methods added to instances of that class:

```
# Including this module in a class prevents instances of that class
# from having singleton methods added to them. Any singleton methods added
# are immediately removed again.
module Strict
  def singleton_method_added(name)
    STDERR.puts "Warning: singleton #{name} added to a Strict object"
    eigenclass = class << self; self; end
    eigenclass.class_eval { remove_method name }
  end
end
```

In addition to `method_added` and `singleton_method_added`, there are hooks for tracking when instance methods and singleton methods are removed or undefined. When an instance method is removed or undefined on a class or module, the class methods `method_removed` and `method_undefined` are invoked on that module. When a singleton method is removed or undefined on an object, the methods `singleton_method_removed` and `singleton_method_undefined` are invoked on that object.

Finally, note that the `method_missing` and `const_missing` methods documented elsewhere in this chapter also behave like hook methods.

8.6 Tracing

Ruby defines a number of features for tracing the execution of a program. These are mainly useful for debugging code and printing informative error messages. Two of the simplest features are actual language keywords: `__FILE__` and `__LINE__`. These keyword expressions always evaluate to the name of the file and the line number within that file on which they appear, and they allow an error message to specify the exact location at which it was generated:

```
STDERR.puts "#{__FILE__}:#{__LINE__}): invalid data"
```

As an aside, note that the methods `Kernel.eval`, `Object.instance_eval`, and `Module.class_eval` all accept a filename (or other string) and a line number as their final two arguments. If you are evaluating code that you have extracted from a file of some sort, you can use these arguments to specify the values of `__FILE__` and `__LINE__` for the evaluation.

You have undoubtedly noticed that when an exception is raised and not handled, the error message printed to the console contains filename and line number information. This information is based on `__FILE__` and `__LINE__`, of course. Every `Exception` object has a *backtrace* associated with it that shows exactly where it was raised, where the method that raised the exception was invoked, where that method was invoked, and so on. The `Exception.backtrace` method returns an array of strings containing this information. The first element of this array is the location at which the exception occurred, and each subsequent element is one stack frame higher.

You needn't raise an exception to obtain a current stack trace, however. The `Kernel.caller` method returns the current state of the call stack in the same form as

Exception.backtrace. With no argument, caller returns a stack trace whose first element is the method that invoked the method that calls caller. That is, caller[0] specifies the location from which the current method was invoked. You can also invoke caller with an argument that specifies how many stack frames to drop from the start of the backtrace. The default is 1, and caller(0)[0] specifies the location at which the caller method is invoked. This means, for example, that caller[0] is the same thing as caller(0)[1] and that caller(2) is the same as caller[1..-1].

Stack traces returned by Exception.backtrace and Kernel.caller also include method names. Prior to Ruby 1.9, you must parse the stack trace strings to extract method names. In Ruby 1.9, however, you can obtain the name (as a symbol) of the currently executing method with Kernel.__method__ or its synonym, Kernel.__callee__. __method__ is useful in conjunction with __FILE__ and __LINE__:

```
raise "Assertion failed in #{__method__} at #{__FILE__}:#{__LINE__}"
```

Note that __method__ returns the name by which a method was originally defined, even if the method was invoked through an alias.

Instead of simply printing the filename and number at which an error occurs, you can take it one step further and display the actual line of code. If your program defines a global constant named SCRIPT_LINES__ and sets it equal to a hash, then the require and load methods add an entry to this hash for each file they load. The hash keys are filenames and the values associated with those keys are arrays that contain the lines of those files. If you want to include the main file (rather than just the files it requires) in the hash, initialize it like this:

```
SCRIPT_LINES__ = {__FILE__ => File.readlines(__FILE__)}
```

If you do this, then you can obtain the current line of source code anywhere in your program with this expression:

```
SCRIPT_LINES__[__FILE__][__LINE__-1]
```

Ruby allows you to trace assignments to global variables with Kernel.trace_var. Pass this method a symbol that names a global variable and a string or block of code. When the value of the named variable changes, the string will be evaluated or the block will be invoked. When a block is specified, the new value of the variable is passed as an argument. To stop tracing the variable, call Kernel.untrace_var. In the following example, note the use of caller[1] to determine the program location at which the variable tracing block was invoked:

```
# Print a message every time $SAFE changes
trace_var(:$SAFE) {|v|
  puts "$SAFE set to #{v} at #{caller[1]}"
}
```

The final tracing method is Kernel.set_trace_func, which registers a Proc to be invoked after every line of a Ruby program. set_trace_func is useful if you want to write a debugger module that allows line-by-line stepping through a program, but we won't cover it in any detail here.

8.7 ObjectSpace and GC

The `ObjectSpace` module defines a handful of low-level methods that can be occasionally useful for debugging or metaprogramming. The most notable method is `each_object`, an iterator that can yield every object (or every instance of a specified class) that the interpreter knows about:

```
# Print out a list of all known classes
ObjectSpace.each_object(Class) {|c| puts c }
```

`ObjectSpace._id2ref` is the inverse of `Object.object_id`: it takes an object ID as its argument and returns the corresponding object, or raises a `RangeError` if there is no object with that ID.

`ObjectSpace.define_finalizer` allows the registration of a `Proc` or a block of code to be invoked when a specified object is garbage collected. You must be careful when registering such a finalizer, however, as the finalizer block is not allowed to use the garbage collected object. Any values required to finalize the object must be captured in the scope of the finalizer block, so that they are available without dereferencing the object. Use `ObjectSpace.undefine_finalizer` to delete all finalizer blocks registered for an object.

The final `ObjectSpace` method is `ObjectSpace.garbage_collect`, which forces Ruby's garbage collector to run. Garbage collection functionality is also available through the GC module. `GC.start` is a synonym for `ObjectSpace.garbage_collect`. Garbage collection can be temporarily disabled with `GC.disable`, and it can be enabled again with `GC.enable`.

The combination of the `_id2ref` and `define_finalizer` methods allows the definition of "weak reference" objects, which hold a reference to a value without preventing the value from being garbage collected if they become otherwise unreachable. See the `WeakRef` class in the standard library (in *lib/weakref.rb*) for an example.

8.8 Custom Control Structures

Ruby's use of blocks, coupled with its parentheses-optional syntax, make it very easy to define iterator methods that look like and behave like control structures. The `loop` method of `Kernel` is a simple example. In this section we develop three more examples. The examples here use Ruby's threading API; you may need to read §9.9 to understand all the details.

8.8.1 Delaying and Repeating Execution: after and every

Example 8-1 defines global methods named **after** and **every**. Each takes a numeric argument that represents a number of seconds and should have a block associated with it. **after** creates a new thread and returns the **Thread** object immediately. The newly created thread sleeps for the specified number of seconds and then calls (with no arguments) the block you provided. **every** is similar, but it calls the block repeatedly, sleeping the specified number of seconds between calls. The second argument to **every** is a value to pass to the first invocation of the block. The return value of each invocation becomes the value passed for the next invocation. The block associated with **every** can use **break** to prevent any future invocations.

Here is some example code that uses **after** and **every**:

```
require 'afterevery'

1.upto(5) {|i| after i { puts i} }  # Slowly print the numbers 1 to 5
sleep(5)                            # Wait five seconds
every 1, 6 do |count|               # Now slowly print 6 to 10
  puts count
  break if count == 10
  count + 1                         # The next value of count
end
sleep(6)                            # Give the above time to run
```

The **sleep** call at the end of this code prevents the example program from exiting before the thread created by **every** can complete its count. With that example of how **after** and **every** are used, we are now ready to present their implementation. Remember to consult §9.9 if you don't understand **Thread.new**.

Example 8-1. The after and every methods

```
#
# Define Kernel methods after and every for deferring blocks of code.
# Examples:
#
#   after 1 { puts "done" }
#   every 60 { redraw_clock }
#
# Both methods return Thread objects. Call kill on the returned objects
# to cancel the execution of the code.
#
# Note that this is a very naive implementation. A more robust
# implementation would use a single global timer thread for all tasks,
# would allow a way to retrieve the value of a deferred block, and would
# provide a way to wait for all pending tasks to complete.
#

# Execute block after sleeping the specified number of seconds.
def after(seconds, &block)
  Thread.new do     # In a new thread...
    sleep(seconds)  # First sleep
    block.call      # Then call the block
```

```
    end              # Return the Thread object right away
  end

  # Repeatedly sleep and then execute the block.
  # Pass value to the block on the first invocation.
  # On subsequent invocations, pass the value of the previous invocation.
  def every(seconds, value=nil, &block)
    Thread.new do              # In a new thread...
      loop do                  # Loop forever (or until break in block)
        sleep(seconds)         # Sleep
        value = block.call(value) # And invoke block
      end                      # Then repeat..
    end                        # every returns the Thread
  end
```

8.8.2 Thread Safety with Synchronized Blocks

When writing programs that use multiple threads, it is important that two threads do
not attempt to modify the same object at the same time. One way to do this is to place
the code that must be made thread-safe in a block associated with a call to the
synchronize method of a Mutex object. Again, this is discussed in detail in §9.9. In
Example 8-2 we take this a step further, and emulate Java's synchronized keyword with
a global method named synchronized. This synchronized method expects a single object
argument and a block. It obtains a Mutex associated with the object, and uses
Mutex.synchronize to invoke the block. The tricky part is that Ruby's object, unlike
Java's objects, do not have a Mutex associated with them. So Example 8-2 also defines
an instance method named mutex in Object. Interestingly, the implementation of this
mutex method uses synchronized in its new keyword-style form!

Example 8-2. Simple synchronized blocks

```
require 'thread'  # Ruby 1.8 keeps Mutex in this library

# Obtain the Mutex associated with the object o, and then evaluate
# the block under the protection of that Mutex.
# This works like the synchronized keyword of Java.
def synchronized(o)
  o.mutex.synchronize { yield }
end

# Object.mutex does not actually exist. We've got to define it.
# This method returns a unique Mutex for every object, and
# always returns the same Mutex for any particular object.
# It creates Mutexes lazily, which requires synchronization for
# thread safety.
class Object
  # Return the Mutex for this object, creating it if necessary.
  # The tricky part is making sure that two threads don't call
  # this at the same time and end up creating two different mutexes.
  def mutex
    # If this object already has a mutex, just return it
    return @__mutex if @__mutex
```

```
    # Otherwise, we've got to create a mutex for the object.
    # To do this safely we've got to synchronize on our class object.
    synchronized(self.class) {
      # Check again: by the time we enter this synchronized block,
      # some other thread might have already created the mutex.
      @__mutex = @__mutex || Mutex.new
    }
    # The return value is @__mutex
  end
end

# The Object.mutex method defined above needs to lock the class
# if the object doesn't have a Mutex yet. If the class doesn't have
# its own Mutex yet, then the class of the class (the Class object)
# will be locked. In order to prevent infinite recursion, we must
# ensure that the Class object has a mutex.
Class.instance_eval { @__mutex = Mutex.new }
```

8.9 Missing Methods and Missing Constants

The method_missing method is a key part of Ruby's method lookup algorithm (see §7.8) and provides a powerful way to catch and handle arbitrary invocations on an object. The const_missing method of Module performs a similar function for the constant lookup algorithm and allows us to compute or lazily initialize constants on the fly. The examples that follow demonstrate both of these methods.

8.9.1 Unicode Codepoint Constants with const_missing

Example 8-3 defines a Unicode module that appears to define a constant (a UTF-8 encoded string) for every Unicode codepoint from U+0000 to U+10FFFF. The only practical way to support this many constants is to use the const_missing method. The code makes the assumption that if a constant is referenced once, it is likely to be used again, so the const_missing method calls Module.const_set to define a real constant to refer to each value it computes.

Example 8-3. Unicode codepoint constants with const_missing
```
# This module provides constants that define the UTF-8 strings for
# all Unicode codepoints. It uses const_missing to define them lazily.
# Examples:
#   copyright = Unicode::U00A9
#   euro = Unicode::U20AC
#   infinity = Unicode::U221E
module Unicode
  # This method allows us to define Unicode codepoint constants lazily.
  def self.const_missing(name)  # Undefined constant passed as a symbol
    # Check that the constant name is of the right form.
    # Capital U followed by a hex number between 0000 and 10FFFF.
    if name.to_s =~ /^U([0-9a-fA-F]{4,5}|10[0-9a-fA-F]{4})$/
      # $1 is the matched hexadecimal number. Convert to an integer.
```

```
        codepoint = $1.to_i(16)
        # Convert the number to a UTF-8 string with the magic of Array.pack.
        utf8 = [codepoint].pack("U")
        # Make the UTF-8 string immutable.
        utf8.freeze
        # Define a real constant for faster lookup next time, and return
        # the UTF-8 text for this time.
        const_set(name, utf8)
      else
        # Raise an error for constants of the wrong form.
        raise NameError, "Uninitialized constant: Unicode::#{name}"
      end
    end
  end
end
```

8.9.2 Tracing Method Invocations with method_missing

Earlier in this chapter, we demonstrated an extension to the Hash class using
method_missing. Now, in Example 8-4, we demonstrate the use of method_missing to
delegate arbitrary calls on one object to another object. In this example, we do this in
order to output tracing messages for the object.

Example 8-4 defines an Object.trace instance method and a TracedObject class. The
trace method returns an instance of TracedObject that uses method_missing to catch
invocations, trace them, and delegate them to the object being traced. You might use
it like this:

```
a = [1,2,3].trace("a")
a.reverse
puts a[2]
puts a.fetch(3)
```

This produces the following tracing output:

```
Invoking: a.reverse() at trace1.rb:66
Returning: [3, 2, 1] from a.reverse to trace1.rb:66
Invoking: a.fetch(3) at trace1.rb:67
Raising: IndexError:index 3 out of array from a.fetch
```

Notice that in addition to demonstrating method_missing, Example 8-4 also demonstrates Module.instance_methods, Module.undef_method, and Kernel.caller.

Example 8-4. Tracing method invocations with method_missing
```
# Call the trace method of any object to obtain a new object that
# behaves just like the original, but which traces all method calls
# on that object. If tracing more than one object, specify a name to
# appear in the output. By default, messages will be sent to STDERR,
# but you can specify any stream (or any object that accepts strings
# as arguments to <<).
class Object
  def trace(name="", stream=STDERR)
    # Return a TracedObject that traces and delegates everything else to us.
    TracedObject.new(self, name, stream)
```

```
      end
end

# This class uses method_missing to trace method invocations and
# then delegate them to some other object. It deletes most of its own
# instance methods so that they don't get in the way of method_missing.
# Note that only methods invoked through the TracedObject will be traced.
# If the delegate object calls methods on itself, those invocations
# will not be traced.
class TracedObject
  # Undefine all of our noncritical public instance methods.
  # Note the use of Module.instance_methods and Module.undef_method.
  instance_methods.each do |m|
    m = m.to_sym  # Ruby 1.8 returns strings, instead of symbols
    next if m == :object_id || m == :__id__ || m == :__send__
    undef_method m
  end

  # Initialize this TracedObject instance.
  def initialize(o, name, stream)
    @o = o            # The object we delegate to
    @n = name         # The object name to appear in tracing messages
    @trace = stream   # Where those tracing messages are sent
  end

  # This is the key method of TracedObject. It is invoked for just
  # about any method invocation on a TracedObject.
  def method_missing(*args, &block)
    m = args.shift      # First arg is the name of the method
    begin
      # Trace the invocation of the method.
      arglist = args.map {|a| a.inspect}.join(', ')
      @trace << "Invoking: #{@n}.#{m}(#{arglist}) at #{caller[0]}\n"
      # Invoke the method on our delegate object and get the return value.
      r = @o.send m, *args, &block
      # Trace a normal return of the method.
      @trace << "Returning: #{r.inspect} from #{@n}.#{m} to #{caller[0]}\n"
      # Return whatever value the delegate object returned.
      r
    rescue Exception => e
      # Trace an abnormal return from the method.
      @trace << "Raising: #{e.class}:#{e} from #{@n}.#{m}\n"
      # And re-raise whatever exception the delegate object raised.
      raise
    end
  end

  # Return the object we delegate to.
  def __delegate
    @o
  end
end
```

8.9.3 Synchronized Objects by Delegation

In Example 8-2, we saw a global method `synchronized`, which accepts an object and executes a block under the protection of the `Mutex` associated with that object. Most of the example consisted of the implementation of the `Object.mutex` method. The `synchronized` method was trivial:

```
def synchronized(o)
  o.mutex.synchronize { yield }
end
```

Example 8-5 modifies this method so that, when invoked without a block, it returns a `SynchronizedObject` wrapper around the object. `SynchronizedObject` is a delegating wrapper class based on `method_missing`. It is much like the `TracedObject` class of Example 8-4, but it is written as a subclass of Ruby 1.9's `BasicObject`, so there is no need to explicitly delete the instance methods of Object. Note that the code in this example does not stand alone; it requires the `Object.mutex` method defined earlier.

Example 8-5. Synchronizing methods with method_missing

```
def synchronized(o)
  if block_given?
    o.mutex.synchronize { yield }
  else
    SynchronizedObject.new(o)
  end
end

# A delegating wrapper class using method_missing for thread safety
# Instead of extending Object and deleting our methods we just extend
# BasicObject, which is defined in Ruby 1.9. BasicObject does not
# inherit from Object or Kernel, so the methods of a BasicObject cannot
# invoke any top-level methods: they are just not there.
class SynchronizedObject < BasicObject
  def initialize(o); @delegate = o;  end
  def __delegate; @delegate; end

  def method_missing(*args, &block)
    @delegate.mutex.synchronize {
      @delegate.send *args, &block
    }
  end
end
```

8.10 Dynamically Creating Methods

One important metaprogramming technique is the use of methods that create methods. The `attr_reader` and `attr_accessor` methods (see §7.1.5) are examples. These private instance methods of `Module` are used like keywords within class definitions. They accept attribute names as their arguments, and dynamically create methods with those names.

The examples that follow are variants on these attribute accessor creation methods and demonstrate two different ways to dynamically create methods like this.

8.10.1 Defining Methods with class_eval

Example 8-6 defines private instance methods of `Module` named `readonly` and `readwrite`. These methods work like `attr_reader` and `attr_accessor` do, and they are here to demonstrate how those methods are implemented. The implementation is actually quite simple: `readonly` and `readwrite` first build a string of Ruby code containing the `def` statements required to define appropriate accessor methods. Next, they evaluate that string of code using `class_eval` (described earlier in the chapter). Using `class_eval` like this incurs the slight overhead of parsing the string of code. The benefit, however, is that the methods we define need not use any reflective APIs themselves; they can query or set the value of an instance variable directly.

Example 8-6. Attribute methods with class_eval

```
class Module
  private      # The methods that follow are both private

  # This method works like attr_reader, but has a shorter name
  def readonly(*syms)
    return if syms.size == 0  # If no arguments, do nothing
    code = ""                 # Start with an empty string of code
    # Generate a string of Ruby code to define attribute reader methods.
    # Notice how the symbol is interpolated into the string of code.
    syms.each do |s|                    # For each symbol
      code << "def #{s}; @#{s}; end\n"   # The method definition
    end
    # Finally, class_eval the generated code to create instance methods.
    class_eval code
  end

  # This method works like attr_accessor, but has a shorter name.
  def readwrite(*syms)
    return if syms.size == 0
    code = ""
    syms.each do |s|
      code << "def #{s}; @#{s} end\n"
      code << "def #{s}=(value); @#{s} = value; end\n"
    end
    class_eval code
  end
end
```

8.10.2 Defining Methods with define_method

Example 8-7 is a different take on attribute accessors. The `attributes` method is something like the `readwrite` method defined in Example 8-6. Instead of taking any number of attribute names as arguments, it expects a single hash object. This hash should have attribute names as its keys, and should map those attribute names to the default values for the attributes. The `class_attrs` method works like `attributes`, but defines class attributes rather than instance attributes.

Remember that Ruby allows the curly braces to be omitted around hash literals when they are the final argument in a method invocation. So the `attributes` method might be invoked with code like this:

```ruby
class Point
  attributes :x => 0, :y => 0
end
```

In Ruby 1.9, we can use the more succinct hash syntax:

```ruby
class Point
  attributes x:0, y:0
end
```

This is another example that leverages Ruby's flexible syntax to create methods that behave like language keywords.

The implementation of the `attributes` method in Example 8-7 is quite a bit different than that of the `readwrite` method in Example 8-6. Instead of defining a string of Ruby code and evaluating it with `class_eval`, the `attributes` method defines the body of the attribute accessors in a block and defines the methods using `define_method`. Because this method definition technique does not allow us to interpolate identifiers directly into the method body, we must rely on reflective methods such as `instance_variable_get`. Because of this, the accessors defined with `attributes` are likely to be less efficient than those defined with `readwrite`.

An interesting point about the `attributes` method is that it does not explicitly store the default values for the attributes in a class variable of any kind. Instead, the default value for each attribute is captured by the scope of the block used to define the method. (See §6.6 for more about closures like this.)

The `class_attrs` method defines class attributes very simply: it invokes `attributes` on the eigenclass of the class. This means that the resulting methods use class instance variables (see §7.1.16) instead of regular class variables.

Example 8-7. Attribute methods with define_method

```ruby
class Module
  # This method defines attribute reader and writer methods for named
  # attributes, but expects a hash argument mapping attribute names to
  # default values. The generated attribute reader methods return the
  # default value if the instance variable has not yet been defined.
  def attributes(hash)
    hash.each_pair do |symbol, default|     # For each attribute/default pair
      getter = symbol                       # Name of the getter method
      setter = :"#{symbol}="                # Name of the setter method
      variable = :"@#{symbol}"              # Name of the instance variable
      define_method getter do               # Define the getter method
        if instance_variable_defined? variable
```

```
            instance_variable_get variable   # Return variable, if defined
          else
            default                          # Otherwise return default
          end
      end

        define_method setter do |value|     # Define setter method
          instance_variable_set variable,    # Set the instance variable
                            value            # To the argument value
        end
      end
    end

    # This method works like attributes, but defines class methods instead
    # by invoking attributes on the eigenclass instead of on self.
    # Note that the defined methods use class instance variables
    # instead of regular class variables.
    def class_attrs(hash)
      eigenclass = class << self; self; end
      eigenclass.class_eval { attributes(hash) }
    end

    # Both methods are private
    private :attributes, :class_attrs
  end
```

8.11 Alias Chaining

As we've seen, metaprogramming in Ruby often involves the dynamic definition of methods. Just as common is the dynamic *modification* of methods. Methods are modified with a technique we'll call *alias chaining*.[*] It works like this:

- First, create an alias for the method to be modified. This alias provides a name for the unmodified version of the method.
- Next, define a new version of the method. This new version should call the unmodified version through the alias, but it can add whatever functionality is needed before and after it does that.

Note that these steps can be applied repeatedly (as long as a different alias is used each time), creating a chain of methods and aliases.

This section includes three alias chaining examples. The first performs the alias chaining statically; i.e., using regular `alias` and `def` statements. The second and third examples are more dynamic; they alias chain arbitrarily named methods using `alias_method`, `define_method`, and `class_eval`.

---

[*] It has also been called *monkey patching*, but since that term was originally used with derision, we avoid it here. The term *duck punching* is sometimes used as a humorous alternative.

8.11.1 Tracing Files Loaded and Classes Defined

Example 8-8 is code that keeps track of all files loaded and all classes defined in a program. When the program exits, it prints a report. You can use this code to "instrument" an existing program so that you better understand what it is doing. One way to use this code is to insert this line at the beginning of the program:

```
require 'classtrace'
```

An easier solution, however, is to use the -r option to your Ruby interpreter:

```
ruby -rclasstrace my_program.rb  --traceout /tmp/trace
```

The -r option loads the specified library before it starts running the program. See §10.1 for more on the Ruby interpreter's command-line arguments.

Example 8-8 uses static alias chaining to trace all invocations of the Kernel.require and Kernel.load methods. It defines an Object.inherited hook to track definitions of new classes. And it uses Kernel.at_exit to execute a block of code when the program terminates. (The END statement described in §5.7 would work here as well.) Besides alias chaining require and load and defining Object.inherited, the only modification to the global namespace made by this code is the definition of a module named ClassTrace. All state required for tracing is stored in constants within this module, so that we don't pollute the namespace with global variables.

Example 8-8. Tracing files loaded and classes defined

```
# We define this module to hold the global state we require, so that
# we don't alter the global namespace any more than necessary.
module ClassTrace
  # This array holds our list of files loaded and classes defined.
  # Each element is a subarray holding the class defined or the
  # file loaded and the stack frame where it was defined or loaded.
  T = [] # Array to hold the files loaded

  # Now define the constant OUT to specify where tracing output goes.
  # This defaults to STDERR, but can also come from command-line arguments
  if x = ARGV.index("--traceout")    # If argument exists
    OUT = File.open(ARGV[x+1], "w")  # Open the specified file
    ARGV[x,2] = nil                  # And remove the arguments
  else
    OUT = STDERR                     # Otherwise default to STDERR
  end
end

# Alias chaining step 1: define aliases for the original methods
alias original_require require
alias original_load load

# Alias chaining step 2: define new versions of the methods
def require(file)
  ClassTrace::T << [file,caller[0]]  # Remember what was loaded where
  original_require(file)             # Invoke the original method
end
```

```
def load(*args)
  ClassTrace::T << [args[0],caller[0]]  # Remember what was loaded where
  original_load(*args)                   # Invoke the original method
end

# This hook method is invoked each time a new class is defined
def Object.inherited(c)
  ClassTrace::T << [c,caller[0]]         # Remember what was defined where
end

# Kernel.at_exit registers a block to be run when the program exits
# We use it to report the file and class data we collected
at_exit {
  o = ClassTrace::OUT
  o.puts "="*60
  o.puts "Files Loaded and Classes Defined:"
  o.puts "="*60
  ClassTrace::T.each do |what,where|
    if what.is_a? Class  # Report class (with hierarchy) defined
      o.puts "Defined: #{what.ancestors.join('<-')} at #{where}"
    else                 # Report file loaded
      o.puts "Loaded: #{what} at #{where}"
    end
  end
}
```

8.11.2 Chaining Methods for Thread Safety

Two earlier examples in this chapter have involved thread safety. Example 8-2 defined a synchronized method (based on an Object.mutex method) that executed a block under the protection of a Mutex object. Then, Example 8-5 redefined the synchronized method so that when it was invoked without a block, it would return a SynchronizedObject wrapper around an object, protecting access to any methods invoked through that wrapper object. Now, in Example 8-9, we augment the synchronized method again so that when it is invoked within a class or module definition, it alias chains the named methods to add synchronization.

The alias chaining is done by our method Module.synchronize_method, which in turn uses a helper method Module.create_alias to define an appropriate alias for any given method (including operator methods like +).

After defining these new Module methods, Example 8-9 redefines the synchronized method again. When the method is invoked within a class or a module, it calls synchronize_method on each of the symbols it is passed. Interestingly, however, it can also be called with no arguments; when used this way, it adds synchronization to whatever instance method is defined next. (It uses the method_added hook to receive notifications when a new method is added.) Note that the code in this example depends on the Object.mutex method of Example 8-2 and the SynchronizedObject class of Example 8-5.

Example 8-9. Alias chaining for thread safety

```ruby
# Define a Module.synchronize_method that alias chains instance methods
# so they synchronize on the instance before running.
class Module
  # This is a helper function for alias chaining.
  # Given a method name (as a string or symbol) and a prefix, create
  # a unique alias for the method, and return the name of the alias
  # as a symbol. Any punctuation characters in the original method name
  # will be converted to numbers so that operators can be aliased.
  def create_alias(original, prefix="alias")
    # Stick the prefix on the original name and convert punctuation
    aka = "#{prefix}_#{original}"
    aka.gsub!(/([\=\|\&\+\-\*\/\^\!\?\~\%\<\>\[\]])/) {
      num = $1[0]                     # Ruby 1.8 character -> ordinal
      num = num.ord if num.is_a? String # Ruby 1.9 character -> ordinal
      '_' + num.to_s
    }

    # Keep appending underscores until we get a name that is not in use
    aka += "_" while method_defined? aka or private_method_defined? aka

    aka = aka.to_sym            # Convert the alias name to a symbol
    alias_method aka, original  # Actually create the alias
    aka                         # Return the alias name
  end

  # Alias chain the named method to add synchronization
  def synchronize_method(m)
    # First, make an alias for the unsynchronized version of the method.
    aka = create_alias(m, "unsync")
    # Now redefine the original to invoke the alias in a synchronized block.
    # We want the defined  method to be able to accept blocks, so we
    # can't use define_method, and must instead evaluate a string with
    # class_eval. Note that everything between %Q{ and the matching }
    # is a double-quoted string, not a block.
    class_eval %Q{
      def #{m}(*args, &block)
        synchronized(self) { #{aka}(*args, &block) }
      end
    }
  end
end

# This global synchronized method can now be used in three different ways.
def synchronized(*args)
  # Case 1: with one argument and a block, synchronize on the object
  # and execute the block
  if args.size == 1 && block_given?
    args[0].mutex.synchronize { yield }

  # Case two: with one argument that is not a symbol and no block
  # return a SynchronizedObject wrapper
  elsif args.size == 1 and not args[0].is_a? Symbol and not block_given?
    SynchronizedObject.new(args[0])
```

```
  # Case three: when invoked on a module with no block, alias chain the
  # named methods to add synchronization. Or, if there are no arguments,
  # then alias chain the next method defined.
  elsif self.is_a? Module and not block_given?
    if (args.size > 0) # Synchronize the named methods
      args.each {|m| self.synchronize_method(m) }
    else
      # If no methods are specified synchronize the next method defined
      eigenclass = class<<self; self; end
      eigenclass.class_eval do # Use eigenclass to define class methods
        # Define method_added for notification when next method is defined
        define_method :method_added do |name|
          # First remove this hook method
          eigenclass.class_eval { remove_method :method_added }
          # Next, synchronize the method that was just added
          self.synchronize_method name
        end
      end
    end

  # Case 4: any other invocation is an error
  else
    raise ArgumentError, "Invalid arguments to synchronize()"
  end
end
```

8.11.3 Chaining Methods for Tracing

Example 8-10 is a variant on Example 8-4 that supports tracing of named methods of
an object. Example 8-4 used delegation and method_missing to define an
Object.trace method that would return a traced wrapper object. This version uses
chaining to alter methods of an object in place. It defines trace! and untrace! to chain
and unchain named methods of an object.

The interesting thing about this example is that it does its chaining in a different way
from Example 8-9; it simply defines singleton methods on the object and uses super
within the singleton to chain to the original instance method definition. No method
aliases are created.

Example 8-10. Chaining with singleton methods for tracing
```
# Define trace! and untrace! instance methods for all objects.
# trace! "chains" the named methods by defining singleton methods
# that add tracing functionality and then use super to call the original.
# untrace! deletes the singleton methods to remove tracing.
class Object
  # Trace the specified methods, sending output to STDERR.
  def trace!(*methods)
    @traced = @traced || []      # Remember the set of traced methods

    # If no methods were specified, use all public methods defined
    # directly (not inherited) by the class of this object
    methods = public_methods(false) if methods.size == 0
```

```ruby
    methods.map! {|m| m.to_sym }  # Convert any strings to symbols
    methods -= @_traced           # Remove methods that are already traced
    return if methods.empty?      # Return early if there is nothing to do
    @_traced |= methods           # Add methods to set of traced methods

    # Trace the fact that we're starting to trace these methods
    STDERR << "Tracing #{methods.join(', ')} on #{object_id}\n"

    # Singleton methods are defined in the eigenclass
    eigenclass = class << self; self; end

    methods.each do |m|           # For each method m
      # Define a traced singleton version of the method m.
      # Output tracing information and use super to invoke the
      # instance method that it is tracing.
      # We want the defined  methods to be able to accept blocks, so we
      # can't use define_method, and must instead evaluate a string.
      # Note that everything between %Q{ and the matching } is a
      # double-quoted string, not a block. Also note that there are
      # two levels of string interpolations here. #{} is interpolated
      # when the singleton method is defined. And \#{} is interpolated
      # when the singleton method is invoked.
      eigenclass.class_eval %Q{
        def #{m}(*args, &block)
          begin
            STDERR << "Entering: #{m}(\#{args.join(', ')})\n"
            result = super
            STDERR << "Exiting: #{m} with \#{result}\n"
            result
          rescue
            STDERR << "Aborting: #{m}: \#{$!.class}: \#{$!.message}"
            raise
          end
        end
      }
    end
  end

  # Untrace the specified methods or all traced methods
  def untrace!(*methods)
    if methods.size == 0    # If no methods specified untrace
      methods = @_traced    # all currently traced methods
      STDERR << "Untracing all methods on #{object_id}\n"
    else                    # Otherwise, untrace
      methods.map! {|m| m.to_sym }  # Convert string to symbols
      methods &= @_traced   # all specified methods that are traced
      STDERR << "Untracing #{methods.join(', ')} on #{object_id}\n"
    end

    @_traced -= methods     # Remove them from our set of traced methods

    # Remove the traced singleton methods from the eigenclass
    # Note that we class_eval a block here, not a string
    (class << self; self; end).class_eval do
```

```
        methods.each do |m|
          remove_method m      # undef_method would not work correctly
        end
      end

      # If no methods are traced anymore, remove our instance var
      if @_traced.empty?
        remove_instance_variable :@_traced
      end
    end
  end
end
```

8.12 Domain-Specific Languages

The goal of metaprogramming in Ruby is often the creation of *domain-specific languages*, or DSLs. A DSL is just an extension of Ruby's syntax (with methods that look like keywords) or API that allows you to solve a problem or represent data more naturally than you could otherwise. For our examples, we'll take the problem domain to be the output of XML formatted data, and we'll define two DSLs—one very simple and one more clever—to tackle this problem.*

8.12.1 Simple XML Output with method_missing

We begin with a simple class named XML for generating XML output. Here's an example of how the XML can be used:

```
pagetitle = "Test Page for XML.generate"
XML.generate(STDOUT) do
  html do
    head do
      title { pagetitle }
      comment "This is a test"
    end
    body do
      h1(:style => "font-family:sans-serif") { pagetitle }
      ul :type=>"square" do
        li { Time.now }
        li { RUBY_VERSION }
      end
    end
  end
end
```

This code doesn't look like XML, and it only sort of looks like Ruby. Here's the output it generates (with some line breaks added for legibility):

```
<html><head>
<title>Test Page for XML.generate</title>
<!-- This is a test -->
```

---

* For a fully realized solution to this problem, see Jim Weirich's Builder API at *http://builder.rubyforge.org*.

```
</head><body>
<h1 style='font-family:sans-serif'>Test Page for XML.generate</h1>
<ul type='square'>
<li>2007-08-19 16:19:58 -0700</li>
<li>1.9.0</li>
</ul></body></html>
```

To implement this class and the XML generation syntax it supports, we rely on:

- Ruby's block structure
- Ruby's parentheses-optional method invocations
- Ruby's syntax for passing hash literals to methods without curly braces
- The `method_missing` method

Example 8-11 shows the implementation for this simple DSL.

Example 8-11. A simple DSL for generating XML output

```ruby
class XML
  # Create an instance of this class, specifying a stream or object to
  # hold the output. This can be any object that responds to <<(String).
  def initialize(out)
    @out = out  # Remember where to send our output
  end

  # Output the specified object as CDATA, return nil.
  def content(text)
    @out << text.to_s
    nil
  end

  # Output the specified object as a comment, return nil.
  def comment(text)
    @out << "<!-- #{text} -->"
    nil
  end

  # Output a tag with the specified name and attributes.
  # If there is a block invoke it to output or return content.
  # Return nil.
  def tag(tagname, attributes={})
    # Output the tag name
    @out << "<#{tagname}"

    # Output the attributes
    attributes.each {|attr,value| @out << " #{attr}='#{value}'" }

    if block_given?
      # This block has content
      @out << '>'                 # End the opening tag
      content = yield             # Invoke the block to output or return content
      if content                  # If any content returned
        @out << content.to_s      # Output it as a string
      end
      @out << "</#{tagname}>"      # Close the tag
```

```
    else
      # Otherwise, this is an empty tag, so just close it.
      @out << '/>'
    end
    nil # Tags output themselves, so they don't return any content
  end

  # The code below is what changes this from an ordinary class into a DSL.
  # First: any unknown method is treated as the name of a tag.
  alias method_missing tag

  # Second: run a block in a new instance of the class.
  def self.generate(out, &block)
    XML.new(out).instance_eval(&block)
  end
end
```

8.12.2 Validated XML Output with Method Generation

The XML class of Example 8-11 is helpful for generating well-formed XML, but it does no error checking to ensure that the output is valid according to any particular XML grammar. In the next example, Example 8-12, we add some simple error checking (though not nearly enough to ensure complete validity—that would require a much longer example). This example is really two DSLs in one. The first is a DSL for defining an XML grammar: a set of tags and the allowed attributes for each tag. You use it like this:

```
class HTMLForm < XMLGrammar
  element :form, :action => REQ,
                 :method => "GET",
                 :enctype => "application/x-www-form-urlencoded",
                 :name => OPT
  element :input, :type => "text", :name => OPT, :value => OPT,
                  :maxlength => OPT, :size => OPT, :src => OPT,
                  :checked => BOOL, :disabled => BOOL, :readonly => BOOL
  element :textarea, :rows => REQ, :cols => REQ, :name => OPT,
                     :disabled => BOOL, :readonly => BOOL
  element :button, :name => OPT, :value => OPT,
                   :type => "submit", :disabled => OPT
end
```

This first DSL is defined by the class method XMLGrammar.element. You use it by sub-classing XMLGrammar to create a new class. The element method expects the name of a tag as its first argument and a hash of legal attributes as the second argument. The keys of the hash are attribute names. These names may map to default values for the attribute, to the constant REQ for required attributes, or to the constant OPT for optional attributes. Calling element generates a method with the specified name in the subclass you are defining.

The subclass of XMLGrammar you define is the second DSL, and you can use it to generate XML output that is valid according to the rules you specified. The XMLGrammar class does

---

not have a `method_missing` method so it won't allow you to use a tag that is not part of the grammar. And the `tag` method for outputting tags performs error checking on your attributes. Use the generated grammar subclass like the `XML` class of Example 8-11:

```
HTMLForm.generate(STDOUT) do
  comment "This is a simple HTML form"
  form :name => "registration",
       :action => "http://www.example.com/register.cgi" do
    content "Name:"
    input :name => "name"
    content "Address:"
    textarea :name => "address", :rows=>6, :cols=>40 do
      "Please enter your mailing address here"
    end
    button { "Submit" }
  end
end
```

Example 8-12 shows the implementation of the `XMLGrammar` class.

Example 8-12. A DSL for validated XML output

```
class XMLGrammar
  # Create an instance of this class, specifying a stream or object to
  # hold the output. This can be any object that responds to <<(String).
  def initialize(out)
    @out = out  # Remember where to send our output
  end

  # Invoke the block in an instance that outputs to the specified stream.
  def self.generate(out, &block)
    new(out).instance_eval(&block)
  end

  # Define an allowed element (or tag) in the grammar.
  # This class method is the grammar-specification DSL
  # and defines the methods that constitute the XML-output DSL.
  def self.element(tagname, attributes={})
    @allowed_attributes ||= {}
    @allowed_attributes[tagname] = attributes

    class_eval %Q{
      def #{tagname}(attributes={}, &block)
        tag(:#{tagname},attributes,&block)
      end
    }
  end

  # These are constants used when defining attribute values.
  OPT = :opt     # for optional attributes
  REQ = :req     # for required attributes
  BOOL = :bool   # for attributes whose value is their own name

  def self.allowed_attributes
    @allowed_attributes
  end
```

```ruby
# Output the specified object as CDATA, return nil.
def content(text)
  @out << text.to_s
  nil
end

# Output the specified object as a comment, return nil.
def comment(text)
  @out << "<!-- #{text} -->"
  nil
end

# Output a tag with the specified name and attribute.
# If there is a block, invoke it to output or return content.
# Return nil.
def tag(tagname, attributes={})
  # Output the tag name
  @out << "<#{tagname}"

  # Get the allowed attributes for this tag.
  allowed = self.class.allowed_attributes[tagname]

  # First, make sure that each of the attributes is allowed.
  # Assuming they are allowed, output all of the specified ones.
  attributes.each_pair do |key,value|
    raise "unknown attribute: #{key}" unless allowed.include?(key)
    @out << " #{key}='#{value}'"
  end

  # Now look through the allowed attributes, checking for
  # required attributes that were omitted and for attributes with
  # default values that we can output.
  allowed.each_pair do |key,value|
    # If this attribute was already output, do nothing.
    next if attributes.has_key? key
    if (value == REQ)
      raise "required attribute '#{key}' missing in <#{tagname}>"
    elsif value.is_a? String
      @out << " #{key}='#{value}'"
    end
  end

  if block_given?
    # This block has content
    @out << '>'              # End the opening tag
    content = yield          # Invoke the block to output or return content
    if content              # If any content returned
      @out << content.to_s  # Output it as a string
    end
    @out << "</#{tagname}>"  # Close the tag
  else
    # Otherwise, this is an empty tag, so just close it.
    @out << '/>'
  end
```

```
      nil # Tags output themselves, so they don't return any content.
  end
end
```

## CHAPTER 9

The Ruby Platform

Ruby's core library defines a rich and powerful API that serves as a platform on which to create your programs. It is well worth your time to study and master this API, particularly the key classes such as String, Array, Hash, Enumerable, and IO. If you aren't familiar with the methods defined by these classes, you may end up spending time reinventing functionality that is already provided for you.

This chapter documents those methods. It is not a comprehensive API reference, but attempts to illustrate, with short code snippets, the use of the important methods of all the important core classes and modules, and a few of the most commonly used classes from the standard library. The aim is to familiarize you with the broad range of existing methods, so that when you need one of them, you will remember that it exists and will be able to find its documentation with *ri*.

This is a long chapter, broken down into sections that cover the following:

- Strings and text processing
- Regular expressions
- Numbers and math
- Dates and times
- The Enumerable module and the Array, Hash and Set collections
- Input/output and files
- Networking
- Threads and concurrency

You'll find that the code early in the chapter takes the form of one-line snippets demonstrating individual methods. Toward the end, however, when documenting networking and threads, the examples become longer and demonstrate how to accomplish common tasks like creating a network client or using threads to concurrently process the items in a collection.

9.1 Strings

Chapter 3explained Ruby's string literal syntax, as well as the String operators for concatenation (+), appends (<<), repetition (*), and indexing ([]). In this section we expand on that coverage by demonstrating the named methods of the String class. The subsections that follow this API overview cover specific areas in more detail.

We begin with methods that provide named alternatives to some of the operators documented in Chapter 3:

```
s = "hello"
s.concat(" world")    # Synonym for <<. Mutating append to s. Returns new s.
s.insert(5, " there") # Same as s[5,0] = " there". Alters s. Returns new s.
s.slice(0,5)          # Same as s[0,5]. Returns a substring.
s.slice!(5,6)         # Deletion. Same as s[5,6]="". Returns deleted substring.
s.eql?("hello world") # True. Same as ==.
```

There are several methods for querying the length of a string:

```
s.length      # => 11: counts characters in 1.9, bytes in 1.8
s.size        # => 11: size is a synonym
s.bytesize    # => 11: length in bytes; Ruby 1.9 only
s.empty?      # => false
"".empty?     # => true
```

String methods for searching a string and for replacing content include the following. We'll revisit some of these when we consider regular expressions later in this section:

```
s = "hello"
# Finding the position of a substring or pattern match
s.index('l')         # => 2: index of first l in string
s.index(?l)          # => 2: works with character codes as well
s.index(/l+/)        # => 2: works with regular expressions, too
s.index('l',3)       # => 3: index of first l in string at or after position 3
s.index('Ruby')      # => nil: search string not found
s.rindex('l')        # => 3: index of rightmost l in string
s.rindex('l',2)      # => 2: index of rightmost l in string at or before 2

# Checking for prefixes and suffixes: Ruby 1.9 and later
s.start_with? "hell" # => true. Note start_with not starts_with
s.end_with? "bells"  # => false

# Testing for presence of substring
s.include?("ll")     # => true: "hello" includes "ll"
s.include?(?H)       # => false: "hello" does not include character H

# Pattern matching with regular expressions
s =~ /[aeiou]{2}/    # => nil: no double vowels in "hello"
s.match(/[aeiou]/) {|m| m.to_s} # => "e": return first vowel

# Splitting a string into substrings based on a delimiter string or pattern
"this is it".split   # => ["this", "is", "it"]: split on spaces by default
"hello".split('l')   # => ["he", "", "o"]
"1, 2,3".split(/,\s*/) # => ["1","2","3"]: comma and optional space delimiter

# Split a string into two parts plus a delimiter. Ruby 1.9 only.
# These methods always return arrays of 3 strings:
"banana".partition("an")  # => ["b", "an", "ana"]
"banana".rpartition("an") # => ["ban", "an", "a"]: start from right
"a123b".partition(/\d+/)  # => ["a", "123", "b"]: works with Regexps, too

# Search and replace the first (sub, sub!) or all (gsub, gsub!)
# occurrences of the specified string or pattern.
# More about sub and gsub when we cover regular expressions later.
s.sub("l", "L")           # => "heLlo": Just replace first occurrence
s.gsub("l", "L")          # => "heLLo": Replace all occurrences
s.sub!(/(.)(.)/, '\2\1')  # => "ehllo": Match and swap first 2 letters
s.sub!(/(.)(.)/, "\\2\\1") # => "hello": Double backslashes for double quotes
# sub and gsub can also compute a replacement string with a block
# Match the first letter of each word and capitalize it
"hello world".gsub(/\b./) {|match| match.upcase } # => "Hello World"
# In Ruby 1.9, you can specify a hash to map matches to replacements
s.gsub(/[aeiou]/,"a"=>0, "e"=>1, "i"=>2)  # => "h1ll0"
```

The last line of this example uses the upcase method to convert a string to uppercase. The String class defines a number of methods for working with case (but it does not define methods for testing the case or category of a character):

```
# Case modification methods
s = "world"     # These methods work with ASCII characters only
s.upcase        # => "WORLD"
s.upcase!       # => "WORLD"; alter s in place
s.downcase      # => "world"
s.capitalize    # => "World": first letter upper, rest lower
s.capitalize!   # => "World": alter s in place
s.swapcase      # => "wORLD": alter case of each letter

# Case insensitive comparison. (ASCII text only)
# casecmp works like <=> and returns -1 for less, 0 for equal, +1 for greater
"world".casecmp("WORLD")  # => 0
"a".casecmp("B")          # => -1 (<=> returns 1 in this case)
```

String defines a number of useful methods for adding and removing whitespace. Most exist in mutating (end with !) and nonmutating versions:

```
s = "hello\r\n"      # A string with a line terminator
s.chomp!             # => "hello": remove one line terminator from end
s.chomp              # => "hello": no line terminator so no change
s.chomp!             # => nil: return of nil indicates no change made
s.chomp("o")         # => "hell": remove "o" from end
$/ = ";"             # Set global record separator $/ to semicolon
"hello;".chomp       # => "hello": now chomp removes semicolons and end

# chop removes trailing character or line terminator (\n, \r, or \r\n)
s = "hello\n"
s.chop!              # => "hello": line terminator removed. s modified.
s.chop               # => "hell": last character removed. s not modified.
"".chop              # => "": no characters to remove
"".chop!             # => nil: nothing changed

# Strip all whitespace (including \t, \r, \n) from left, right, or both
# strip!, lstrip! and rstrip! modify the string in place.
s = "\t hello \n"    # Whitespace at beginning and end
s.strip              # => "hello"
s.lstrip             # => "hello \n"
s.rstrip             # => "\t hello"

# Left-justify, right-justify, or center a string in a field n-characters wide.
# There are no mutator versions of these methods. See also printf method.
s = "x"
s.ljust(3)           # => "x  "
s.rjust(3)           # => "  x"
s.center(3)          # => " x "
s.center(5, '-')     # => "--x--": padding other than space are allowed
s.center(7, '-=')    # => "-=-x-=-": multicharacter padding allowed
```

Strings may be enumerated byte-by-byte or line-by-line with the each_byte and each_line iterators. In Ruby 1.8, the each method is a synonym for each_line, and the String class includes Enumerable. Avoid using each and its related iterators because

Ruby 1.9 removes the each method and no longer makes strings Enumerable. Ruby 1.9 (and the jcode library in Ruby 1.8) adds an each_char iterator and enables character-by-character enumeration of strings:

```
s = "A\nB"                       # Three ASCII characters on two lines
s.each_byte {|b| print b, " " }  # Prints "65 10 66 "
s.each_line {|l| print l.chomp}  # Prints "AB"

# Sequentially iterate characters as 1-character strings
# Works in Ruby 1.9, or in 1.8 with the jcode library:
s.each_char { |c| print c, " " } # Prints "A \n B "

# Enumerate each character as a 1-character string
# This does not work for multibyte strings in 1.8
# It works (inefficiently) for multibyte strings in 1.9:
0.upto(s.length-1) {|n| print s[n,1], " "}

# In Ruby 1.9, bytes, lines, and chars are aliases
s.bytes.to_a                     # => [65,10,66]: alias for each_byte
s.lines.to_a                     # => ["A\n","B"]: alias for each_line
s.chars.to_a                     # => ["A", "\n", "B"] alias for each_char
```

String defines a number of methods for parsing numbers from strings, and for converting strings to symbols:

```
"10".to_i          # => 10: convert string to integer
"10".to_i(2)       # => 2: argument is radix: between base-2 and base-36
"10x".to_i         # => 10: nonnumeric suffix is ignored. Same for oct, hex
" 10".to_i         # => 10: leading whitespace ignored
"ten".to_i         # => 0: does not raise exception on bad input
"10".oct           # => 8: parse string as base-8 integer
"10".hex           # => 16: parse string as hexadecimal integer
"0xff".hex         # => 255: hex numbers may begin with 0x prefix
" 1.1 dozen".to_f  # => 1.1: parse leading floating-point number
"6.02e23".to_f     # => 6.02e+23: exponential notation supported

"one".to_sym       # => :one -- string to symbol conversion
"two".intern       # => :two -- intern is a synonym for to_sym
```

Finally, here are some miscellaneous String methods:

```
# Increment a string:
"a".succ                    # => "b": the successor of "a". Also, succ!
"aaz".next                  # => "aba": next is a synonym. Also, next!
"a".upto("e") {|c| print c } # Prints "abcde. upto iterator based on succ.

# Reverse a string:
"hello".reverse     # => "olleh". Also reverse!

# Debugging
"hello\n".dump      # => "\"hello\\n\"": Escape special characters
"hello\n".inspect   # Works much like dump

# Translation from one set of characters to another
"hello".tr("aeiou", "AEIOU") # => "hEllO": capitalize vowels. Also tr!
"hello".tr("aeiou", " ")     # => "h ll ": convert vowels to spaces
```

```
"bead".tr_s("aeiou", " ")      # => "b d": convert and remove duplicates

# Checksums
"hello".sum            # => 532: weak 16-bit checksum
"hello".sum(8)         # => 20: 8 bit checksum instead of 16 bit
"hello".crypt("ab")    # => "abloJrMf6tlhw": one way cryptographic checksum
                       # Pass two alphanumeric characters as "salt"
                       # The result may be platform-dependent

# Counting letters, deleting letters, and removing duplicates
"hello".count('aeiou')  # => 2: count lowercase vowels
"hello".delete('aeiou') # => "hll": delete lowercase vowels. Also delete!
"hello".squeeze('a-z')  # => "helo": remove runs of letters. Also squeeze!
# When there is more than one argument, take the intersection.
# Arguments that begin with ^ are negated.
"hello".count('a-z', '^aeiou')   # => 3: count lowercase consonants
"hello".delete('a-z', '^aeiou')  # => "eo: delete lowercase consonants
```

9.1.1 Formatting Text

As you know, Ruby's double-quoted string literals allow arbitrary Ruby expressions to be interpolated into strings. For example:

```
n, animal = 2, "mice"
"#{n+1} blind #{animal}"  # => '3 blind mice'
```

This string-literal interpolation syntax was documented in Chapter 3. Ruby also supports another technique for interpolating values into strings: the String class defines a format operator %, and the Kernel module defines global printf and sprintf methods. These methods and the % operator are very much like the printf function popularized by the C programming language. One advantage of printf-style formatting over regular string literal interpolation is that it allows precise control over field widths, which makes it useful for ASCII report generation. Another advantage is that it allows you to specify the number of significant digits to display in floating-point numbers, which is useful in scientific (and sometimes financial) applications. Finally, printf-style formatting decouples the values to be formatted from the string into which they are interpolated. This can be helpful for internationalization and localization of applications.

Examples using the % operator follow. See Kernel.sprintf for complete documentation of the formatting directives used by these methods:

```
# Alternatives to the interpolation above
printf('%d blind %s', n+1, animal) # Prints '3 blind mice', returns nil
sprintf('%d blind %s', n+1, animal) # => '3 blind mice'
'%d blind %s' % [n+1, animal]  # Use array on right if more than one argument

# Formatting numbers
'%d' % 10         # => '10': %d for decimal integers
'%x' % 10         # => 'a': hexadecimal integers
'%X' % 10         # => 'A': uppercase hexadecimal integers
'%o' % 10         # => '12': octal integers
```

```
'%f' % 1234.567   # => '1234.567000': full-length floating-point numbers
'%e' % 1234.567   # => '1.234567e+03': force exponential notation
'%E' % 1234.567   # => '1.234567e+03': exponential with uppercase E
'%g' % 1234.567   # => '1234.57': six significant digits
'%g' % 1.23456E12 # => '1.23456e+12': Use %f or %e depending on magnitude

# Field width
'%5s' % '<<<'     # '  <<<': right-justify in field five characters wide
'%-5s' % '>>>'    # '>>>  ': left-justify in field five characters wide
'%5d' % 123       # '  123': field is five characters wide
'%05d' % 123      # '00123': pad with zeros in field five characters wide

# Precision
'%.2f' % 123.456  # '123.46': two digits after decimal place
'%.2e' % 123.456  # '1.23e+02': two digits after decimal = three significant digits
'%.6e' % 123.456  # '1.234560e+02': note added zero
'%.4g' % 123.456  # '123.5': four significant digits

# Field and precision combined
'%6.4g' % 123.456 # ' 123.5': four significant digits in field six chars wide
'%3s' % 'ruby'    # 'ruby': string argument exceeds field width
'%3.3s' % 'ruby'  # 'rub': precision forces truncation of string

# Multiple arguments to be formatted
args = ['Syntax Error', 'test.rb', 20]  # An array of arguments
"%s: in '%s' line %d" % args      # => "Syntax Error: in 'test.rb' line 20"
# Same args, interpolated in different order!  Good for internationalization.
"%2$s:%3$d: %1$s" % args          # => "test.rb:20: Syntax Error"
```

9.1.2 Packing and Unpacking Binary Strings

Ruby's strings can hold binary data as well as textual data. A pair of methods, Array.pack and String.unpack, can be helpful if you are working with binary file formats or binary network protocols. Use Array.pack to encode the elements of an array into a binary string. And use String.unpack to decode a binary string, extracting values from it and returning those values in an array. Both the encoding and decoding operations are under the control of a format string where letters specify the datatype and encoding and numbers specify the number of repetitions. The creation of these format strings is fairly arcane, and you can find a complete list of letter codes in the documentation for Array.pack and String.unpack. Here are some simple examples:

```
a = [1,2,3,4,5,6,7,8,9,10] # An array of 10 integers
b = a.pack('i10')          # Pack 10 4-byte integers (i) into binary string b
c = b.unpack('i*')         # Decode all (*) the 4-byte integers from b
c == a                     # => true

m = 'hello world'          # A message to encode
data = [m.size, m]         # Length first, then the bytes
template = 'Sa*'           # Unsigned short, any number of ASCII chars
b = data.pack(template)    # => "\v\000hello world"
b.unpack(template)         # => [11, "hello world"]
```

9.1.3 Strings and Encodings

The `String` methods `encoding`, `encode`, `encode!`, and `force_encoding` and the `Encoding` class were described in §3.2.6. You may want to reread that section now if you will be writing programs using Unicode or other multibyte character encodings.

9.2 Regular Expressions

A *regular expression* (also known as a regexp or regex) describes a textual pattern. Ruby's `Regexp` class[*] implements regular expressions, and both `Regexp` and `String` define pattern matching methods and operators. Like most languages that support regular expressions, Ruby's `Regexp` syntax follows closely (but not precisely) the syntax of Perl 5.

9.2.1 Regexp Literals

Regular expression literals are delimited by forward slash characters:

```
/Ruby?/  # Matches the text "Rub" followed by an optional "y"
```

The closing slash character isn't a true delimiter because a regular expression literal may be followed by one or more optional flag characters that specify additional information about the how pattern matching is to be done. For example:

```
/ruby?/i  # Case-insensitive: matches "ruby" or "RUB", etc.
/./mu     # Matches Unicode characters in Multiline mode
```

The allowed modifier characters are shown in Table 9-1.

Table 9-1. Regular expression modifier characters

Modifier	Description
i	Ignore case when matching text.
m	The pattern is to be matched against multiline text, so treat newline as an ordinary character: allow . to match newlines.
x	Extended syntax: allow whitespace and comments in regexp.
o	Perform #{ } interpolations only once, the first time the regexp literal is evaluated.
u,e,s,n	Interpret the regexp as Unicode (UTF-8), EUC, SJIS, or ASCII. If none of these modifiers is specified, the regular expression is assumed to use the source encoding.

Like string literals delimited with `%Q`, Ruby allows you to begin your regular expressions with `%r` followed by a delimiter of your choice. This is useful when the pattern you are describing contains a lot of forward slash characters that you don't want to escape:

---

[*] JavaScript programmers should note that the Ruby class has a lowercase e, unlike the JavaScript `RegExp` class.

```
%r|/|          # Matches a single slash character, no escape required
%r[</(.*)>]i   # Flag characters are allowed with this syntax, too
```

Regular expression syntax gives special meaning to the characters (), [], {}, ., ?, +, *, |, ^, and $. If you want to describe a pattern that includes one of these characters literally, use a backslash to escape it. If you want to describe a pattern that includes a backslash, double the backslash:

```
/\(\)/         # Matches open and close parentheses
/\\/           # Matches a single backslash
```

Regular expression literals behave like double-quoted string literals and can include escape characters such as \n, \t, and (in Ruby 1.9) \u (see Table 3-1 in Chapter 3 for a complete list of escape sequences):

```
money = /[$\u20AC\u{a3}\u{a5}]/ # match dollar,euro,pound, or yen sign
```

Also like double-quoted string literals, Regexp literals allow the interpolation of arbitrary Ruby expressions with the #{} syntax:

```
prefix = ","
/#{prefix}\t/   # Matches a comma followed by an ASCII TAB character
```

Note that interpolation is done early, before the content of the regular expression is parsed. This means that any special characters in the interpolated expression become part of the regular expression syntax. Interpolation is normally done anew each time a regular expression literal is evaluated. If you use the o modifier, however, this interpolation is only performed once, the first time the code is parsed. The behavior of the o modifier is best demonstrated by example:

```
[1,2].map{|x| /#{x}/}   # => [/1/, /2/]
[1,2].map{|x| /#{x}/o}  # => [/1/, /1/]
```

9.2.2 Regexp Factory Methods

As an alternative to regexp literals, you can also create regular expressions with Regexp.new, or its synonym, Regexp.compile:

```
Regexp.new("Ruby?")                        # /Ruby?/
Regexp.new("ruby?", Regexp::IGNORECASE)    # /ruby?/i
Regexp.compile(".", Regexp::MULTILINE, "u") # /./mu
```

Use the Regexp.escape to escape special regular expression characters in a string before passing them to the Regexp constructor:

```
pattern = "[a-z]+"                   # One or more letters
suffix = Regexp.escape("()")         # Treat these characters literally
r = Regexp.new(pattern + suffix)     # /[a-z]+\(\)/
```

In Ruby 1.9 (and 1.8.7), the factory method Regexp.union creates a pattern that is the "union" of any number of strings or Regexp objects. (That is, the resulting pattern matches any of the strings matched by its constituent patterns.) Pass any number of arguments or a single array of strings and patterns. This factory method is good for creating patterns that match any word in a list of words. Strings passed to Regexp.union are automatically escaped, unlike those passed to new and compile:

```
# Match any one of five language names.
pattern = Regexp.union("Ruby", "Perl", "Python", /Java(Script)?/)
# Match empty parens, brackets, or braces. Escaping is automatic:
Regexp.union("()", "[]", "{}")   # => /\(\)|\[\]|\{\}/
```

9.2.3 Regular Expression Syntax

Many programming languages support regular expressions, using the syntax popularized by Perl. This book does not include a complete discussion of that syntax, but the following examples walk you through the elements of regular expression grammar. The tutorial is followed by Table 9-2, which summarizes the syntax. The tutorial's focus is on Ruby 1.8 regular expression syntax, but some of the features available only in Ruby 1.9 are demonstrated as well. For book-length coverage of regular expressions, see *Mastering Regular Expressions* by Jeffrey E. F. Friedl (O'Reilly).

```
# Literal characters
/ruby/            # Match "ruby". Most characters simply match themselves.
/¥/               # Matches Yen sign. Multibyte characters are suported
                  # in Ruby 1.9 and Ruby 1.8.

# Character classes
/[Rr]uby/         # Match "Ruby" or "ruby"
/rub[ye]/         # Match "ruby" or "rube"
/[aeiou]/         # Match any one lowercase vowel
/[0-9]/           # Match any digit; same as /[0123456789]/
/[a-z]/           # Match any lowercase ASCII letter
/[A-Z]/           # Match any uppercase ASCII letter
/[a-zA-Z0-9]/     # Match any of the above
/[^aeiou]/        # Match anything other than a lowercase vowel
/[^0-9]            # Match anything other than a digit

# Special character classes
/./               # Match any character except newline
/./m              # In multiline mode . matches newline, too
/\d/              # Match a digit /[0-9]/
/\D/              # Match a nondigit: /[^0-9]/
/\s/              # Match a whitespace character: /[ \t\r\n\f]/
/\S/              # Match nonwhitespace: /[^ \t\r\n\f]/
/\w/              # Match a single word character: /[A-Za-z0-9_]/
/\W/              # Match a nonword character: /[^A-Za-z0-9_]/

# Repetition
/ruby?/           # Match "rub" or "ruby": the y is optional
/ruby*/           # Match "rub" plus 0 or more ys
/ruby+/           # Match "rub" plus 1 or more ys
/\d{3}/           # Match exactly 3 digits
/\d{3,}/          # Match 3 or more digits
/\d{3,5}/         # Match 3, 4, or 5 digits

# Nongreedy repetition: match the smallest number of repetitions
```

```
/<.*>/              # Greedy repetition: matches "<ruby>perl>"
/<.*?>/             # Nongreedy: matches "<ruby>" in "<ruby>perl>"
                    # Also nongreedy: ??, +?, and {n,m}?

# Grouping with parentheses
/\D\d+/             # No group: + repeats \d
/(\D\d)+/           # Grouped: + repeats \D\d pair
/([Rr]uby(, )?)+/   # Match "Ruby", "Ruby, ruby, ruby", etc.

# Backreferences: matching a previously matched group again
/([Rr])uby&\1ails/  # Match ruby&rails or Ruby&Rails
/(['"])[^\1]*\1/    # Single or double-quoted string
                    #    \1 matches whatever the 1st group matched
                    #    \2 matches whatever the 2nd group matched, etc.

# Named groups and backreferences in Ruby 1.9: match a 4-letter palindrome
/(?<first>\w)(?<second>\w)\k<second>\k<first>/
/(?'first'\w)(?'second'\w)\k'second'\k'first'/ # Alternate syntax

# Alternatives
/ruby|rube/         # Match "ruby" or "rube"
/rub(y|le))/        # Match "ruby" or "ruble"
/ruby(!+|\?)/       # "ruby" followed by one or more ! or one ?

# Anchors: specifying match position
/^Ruby/             # Match "Ruby" at the start of a string or internal line
/Ruby$/             # Match "Ruby" at the end of a string or line
/\ARuby/            # Match "Ruby" at the start of a string
/Ruby\Z/            # Match "Ruby" at the end of a string
/\bRuby\b/          # Match "Ruby" at a word boundary
/\brub\B/           # \B is nonword boundary:
                    #    match "rub" in "rube" and "ruby" but not alone
/Ruby(?=!)/         # Match "Ruby", if followed by an exclamation point
/Ruby(?!!)/         # Match "Ruby", if not followed by an exclamation point

# Special syntax with parentheses
/R(?#comment)/      # Matches "R". All the rest is a comment
/R(?i)uby/          # Case-insensitive while matching "uby"
/R(?i:uby)/         # Same thing
/rub(?:y|le))/      # Group only without creating \1 backreference

# The x option allows comments and ignores whitespace
/   # This is not a Ruby comment. It is a literal part
    # of the regular expression, but is ignored.
  R         # Match a single letter R
  (uby)+    # Followed by one or more "uby"s
  \         # Use backslash for a nonignored space
/x          # Closing delimiter. Don't forget the x option!
```

Table 9-2 summarizes the syntax rules demonstrated by this code.

Table 9-2. Regular expression syntax

Syntax	Matches
Character classes	
.	Matches any single character except newline. Using m option allows it to match newline as well.
[...]	Matches any single character in brackets.
[^...]	Matches any single character not in brackets.
\w	Matches word characters.
\W	Matches nonword characters.
\s	Matches whitespace. Equivalent to [\t\n\r\f].
\S	Matches nonwhitespace.
\d	Matches digits. Equivalent to [0–9].
\D	Matches nondigits.
Sequences, alternatives, groups, and references	
ab	Matches expression *a* followed by expression *b*.
a | b	Matches either expression *a* or expression *b*.
(*re*)	Grouping: groups *re* into a single syntactic unit that can be used with *, +, ?, |, and so on. Also "captures" the text that matches *re* for later use.
(?: *re*)	Groups as with ( ), but does not capture the matched text.
(?< *name* > *re*)	Groups a subexpression and captures the text that matches *re* as with ( ), and also labels the subexpression with *name*. Ruby 1.9.
(?' *name* ' *re*)	A named capture, as above. Single quotes may optionally replace angle brackets around *name*. Ruby 1.9.
\1...\9	Matches the same text that matched the *n*th grouped subexpression.
\10...	Matches the same text that matched the *n*th grouped subexpression if there are that many previous subexpressions. Otherwise, matches the character with the specified octal encoding.
\k< *name* >	Matches the same text that matched the named capturing group *name*.
\g< *n* >	Matches group *n* again. *n* can be a group name or a group number. Contrast \g, which rematches or reexecutes the specified group, with an ordinary back reference that tries to match the same text that matched the first time. Ruby 1.9.
Repetition	*By default, repetition is "greedy"—as many occurrences as possible are matched. For "reluctant" matching, follow a *, +, ?, or {} quantifier with a ? . This will match as few occurrences as possible while still allowing the rest of the expression to match. In Ruby 1.9, follow a quantifier with a + for "possessive" (non-backtracking) behavior.*
re *	Matches zero or more occurrences of *re*.
re +	Matches one or more occurrences of *re*.
re ?	Optional: matches zero or one occurrence of *re*.
re { *n* }	Matches exactly *n* occurrences of *re*.
re { *n* ,}	Matches *n* or more occurrences of *re*.
re { *n* , *m* }	Matches at least *n* and at most *m* occurrences of *re*.

Syntax	Matches
Anchors	*Anchors do not match characters but instead match the zero-width positions between characters, "anchoring" the match to a position at which a specific condition holds.*
^	Matches beginning of line.
$	Matches end of line.
\A	Matches beginning of string.
\Z	Matches end of string. If string ends with a newline, it matches just before newline.
\z	Matches end of string.
\G	Matches point where last match finished.
\b	Matches word boundaries when outside brackets. Matches backspace (0x08) when inside brackets.
\B	Matches nonword boundaries.
(?= *re*)	Positive lookahead assertion: ensures that the following characters match *re*, but doesn't include those characters in the matched text.
(?! *re*)	Negative lookahead assertion: ensures that the following characters do not match *re*.
(?<= *re*)	Positive lookbehind assertion: ensures that the preceding characters match *re*, but doesn't include those characters in the matched text. Ruby 1.9.
(?<! *re*)	Negative lookbehind assertion: ensures that the preceding characters do not match *re*. Ruby 1.9.
Miscellaneous	
(? *onflags* - *offflags*)	Doesn't match anything, but turns on the flags specified by *onflags*, and turns off the flags specified by *offflags*. These two strings are combinations in any order of the modifier letters i, m, and x. Flag settings specified in this way take effect at the point that they appear in the expression and persist until the end of the expression, or until the end of the parenthesized group of which they are a part, or until overridden by another flag setting expression.
(? *onflags* - *offflags* : *x*)	Matches *x*, applying the specified flags to this subexpression only. This is a noncapturing group, like (?:...), with the addition of flags.
(?#...)	Comment: all text within parentheses is ignored.
(?> *re*)	Matches *re* independently of the rest of the expression, without considering whether the match causes the rest of the expression to fail to match. Useful to optimize certain complex regular expressions. The parentheses do not capture the matched text.

9.2.4 Pattern Matching with Regular Expressions

=~ is Ruby's basic pattern-matching operator. One operand must be a regular expression and one must be a string. (It is implemented equivalently by both Regexp and String, so it doesn't matter whether the regular expression is on the left or the right.) The =~ operator checks its string operand to see if it, or any substring, matches the pattern specified by the regular expression. If a match is found, the operator returns the string index at which the first match begins. Otherwise, it returns nil:

```
pattern = /Ruby?/i    # Match "Rub" or "Ruby", case-insensitive
pattern =~ "backrub"  # Returns 4.
```

```
"rub ruby" =~ pattern    # 0
pattern =~ "r"           # nil
```

After using the =~ operator, we may be interested in things other than the position at which the matched text begins. After any successful (non-nil) match, the global variable $~ holds a MatchData object which contains complete information about the match:

```
"hello" =~ /e\w{2}/      # 1: Match an e followed by 2 word characters
$~.string                # "hello": the complete string
$~.to_s                  # "ell": the portion that matched
$~.pre_match             # "h": the portion before the match
$~.post_match            # "o": the portion after the match
```

$~ is a special thread-local and method-local variable. Two threads running concurrently will see distinct values of this variable. And a method that uses the =~ operator does not alter the value of $~ seen by the calling method. We'll have more to say about $~ and related global variables later. An object-oriented alternative to this magical and somewhat cryptic variable is Regexp.last_match. Invoking this method with no arguments returns the same value as a reference to $~.

A MatchData object is more powerful when the Regexp that was matched contains subexpressions in parentheses. In this case, the MatchData object can tell us the text (and the starting and ending offsets of that text) that matched each subexpression:

```
# This is a pattern with three subpatterns
pattern = /(Ruby|Perl)(\s+)(rocks|sucks)!/
text = "Ruby\trocks!"     # Text that matches the pattern
pattern =~ text           # => 0: pattern matches at the first character
data = Regexp.last_match   # => Get match details
data.size                 # => 4: MatchData objects behave like arrays
data[0]                   # => "Ruby\trocks!": the complete matched text
data[1]                   # => "Ruby": text matching first subpattern
data[2]                   # => "\t": text matching second subpattern
data[3]                   # => "rocks": text matching third subpattern
data[1,2]                 # => ["Ruby", "\t"]
data[1..3]                # => ["Ruby", "\t", "rocks"]
data.values_at(1,3)       # => ["Ruby", "rocks"]: only selected indexes
data.captures             # => ["Ruby", "\t", "rocks"]: only subpatterns
Regexp.last_match(3)      # => "rocks": same as Regexp.last_match[3]

# Start and end positions of matches
data.begin(0)             # => 0: start index of entire match
data.begin(2)             # => 4: start index of second subpattern
data.end(2)               # => 5: end index of second subpattern
data.offset(3)            # => [5,10]: start and end of third subpattern
```

In Ruby 1.9, if a pattern includes named captures, then a MatchData obtained from that pattern can be used like a hash, with the names of capturing groups (as strings or symbols) as keys. For example:

```
# Ruby 1.9 only
pattern = /(?<lang>Ruby|Perl) (?<ver>\d(\.\d)+) (?<review>rocks|sucks)!/
if (pattern =~ "Ruby 1.9.1 rocks!")
  $~[:lang]               # => "Ruby"
```

```
      $~[:ver]              # => "1.9.1"
      $~["review"]          # => "rocks"
      $~.offset(:ver)       # => [5,10] start and end offsets of version number
    end
    # Names of capturing groups and a map of group names to group numbers
    pattern.names           # => ["lang", "ver", "review"]
    pattern.named_captures  # => {"lang"=>[1],"ver"=>[2],"review"=>[3]}
```

> ## Named Captures and Local Variables
>
> In Ruby 1.9, if a regular expression containing named captures appears literally on the lefthand side of the =~ operator, then the names of the capturing groups are taken to be local variables, and the text that matches is assigned to those variables. If the match fails, then the variables are assigned nil. Here is an example:
>
> ```
> # Ruby 1.9 only
> if /(?<lang>\w+) (?<ver>\d+\.(\d+)+) (?<review>\w+)/ =~ "Ruby 1.9 rules!"
>   lang    # => "Ruby"
>   ver     # => "1.9"
>   review  # => "rules"
> end
> ```
>
> This is magical behavior, but it only occurs when a regular expression appears literally in your code. If a pattern is stored in a variable or a constant or is returned by a method, or if the pattern appears on the righthand side, then the =~ operator does not perform this special local variable assignment. If Ruby is invoked with the -w option, then it issues a warning if the =~ operator overwrites a variable that is already defined.

In addition to the =~ operator, the Regexp and String classes also define a match method. This method is like the match operator, except that instead of returning the index at which a match is found, it returns the MatchData object, or nil if no matching text is found. Use it like this:

```
    if data = pattern.match(text)  # Or: data = text.match(pattern)
      handle_match(data)
    end
```

In Ruby 1.9, you can also associate a block with a call to match. If no match is found, the block is ignored, and match returns nil. If a match is found, however, the MatchData object is passed to the block, and the match method returns whatever the block returns. So in Ruby 1.9, this code can be more succinctly written like this:

```
    pattern.match(text) {|data| handle_match(data) }
```

Another change in Ruby 1.9 is that the match methods optionally accept an integer as the second argument to specify the starting position of the search.

9.2.4.1 Global variables for match data

Ruby adopts Perl's regular expression syntax and, like Perl, sets special global variables after each match. If you are a Perl programmer, you may find these special variables useful. If you are a not a Perl programmer, you may find them unreadable! Table 9-3 summarizes these variables. The variables listed in the second column are aliases that are available if you require 'English'.

Table 9-3. Special global regular expression variables

Global	English	Alternative
$~	$LAST_MATCH_INFO	Regexp.last_match
$&	$MATCH	Regexp.last_match[0]
$`	$PREMATCH	Regexp.last_match.pre_match
$'	$POSTMATCH	Regexp.last_match.post_match
$1	none	Regexp.last_match[1]
$2, etc.	none	Regexp.last_match[2], etc.
$+	$LAST_PAREN_MATCH	Regexp.last_match[-1]

$~ is the most important of the variables listed in Table 9-3. All the others are derived from it. If you set $~ to a MatchData object, the values of the other special globals change. The other global variables are read-only and cannot be set directly. Finally, it is important to remember that $~ and the variables derived from it are all thread-local and method-local. This means that two Ruby threads can perform matches at the same time without interfering with each other and it means that the value of these variables, as seen by your code, will not change when your code calls a method that performs a pattern match.

9.2.4.2 Pattern matching with strings

The String class defines a number of methods that accept Regexp arguments. If you index a string with a regular expression, then the portion of the string that matches the pattern is returned. If the Regexp is followed by an integer, then the corresponding element of the MatchData is returned:

```
"ruby123"[/\d+/]              # "123"
"ruby123"[/([a-z]+)(\d+)/,1]  # "ruby"
"ruby123"[/([a-z]+)(\d+)/,2]  # "123"
```

The slice method is a synonym for the string index operator []. The slice! variant returns the same value as slice but also has the side effect of deleting the returned substring from the string:

```
r = "ruby123"
r.slice!(/\d+/)  # Returns "123", changes r to "ruby"
```

The split method splits a string into an array of substrings, using a string or regular expression as its delimiter:

```
s = "one, two, three"
s.split          # ["one,","two,","three"]: whitespace delimiter by default
```

```
s.split(", ")      # ["one","two","three"]: hardcoded delimiter
s.split(/\s*,\s*/) # ["one","two","three"]: space is optional around comma
```

The index method searches a string for a character, substring, or pattern, and returns the start index. With a Regexp argument, it works much like the =~ operator, but it also allows a second argument that specifies the character position at which to begin the search. This allows you to find matches other than the first:

```
text = "hello world"
pattern = /l/
first = text.index(pattern)        # 2: first match starts at char 2
n = Regexp.last_match.end(0)       # 3: end position of first match
second = text.index(pattern, n)    # 3: search again from there
last = text.rindex(pattern)        # 9: rindex searches backward from end
```

9.2.4.3 Search and replace

Some of the most important String methods that use regular expressions are sub (for substitute) and gsub (for global substitute), and their in-place variants sub! and gsub!. All of these methods perform a search-and-replace operation using a Regexp pattern. sub and sub! replace the first occurrence of the pattern. gsub and gsub! replace all occurrences. sub and gsub return a new string, leaving the original unmodified. sub! and gsub! modify the string on which they are called. If any modifications are made to the string, these mutator methods return the modified string. If no modifications are made, they return nil (which makes the methods suitable for use in if statements and while loops):

```
phone = gets              # Read a phone number
phone.sub!(/#.*$/, "")    # Delete Ruby-style comments
phone.gsub!(/\D/,' '=>'-') # 1.9: remove non-digits but map space to hyphen
```

These search-and-replace methods do not require the use of regular expressions; you can also use an ordinary string as the text to be replaced:

```
text.gsub!("rails", "Rails")     # Change "rails" to "Rails" throughout
```

However, regular expressions really are more flexible. If you want to capitalize "rails" without modifying "grails", for example, use a Regexp:

```
text.gsub!(/\brails\b/, "Rails") # Capitalize the word "Rails" throughout
```

The reason that the search-and-replace methods are covered in this subsection on their own is that the replacement does not need to be an ordinary string of text. (Replacement strings specified in a hash must be ordinary strings, however.) Suppose you want a replacement string that depends on the details of the match found. The search-and-replace methods process the replacement string before performing replacements. If the string contains a backslash followed by a single digit, then that digit is used as an index into the $~ object, and the text from the MatchData object is used in place of the backslash and the digit. For example, if the string contains the escape sequence \0, the entire matched text is used. If the replacement string contains \1, then the text that matches the first subexpression is used in the replacement. The following code does a case-insensitive search for the word "ruby" and puts HTML bold tags around it, preserving the word's capitalization:

```
text.gsub(/\bruby\b/i, '<b>\0</b>')
```

Note that if you use a double-quoted replacement string, you must double the backslash character.

You might be tempted to try the same thing using normal double-quoted string interpolation:

```
text.gsub(/\bruby\b/i, "<b>#{$&}</b>")
```

This does not work, however, because in this case the interpolation is performed on the string literal before it is passed to gsub. This is before the pattern has been matched, so variables like $& are undefined or hold values from a previous match.

In Ruby 1.9, you can refer to named capturing groups using the \k named backreference syntax:

```
# Strip pairs of quotes from a string
re = /(?<quote>['"])(?<body>[^'"]*)\k<quote>/
puts "These are 'quotes'".gsub(re, '\k<body>')
```

Replacement strings can also refer to text other than that matched by capturing groups. Use \&, \`, \', and \+ to substitute in the value of $&, $`, $', and $+.

Instead of using a static replacement string, the search-and-replace methods can also be called with a block of code that computes the replacement string dynamically. The argument to the block is the text that matched the pattern:

```
# Use consistent capitalization for the names of programming languages
text = "RUBY Java perl PyThOn"      # Text to modify
lang = /ruby|java|perl|python/i     # Pattern to match
text.gsub!(lang) {|l| l.capitalize }  # Fix capitalization
```

Within the block of code, you can use $~ and the related global variables listed earlier in Table 9-3:

```
pattern = /(['"])([^\1]*)\1/   # Single- or double-quoted string
text.gsub!(pattern) do
  if ($1 == '"')   # If it was a double-quoted string
    "'#$2'"        # replace with single-quoted
  else             # Otherwise, if single-quoted
    "\"#$2\""      # replace with double-quoted
  end
end
```

9.2.4.4 Regular expression encoding

In Ruby 1.9, Regexp objects have an encoding method just like strings do. You can explicitly specify the encoding of a regular expression with modifiers: u for UTF-8, s for SJIS, e for EUC-JP, and n for none. You can also explicitly specify UTF-8 encoding by including a \u escape in the regular expression. If you don't explicitly specify an encoding, then the source encoding is used. But if all the characters in the regexp are ASCII, then ASCII is used, even if the source encoding is some superset of ASCII.

Ruby 1.9 pattern-matching operations raise an exception if you attempt to match a pattern and a string that have incompatible encodings. The `fixed_encoding?` method returns `true` if a Regexp has an encoding other than ASCII. If `fixed_encoding?` returns `false`, then it is safe to use that pattern to match against any string whose encoding is ASCII or a superset of ASCII.

9.3 Numbers and Math

Chapter 3 covered the various `Numeric` subclasses in Ruby, explained how to write numeric literals in Ruby, and documented Ruby's integer and floating-point arithmetic. Here we expand on that chapter to cover numeric APIs and other math-related classes.

9.3.1 Numeric Methods

`Numeric` and its subclasses define a number of useful predicates for determining the class or testing the value of a number. Some of these predicates work only for `Float` values, and some work only for `Integer` values:

```
# General Predicates
0.zero?         # => true (is this number zero?)
1.0.zero?       # => false
0.0.nonzero?    # => nil (works like false)
1.nonzero?      # => 1 (works like true)
1.integer?      # => true
1.0.integer?    # => false
1.scalar?       # => true: not a complex number. Ruby 1.9.
1.0.scalar?     # => true: not a complex number. Ruby 1.9.
Complex(1,2).scalar? # => false: a complex number. require 'complex' in 1.8

# Integer predicates
0.even?         # => true (Ruby 1.9)
0.odd?          # => false

# Float predicates
ZERO, INF, NAN = 0.0, 1.0/0.0, 0.0/0.0  # Constants for testing

ZERO.finite?    # => true: is this number finite?
INF.finite?     # => false
NAN.finite?     # => false

ZERO.infinite?  # => nil: is this number infinite? Positive or negative?
INF.infinite?   # => 1
-INF.infinite?  # => -1
NAN.infinite?   # => nil

ZERO.nan?       # => false: is this number not-a-number?
INF.nan?        # => false
NAN.nan?        # => true
```

Numeric and its subclasses define various methods for rounding numbers:

```
# Rounding methods
1.1.ceil     # =>  2: ceiling: smallest integer >= its argument
-1.1.ceil    # => -1: ceiling: smallest integer >= its argument
1.9.floor    # =>  1: floor: largest integer <= its argument
-1.9.floor   # => -2: floor: largest integer <= its argument
1.1.round    # =>  1: round to nearest integer
0.5.round    # =>  1: round toward infinity when halfway between integers
-0.5.round   # => -1: or round toward negative infinity
1.1.truncate # =>  1: chop off fractional part: round toward zero
-1.1.to_i    # => -1: synonym for truncate
```

Here are a few other numeric methods and constants of interest:

```
# For any Numeric value n, in Ruby 1.9
[n.abs, n<=>0]                 # Absolute value and sign
[n.abs, n.angle]               # Magnitude and angle (or use n.polar)
[n.numerator, n.denominator]   # Numerator and denominator
[n.real, n.imag]               # Real and imaginary parts


# Floating point constants: may be implementation dependent
[Float::MAX, Float::MIN]    # => [1.79769313486232e+308,2.2250738585072e-308]
Float::EPSILON # => 2.22044604925031e-16: difference between adjacent floats
```

9.3.2 The Math Module

The Math module defines constants PI and E, and methods for trigonometry and logarithms, plus a few miscellaneous methods. The methods of Math are "module functions" (see §7.5.3), which means that they can be invoked through the Math namespace or included and invoked as if they were global functions. Here are some examples:

```
# Constants
Math::PI            # => 3.14159265358979
Math::E             # => 2.71828182845905

# Roots
Math.sqrt(25.0)     # => 5.0: square root
Math.cbrt(27.0)     # => 3.0: cube root; Ruby 1.9 and later
27.0**(1.0/3.0)     # => 3.0: cube root computed with ** operator

# Logarithms
Math.log10(100.0)   # => 2.0: base-10 logarithm
Math.log(Math::E**3) # => 3.0: natural (base-e) logarithm
Math.log2(8)        # => 3.0: base-2 logarithm. Ruby 1.9 and later.
Math.log(16, 4)     # => 2.0: 2nd arg to log() is the base. Ruby 1.9.
Math.exp(2)         # => 7.38905609893065: same as Math::E**2

# Trigonometry
include Math         # Save typing: we can now omit Math prefix.
sin(PI/2)           # => 1.0: sine. Argument is in radians, not degrees.
cos(0)              # => 1.0: cosine.
tan(PI/4)           # => 1.0: tangent.
asin(1.0)/PI        # => 0.5: arcsine. See also acos and atan.
sinh(0)             # => 0.0: hyperbolic sine. Also cosh, tanh.
```

```
asinh(1.0)              # => 0.0: inverse sinh. Also acosh, atanh.

# Convert cartesian point (x,y) to polar coordinates (theta, r)
theta = atan2(y,x)      # Angle between X axis and line (0,0)-(x,y)
r = hypot(x,y)          # Hypotenuse: sqrt(x**2 + y**2)

# Miscellaneous Functions
f,e = frexp(1024.0)     # => [0.5, 11]: decompose x into [f,e], x = f*2**e
x = ldexp(f, e)         # => 1024: compute x = f*2**e
erf(0.0)                # => 0.0: error function
erfc(0.0)               # => 1.0: 1-erf(x): complementary error function
gamma(5)                # => 24.0: floating-point factorial function
lgamma(100)             # => [359.134205369575, 1]: logarithmic gamma
```

9.3.3 Decimal Arithmetic

The BigDecimal class from the standard library is a useful alternative to Float, particularly for financial computations where you want to avoid the rounding error inherent in the use of a binary floating-point arithmetic (see §3.1.4). BigDecimal objects can have an unlimited number of significant digits and practically unlimited size (exponents over 1 billion are supported). Most importantly, they use decimal arithmetic and offer precise control over rounding modes. Here is example BigDecimal code:

```
require "bigdecimal"      # Load standard library
dime = BigDecimal("0.1")  # Pass a string to constructor, not a Float
4*dime-3*dime == dime     # true with BigDecimal, but false if we use Float

# Compute monthly interest payments on a mortgage with BigDecimal.
# Use "Banker's Rounding" mode, and limit computations to 20 digits
BigDecimal.mode(BigDecimal::ROUND_MODE, BigDecimal::ROUND_HALF_EVEN)
BigDecimal.limit(20)
principal = BigDecimal("200000")  # Always pass strings to constructor
apr = BigDecimal("6.5")           # Annual percentage rate interest
years = 30                        # Term of mortgage in years
payments = years*12               # 12 monthly payments in a year
interest = apr/100/12             # Convert APR to monthly fraction
x = (interest+1)**payments        # Note exponentiation with BigDecimal
monthly = (principal * interest * x)/(x-1)  # Compute monthly payment
monthly = monthly.round(2)        # Round to two decimal places
monthly = monthly.to_s("f")       # Convert to human-readable string
```

Use *ri* for more details on the BigDecimal API, and for complete documentation see the file *ext/bigdecimal/bigdecimal_en.html* in the Ruby source distribution.

9.3.4 Complex Numbers

The Complex class represents complex numbers. It is a core class in 1.9 and part of the standard library in 1.8. Requiring the "complex" module (in either 1.8 or 1.9) redefines the methods of the Math module so that they can accept and return complex numbers. In Ruby 1.9 you can instead require "cmath" to define a CMath module that defines complex-enabled versions of the Math methods. Examples:

```
require "complex"          # Ruby 1.8 and for complex Math methods in 1.9
c = Complex(0.5,-0.2)      # => .5-.2i.
Complex.polar(1,Math::PI/2) # => Complex(0.0,1.0): create with polar coords
i = 1.im                   # => Complex(0,1): multiply by i
(2.re - 3.5.im).to_s       # => "2-3.5i": re method in Ruby 1.9 only
r,i = c.real, c.imag       # => [0.5,-0.2]: Real part, imaginary part
m,a = c.polar              # => [magnitude, angle]: Same as [c.abs,c.angle]
d = c.conj                 # => .5+.2i: change sign of imaginary part
z = "0+0i".to_c            # String-to-Complex conversion function
10.times { z = z*z + c }   # Arithmetic operators work on Complex numbers
1.im**2                    # => Complex(-1,0): i*i == -1
x = Math.sin(z)            # 'complex' module redefines Math functions
require 'cmath'            # Ruby 1.9: Define CMath module for complex math
CMath.sqrt(-1)==Complex::I # => true
```

9.3.5 Rational Numbers

The `Rational` class represents rational numbers (the quotient of two integers).
`Rational` is built-in to Ruby 1.9 and is part of the standard library in Ruby 1.8. Division
with the `quo` method returns a `Rational` value if both arguments are integers. Some
examples:

```
require "rational"            # Only necessary in Ruby 1.8
penny = Rational(1, 100)      # A penny is 1/100th
nickel = "5/100".to_r         # String-to-Rational conversion: Ruby 1.9 only
dime = 10.quo 100             # => Rational(1,10)
change = 2*dime + 3*penny     # => Rational(23,100)
change.numerator              # => 23: top of the fraction
change.denominator            # => 100: bottom of the fraction
change.to_f                   # => 0.23: convert to Float
(nickel * dime).to_s          # => "1/200": to_s returns fractions
```

9.3.6 Vectors and Matrices

The `matrix` library defines `Matrix` and `Vector` classes to represent matrices and vectors
of numbers as well as operators to perform arithmetic on them. A discussion of linear
algebra is well beyond the scope of this book, but the following example code uses the
`Vector` class to represent a two-dimensional point, and uses 2×2 `Matrix` objects to
represent scaling and rotation transformations of the point:

```
require "matrix"

# Represent the point (1,1) as the vector [1,1]
unit = Vector[1,1]

# The identity transformation matrix
identity = Matrix.identity(2)  # 2x2 matrix
identity*unit == unit          # true: no transformation

# This matrix scales a point by sx,sy
sx,sy = 2.0, 3.0;
scale = Matrix[[sx,0], [0, sy]]
```

```
scale*unit              # => [2.0, 3.0]: scaled point

# This matrix rotates counterclockwise around the origin
theta = Math::PI/2      # 90 degrees
rotate = Matrix[[Math.cos(theta), -Math.sin(theta)],
                [Math.sin(theta),  Math.cos(theta)]]
rotate*unit             # [-1.0, 1.0]: 90 degree rotation

# Two transformations in one
scale * (rotate*unit)  # [-2.0, 3.0]
```

9.3.7 Random Numbers

Random numbers are generated in Ruby with the global `Kernel.rand` function. With no arguments, it returns a pseudorandom `Float` greater than or equal to `0.0` and less than `1.0`. With an integer argument *max*, it returns a pseudorandom integer greater than or equal to `0` and less than *max*. For example:

```
rand        # => 0.964395196505186
rand        # => 0.390523655919935
rand(100)   # => 81
rand(100)   # => 32
```

If you need a repeatable sequence of pseudorandom numbers (for testing, perhaps), seed the random number generator with a known value:

```
srand(0)                    # Known seed
[rand(100),rand(100)]       # => [44,47]: pseudorandom sequence
srand(0)                    # Reset the seed to repeat the sequence
[rand(100),rand(100)]       # => [44,47]
```

For cryptographically secure random numbers, use the `SecureRandom` module, which is part of the standard library in Ruby 1.9 and 1.8.7.

9.4 Dates and Times

The `Time` class represents dates and times. It is a thin layer over the system date and time functionality provided by the operating system. On some platforms, therefore, this class may be unable to represent dates before 1970 or after 2038. The `Date` and `DateTime` classes in the standard `date` library are not constrained in this way, but are not demonstrated here:

```
# Creating Time objects
Time.now        # Returns a time object that represents the current time
Time.new        # A synonym for Time.now

Time.local(2007, 7, 8)          # July 8, 2007
Time.local(2007, 7, 8, 9, 10)   # July 8, 2007, 09:10am, local time
Time.utc(2007, 7, 8, 9, 10)     # July 8, 2007, 09:10 UTC
Time.gm(2007, 7, 8, 9, 10, 11)  # July 8, 2007, 09:10:11 GMT (same as UTC)

# One microsecond before the new millennium began in London
```

```
# We'll use this Time object in many examples below.
t = Time.utc(2000, 12, 31, 23, 59, 59, 999999)

# Components of a Time
t.year    # => 2000
t.month   # => 12: December
t.day     # => 31
t.wday    # => 0: day of week: 0 is Sunday
t.yday    # => 366: day of year: 2000 was a leap year
t.hour    # => 23: 24-hour clock
t.min     # => 59
t.sec     # => 59
t.usec    # => 999999: microseconds, not milliseconds
t.zone    # => "UTC": timezone name

# Get all components in an array that holds
# [sec,min,hour,day,month,year,wday,yday,isdst,zone]
# Note that we lose microseconds
values = t.to_a    # => [59, 59, 23, 31, 12, 2000, 0, 366, false, "UTC"]

# Arrays of this form can be passed to Time.local and Time.utc
values[5] += 1     # Increment the year
Time.utc(*values) # => Mon Dec 31 23:59:59 UTC 2001

# Timezones and daylight savings time
t.zone       # => "UTC": return the timezone
t.utc?       # => true: t is in UTC time zone
t.utc_offset # => 0: UTC is 0 seconds offset from UTC
t.localtime  # Convert to local timezone. Mutates the Time object!
t.zone       # => "PST" (or whatever your timezone is)
t.utc?       # => false
t.utc_offset # => -28800: 8 hours before UTC
t.gmtime     # Convert back to UTC. Another mutator.
t.getlocal   # Return a new Time object in local zone
t.getutc     # Return a new Time object in UTC
t.isdst      # => false: UTC does not have DST. Note no ?.
t.getlocal.isdst # => false: no daylight savings time in winter.

# Weekday predicates: Ruby 1.9
t.sunday?    # => true
t.monday?    # => false
t.tuesday?   # etc.

# Formatting Times and Dates
t.to_s       # => "Sun Dec 31 23:59:59 UTC 2000": Ruby 1.8
t.to_s       # => "2000-12-31 23:59:59 UTC": Ruby 1.9 uses ISO-8601
t.ctime      # => "Sun Dec 31 23:59:59 2000": another basic format

# strftime interpolates date and time components into a template string
# Locale-independent formatting
t.strftime("%Y-%m-%d %H:%M:%S") # => "2000-12-31 23:59:59": ISO-8601 format
t.strftime("%H:%M")             # => "23:59": 24-hour time
t.strftime("%I:%M %p")          # => "11:59 PM": 12-hour clock

# Locale-dependent formats
```

```ruby
t.strftime("%A, %B %d")       # => "Sunday, December 31"
t.strftime("%a, %b %d %y")    # => "Sun, Dec 31 00": 2-digit year
t.strftime("%x")              # => "12/31/00": locale-dependent format
t.strftime("%X")              # => "23:59:59"
t.strftime("%c")              # same as ctime

# Parsing Times and Dates
require 'parsedate'   # A versatile date/time parsing library
include ParseDate     # Include parsedate() as a global function
datestring = "2001-01-01"
values = parsedate(datestring)  # [2001, 1, 1, nil, nil, nil, nil, nil]
t = Time.local(*values)         # => Mon Jan 01 00:00:00 -0800 2001
s = t.ctime                     # => "Mon Jan  1 00:00:00 2001"
Time.local(*parsedate(s))==t    # => true

s = "2001-01-01 00:00:00-0500"  # midnight in New York
v = parsedate(s)                # => [2001, 1, 1, 0, 0, 0, "-0500", nil]
t = Time.local(*v)              # Loses time zone information!

# Time arithmetic
now = Time.now        # Current time
past = now - 10       # 10 seconds ago. Time - number => Time
future = now + 10     # 10 seconds from now Time + number => Time
future - now          # => 10   Time - Time => number of seconds

# Time comparisons
past <=> future       # => -1
past < future         # => true
now >= future         # => false
now == now            # => true

# Helper methods for working with time units other than seconds
class Numeric
  # Convert time intervals to seconds
  def milliseconds; self/1000.0; end
  def seconds; self; end
  def minutes; self*60; end
  def hours; self*60*60; end
  def days; self*60*60*24; end
  def weeks; self*60*60*24*7; end

  # Convert seconds to other intervals
  def to_milliseconds; self*1000; end
  def to_seconds; self; end
  def to_minutes; self/60.0; end
  def to_hours; self/(60*60.0); end
  def to_days; self/(60*60*24.0); end
  def to_weeks; self/(60*60*24*7.0); end
end

expires = now + 10.days    # 10 days from now
expires - now              # => 864000.0 seconds
(expires - now).to_hours   # => 240.0 hours

# Time represented internally as seconds since the (platform-dependent) epoch
```

```
t = Time.now.to_i      # => 1184036194 seconds since epoch
Time.at(t)             # => seconds since epoch to Time object
t = Time.now.to_f      # => 1184036322.90872: includes 908720 microseconds
Time.at(0)             # => Wed Dec 31 16:00:00 -0800 1969: epoch in local time
```

9.5 Collections

This section documents Ruby's *collection* classes. A collection is any class that represents a collection of values. `Array` and `Hash` are the key collection classes in Ruby, and the standard library adds a `Set` class. Each of these collection classes mixes in the `Enumerable` module, which means that `Enumerable` methods are universal collection methods.

9.5.1 Enumerable Objects

The `Enumerable` module is a mixin that implements a number of useful methods on top of the each iterator. The `Array`, `Hash`, and `Set` classes described below all include `Enumerable` and therefore implement all of the methods described here. `Range` and `IO` are other noteworthy enumerable classes. `Enumerable` was covered briefly in §5.3.2. This section provides more detailed coverage.

Note that some enumerable classes have a natural enumeration order that their each method follows. Arrays, for example, enumerate their elements in order of increasing array index. `Range` enumerates in ascending order. And `IO` objects enumerate lines of text in the order in which they are read from the underlying file or socket. In Ruby 1.9, `Hash` and `Set` (which is based on `Hash`) enumerate their elements in the order in which they were inserted. Prior to Ruby 1.9, however, these classes enumerate their elements in what is essentially an arbitrary order.

Many `Enumerable` methods return a processed version of the enumerable collection or a selected subcollection of its elements. Usually, if an `Enumerable` method returns a collection (rather than a single value selected from a collection), the collection is an `Array`. This is not always the case, however. The `Hash` class overrides the `reject` method so that it returns a `Hash` object instead of an array, for example. Whatever the precise return value, it is certain that a collection returned by an `Enumerable` method will itself be enumerable.

9.5.1.1 Iterating and converting collections

By definition, any `Enumerable` object must have an each iterator. `Enumerable` provides a simple variant `each_with_index`, which yields an element of the collection and an integer. For arrays, the integer is the array index. For `IO` objects, the integer is the line number (starting at 0). For other objects, the integer is what the array index would be if the collection was converted to an array:

```
(5..7).each {|x| print x }               # Prints "567"
(5..7).each_with_index {|x,i| print x,i } # Prints "506172"
```

In Ruby 1.9, Enumerable defines cycle, which iterates repeatedly through the elements of the collection, looping forever until the block you provide explicitly terminates the iteration with break or return or by raising an exception. During its first pass through the Enumerable object, cycle saves the elements into an array and then subsequently iterates from the array. This means that after the first pass through the collection, modifications to that collection do not affect the behavior of cycle.

each_sliceand each_cons are iterators that yield subarrays of a collection. They are available in Ruby 1.8 with require 'enumerator' and are part of the core library in Ruby 1.9 (and 1.8.7). each_slice(n) iterates the enumerable values in "slices" of size n:

```
(1..10).each_slice(4) {|x| print x } # Prints "[1,2,3,4][5,6,7,8][9,10]"
```

each_cons is similar to each_slice, but it uses a "sliding window" on the enumerable collection:

```
(1..5).each_cons(3) {|x| print x }     # Prints "[1,2,3][2,3,4][3,4,5]"
```

The collect method applies a block to each element of a collection and collects the return values of the block into a new array. map is a synonym; it maps the elements of a collection to the elements of an array by applying a block to each element:

```
data = [1,2,3,4]                        # An enumerable collection
roots = data.collect {|x| Math.sqrt(x)} # Collect roots of our data
words = %w[hello world]                 # Another collection
upper = words.map {|x| x.upcase }       # Map to uppercase
```

The zip method interleaves the elements of one enumerable collection with the elements of zero or more other collections, and yields an array of elements (one from each collection) to the associated block. If no block is provided, the return value is an array of arrays:

```
(1..3).zip([4,5,6]) {|x| print x.inspect } # Prints "[1,4][2,5][3,6]"
(1..3).zip([4,5,6],[7,8]) {|x| print x}  # Prints "14725836"
(1..3).zip('a'..'c') {|x,y| print x,y }  # Prints "1a2b3c"
p (1..3).zip('a'..'z')                    # Prints [[1,"a"],[2,"b"],[3,"c"]]
p (1..3).zip('a'..'b')                    # Prints [[1,"a"],[2,"b"],[3,nil]]
```

Enumerable defines a to_a method (and a synonym entries) that converts any enumerable collection into an array. to_a is included in this section because the conversion obviously involves iterating the collection. The elements of the resulting array appear in whatever order the each iterator yields them:

```
(1..3).to_a      # => [1,2,3]
(1..3).entries   # => [1,2,3]
```

If you require 'set', all Enumerable objects gain a to_set conversion method as well. Sets are described in detail in §9.5.4:

```
require 'set'
(1..3).to_set    # => #<Set: {1, 2, 3}>
```

9.5.1.2 Enumerators and external iterators

Enumerators and their use as external iterators are fully documented in §5.3.4 and §5.3.5. This section is just a brief recap, with examples, of the detailed descriptions in Chapter 5.

Enumerators are of class `Enumerable::Enumerator`, which has a surprisingly small number of methods for such a powerful iteration construct. Enumerators are primarily a feature of Ruby 1.9 (and 1.8.7) but some enumerator functionality is available in Ruby 1.8 by requiring the `enumerator` library. Create an `Enumerator` with `to_enum` or its alias `enum_for`, or simply by calling an iterator method without the block it expects:

```
e = [1..10].to_enum                  # Uses Range.each
e = "test".enum_for(:each_byte)      # Uses String.each_byte
e = "test".each_byte                 # Uses String.each_byte
```

`Enumerator` objects are `Enumerable` objects with an `each` method that is based on some other iterator method of some other object. In addition to being `Enumerable` proxy objects, an enumerator also behaves as an external iterator. To obtain the elements of a collection using an external iterator, simply call `next` repeatedly until it raises `StopIteration`. The `Kernel.loop` iterator rescues `StopIteration` for you. After `next` raises `StopIteration`, a subsequent call will typically begin a new iteration, assuming the underlying iterator method allows repeated iterations (iterators reading from a file don't allow that, for example). If repeated iterations are possible, you can restart an external iterator before `StopIteration` has been raised by calling `rewind`:

```
"Ruby".each_char.max       # => "y"; Enumerable method of Enumerator
iter = "Ruby".each_char    # Create an Enumerator
loop { print iter.next }   # Prints "Ruby"; use it as external iterator
print iter.next            # Prints "R": iterator restarts automatically
iter.rewind                # Force it to restart now
print iter.next            # Prints "R" again
```

Given any enumerator e, you can obtain a new enumerator with `e.with_index`. As the name implies, this new enumerator yields an index (or iteration number) along with whatever value the original iterator would yield:

```
# Print "0:R\n1:u\n2:b\n3:y\n"
"Ruby".each_char.with_index.each {|c,i| puts "#{i}:#{c} }
```

Finally, note that enumerators, like all `Enumerable` objects, are *splattable*: you can prefix an enumerator with an asterisk to expand it into individual values for method invocation or parallel assignment.

9.5.1.3 Sorting collections

One of the most important methods of `Enumerable` is `sort`. It converts the enumerable collection to an array and sorts the elements of that array. By default, the sort is done according to the `<=>` method of the elements. If a block is provided, however, then it is passed pairs of elements and should return -1, 0, or +1 to indicate their relative order:

```
w = Set['apple','Beet','carrot']  # A set of words to sort
w.sort                             # ['Beet','apple','carrot']: alphabetical
w.sort {|a,b| b<=>a }              # ['carrot','apple','Beet']: reverse
w.sort {|a,b| a.casecmp(b) }       # ['apple','Beet','carrot']: ignore case
w.sort {|a,b| b.size<=>a.size}     # ['carrot','apple','Beet']: reverse length
```

If the block you associate with **sort** must do substantial computation in order to perform its comparison, then it is more efficient to use **sort_by** instead. The block associated with **sort_by** will be called once for each element in the collection, and should return a numeric "sort key" for that element. The collection will then be sorted by ascending order of the sort key. This way, a sort key is only computed once for each element, rather than twice for each comparison:

```
# Case-insensitive sort
words = ['carrot', 'Beet', 'apple']
words.sort_by {|x| x.downcase}      # => ['apple', 'Beet', 'carrot']
```

9.5.1.4 Searching collections

Enumerable defines several methods for searching for single elements within a collection. **include?** and its synonym **member?** search for an element equal to (using ==) their argument:

```
primes = Set[2, 3, 5, 7]
primes.include? 2     # => true
primes.member? 1      # => false
```

The **find** method, and its synonym **detect**, apply the associated block to each element of the collection in turn. If the block returns anything other than **false** or **nil**, then **find** returns that element and stops iterating. If the block always returns **nil** or **false**, then **find** returns **nil**:

```
# Find the first subarray that includes the number 1
data = [[1,2], [0,1], [7,8]]
data.find {|x| x.include? 1}      # => [1,2]
data.detect {|x| x.include? 3}    # => nil: no such element
```

The **find_index** method (new in Ruby 1.9) is like the **index** method of **Array**: it returns the index of a specific element or of the first element that matches a block:

```
data.find_index [0,1]            # => 1: the second element matches
data.find_index {|x| x.include? 1} # => 0: the first element matches
data.find_index {|x| x.include? 3} # => nil: no such element
```

Note that the return value of **find_index** is not terribly useful for collections like hashes and sets that do not use numeric indexes.

Enumerable defines other searching methods that return a collection of matches rather than a single match. We cover these methods in the next section.

9.5.1.5 Selecting subcollections

The select method selects and returns elements of a collection for which a block returns a non-nil, non-false value. A synonym for this method is find_all; it works like the find method but returns an array of all matching elements:

```
(1..8).select {|x| x%2==0}    # => [2,4,6,8]: select even elements
(1..8).find_all {|x| x%2==1}  # => [1,3,5,7]: find all odd elements
```

reject is the opposite of select; the elements in the returned array are those for which the block returns false or nil.

```
primes = [2,3,5,7]
primes.reject {|x| x%2==0}  # => [3,5,7]: reject the even ones
```

If you want both to select and reject elements of a collection, use partition. It returns an array of two arrays. The first subarray holds elements for which the block is true, and the second subarray holds elements for which the block is false:

```
(1..8).partition {|x| x%2==0}  # => [[2, 4, 6, 8], [1, 3, 5, 7]]
```

The group_by method of Ruby 1.9 is a generalization of partition. Rather than treating the block as a predicate and returning two groups, group_by takes the return value of the block and uses it as a hash key. It maps that key to an array of all collection elements for which the block returned that value. For example:

```
# Group programming languages by their first letter
langs = %w[ java perl python ruby ]
groups = langs.group_by {|lang| lang[0] }
groups # => {"j"=>["java"], "p"=>["perl", "python"], "r"=>["ruby"]}
```

grep returns an array of elements that match the argument value, determining matching with the case equality operator (===) of the argument. When used with a regular expression argument, this method works like the Unix command-line utility *grep*. If a block is associated with the call, it is used to process matching elements, as if collect or map were called on the results of grep:

```
langs = %w[ java perl python ruby ]
langs.grep(/^p/)                  # => [perl, python]: start with 'p'
langs.grep(/^p/) {|x| x.capitalize} # => [Perl, Python]: fix caps
data = [1, 17, 3.0, 4]
ints = data.grep(Integer)         # => [1, 17, 4]: only integers
small = ints.grep(0..9)           # [1,4]: only in range
```

In Ruby 1.9, the selection methods described previously are augmented by first, take, drop, take_while, and drop_while. first returns the first element of an Enumerable object, or, given an integer argument *n*, an array containing the first *n* elements. take and drop expect an integer argument. take behaves just like first; it returns an array of the first *n* elements of the Enumerable receiver object. drop does the opposite; it returns an array of all elements of the Enumerable except for the first *n*:

```
p (1..5).first(2)    # => [1,2]
p (1..5).take(3)     # => [1,2,3]
p (1..5).drop(3)     # => [4,5]
```

`take_while` and `drop_while` expect a block instead of an integer argument. `take_while` passes elements of the `Enumerable` object to the block in turn, until the block returns `false` or `nil` for the first time. Then it returns an array of the previous elements for which the block returned `true`. `drop` also passes elements to the block in turn until the block returns `false` or `nil` for the first time. Then, however, it returns an array containing the element for which the block returned `false` and all subsequent elements:

```
[1,2,3,nil,4].take_while {|x| x }  # => [1,2,3]: take until nil
[nil, 1, 2].drop_while {|x| !x }   # => [1,2]: drop leading nils
```

The `Array` class defines its own efficient versions of these taking and dropping methods that do not require arrays to be iterated with `each`.

9.5.1.6 Reducing collections

Sometimes we want to *reduce* an enumerable collection to a single value that captures some property of the collection. `min` and `max` are methods that perform a reduction, returning the smallest or largest element of the collection (assuming that the elements are mutually comparable with `<=>`):

```
[10, 100, 1].min   # => 1
['a','c','b'].max   # => 'c'
[10, 'a', []].min   # => ArgumentError: elements not comparable
```

`min` and `max` can take a block like `sort` can, to compare two elements. In Ruby 1.9, it is easier to use `min_by` and `max_by` instead:

```
langs = %w[java perl python ruby]     # Which has the longest name?
langs.max {|a,b| a.size <=> b.size } # => "python": block compares 2
langs.max_by {|word| word.length }   # => "python": Ruby 1.9 only
```

Ruby 1.9 also defines `minmax` and `minmax_by`, which compute both the minimum and maximum value of a collection and return them as a two-element array [`min`,`max`]:

```
(1..100).minmax              # => [1,100] min, max as numbers
(1..100).minmax_by {|n| n.to_s }  # => [1,99]  min, max as strings
```

`any?` and `all?` are predicates that also perform reductions. They apply a predicate block to elements of the collection. `all?` returns `true` if the predicate is true (that is, not `nil` and not `false`) for *all* elements of the collection. `any?` returns `true` if the predicate is true for any one of the elements. In Ruby 1.9, `none?` returns `true` only if the predicate never returns a true value. Also in 1.9, `one?` returns `true` only if the predicate returns a true value for one, and only one, element of the collection. Invoked without blocks, these methods simply test the elements of the collection themselves:

```
c = -2..2
c.all? {|x| x>0}   # => false: not all values are > 0
c.any? {|x| x>0}   # => true: some values are > 0
c.none? {|x| x>2}  # => true: no values are > 2
c.one? {|x| x>0}   # => false: more than one value is > 0
c.one? {|x| x>2}   # => false: no values are > 2
c.one? {|x| x==2}  # => true: one value == 2
[1, 2, 3].all?     # => true: no values are nil or false
```

```
[nil, false].any?    # => false: no true values
[].none?             # => true: no non-false, non-nil values
```

Another Ruby 1.9 addition is the count method: it returns the number of elements in the collection that equal a specified value, or the number for which an associated block returns true:

```
a = [1,1,2,3,5,8]
a.count(1)              # => 2: two elements equal 1
a.count {|x| x % 2 == 1}  # => 4: four elements are odd
```

Finally, inject is a general purpose method for reducing a collection. Ruby 1.9 defines reduce as an alias for inject. The block associated with a call to inject expects two arguments. The first is an accumulated value; the second is an element from the collection. The accumulated value for the first iteration is the argument passed to inject. The block return value on one iteration becomes the accumulated value for the next iteration. The return value after the last iteration becomes the return value of inject. Here are some examples:

```
# How many negative numbers?
(-2..10).inject(0) {|num, x| x<0 ? num+1 : num }  # => 2

# Sum of word lengths
%w[pea queue are].inject(0) {|total, word| total + word.length }  # => 11
```

If no argument is passed to inject, then the first time the block is invoked, it is passed the first two elements of the collection. (Or, if there is only one element in the collection, inject simply returns that element.) This form of inject is useful for a number of common operations:

```
sum = (1..5).inject {|total,x| total + x}  # => 15
prod = (1..5).inject {|total,x| total * x} # => 120
max = [1,3,2].inject {|m,x| m>x ? m : x}   # => 3
[1].inject {|total,x| total + x}           # => 1: block never called
```

In Ruby 1.9, you can pass a symbol that names a method (or operator) to inject instead of specifying a block. Each element in the collection will be passed to the named method of the accumulated value, and its result will become the new accumulated value. It is common to use the reduce synonym when invoking the method with a symbol in this way:

```
sum = (1..5).reduce(:+)                # => 15
prod = (1..5).reduce(:*)               # => 120
letters = ('a'..'e').reduce("-", :concat)  # => "-abcde"
```

9.5.2 Arrays

Arrays are probably the most fundamental and commonly used data structure in Ruby programming. We covered array literals and indexing operators in §3.3. This section builds on that earlier one, demonstrating the rich API implemented by the Array class.

9.5.2.1 Creating arrays

Arrays can be created with array literals, or with the classmethod `Array.new` or the class operator `Array.[]`. Examples:

```
[1,2,3]            # Basic array literal
[]                 # An empty array
[]                 # Arrays are mutable: this empty array is different
%w[a b c]          # => ['a', 'b', 'c']: array of words
Array[1,2,3]       # => [1,2,3]: just like an array literal

# Creating arrays with the new() method
empty = Array.new          # []: returns a new empty array
nils = Array.new(3)        # [nil, nil, nil]: three nil elements
copy = Array.new(nils)     # Make a new copy of an existing array
zeros = Array.new(4, 0)    # [0, 0, 0, 0]: four 0 elements
count = Array.new(3){|i| i+1} # [1,2,3]: three elements computed by block

# Be careful with repeated objects
a=Array.new(3,'a')  # => ['a','a','a']: three references to the same string
a[0].upcase!        # Capitalize the first element of the array
a                   # => ['A','A','A']: they are all the same string!
a=Array.new(3){'b'} # => ['b','b','b']: three distinct string objects
a[0].upcase!;       # Capitalize the first one
a                   # => ['B','b','b']: the others are still lowercase
```

In addition to the `Array` factory methods, a number of other classes define `to_a` methods that return arrays. In particular, any `Enumerable` object, such as a `Range` or `Hash`, can be converted to an array with `to_a`. Also, array operators, such as `+`, and many array methods, such as `slice`, create and return new arrays rather than altering the receiving array in place.

9.5.2.2 Array size and elements

The following code shows how to determine the length of an array, and demonstrates a variety of ways to extract elements and subarrays from an array:

```
# Array length
[1,2,3].length     # => 3
[].size            # => 0: synonym for length
[].empty?          # => true
[nil].empty?       # => false
[1,2,nil].nitems   # => 2: number of non-nil elements
[1,2,3].nitems {|x| x>2} # => 1: # of elts matching block (Ruby 1.9 + 1.8.7)

# Indexing single elements
a = %w[a b c d]    # => ['a', 'b', 'c', 'd']
a[0]               # => 'a': first element
a[-1]              # => 'd': last element
a[a.size-1]        # => 'd': last element
a[-a.size]         # => 'a': first element
a[5]               # => nil: no such element
a[-5]              # => nil: no such element
a.at(2)            # => 'c': just like [] for single integer argument
```

```
a.fetch(1)          # => 'b': also like [] and at
a.fetch(-1)         # => 'd': works with negative args
a.fetch(5)          # => IndexError!: does not allow out-of-bounds
a.fetch(-5)         # => IndexError!: does not allow out-of-bounds
a.fetch(5, 0)       # => 0: return 2nd arg when out-of-bounds
a.fetch(5){|x|x*x}  # => 25: compute value when out-of-bounds
a.first             # => 'a': the first element
a.last              # => 'd': the last element
a.choice            # Ruby 1.9: return one element at random

# Indexing subarrays
a[0,2]              # => ['a','b']: two elements, starting at 0
a[0..2]             # => ['a','b','c']: elements with index in range
a[0...2]            # => ['a','b']: three dots instead of two
a[1,1]              # => ['b']: single element, as an array
a[-2,2]             # => ['c','d']: last two elements
a[4,2]              # => []: empty array right at the end
a[5,1]              # => nil: nothing beyond that
a.slice(0..1)       # => ['a','b']: slice is synonym for []
a.first(3)          # => ['a','b','c']: first three elements
a.last(1)           # => ['d']: last element as an array

# Extracting arbitrary values
a.values_at(0,2)        # => ['a','c']
a.values_at(4, 3, 2, 1) # => [nil, 'd','c','b']
a.values_at(0, 2..3, -1) # => ['a','c','d','d']
a.values_at(0..2,1..3)  # => ['a','b','c','b','c','d']
```

9.5.2.3 Altering array elements

The following code demonstrates how to change the value of individual array elements, insert values into an array, delete values from an array, and replace values with other values:

```
a = [1,2,3]         # Start with this array
# Changing the value of elements
a[0] = 0            # Alter an existing element: a is [0,2,3]
a[-1] = 4           # Alter the last element: a is [0,2,4]
a[1] = nil          # Set the 2nd element to nil: a is [0,nil,4]

# Appending to an array
a = [1,2,3]         # Start over with this array
a[3] = 4            # Add a fourth element to it: a is [1,2,3,4]
a[5] = 6            # We can skip elements: a is [1,2,3,4,nil,6]
a << 7              # => [1,2,3,4,nil,6,7]
a << 8 << 9         # => [1,2,3,4,nil,6,7,8,9] operator is chainable
a = [1,2,3]         # Start over with short array
a + a               # => [1,2,3,1,2,3]: + concatenates into new array
a.concat([4,5])     # => [1,2,3,4,5]: alter a in place: note no !

# Inserting elements with insert
a = ['a', 'b', 'c']
a.insert(1, 1, 2)   # a now holds ['a',1,2,'b','c']. Like a[1,0] = [1,2]

# Removing (and returning) individual elements by index
```

```
a = [1,2,3,4,5,6]
a.delete_at(4)      # => 5: a is now [1,2,3,4,6]
a.delete_at(-1)     # => 6: a is now [1,2,3,4]
a.delete_at(4)      # => nil: a is unchanged

# Removing elements by value
a.delete(4)         # => 4: a is [1,2,3]
a[1] = 1            # a is now [1,1,3]
a.delete(1)         # => 1: a is now [3]: both 1s removed
a = [1,2,3]
a.delete_if {|x| x%2==1} # Remove odd values: a is now [2]
a.reject! {|x| x%2==0}   # Like delete_if: a is now []

# Removing elements and subarrays with slice!
a = [1,2,3,4,5,6,7,8]
a.slice!(0)         # => 1: remove element 0: a is [2,3,4,5,6,7,8]
a.slice!(-1,1)      # => [8]: remove subarray at end: a is [2,3,4,5,6,7]
a.slice!(2..3)      # => [4,5]: works with ranges: a is [2,3,6,7]
a.slice!(4,2)       # => []: empty array just past end: a unchanged
a.slice!(5,2)       # => nil: a now holds [2,3,6,7,nil]!

# Replacing subarrays with []=
# To delete, assign an empty array
# To insert, assign to a zero-width slice
a = ('a'..'e').to_a  # => ['a','b','c','d','e']
a[0,2] = ['A','B']   # a now holds ['A', 'B', 'c', 'd', 'e']
a[2...5]=['C','D','E'] # a now holds ['A', 'B', 'C', 'D', 'E']
a[0,0] = [1,2,3]     # Insert elements at the beginning of a
a[0..2] = []         # Delete those elements
a[-1,1] = ['Z']      # Replace last element with another
a[-1,1] = 'Z'        # For single elements, the array is optional
a[1,4] = nil         # Ruby 1.9: a now holds ['A',nil]
                     # Ruby 1.8: a now holds ['A']: nil works like []

# Other methods
a = [4,5]
a.replace([1,2,3])   # a now holds [1,2,3]: a copy of its argument
a.fill(0)            # a now holds [0,0,0]
a.fill(nil,1,3)      # a now holds [0,nil,nil,nil]
a.fill('a',2..4)     # a now holds [0,nil,'a','a','a']
a[3].upcase!         # a now holds [0,nil,'A','A','A']
a.fill(2..4) { 'b' } # a now holds [0,nil,'b','b','b']
a[3].upcase!         # a now holds [0,nil,'b','B','b']
a.compact            # => [0,'b','B','b']: copy with nils removed
a.compact!           # Remove nils in place: a now holds [0,'b','B','b']
a.clear              # a now holds []
```

9.5.2.4 Iterating, searching, and sorting arrays

Array mixes in the Enumerable module, so all of the Enumerable iterators are available. In addition, the Array class defines some important iterators and related searching and sorting methods of its own. In Ruby 1.9 and 1.8.7, array iterators return an enumerator when invoked without a block:

```
a = ['a','b','c']
a.each {| elt| print elt }          # The basic each iterator prints "abc"
a.reverse_each {|e| print e}        # Array-specific: prints "cba"
a.cycle {|e| print e }              # Ruby 1.9: prints "abcabcabc..." forever
a.each_index {|i| print i}          # Array-specific: prints "012"
a.each_with_index{|e,i| print e,i}  # Enumerable: prints "a0b1c2"
a.map {|x| x.upcase}                # Enumerable: returns ['A','B','C']
a.map! {|x| x.upcase}               # Array-specific: alters a in place
a.collect! {|x| x.downcase!}        # collect! is synonym for map!

# Searching methods
a = %w[h e l l o]
a.include?('e')                     # => true
a.include?('w')                     # => false
a.index('l')                        # => 2: index of first match
a.index('L')                        # => nil: no match found
a.rindex('l')                       # => 3: search backwards
a.index {|c| c =~ /[aeiou]/}        # => 1: index of 1st vowel. 1.9 and 1.8.7
a.rindex {|c| c =~ /[aeiou]/}       # => 4: index of last vowel. 1.9 and 1.8.7

# Sorting
a.sort    # => %w[e h l l o]: copy a and sort the copy
a.sort!   # Sort in place: a now holds ['e','h','l','l','o']
a = [1,2,3,4,5]              # A new array to sort into evens and odds
a.sort! {|a,b| a%2 <=> b%2}  # Compare elements modulo 2

# Shuffling arrays: the opposite of sorting; Ruby 1.9 only
a = [1,2,3]      # Start ordered
puts a.shuffle  # Shuffle randomly. E.g.: [3,1,2]. Also shuffle!
```

9.5.2.5 Array comparison

Two arrays are equal if and only if they have the same number of elements, the elements have the same values, and they appear in the same order. The == method tests the equality of its elements with ==, and the eql? method tests the equality of its elements by calling eql? on them. In most cases, these two equality-testing methods return the same result.

The Array class is not Comparable, but it does implement the <=> operator and defines an ordering for arrays. This ordering is analogous to string ordering, and arrays of character codes are sorted in the same way that the corresponding String objects are. Arrays are compared element-by-element from index 0. If any pair of elements is not equal, then the array-comparison method returns the same value as the element comparison did. If all pairs of elements are equal, and the two arrays have the same length, then the arrays are equal and <=> returns 0. Otherwise, one of the arrays is a prefix of the other. In this case, the longer array is greater than the shorter array. Note that the empty array [] is a prefix of every other array and is always less than any nonempty array. Also, if a pair of array elements is incomparable (if one is a number and one is a string, for example), then <=> returns nil rather than returning –1, 0, or +1:

```
[1,2] <=> [4,5]     # => -1 because 1 < 4
[1,2] <=> [0,0,0]   # => +1 because 1 > 0
```

```
[1,2] <=> [1,2,3]     # => -1 because first array is shorter
[1,2] <=> [1,2]       # => 0: they are equal
[1,2] <=> []          # => +1 [] always less than a nonempty array
```

9.5.2.6 Arrays as stacks and queues

The push and pop add and remove elements from the end of an array. They allow you
to use an array as a last-on-first-off stack:

```
a = []
a.push(1)    # => [1]: a is now [1]
a.push(2,3)  # => [1,2,3]: a is now [1,2,3]
a.pop        # => 3: a is now [1,2]
a.pop        # => 2: a is now [1]
a.pop        # => 1: a is now []
a.pop        # => nil: a is still []
```

shift is like pop, but it removes and returns the first element of an array instead of the
last element. unshift is like push, but it adds elements at the beginning of the array
instead of the end. You can use push and shift to implement a first-in-first-out queue:

```
a = []
a.push(1)    # => [1]: a is [1]
a.push(2)    # => [1,2]: a is [1,2]
a.shift      # => 1: a is [2]
a.push(3)    # => [2,3]: a is [2,3]
a.shift      # => 2: a is [3]
a.shift      # => 3: a is []
a.shift      # => nil: a is []
```

9.5.2.7 Arrays as sets

The Array class implements the &, |, and - operators to perform set-like intersection,
union, and difference operations. Furthermore, it defines include? to test for the pres-
ence (membership) of a value in an array. It even defines uniq and uniq! to remove
duplicate values from an array (sets don't allow duplicates). Array is not an efficient set
implementation (for that, see the Set class in the standard library), but it may be
convenient to use it to represent small sets:

```
[1,3,5] & [1,2,3]        # => [1,3]: set intersection
[1,1,3,5] & [1,2,3]      # => [1,3]: duplicates removed
[1,3,5] | [2,4,6]        # => [1,3,5,2,4,6]: set union
[1,3,5,5] | [2,4,6,6]    # => [1,3,5,2,4,6]: duplicates removed
[1,2,3] - [2,3]          # => [1]: set difference
[1,1,2,2,3,3] - [2, 3]   # => [1,1]: not all duplicates removed

small = 0..10.to_a       # A set of small numbers
even = 0..50.map {|x| x*2} # A set of even numbers
smalleven = small & even  # Set intersection
smalleven.include?(8)     # => true: test for set membership

[1, 1, nil, nil].uniq    # => [1, nil]: remove dups. Also uniq!
```

Note that the & and | - operators do not specify the order of the elements in the arrays they return. Only use these operators if your array truly represents an unordered set of values.

In Ruby 1.9, the `Array` class defines set combinatorics methods for computing permutations, combinations, and Cartesian products:

```
a = [1,2,3]

# Iterate all possible 2-element subarrays (order matters)
a.permutation(2) {|x| print x }  # Prints "[1,2][1,3][2,1][2,3][3,1][3,2]"

# Iterate all possible 2-element subsets (order does not matter)
a.combination(2) {|x| print x }  # Prints "[1, 2][1, 3][2, 3]"

# Return the Cartesian product of the two sets
a.product(['a','b'])        # => [[1,"a"],[1,"b"],[2,"a"],[2,"b"],[3,"a"],[3,"b"]]
[1,2].product([3,4],[5,6])  # => [[1,3,5],[1,3,6],[1,4,5],[1,4,6], etc... ]
```

9.5.2.8 Associative array methods

The `assoc` and `rassoc` methods allow you to treat an array as an associative array or hash. For this to work, the array must be an array of arrays, typically like this:

```
[[key1, value1], [key2, value2], [key3, value3], ...]
```

The `Hash` class defines methods that convert a hash to a nested array of this form. The `assoc` methods looks for a nested array whose first element matches the supplied argument. It returns the first matching nested array. The `rassoc` method does the same thing, but returns the first nested array whose second element matches:

```
h = { :a => 1, :b => 2}   # Start with a hash
a = h.to_a                 # => [[:b,2], [:a,1]]: associative array
a.assoc(:a)                # => [:a,1]: subarray for key :a
a.assoc(:b).last           # => 2: value for key :b
a.rassoc(1)                # => [:a,1]: subarray for value 1
a.rassoc(2).first          # => :b: key for value 2
a.assoc(:c)                # => nil
a.transpose                # => [[:a, :b], [1, 2]]: swap rows and cols
```

9.5.2.9 Miscellaneous array methods

`Array` defines a few miscellaneous methods that do not fit in any of the previous categories:

```
# Conversion to strings
[1,2,3].join         # => "123": convert elements to string and join
[1,2,3].join(", ")   # => "1, 2, 3": optional delimiter
[1,2,3].to_s         # => "[1, 2, 3]" in Ruby 1.9
[1,2,3].to_s         # => "123" in Ruby 1.8
[1,2,3].inspect      # => "[1, 2, 3]": better for debugging in 1.8

# Binary conversion with pack. See also String.unpack.
[1,2,3,4].pack("CCCC")   # => "\001\002\003\004"
```

```
[1,2].pack('s2')        # => "\001\000\002\000"
[1234].pack("i")        # => "\322\004\000\000"

# Other methods
[0,1]*3                 # => [0,1,0,1,0,1]: * operator repeats
[1, [2, [3]]].flatten   # => [1,2,3]: recursively flatten; also flatten!
[1, [2, [3]]].flatten(1) # => [1,2,[3]]: specify # of levels; Ruby 1.9
[1,2,3].reverse         # => [3,2,1]: also reverse!
a=[1,2,3].zip([:a,:b,:c]) # => [[1,:a],[2,:b],[3,:c]]: Enumerable method
a.transpose             # => [[1,2,3],[:a,:b,:c]]: swap rows/cols
```

9.5.3 Hashes

Hashes were introduced in §3.4, which explained hash literal syntax and the [] and
[]= operators for retrieving and storing key/value pairs in a hash. This section covers
the Hash API in more detail. Hashes use the same square-bracket operators as arrays
do, and you'll notice that many Hash methods are similar to Array methods.

9.5.3.1 Creating hashes

Hashes can be created with literals, the Hash.new method, or the [] operator of the
Hash class itself:

```
{ :one => 1, :two => 2 } # Basic hash literal syntax
{ :one, 1, :two, 2 }     # Same, with deprecated Ruby 1.8 syntax
{ one: 1, two: 2 }       # Same, Ruby 1.9 syntax. Keys are symbols.
{}                       # A new, empty, Hash object
Hash.new                 # => {}: creates empty hash
Hash[:one, 1, :two, 2]   # => {one:1, two:2}
```

Recall from §6.4.4 that you can omit the curly braces around a hash literal that is the
final argument in a method invocation:

```
puts :a=>1, :b=>2   # Curly braces omitted in invocation
puts a:1, b:2       # Ruby 1.9 syntax works too
```

9.5.3.2 Indexing hashes and testing membership

Hashes are very efficient at looking up the value associated with a given key. It is also
possible (though not efficient) to find a key with which a value is associated. Note,
however, that many keys can map to the same value, and in this case, the key returned
is arbitrary:

```
h = { :one => 1, :two => 2 }
h[:one]       # => 1: find value associated with a key
h[:three]     # => nil: the key does not exist in the hash
h.assoc :one  # => [:one, 1]: find key/value pair. Ruby 1.9.

h.index 1     # => :one: search for key associated with a value
h.index 4     # => nil: no mapping to this value exists
h.rassoc 2    # => [:two, 2]: key/value pair matching value. Ruby 1.9.
```

Hash defines several synonymous methods for testing membership:

```
h = { :a => 1, :b => 2 }
# Checking for the presence of keys in a hash: fast
h.key?(:a)       # true: :a is a key in h
h.has_key?(:b)   # true: has_key? is a synonym for key?
h.include?(:c)   # false: include? is another synonym
h.member?(:d)    # false: member? is yet another synonym

# Checking for the presence of values: slow
h.value?(1)       # true: 1 is a value in h
h.has_value?(3)   # false: has_value? is a synonym for value?
```

The fetch method is an alternative to [] when querying values in a hash. It provides options for handling the case where a key does not exist in the hash:

```
h = { :a => 1, :b => 2 }
h.fetch(:a)      # => 1: works like [] for existing keys
h.fetch(:c)      # Raises IndexError for nonexistent key
h.fetch(:c, 33)  # => 33: uses specified value if key is not found
h.fetch(:c) {|k| k.to_s } # => "c": calls block if key not found
```

If you want to extract more than one value from a hash at once, use values_at:

```
h = { :a => 1, :b => 2, :c => 3 }
h.values_at(:c)         # => [3]: values returned in an array
h.values_at(:a, :b)     # => [1, 2]: pass any # of args
h.values_at(:d, :d, :a) # => [nil, nil, 1]
```

You can extract keys and values selected by a block with the select method:

```
h = { :a => 1, :b => 2, :c => 3 }
h.select {|k,v| v % 2 == 0 } # => [:b,2] Ruby 1.8
h.select {|k,v| v % 2 == 0 } # => {:b=>2} Ruby 1.9
```

This method overrides Enumerable.select. In Ruby 1.8, select returns an array of key/value pairs. It has been modified in Ruby 1.9 so that it returns a hash of the selected keys and values instead.

9.5.3.3 Storing keys and values in a hash

Associate a value with a key in a hash with the []= operator or its synonym, the store method:

```
h = {}         # Start with an empty hash
h[:a] = 1      # Map :a=>1. h is now {:a=>1}
h.store(:b,2)  # More verbose: h is now {:a=>1, :b=>2}
```

To replace all the key/value pairs in a hash with copies of the pairs from another hash, use replace:

```
# Replace all of the pairs in h with those from another hash
h.replace({1=>:a, 2=>:b}) # h is now equal to the argument hash
```

The merge, merge!, and update methods allow you to merge the mappings from two hashes:

```
# Merge hashes h and j into new hash k.
# If h and j share keys, use values from j
```

```
k = h.merge(j)
{:a=>1,:b=>2}.merge(:a=>3,:c=>3)  # => {:a=>3,:b=>2,:c=>3}
h.merge!(j)   # Modifies h in place.

# If there is a block, use it to decide which value to use
h.merge!(j) {|key,h,j| h }       # Use value from h
h.merge(j) {|key,h,j| (h+j)/2 } # Use average of two values

# update is a synonym for merge!
h = {a:1,b:2}    # Using Ruby 1.9 syntax and omitting braces
h.update(b:4,c:9) {|key,old,new| old }  # h is now {a:1, b:2, c:9}
h.update(b:4,c:9) # h is now {a:1, b:4, c:9}
```

9.5.3.4 Removing hash entries

You can't remove a key from a hash simply by mapping it to `nil`. Instead, use the delete method:

```
h = {:a=>1, :b=>2}
h[:a] = nil       # h now holds {:a=> nil, :b=>2 }
h.include? :a     # => true
h.delete :b       # => 2: returns deleted value: h now holds {:a=>nil}
h.include? :b     # => false
h.delete :b       # => nil: key not found
# Invoke block if key not found
h.delete(:b) {|k| raise IndexError, k.to_s } # IndexError!
```

You can delete multiple key/value pairs from a hash using the `delete_if` and `reject!` iterators (and the `reject` iterator which operates on a copy of its receiver). Note that `reject` overrides the `Enumerable` method by the same name and returns a hash rather than an array:

```
h = {:a=>1, :b=>2, :c=>3, :d=>"four"}
h.reject! {|k,v| v.is_a? String }   # => {:a=>1, :b=>2, :c=>3 }
h.delete_if {|k,v| k.to_s < 'b' }   # => {:b=>2, :c=>3 }
h.reject! {|k,v| k.to_s < 'b' }     # => nil: no change
h.delete_if {|k,v| k.to_s < 'b' }   # => {:b=>2, :c=>3 }: unchanged hash
h.reject {|k,v| true }              # => {}: h is unchanged
```

Finally, you can remove all key/value pairs from a hash with the `clear` method. This method does not end with an exclamation mark, but it alters its receiver in place:

```
h.clear    # h is now {}
```

9.5.3.5 Arrays from hashes

Hash defines methods for extracting hash data into arrays:

```
h = { :a=>1, :b=>2, :c=>3 }
# Size of hash: number of key/value pairs
h.length    # => 3
h.size      # => 3: size is a synonym for length
h.empty?    # => false
{}.empty?   # => true
```

```
h.keys        # => [:b, :c, :a]: array of keys
h.values      # => [2,3,1]: array of values
h.to_a        # => [[:b,2],[:c,3],[:a,1]]: array of pairs
h.flatten     # => [:b, 2, :c, 3, :a, 1]: flattened array. Ruby 1.9
h.sort        # => [[:a,1],[:b,2],[:c,3]]: sorted array of pairs
h.sort {|a,b| a[1]<=>b[1] } # Sort pairs by value instead of key
```

9.5.3.6 Hash iterators

It is not usually necessary to extract hash keys, values, or pairs as an array, because the Hash class is Enumerable and defines other useful iterators as well. In Ruby 1.8, Hash objects make no guarantees about the order in which their values are iterated. In Ruby 1.9, however, hash elements are iterated in their insertion order, and that is the order shown in the following examples:

```
h = { :a=>1, :b=>2, :c=>3 }

# The each() iterator iterates [key,value] pairs
h.each {|pair| print pair }    # Prints "[:a, 1][:b, 2][:c, 3]"

# It also works with two block arguments
h.each do |key, value|
  print "#{key}:#{value} "     # Prints "a:1 b:2 c:3"
end

# Iterate over keys or values or both
h.each_key {|k| print k }      # Prints "abc"
h.each_value {|v| print v }    # Prints "123"
h.each_pair {|k,v| print k,v } # Prints "a1b2c3". Like each
```

The each iterator yields an array containing the key and value. Block invocation syntax allows this array to be automatically expanded into separate key and value parameters. In Ruby 1.8, the each_pair iterator yields the key and value as two separate values (which may have a slight performance advantage). In Ruby 1.9, each_pair is simply a synonym for each.

Although it is not an iterator, the shift method can be used to iterate through the key/value pairs of a hash. Like the array method of the same name, it removes and returns one element (one [key,value] array in this case) from the hash:

```
h = { :a=> 1, :b=>2 }
print h.shift[1] while not h.empty?   # Prints "12"
```

9.5.3.7 Default values

Normally, if you query the value of a key with which no value has been associated, the hash returns nil:

```
empty = {}
empty["one"]    # nil
```

You can alter this behavior, however, by specifying a default value for the hash:

```
empty = Hash.new(-1)      # Specify a default value when creating hash
empty["one"]              # => -1
empty.default = -2        # Change the default value to something else
empty["two"]              # => -2
empty.default             # => -2: return the default value
```

Instead of providing a single default value, you can provide a block of code to compute values for keys that do not have an associated value:

```
# If the key is not defined, return the successor of the key.
plus1 = Hash.new {|hash, key| key.succ }
plus1[1]       # 2
plus1["one"]   # "onf": see String.succ
plus1.default_proc  # Returns the Proc that computes defaults
plus1.default(10)   # => 11: default returned for key 10
```

When using a default block like this, it is common to associate the computed value with the key, so that the computation does not need to be redone if the key is queried again. This is an easy-to-implement form of lazy evaluation (and it explains why the default block is passed the hash object itself along with the key):

```
# This lazily initialized hash maps integers to their factorials
fact = Hash.new {|h,k| h[k] = if k > 1: k*h[k-1] else 1 end }
fact       # {}: it starts off empty
fact[4]    # 24: 4! is 24
fact       # {1=>1, 2=>2, 3=>6, 4=>24}: the hash now has entries
```

Note that setting the `default` property of a hash overrides any block passed to the `Hash.new` constructor.

If you are not interested in default values for a hash, or if you want to override them with your own default, use the `fetch` method to retrieve values instead of using square brackets. `fetch` was covered earlier:

```
fact.fetch(5)   # IndexError: key not found
```

9.5.3.8 Hashcodes, key equality, and mutable keys

In order for an object to be used as a hash key, it must have a `hash` method that returns an integer "hashcode" for the object. Classes that do not define their own `eql?` method can simply use the `hash` method they inherit from `Object`. If you define an `eql?` method for testing object equality, however, you must define a corresponding `hash` method. If two distinct objects are considered equal, their `hash` methods must return the same value. Ideally, two objects that are not equal should have different hashcodes. This topic was covered in §3.4.2, and §7.1.9 includes an example `hash` implementation.

As noted in §3.4.2, you must be careful any time you use a mutable object as a hash key. (Strings are a special case: the `Hash` class makes a private internal copy of string keys.) If you do use mutable keys and mutate one of them, you must call `rehash` on the `Hash` object in order to ensure that it works right:

```
key = {:a=>1}      # This hash will be a key in another hash!
h = { key => 2 }   # This hash has a mutable key
```

```
h[key]          # => 2: get value associated with key
key.clear       # Mutate the key
h[key]          # => nil: no value found for mutated key
h.rehash        # Fix up the hash after mutation
h[key]          # => 2: now the value is found again
```

9.5.3.9 Miscellaneous hash methods

The `invert` method does not fit into any of the previous categories. `invert` swaps keys and values in a hash:

```
h = {:a=>1, :b=>2}
h.invert        # => {1=>:a, 2=>:b}: swap keys and values
```

As was the case for `Array`, the `Hash.to_s` method is not very useful in Ruby 1.8, and you may prefer to use `inspect` to convert to a string in hash literal form. In Ruby 1.9, `to_s` and `inspect` are the same:

```
{:a=>1, :b=>2}.to_s    # => "a1b2" in Ruby 1.8; "{:a=>1, :b=>2}" in 1.9
{:a=>1, :b=>2}.inspect # => "{:a=>1, :b=>2}" for both versions
```

9.5.4 Sets

A *set* is simply a collection of values, without duplicates. Unlike an array, the elements of a set have no order. A hash can be considered a set of key/value pairs. Conversely, a set can be implemented using a hash in which set elements are stored as keys and values are ignored. A *sorted set* is a set that imposes an ordering on its elements (but does not allow random access to them as an array does). A characteristic feature of set implementations is that they feature fast membership testing, insertion, and deletion operations.

Ruby does not offer a built-in set type, but the standard library includes the `Set` and `SortedSet` classes, which you can use if you first:

```
require 'set'
```

The `Set` API is similar in many ways to the `Array` and `Hash` APIs. A number of `Set` methods and operators accept any `Enumerable` object as their argument.

SortedSet

The `SortedSet` class inherits from `Set` and does not define any new methods of its own; it simply guarantees that the elements of the set will be iterated (or printed or converted to arrays) in sorted order. `SortedSet` does not allow you to provide a custom block to compare set elements, and requires that all set elements are mutually comparable according to their default `<=>` operator. Because the `SortedSet` API is no different than the basic `Set` API, it will not be covered here.

9.5.4.1 Creating sets

Because Set is not a core Ruby class, there is no literal syntax for creating sets. The set library adds a to_set method to the Enumerable module, and a set can be created from any enumerable object with this method:

```
(1..5).to_set          # => #<Set: {5, 1, 2, 3, 4}>
[1,2,3].to_set         # => #<Set: {1, 2, 3}>
```

Alternatively, any enumerable object can be passed to Set.new. If a block is provided, it is used (as with the map iterator) to preprocess the enumerated values before adding them to the set:

```
Set.new(1..5)              # => #<Set: {5, 1, 2, 3, 4}>
Set.new([1,2,3])           # => #<Set: {1, 2, 3}>
Set.new([1,2,3]) {|x| x+1} # => #<Set: {2, 3, 4}>
```

If you prefer to enumerate the members of your set without first placing them in an array or other enumerable object, use the [] operator of the Set class:

```
Set["cow", "pig", "hen"]   # => #<Set: {"cow", "pig", "hen"}>
```

9.5.4.2 Testing, comparing, and combining Sets

The most common operation on sets is usually membership testing:

```
s = Set.new(1..3)  # => #<Set: {1, 2, 3}>
s.include? 1       # => true
s.member? 0        # => false: member? is a synonym
```

It is also possible to test sets for membership in other sets. A set S is a *subset* of T if all the elements of S are also elements of T. We can also say that T is a *superset* of S. If two sets are equal, then they are both subsets and supersets of each other. S is a *proper subset* of T if it is a subset of T but not equal to T. In this case, T is a *proper superset* of S:

```
s = Set[2, 3, 5]
t = Set[2, 3, 5, 7]
s.subset? t              # => true
t.subset? s              # => false
s.proper_subset? t       # => true
t.superset? s            # => true
t.proper_superset? s     # => true
s.subset? s              # => true
s.proper_subset? s       # => false
```

Set defines the same size methods as **Array** and **Hash** do:

```
s = Set[2, 3, 5]
s.length           # => 3
s.size             # => 3: a synonym for length
s.empty?           # => false
Set.new.empty?     # => true
```

New sets can be created by combining two existing sets. There are several ways this can be done, and Set defines the operators &, |, -, and ^ (plus named method aliases) to represent them:

```
# Here are two simple sets
primes = Set[2, 3, 5, 7]
odds = Set[1, 3, 5, 7, 9]

# The intersection is the set of values that appear in both
primes & odds              # => #<Set: {5, 7, 3}>
primes.intersection(odds)  # this is an explicitly named alias

# The union is the set of values that appear in either
primes | odds              # => #<Set: {5, 1, 7, 2, 3, 9}>
primes.union(odds)         # an explicitly named alias

# a-b: is the elements of a except for those also in b
primes-odds                # => #<Set: {2}>
odds-primes                # => #<Set: {1, 9}>
primes.difference(odds)    # A named method alias

# a^b is the set of values that appear in one set but not both: (a|b)-(a&b)
primes ^ odds              # => #<Set: {1, 2, 9}>
```

The Set class also defines mutating variants of some of these methods; we'll consider them shortly.

9.5.4.3 Adding and deleting set elements

This section describes methods that add or remove elements from a set. They are mutator methods that modify the receiver set in place rather than returning a modified copy and leaving the original unchanged. Because these methods do not exist in non-mutating versions, they do not have an exclamation point suffix.

The << operator adds a single element to a set:

```
s = Set[]            # start with an empty set
s << 1               # => #<Set: {1}>
s.add 2              # => #<Set: {1, 2}>: add is a synonym for <<
s << 3 << 4 << 5     # => #<Set: {5, 1, 2, 3, 4}>: can be chained
s.add 3              # => #<Set: {5, 1, 2, 3, 4}>: value unchanged
s.add? 6             # => #<Set: {5, 6, 1, 2, 3, 4}>
s.add? 3             # => nil: the set was not changed
```

To add more than one value to a set, use the merge method, which can take any enumerable object as its argument. merge is effectively a mutating version of the union method:

```
s = (1..3).to_set  # => #<Set: {1, 2, 3}>
s.merge(2..5)      # => #<Set: {5, 1, 2, 3, 4}>
```

To remove a single element from a set, use delete or delete?, which are analogous to add and add? but do not have an operator equivalent:

```
s = (1..3).to_set    # => #<Set: {1, 2, 3}>
s.delete 1           # => #<Set: {2, 3}>
s.delete 1           # => #<Set: {2, 3}>: unchanged
s.delete? 1          # => nil: returns nil when no change
s.delete? 2          # => #<Set: {3}>: otherwise returns set
```

Remove multiple values from a set at once with subtract. The argument to this method can be any enumerable object, and the method acts as a mutating version of the difference method:

```
s = (1..3).to_set    # => #<Set: {1, 2, 3}>
s.subtract(2..10)    # => #<Set: {1}>
```

To selectively delete elements from a set, use delete_if or reject!. Just as with the Array and Hash classes, these two methods are equivalent except for their return value when the set is unmodified. delete_if always returns the receiver set. reject! returns the receiver set if it was modified, or nil if no values were removed from it:

```
primes = Set[2, 3, 5, 7]        # set of prime numbers
primes.delete_if {|x| x%2==1}   # => #<Set: {2}>: remove odds
primes.delete_if {|x| x%2==1}   # => #<Set: {2}>: unchanged
primes.reject! {|x| x%2==1}     # => nil: unchanged

# Do an in-place intersection like this:
s = (1..5).to_set
t = (4..8).to_set
s.reject! {|x| not t.include? x}  # => #<Set: {5, 4}>
```

Finally, the clear and replace methods work just as they do for arrays and hashes:

```
s = Set.new(1..3) # Initial set
s.replace(3..4)   # Replace all elements.  Argument is any enumerable
s.clear           # => #<Set: {}>
s.empty?          # => true
```

9.5.4.4 Set iterators

Sets are Enumerable, and the Set class defines an each iterator that yields each of the set elements once. In Ruby 1.9, Set behaves like the Hash class on which it is implemented and iterates elements in the order in which they were inserted. Prior to Ruby 1.9 the iteration order is arbitrary. For SortedSet, the elements are yielded in their ascending sorted order. In addition, the map! iterator transforms each element of the set with a block, altering the set in place. collect! is a synonym:

```
s = Set[1, 2, 3, 4, 5] # => #<Set: {5, 1, 2, 3, 4}>
s.each {|x| print x }  # prints "51234": arbitrary order before Ruby 1.9
s.map! {|x| x*x }      # => #<Set: {16, 1, 25, 9, 4}>
s.collect! {|x| x/2 }  # => #<Set: {0, 12, 2, 8, 4}>
```

9.5.4.5 Miscellaneous set methods

Set defines powerful methods for partitioning sets into subsets and for flattening sets of subsets into single larger sets. In addition, it defines a few mundane methods that we will cover first:

```
s = (1..3).to_set
s.to_a          # => [1, 2, 3]
s.to_s          # => "#<Set:0xb7e8f938>": not useful
s.inspect       # => "#<Set: {1, 2, 3}>": useful
s == Set[3,2,1] # => true: uses eql? to compare set elements
```

The classify method expects a block and yields each set element to that block in turn. The return value is a hash that maps block return values to sets of elements that returned that value:

```
# Classify set elements as even or odd
s = (0..3).to_set       # => #<Set: {0, 1, 2, 3}>
s.classify {|x| x%2}    # => {0=>#<Set: {0, 2}>, 1=>#<Set: {1, 3}>}
```

The divide method is similar but returns a set of subsets rather than hash mapping values to subsets:

```
s.divide {|x| x%2}  # => #<Set: {#<Set: {0, 2}>, #<Set: {1, 3}>}>
```

divide works completely differently if the associated block expects two arguments. In this case, the block should return true if the two values belong in the same subset, and false otherwise:

```
s = %w[ant ape cow hen hog].to_set # A set of words
s.divide {|x,y| x[0] == y[0]}      # Divide into subsets by first letter
# => #<Set:{#<Set:{"hog", "hen"}>, #<Set:{"cow"}>, #<Set:{"ape", "ant"}>}>
```

If you have a set of sets (which may themselves include sets, recursively), you can flatten it, effectively merging (by union) all the contained sets with the flatten method, or the flatten! method, which performs the operation in place:

```
s = %w[ant ape cow hen hog].to_set # A set of words
t = s.divide {|x,y| x[0] == y[0]}  # Divide it into subsets
t.flatten!                         # Flatten the subsets
t == s                             # => true
```

9.6 Files and Directories

The File class defines quite a few class methods for working with files as entries in a filesystem: methods for testing the size or existence of a named file, for example, and methods for separating a filename from the directory name that precedes it. These are class methods and they do not operate on File objects; instead, filenames are specified as strings. Similarly, the Dir class defines class methods for working with and reading filenames from filesystem directories. The subsections that follow demonstrate how to:

- Work with and manipulate filenames and directory names

- List directories
- Test files to determine their type, size, modification time, and other attributes
- Delete, rename, and perform similar operations on files and directories

Note that the methods described here query and manipulate files, but do not read or write file *content*. Reading and writing files is covered in §9.7.

Specifying Filenames in Ruby 1.9

Many of the file and directory methods described in this section expect one or more arguments that name files. Normally, you specify filenames and directory paths as strings. In Ruby 1.9, you can also use nonstring objects if they have a **to_path** method that returns a string.

9.6.1 File and Directory Names

The class methods of the `File` and `Dir` classes operate on files and directories specified by name. Ruby uses Unix-style filenames with / as the directory separator character. You can use the forward slash character in your filenames, even when using Ruby on a Windows platform. On Windows, Ruby can also handle filenames that use the backslash character and that include drive letter prefixes. The constant `File::SEPARATOR` should be '/' in all implementations. `File::ALT_SEPARATOR` is '\' on Windows, and is `nil` on other platforms.

The `File` class defines some methods for manipulating filenames:

```
full = '/home/matz/bin/ruby.exe'
file=File.basename(full)       # => 'ruby.exe': just the local filename
File.basename(full, '.exe')    # => 'ruby': with extension stripped
dir=File.dirname(full)         # => '/home/matz/bin': no / at end
File.dirname(file)             # => '.': current directory
File.split(full)               # => ['/home/matz/bin', 'ruby.exe']
File.extname(full)             # => '.exe'
File.extname(file)             # => '.exe'
File.extname(dir)              # => ''
File.join('home','matz')       # => 'home/matz': relative
File.join('','home','matz')    # => '/home/matz': absolute
```

The `File.expand_path` method converts a relative path to a fully qualified path. If the optional second argument is supplied, it is first prepended as a directory to the first argument. The result is then converted to an absolute path. If it begins with a Unix-style ~, the directory is relative to the current or specified user's home directory. Otherwise, the directory is resolved relative to the current working directory (see `Dir.chdir` below to change the working directory):

```
Dir.chdir("/usr/bin")      # Current working directory is "/usr/bin"
File.expand_path("ruby")        # => "/usr/bin/ruby"
File.expand_path("~/ruby")      # => "/home/david/ruby"
File.expand_path("~matz/ruby") # => "/home/matz/ruby"
```

```
File.expand_path("ruby", "/usr/local/bin") # => "/usr/local/bin/ruby"
File.expand_path("ruby", "../local/bin")   # => "/usr/local/bin/ruby"
File.expand_path("ruby", "~/bin")          # => "/home/david/bin/ruby"
```

The `File.identical?` method tests whether two filenames refer to the same file. This might be because the names are the same, but it is a more useful method when the names differ. Two different names might refer to the same file if one is a relative filename and the other is absolute, for example. One might include ".." to go up a level and then down again. Or, two different names might refer to the same file if one name is a symbolic link or shortcut (or hard link on platforms that support it) to the other. Note, however, that `File.identical?` only returns `true` if the two names refer to the same file and that file actually exists. Also note that `File.identical?` does not expand the ~ character for home directories the way that `File.expand_path` does:

```
File.identical?("ruby", "ruby")           # => true if the file exists
File.identical?("ruby", "/usr/bin/ruby")  # => true if CWD is /usr/bin
File.identical?("ruby", "../bin/ruby")    # => true if CWD is /usr/bin
File.identical?("ruby", "ruby1.9")        # => true if there is a link
```

Finally, `File.fnmatch` tests whether a filename matches a specified pattern. The pattern is not a regular expression, but is like the file-matching patterns used in shells. "?" matches a single character. "*" matches any number of characters. And "**" matches any number of directory levels. Characters in square brackets are alternatives, as in regular expressions. `fnmatch` does not allow alternatives in curly braces (as the `Dir.glob` method described below does). `fnmatch` should usually be invoked with a third argument of `File::FNM_PATHNAME`, which prevents "*" from matching "/". Add `File::FNM_DOTMATCH` if you want "hidden" files and directories whose names begin with "." to match. Only a few examples of `fnmatch` are given here. Use `ri File.fnmatch` for complete details. Note that `File.fnmatch?` is a synonym:

```
File.fnmatch("*.rb", "hello.rb")     # => true
File.fnmatch("*.[ch]", "ruby.c")     # => true
File.fnmatch("*.[ch]", "ruby.h")     # => true
File.fnmatch("?.txt", "ab.txt")      # => false
flags = File::FNM_PATHNAME | File::FNM_DOTMATCH
File.fnmatch("lib/*.rb", "lib/a.rb", flags)     # => true
File.fnmatch("lib/*.rb", "lib/a/b.rb", flags)   # => false
File.fnmatch("lib/**/*.rb", "lib/a.rb", flags)  # => true
File.fnmatch("lib/**/*.rb", "lib/a/b.rb", flags) # => true
```

9.6.2 Listing Directories

The easiest way to list the contents of a directory is with the `Dir.entries` method or the `Dir.foreach` iterator:

```
# Get the names of all files in the config/ directory
filenames = Dir.entries("config")        # Get names as an array
Dir.foreach("config") {|filename| ... }  # Iterate names
```

The names returned by these methods are not guaranteed to be in any particular order, and (on Unix-like platforms) include "." (the current directory) and ".." (the parent directory). To obtain a list of files that match a given pattern, use the Dir.[] operator:

```
Dir['*.data']        # Files with the "data" extension
Dir['ruby.*']        # Any filename beginning with "ruby."
Dir['?']             # Any single-character filename
Dir['*.[ch]']        # Any file that ends with .c or .h
Dir['*.{java,rb}']   # Any file that ends with .java or .rb
Dir['*/*.rb']        # Any Ruby program in any direct sub-directory
Dir['**/*.rb']       # Any Ruby program in any descendant directory
```

A more powerful alternative to Dir[] is Dir.glob. (The verb "glob" is an old Unix term for filename matching in a shell.) By default, this method works like Dir[], but if passed a block, it yields the matching filenames one at a time rather than returning an array. Also, the glob method accepts an optional second argument. If you pass the constant File::FNM_DOTMATCH (see File.fnmatch previously) as this second argument, then the result will include files whose names begin with "." (on Unix systems, these files are hidden and are not returned by default):

```
Dir.glob('*.rb') {|f| ... }       # Iterate all Ruby files
Dir.glob('*')                     # Does not include names beginning with '.'
Dir.glob('*',File::FNM_DOTMATCH)  # Include . files, just like Dir.entries
```

The directory listing methods shown here, and all File and Dir methods that resolve relative pathnames, do so relative to the "current working directory," which is a value global to the Ruby interpreter process. Query and set the CWD with the getwd and chdir methods:

```
puts Dir.getwd          # Print current working directory
Dir.chdir("..")         # Change CWD to the parent directory
Dir.chdir("../sibling") # Change again to a sibling directory
Dir.chdir("/home")      # Change to an absolute directory
Dir.chdir              # Change to user's home directory
home = Dir.pwd          # pwd is an alias for getwd
```

If you pass a block to the chdir method, the directory will be restored to its original value when the block exits. Note, however, that while the directory change is limited in duration, it is still global in scope and affects other threads. Two threads may not call Dir.chdir with a block at the same time.

9.6.3 Testing Files

File defines a slew of methods to obtain metadata about a named file or directory. Many of the methods return low-level information that is OS-dependent. Only the most portable and broadly useful are demonstrated here. Use *ri* on the File and File::Stat classes for a complete list of methods.

The following simple methods return basic information about a file. Most are predicates that return true or false:

```
f = "/usr/bin/ruby"        # A filename for the examples below

# File existence and types.
File.exist?(f)             # Does the named file exist? Also: File.exists?
File.file?(f)              # Is it an existing file?
File.directory?(f)         # Or is it an existing directory?
File.symlink?(f)           # Either way, is it a symbolic link?

# File size methods. Use File.truncate to set file size.
File.size(f)               # File size in bytes.
File.size?(f)              # Size in bytes or nil if empty file.
File.zero?(f)              # True if file is empty.

# File permissions. Use File.chmod to set permissions (system dependent).
File.readable?(f)          # Can we read the file?
File.writable?(f)          # Can we write the file? No "e" in "writable"
File.executable?(f)        # Can we execute the file?
File.world_readable?(f)    # Can everybody read it? Ruby 1.9.
File.world_writable?(f)    # Can everybody write it? Ruby 1.9.

# File times/dates. Use File.utime to set the times.
File.mtime(f)              # => Last modification time as a Time object
File.atime(f)              # => Last access time as a Time object
```

Another way to determine the type (file, directory, symbolic link, etc.) of a filename is with **ftype**, which returns a string that names the type. Assume that */usr/bin/ruby* is a symbolic link (or shortcut) to **/usr/bin/ruby1.9**:

```
File.ftype("/usr/bin/ruby")    # => "link"
File.ftype("/usr/bin/ruby1.9") # => "file"
File.ftype("/usr/lib/ruby")    # => "directory"
File.ftype("/usr/bin/ruby3.0") # SystemCallError: No such file or directory
```

If you are interested in multiple pieces of information about a file, it may be more efficient to call **stat** or **lstat**. (**stat** follows symbolic links; **lstat** returns information about the link itself.) These methods return a **File::Stat** object, which has instance methods with the same names (but without arguments) as the class methods of **File**. The efficiency of using **stat** is that Ruby only has to make one call to the OS to obtain all file metadata. Your Ruby program can then obtain that information from the **File::Stat** object as it needs it:

```
s = File.stat("/usr/bin/ruby")
s.file?          # => true
s.directory?     # => false
s.ftype          # => "file"
s.readable?      # => true
s.writable?      # => false
s.executable?    # => true
s.size           # => 5492
s.atime          # => Mon Jul 23 13:20:37 -0700 2007
```

Use *ri* on **File::Stat** for a full list of its methods. One final general-purpose file testing method is **Kernel.test**. It exists for historical compatibility with the Unix shell command *test*. The `test` method is largely obviated by the class methods of the `File` class, but you may see it used in existing Ruby scripts. Use *ri* for complete details:

```
# Testing single files
test ?e, "/usr/bin/ruby"    # File.exist?("/usr/bin/ruby")
test ?f, "/usr/bin/ruby"    # File.file?("/usr/bin/ruby")
test ?d, "/usr/bin/ruby"    # File.directory?("/usr/bin/ruby")
test ?r, "/usr/bin/ruby"    # File.readable?("/usr/bin/ruby")
test ?w, "/usr/bin/ruby"    # File.writeable?("/usr/bin/ruby")
test ?M, "/usr/bin/ruby"    # File.mtime("/usr/bin/ruby")
test ?s, "/usr/bin/ruby"    # File.size?("/usr/bin/ruby")

# Comparing two files f and g
test ?-, f, g               # File.identical(f,g)
test ?<, f, g               # File(f).mtime < File(g).mtime
test ?>, f, g               # File(f).mtime > File(g).mtime
test ?=, f, g               # File(f).mtime == File(g).mtime
```

9.6.4 Creating, Deleting, and Renaming Files and Directories

The `File` class does not define any special methods for creating a file. To create one, simply open it for writing, write zero or more bytes, and close it again. If you don't want to clobber an existing file, open it in append mode:

```
# Create (or overwrite) a file named "test"
File.open("test", "w") {}
# Create (but do not clobber) a file named "test"
File.open("test", "a") {}
```

To copy a file, use `File.copy_stream`, specifying filenames as the source and destination:

```
File.copy_stream("test", "test.backup")
```

To change the name of a file, use `File.rename`:

```
File.rename("test", "test.old")    # Current name, then new name
```

To create a symbolic link to a file, use `File.symlink`:

```
File.symlink("test.old", "oldtest") # Link target, link name
```

On systems that support it, you can create a "hard link" with `File.link`:

```
File.link("test.old", "test2")    # Link target, link name
```

Finally, to delete a file or link, use `File.delete`, or its synonym `File.unlink`:

```
File.delete("test2")   # May also be called with multiple args
File.unlink("oldtest") # to delete multiple named files
```

On systems that support it, use `File.truncate` to truncate a file to a specified number (possibly zero) of bytes. Use `File.utime` to set the access and modification times of a file. And use the platform-dependent method `File.chmod` to change the permissions of a file:

```
f = "log.messages"          # Filename
atime = mtime = Time.now    # New access and modify times
File.truncate(f, 0)         # Erase all existing content
File.utime(atime, mtime, f) # Change times
File.chmod(0600, f)         # Unix permissions -rw-------; note octal arg
```

To create a new directory, use `Dir.mkdir`. To delete a directory, use `Dir.rmdir` or one of its synonyms, `Dir.delete` or `Dir.unlink`. The directory must be empty before it can be deleted:

```
Dir.mkdir("temp")               # Create a directory
File.open("temp/f", "w") {}     # Create a file in it
File.open("temp/g", "w") {}     # Create another one
File.delete(*Dir["temp/*"])     # Delete all files in the directory
Dir.rmdir("temp")               # Delete the directory
```

9.7 Input/Output

An `IO` object is a stream: a readable source of bytes or characters or a writable sink for bytes or characters. The `File` class is a subclass of `IO`. `IO` objects also represent the "standard input" and "standard output" streams used to read from and write to the console. The `stringio` module in the standard library allows us to create a stream wrapper around a string object. Finally, the socket objects used in networking (described later in this chapter) are also `IO` objects.

9.7.1 Opening Streams

Before we can perform input or output, we must have an `IO` object to read from or write to. The `IO` class defines factory methods `new`, `open`, `popen`, and `pipe`, but these are low-level methods with operating system dependencies, and they are not documented here. The subsections that follow describe more common ways to obtain `IO` objects. (And §9.8 includes examples that create `IO` objects that communicate across the network.)

9.7.1.1 Opening files

One of the most common kinds of `IO` is the reading and writing of files. The `File` class defines some utility methods (described below) that read the entire contents of a file with one call. Often, however, you will instead open a file to obtain a `File` object and then use `IO` methods to read from or write to the file.

Use `File.open` (or `File.new`) to open a file. The first argument is the name of the file. This is usually specified as a string, but in Ruby 1.9, you can use any object with a `to_path` method. Filenames are interpreted relative to the current working directory unless they are specified with an absolute path. Use forward slash characters to separate directories—Ruby automatically converts them into backslashes on Windows. The second argument to `File.open` is a short string that specifies how the file should be opened:

```
f = File.open("data.txt", "r")    # Open file data.txt for reading
out = File.open("out.txt", "w")   # Open file out.txt for writing
```

The second argument to `File.open` is a string that specifies the "file mode." It must begin with one of the values in the following table. Add "b" to the mode string to prevent automatic line terminator conversion on Windows platforms. For text files, you may add the name of a character encoding to the mode string. For binary files, you should add ":binary" to the string. This is explained in §9.7.2.

Mode	Description
"r"	Open for reading. The default mode.
"r+"	Open for reading and writing. Start at beginning of file. Fail if file does not exist.
"w"	Open for writing. Create a new file or truncate an existing one.
"w+"	Like "w", but allows reading of the file as well.
"a"	Open for writing, but append to the end of the file if it already exists.
"a+"	Like "a", but allows reads also.

`File.open` (but not `File.new`) may be followed by a block. If a block is provided, then `File.open` doesn't return the `File` object but instead passes it to the block, and automatically closes it when the block exits. The return value of the block becomes the return value of `File.open`:

```
File.open("log.txt", "a") do |log|     # Open for appending
  log.puts("INFO: Logging a message")  # Output to the file
end                                    # Automatically closed
```

9.7.1.2 Kernel.open

The `Kernel` method open works like `File.open` but is more flexible. If the filename begins with |, it is treated as an operating system command, and the returned stream is used for reading from and writing to that command process. This is platform-dependent, of course:

```
# How long has the server been up?
uptime = open("|uptime") {|f| f.gets }
```

If the `open-uri` library has been loaded, then open can also be used to read from http and ftp URLs as if they were files:

```
require "open-uri"                          # Required library
f = open("http://www.davidflanagan.com/")   # Webpage as a file
webpage = f.read                            # Read it as one big string
f.close                                     # Don't forget to close!
```

In Ruby 1.9, if the argument to open has a method named to_open, then that method is called and should return an opened IO object.

9.7.1.3 StringIO

Another way to obtain an IO object is to use the `stringio` library to read from or write to a string:

```
require "stringio"
input = StringIO.open("now is the time")  # Read from this string
buffer = ""
output = StringIO.open(buffer, "w")       # Write into buffer
```

The `StringIO` class is not a subclass of `IO`, but it defines many of the same methods as `IO` does, and duck typing usually allows us to use a `StringIO` object in place of an `IO` object.

9.7.1.4 Predefined streams

Ruby predefines a number of streams that can be used without being created or opened. The global constants `STDIN`, `STDOUT`, and `STDERR` are the standard input stream, the standard output stream, and the standard error stream, respectively. By default, these streams are connected to the user's console or a terminal window of some sort. Depending on how your Ruby script is invoked, they may instead use a file, or even another process, as a source of input or a destination for output. Any Ruby program can read from standard input and write to standard output (for normal program output) or standard error (for error messages that should be seen even if the standard output is redirected to a file). The global variables `$stdin`, `$stdout`, and `$stderr` are initially set to the same values as the stream constants. Global functions like `print` and `puts` write to `$stdout` by default. If a script alters the value of this global variable, it will change the behavior of those methods. The true "standard output" will still be available through `STDOUT`, however.

Another predefined stream is `ARGF`, or `$<`. This stream has special behavior intended to make it simple to write scripts that read the files specified on the command line or from standard input. If there are command-line arguments to the Ruby script (in the `ARGV` or `$*` array), then the `ARGF` stream acts as if those files had been concatenated together and the single resulting file opened for reading. In order for this to work properly, a Ruby script that accepts command-line options other than filenames must first process those options and remove them from the `ARGV` array. If the `ARGV` array is empty, then `ARGF` is the same as `STDIN`. (See §10.3.1 for further details about the `ARGF` stream.)

Finally, the `DATA` stream is designed for reading text that appears after the end of your Ruby script. This works only if your script includes the token `__END__` on a line by itself. That token marks the end of the program text. Any lines after the token may be read with the `DATA` stream.

9.7.2 Streams and Encodings

One of the most significant changes in Ruby 1.9 is support for multibyte character encodings. We saw in §3.2 that there were many changes to the String class. There are similar changes to the IO class.

In Ruby 1.9, every stream can have two encodings associated with it. These are known as the external and internal encodings, and are returned by the external_encoding and internal_encoding methods of an IO object. The external encoding is the encoding of the text as stored in the file. The internal encoding is the encoding used to represent the text within Ruby. If the external encoding is also the desired internal encoding, there is no need to specify an internal encoding: strings read from the stream will have the external encoding associated with them (as by the String method force_encoding). If, on the other hand, you'd like the internal representation of the text to be different than the external representation, you can specify an internal encoding and Ruby will transcode from the external to the internal when reading and to the external when writing.

Specify the encoding of any IO object (including pipes and network sockets) with the set_encoding method. With two arguments, it specifies an external encoding and an internal encoding. You can also specify two encodings with a single string argument, which consists of two encoding names separated by a colon. Normally, however, a single argument specifies just an external encoding. The arguments can be strings or Encoding objects. The external encoding is always specified first, followed, optionally, by an internal encoding. For example:

```
f.set_encoding("iso-8859-1", "utf-8") # Latin-1, transcoded to UTF-8
f.set_encoding("iso-8859-1:utf-8")    # Same as above
f.set_encoding(Encoding::UTF-8)       # UTF-8 text
```

set_encoding works for any kind of IO object. For files, however, it is often easiest to specify encoding when you open the file. You can do this by appending the encoding names to the file mode string. For example:

```
in = File.open("data.txt", "r:utf-8");        # Read UTF-8 text
out = File.open("log", "a:utf-8");            # Write UTF-8 text
in = File.open("data.txt", "r:iso8859-1:utf-8"); # Latin-1 transcoded to UTF-8
```

Note that it is not usually necessary to specify two encodings for a stream that is to be used for output. In that case, the internal encoding is specified by the String objects that are written to the stream.

If you specify no encoding at all, then Ruby defaults to the default external encoding (see §2.4.2) when reading from files, and defaults to no encoding (i.e., the ASCII-8BIT/ BINARY encoding) when writing to files or when reading or writing from pipes and sockets.

The default external encoding is, by default, derived from the user's locale settings and is often a multibyte encoding. In order to read binary data from a file, therefore, you must explicitly specify that you want unencoded bytes, or you'll get characters in the default external encoding. To do this, open a file with mode `"r:binary"`, or pass `Encoding::BINARY` to `set_encoding` after opening the file:

```
File.open("data", "r:binary")  # Open a file for reading binary data
```

On Windows, you should open binary files with mode `"rb:binary"` or call `binmode` on the stream. This disables the automatic newline conversion performed by Windows, and is only necessary on that platform.

Not every stream-reading method honors the encoding of a stream. Some lower-level reading methods take an argument that specifies the number of bytes to read. By their nature, these methods return unencoded strings of bytes rather than strings of text. The methods that do not specify a length to read do honor the encoding.

9.7.3 Reading from a Stream

The `IO` class defines a number of methods for reading from streams. They work only if the stream is readable, of course. You can read from `STDIN`, `ARGF`, and `DATA`, but not from `STDOUT` or `STDERR`. Files and `StringIO` objects are opened for reading by default, unless you explicitly open them for writing only.

9.7.3.1 Reading lines

`IO` defines a number of ways to read lines   from a stream:

```
lines = ARGF.readlines           # Read all input, return an array of lines
line = DATA.readline             # Read one line from stream
print l while l = DATA.gets      # Read until gets returns nil, at EOF
DATA.each {|line| print line }   # Iterate lines from stream until EOF
DATA.each_line                   # An alias for each
DATA.lines                       # An enumerator for each_line: Ruby 1.9
```

Here are some important notes on these line-reading methods. First, the `readline` and the `gets` method differ only in their handling of EOF (end-of-file: the condition that occurs when there is no more to read from a stream). `gets` returns `nil` if it is invoked on a stream at EOF. `readline` instead raises an `EOFError`. If you do not know how many lines to expect, use `gets`. If you expect another line (and it is an error if it is not there), then use `readline`. You can check whether a stream is already at EOF with the `eof?` method.

Second, `gets` and `readline` implicitly set the global variable `$_` to the line of text they return. A number of global methods, such as `print`, use `$_` if they are not explicitly passed an argument. Therefore, the `while` loop in the code above could be written more succinctly as:

```
print while DATA.gets
```

Relying on `$_` is useful for short scripts, but in longer programs, it is better style to explicitly use variables to store the lines of input you've read.

Third, these methods are typically used for text (instead of binary) streams, and a "line" is defined as a sequence of bytes up to and including the default line terminator (newline on most platforms). The lines returned by these methods include the line terminator (although the last line in a file may not have one). Use `String.chomp!` to strip it off. The special global variable `$/` holds the line terminator. You can set `$/` to alter the default behavior of all the line-reading methods, or you can simply pass an alternate separator to any of the methods (including the `each` iterator). You might do this when reading comma-separated fields from a file, for example, or when reading a binary file that has some kind of "record separator" character. There are two special cases for the line terminator. If you specify `nil`, then the line-reading methods keep reading until EOF and return the entire contents of the stream as a single line. If you specify the empty string "" as the line terminator, then the line-reading methods read a paragraph at a time, looking for a blank line as the separator.

In Ruby 1.9, `gets` and `readline` accept an optional integer as the first argument or as the second after a separator string. If specified, this integer specifies the maximum number of bytes to read from the stream. This limit argument exists to prevent accidental reads of unexpectedly long lines, and these methods are exceptions to the previously cited rule; they return encoded character strings despite the fact that they have a limit argument measured in bytes.

Finally, the line-reading methods `gets`, `readline`, and the `each` iterator (and its `each_line` alias) keep track of the number of lines they've read. You can query the line number of the most recently read line with the `lineno` method, and you can set that line number with `lineno=` accessor. Note that `lineno` does not actually count the number of newlines in a file. It counts the number of times line-reading methods have been called, and may return different results if you use different line separator characters:

```
DATA.lineno = 0    # Start from line 0, even though data is at end of file
DATA.readline      # Read one line of data
DATA.lineno        # => 1
$.                 # => 1: magic global variable, implicitly set
```

9.7.3.2 Reading entire files

IO defines three class methods for reading files without ever opening an IO stream. `IO.read` reads an entire file (or a portion of a file) and returns it as a single string. `IO.readlines` reads an entire named file into an array of lines. And `IO.foreach` iterates over the lines of a named file. In Ruby 1.9, you can pass a hash to these methods to specify the mode string and/or encoding of the file being read:

```
data = IO.read("data")                   # Read and return the entire file
data = IO.read("data", mode:"rb")        # Open with mode string "rb"
data = IO.read("data", encoding:"binary") # Read unencoded bytes
data = IO.read("data", 4, 2)             # Read 4 bytes starting at byte 2
data = IO.read("data", nil, 6)           # Read from byte 6 to end-of-file

# Read lines into an array
words = IO.readlines("/usr/share/dict/words")
```

```
# Read lines one at a time and initialize a hash
words = {}
IO.foreach("/usr/share/dict/words") {|w| words[w] = true}
```

In Ruby 1.9 you can use IO.copy_stream to read a file (or a portion) and write its content to a stream:

```
IO.copy_stream("/usr/share/dict/words", STDOUT) # Print the dictionary
IO.copy_stream("/usr/share/dict/words", STDOUT, 10, 100) # Print bytes 100-109
```

Although these class methods are defined by the IO class, they operate on named files, and it is also common to see them invoked as class methods of File: File.read, File.readlines, File.foreach, and File.copy_stream.

The IO class also defines an instance method named read, which is similar to the class method with the same name; with no arguments it reads text until the end of the stream and returns it as an encoded string:

```
# An alternative to text = File.read("data.txt")
f = File.open("data.txt")  # Open a file
text = f.read              # Read its contents as text
f.close                    # Close the file
```

The IO.read instance method can also be used with arguments to read a specified number of bytes from the stream. That use is described in the next section.

9.7.3.3 Reading bytes and characters

The IO class also defines methods for reading a stream one or more bytes or characters at a time, but these methods have changed substantially between Ruby 1.8 and Ruby 1.9 because Ruby's definition of a character has changed.

In Ruby 1.8, bytes and characters are the same thing, and the getc and readchar methods read a single byte and return it as a Fixnum. Like gets, getc returns nil at EOF. And like readline, readchar raises EOFError if it is called at EOF.

In Ruby 1.9, getc and readchar have been modified to return a string of length 1 instead of a Fixnum. When reading from a stream with a multibyte encoding, these methods read as many bytes as necessary to read a complete character. If you want to read a string a byte at a time in Ruby 1.9, use the new methods getbyte and readbyte. getbyte is like getc and gets: it returns nil at EOF. And readbyte is like readchar and readline: it raises EOFError.

Programs (like parsers) that read a stream one character at a time sometimes need to push a single character back into the stream's buffer, so that it will be returned by the next read call. They can do this with ungetc. This method expects a Fixnum in Ruby 1.8 and a single character string in Ruby 1.9. The character pushed back will be returned by the next call to getc or readchar:

```
f = File.open("data", "r:binary") # Open data file for binary reads
c = f.getc                         # Read the first byte as an integer
```

```
f.ungetc(c)                    # Push that byte back
c = f.readchar                 # Read it back again
```

You can also iterate and enumerate the characters and bytes of a stream:

```
f.each_byte {|b| ... }         # Iterate through remaining bytes
f.bytes                        # An enumerator for each_byte: Ruby 1.9
f.each_char {|c} ...}          # Iterate characters: Ruby 1.9
f.chars                        # An enumerator for each_char: Ruby 1.9
```

If you want to read more than one byte at a time, you have a choice of five methods, each with slightly different behavior:

readbytes(n)

Read exactly n bytes and return them as a string. Block, if necessary, until n bytes arrive. Raise EOFError if EOF occurs before n bytes are available.

readpartial(n, buffer=nil)

Read between 1 and n bytes and return them as a new binary string, or, if a String object is passed as the second argument, store them in that string (overwriting whatever text it contains). If one or more bytes are available for reading, this method returns them (up to a maximum of n) immediately. It blocks only if no bytes are available. This method raises EOFError if called when the stream is at EOF.

read(n=nil, buffer=nil)

Read n bytes (or fewer, if EOF is reached), blocking if necessary, until the bytes are ready. The bytes are returned as a binary string. If the second argument is an existing String object, then the bytes are stored in that object (replacing any existing content) and the string is returned. If the stream is at EOF and n is specified, it returns nil. If called at EOF and n is omitted or is nil, then it returns the empty string "".

If n is nil or is omitted, then this method reads the rest of the stream and returns it as an encoded character string rather than an unencoded byte string.

read_nonblock(n, buffer=nil)

Read the bytes (up to a maximum of n) that are currently available for reading, and return them as a string, using the buffer string if it is specified. This method does not block. If there is no data ready to be read on the stream (this might occur with a networking socket or with STDIN, for example) this method raises a SystemCallError. If called at EOF, this method raises EOFError.

This method is new in Ruby 1.9. (Ruby 1.9 also defines other nonblocking IO methods, but they are low-level and are not covered here.)

sysread(n)

This method works like readbytes but operates at a lower level without buffering. Do not mix calls to sysread with any other line- or byte-reading methods; they are incompatible.

Here is some example code you might use when reading a binary file:

```
f = File.open("data.bin", "rb:binary")  # No newline conversion, no encoding
magic = f.readbytes(4)       # First four bytes identify filetype
exit unless magic == "INTS"  # Magic number spells "INTS" (ASCII)
bytes = f.read               # Read the rest of the file
                             # Encoding is binary, so this is a byte string
data = bytes.unpack("i*")    # Convert bytes to an array of integers
```

9.7.4 Writing to a Stream

The IO methods for writing to a stream mirror those for reading. The STDOUT and STDERR streams are writable, as are files opened in any mode other than "r" or "rb".

IO defines a single putc method for writing single bytes or characters to a stream. This method accepts either a byte value or a single-character string as its argument, and therefore has not changed between Ruby 1.8 and 1.9:

```
o = STDOUT
# Single-character output
o.putc(65)        # Write single byte 65 (capital A)
o.putc("B")       # Write single byte 66 (capital B)
o.putc("CD")      # Write just the first byte of the string
```

The IO class defines a number of other methods for writing arbitrary strings. These methods differ from each other in the number of arguments they accept and whether or not line terminators are added. Recall that in Ruby 1.9, textual output is transcoded to the external encoding of the stream, if one was specified:

```
o = STDOUT
# String output
o << x            # Output x.to_s
o << x << y       # May be chained: output x.to_s + y.to_s
o.print           # Output $_ + $\
o.print s         # Output s.to_s + $\
o.print s,t       # Output s.to_s + t.to_s + $\
o.printf fmt,*args # Outputs fmt%[args]
o.puts            # Output newline
o.puts x          # Output x.to_s.chomp plus newline
o.puts x,y        # Output x.to_s.chomp, newline, y.to_s.chomp, newline
o.puts [x,y]      # Same as above
o.write s         # Output s.to_s, returns s.to_s.length
o.syswrite s      # Low-level version of write
```

Output streams are appendable, like strings and arrays are, and you can write values to them with the << operator. puts is one of the most common output methods. It converts each of its arguments to a string, and writes each one to the stream. If the string does not already end with a newline character, it adds one. If any of the arguments to puts is an array, the array is recursively expanded, and each element is printed on its own line as if it were passed directly as an argument to puts. The print method converts its arguments to strings, and outputs them to the stream. If the global field separator $, has been changed from its default value of nil, then that value is output between each of the arguments to print. If the output record separator $/ has been changed from its default value of nil, then that value is output after all arguments are printed.

The `printf` method expects a format string as its first argument, and interpolates the values of any additional arguments into that format string using the `String %` operator. It then outputs the interpolated string with no newline or record separator.

`write` simply outputs its single argument as `<<` does, and returns the number of bytes written. Finally, `syswrite` is a low-level, unbuffered, nontranscoding version of `write`. If you use `syswrite`, you must use that method exclusively, and not mix it with any other writing methods.

9.7.5 Random Access Methods

Some streams, such as those that represent network sockets, or user input at the console, are sequential streams: once you have read or written from them, you cannot go back. Other streams, such as those that read from or write to files or strings, allow random access with the methods described here. If you attempt to use these methods on a stream that does not allow random access, they will raise a `SystemCallException`:

```
f = File.open("test.txt")
f.pos       # => 0: return the current position in bytes
f.pos = 10  # skip to position 10
f.tell      # => 10: a synonym for pos
f.rewind    # go back to position 0, reset lineno to 0, also
f.seek(10, IO::SEEK_SET)  # Skip to absolute position 10
f.seek(10, IO::SEEK_CUR)  # Skip 10 bytes from current position
f.seek(-10, IO::SEEK_END) # Skip 10 bytes from end
f.seek(0, IO::SEEK_END)   # Skip to very end of file
f.eof?                    # => true: we're at the end
```

If you use `sysread` or `syswrite` in your program, then use `sysseek` instead of `seek` for random access. `sysseek` is like `seek` except that it returns the new file position after each call:

```
pos = f.sysseek(0, IO::SEEK_CUR)  # Get current position
f.sysseek(0, IO::SEEK_SET)        # Rewind stream
f.sysseek(pos, IO::SEEK_SET)      # Return to original position
```

9.7.6 Closing, Flushing, and Testing Streams

When you are done reading from or writing to a stream, you must close it with the `close` method. This flushes any buffered input or output, and also frees up operating system resources. A number of stream-opening methods allow you to associate a block with them. They pass the open stream to the block, and automatically close the stream when the block exits. Managing streams in this way ensures that they are properly closed even when exceptions are raised:

```
File.open("test.txt") do |f|
  # Use stream f here
  # Value of this block becomes return value of the open method
end # f is automatically closed for us here
```

The alternative to using a block is to use an **ensure** clause of your own:

```
begin
  f = File.open("test.txt")
  # use stream f here
ensure
  f.close if f
end
```

Network sockets are implemented using IO objects that have separate read and write streams internally. You can use `close_read` and `close_write` to close these internal streams individually. Although files can be opened for reading and writing at the same time, you cannot use `close_read` and `close_write` on those IO objects.

Ruby's output methods (except `syswrite`) buffer output for efficiency. The output buffer is flushed at reasonable times, such as when a newline is output or when data is read from a corresponding input stream. There are times, however, when you may need to explicitly flush the output buffer to force output to be sent right away:

```
out.print 'wait>' # Display a prompt
out.flush         # Manually flush output buffer to OS
sleep(1)          # Prompt appears before we go to sleep

out.sync = true   # Automatically flush buffer after every write
out.sync = false  # Don't automatically flush
out.sync          # Return current sync mode
out.fsync         # Flush output buffer and ask OS to flush its buffers
                  # Returns nil if unsupported on current platform
```

IO defines several predicates for testing the state of a stream:

```
f.eof?     # true if stream is at EOF
f.closed?  # true if stream has been closed
f.tty?     # true if stream is interactive
```

The only one of these methods that needs explanation is `tty?`. This method, and its alias `isatty` (with no question mark), returns `true` if the stream is connected to an interactive device such as a terminal window or a keyboard with (presumably) a human at it. They return `false` if the stream is a noninteractive one, such as a file, pipe, or socket. A program can use `tty?` to avoid prompting a user for input if `STDIN` has actually been redirected and is coming from a file, for example.

9.8 Networking

Ruby's networking capabilities are provided by the standard library rather than by core classes. For this reason, the subsections that follow do not attempt to enumerate each available class or method. Instead, they demonstrate how to accomplish common networking tasks with simple examples. Use *ri* for more complete documentation.

At the lowest level, networking is accomplished with sockets, which are a kind of IO object. Once you have a socket opened, you can read data from, or write data to, another computer just as if you were reading from or writing to a file. The socket class hierarchy is somewhat confusing, but the details are not important in the following examples. Internet clients use the `TCPSocket` class, and Internet servers use the `TCPServer` class (also a socket). All socket classes are part of the standard library, so to use them in your Ruby program, you must first write:

```
require 'socket'
```

9.8.1 A Very Simple Client

To write Internet client applications, use the `TCPSocket` class. Obtain a `TCPSocket` instance with the `TCPSocket.open` class method, or with its synonym `TCPSocket.new`. Pass the name of the host to connect to as the first argument and the port as the second argument. (The port should be an integer between 1 and 65535, specified as a `Fixnum` or `String` object. Different internet protocols use different ports. Web servers use port 80 by default, for example. You may also pass the name of an Internet service, such as "http", as a string, in place of a port number, but this is not well documented and may be system dependent.)

Once you have a socket open, you can read from it like any `IO` object. When done, remember to close it, as you would close a file. The following code is a very simple client that connects to a given host and port, reads any available data from the socket, and then exits:

```
require 'socket'              # Sockets are in standard library

host, port = ARGV            # Host and port from command line

s = TCPSocket.open(host, port)  # Open a socket to host and port
while line = s.gets          # Read lines from the socket
  puts line.chop             # And print with platform line terminator
end
s.close                      # Close the socket when done
```

Like `File.open`, the `TCPSocket.open` method can be invoked with a block. In that form, it passes the open socket to the block and automatically closes the socket when the block returns. So we can also write this code like this:

```
require 'socket'
host, port = ARGV
TCPSocket.open(host, port) do |s| # Use block form of open
  while line = s.gets
    puts line.chop
  end
end                          # Socket automatically closed
```

This client code for use with services like the old-style (and now defunct) Unix "daytime" service. With services like these, the client doesn't make a query; the client simply connects and the server sends a response. If you can't find an Internet host running a server to test the client with, don't despair—the next section shows how to write an equally simple time server.

9.8.2 A Very Simple Server

To write Internet servers, we use the TCPServer class. In essence, a TCPServer object is a factory for TCPSocket objects. Call TCPServer.open to specify a port for your service and create a TCPServer object. Next, call the accept method of the returned TCPServer object. This method waits until a client connects to the port you specified, and then returns a TCPSocket object that represents the connection to that client.

The following code shows how we might write a simple time server. It listens for connections on port 2000. When a client connects to that port, it sends the current time to the client and closes the socket, thereby terminating the connection with the client:

```
require 'socket'                # Get sockets from stdlib

server = TCPServer.open(2000)   # Socket to listen on port 2000
loop {                          # Infinite loop: servers run forever
  client = server.accept        # Wait for a client to connect
  client.puts(Time.now.ctime)   # Send the time to the client
  client.close                  # Disconnect from the client
}
```

To test this code, run it in the background or in another terminal window. Then, run the simple client code from above with a command like this:

```
ruby client.rb localhost 2000
```

9.8.3 Datagrams

Most Internet protocols are implemented using TCPSocket and TCPServer, as shown earlier. A lower-overhead alternative is to use UDP datagrams, with the UDPSocket class. UDP allows computers to send individual packets of data to other computers, without the overhead of establishing a persistent connection. The following client and server code demonstrate: the client sends a datagram containing a string of text to a specified host and port. The server, which should be running on that host and listening on that port, receives the text, converts it to uppercase (not much of a service, I know), and sends it back in a second datagram.

The client code is first. Note that although UDPSocket objects are IO objects, datagrams are pretty different from other IO streams. For this reason, we avoid using IO methods and use the lower-level sending and receiving methods of UDPSocket. The second argument to the send method specifies flags. It is required, even though we are not setting any flags. The argument to recvfrom specifies the maximum amount of data we are interested in receiving. In this case, we limit our client and server to transferring 1 kilobyte:

```
require 'socket'                    # Standard library

host, port, request = ARGV          # Get args from command line

ds = UDPSocket.new                  # Create datagram socket
ds.connect(host, port)              # Connect to the port on the host
ds.send(request, 0)                 # Send the request text
response,address = ds.recvfrom(1024) # Wait for a response (1kb max)
puts response                       # Print the response
```

The server code uses the UDPSocket class just as the client code does—there is no special UDPServer class for datagram-based servers. Instead of calling connect to connect the socket, our server calls bind to tell the socket what port to listen on. The server then uses send and recvfrom, just as the client does, but in the opposite order. It calls recvfrom to wait until it receives a datagram on the specified port. When that happens, it converts the text it receives to uppercase and sends it back. An important point to notice is that the recvfrom method returns two values. The first is the received data. The second is an array containing information about where that data came from. We extract host and port information from that array and use it to send the response back to the client:

```
require 'socket'                    # Standard library

port = ARGV[0]                      # The port to listen on

ds = UDPSocket.new                  # Create new socket
ds.bind(nil, port)                  # Make it listen on the port
loop do                             # Loop forever
  request,address=ds.recvfrom(1024) # Wait to receive something
  response = request.upcase         # Convert request text to uppercase
  clientaddr = address[3]           # What ip address sent the request?
  clientname = address[2]           # What is the host name?
  clientport = address[1]           # What port was it sent from
  ds.send(response, 0,              # Send the response back...
          clientaddr, clientport)   # ...where it came from
  # Log the client connection
  puts "Connection from: #{clientname} #{clientaddr} #{clientport}"
end
```

9.8.4 A More Complex Client

The following code is a more fully developed Internet client in the style of *telnet*. It connects to the specified host and port and then loops, reading a line of input from the console, sending it to the server, and then reading and printing the server's response. It demonstrates how to determine the local and remote addresses of the network connection, adds exception handling, and uses the IO methods read_nonblock and readpartial described earlier in this chapter. The code is well-commented and should be self-explanatory:

```
require 'socket'     # Sockets from standard library
```

```
host, port = ARGV      # Network host and port on command line

begin                  # Begin for exception handling
  # Give the user some feedback while connecting.
  STDOUT.print "Connecting..."       # Say what we're doing
  STDOUT.flush                       # Make it visible right away
  s = TCPSocket.open(host, port)     # Connect
  STDOUT.puts "done"                 # And say we did it

  # Now display information about the connection.
  local, peer = s.addr, s.peeraddr
  STDOUT.print "Connected to #{peer[2]}:#{peer[1]}"
  STDOUT.puts " using local port #{local[1]}"

  # Wait just a bit, to see if the server sends any initial message.
  begin
    sleep(0.5)                       # Wait half a second
    msg = s.read_nonblock(4096)      # Read whatever is ready
    STDOUT.puts msg.chop             # And display it
  rescue SystemCallError
    # If nothing was ready to read, just ignore the exception.
  end

  # Now begin a loop of client/server interaction.
  loop do
    STDOUT.print '> '    # Display prompt for local input
    STDOUT.flush         # Make sure the prompt is visible
    local = STDIN.gets   # Read line from the console
    break if !local      # Quit if no input from console

    s.puts(local)        # Send the line to the server
    s.flush              # Force it out

    # Read the server's response and print out.
    # The server may send more than one line, so use readpartial
    # to read whatever it sends (as long as it all arrives in one chunk).
    response = s.readpartial(4096) # Read server's response
    puts(response.chop)            # Display response to user
  end
rescue             # If anything goes wrong
  puts $!          # Display the exception to the user
ensure             # And no matter what happens
  s.close if s     # Don't forget to close the socket
end
```

9.8.5 A Multiplexing Server

The simple time server shown earlier in this section never maintained a connection with any client—it would simply tell the client the time and disconnect. Many more sophisticated servers maintain a connection, and in order to be useful, they must allow multiple clients to connect and interact at the same time. One way to do this is with threads—each client runs in its own thread. We'll see an example of a multithreaded server later in this chapter. The alternative that we'll consider here is to write a multi-plexing server using the `Kernel.select` method.

When a server has multiple clients connected, it cannot call a blocking method like `gets` on the socket of any one client. If it blocks waiting for input from one client, it won't be able to receive input from other clients or accept connections from new clients. The `select` method solves this problem; it allows us to block on a whole array of IO objects, and returns when there is activity on any one of those objects. The return value of `select` is an array of arrays of IO objects. The first element of the array is the array of streams (sockets, in this case) that have data to be read (or a connection to be accepted).

With that explanation of `select`, you should be able to understand the following server code. The service it implements is trivial—it simply reverses each line of client input and sends it back. It is the mechanism for handling multiple connections that is interesting. Note that we use `select` to monitor both the `TCPServer` object and each of the client `TCPSocket` objects. Also note that the server handles the case where a client asks to disconnect as well as the case where the client disconnects unexpectedly:

```
# This server reads a line of input from a client, reverses
# the line and sends it back. If the client sends the string "quit"
# it disconnects. It uses Kernel.select to handle multiple sessions.

require 'socket'

server = TCPServer.open(2000) # Listen on port 2000
sockets = [server]            # An array of sockets we'll monitor
log = STDOUT                  # Send log messages to standard out
while true                    # Servers loop forever
  ready = select(sockets)     # Wait for a socket to be ready
  readable = ready[0]         # These sockets are readable

  readable.each do |socket|          # Loop through readable sockets
    if socket == server              # If the server socket is ready
      client = server.accept         # Accept a new client
      sockets << client              # Add it to the set of sockets
      # Tell the client what and where it has connected.
      client.puts "Reversal service v0.01 running on #{Socket.gethostname}"
      # And log the fact that the client connected
      log.puts "Accepted connection from #{client.peeraddr[2]}"
    else                             # Otherwise, a client is ready
      input = socket.gets            # Read input from the client

      # If no input, the client has disconnected
      if !input
        log.puts "Client on #{socket.peeraddr[2]} disconnected."
        sockets.delete(socket)       # Stop monitoring this socket
        socket.close                 # Close it
        next                         # And go on to the next
      end

      input.chop!                    # Trim client's input
```

```
        if (input == "quit")            # If the client asks to quit
          socket.puts("Bye!");          # Say goodbye
          log.puts "Closing connection to #{socket.peeraddr[2]}"
          sockets.delete(socket)        # Stop monitoring the socket
          socket.close                  # Terminate the session
        else                            # Otherwise, client is not quitting
          socket.puts(input.reverse)    # So reverse input and send it back
        end
      end
    end
  end
end
```

9.8.6 Fetching Web Pages

We can use the socket library to implement any Internet protocol. Here, for example,
is code to fetch the content of a web page:

```
require 'socket'          # We need sockets

host = 'www.example.com'  # The web server
port = 80                 # Default HTTP port
path = "/index.html"      # The file we want

# This is the HTTP request we send to fetch a file
request = "GET #{path} HTTP/1.0\r\n\r\n"

socket = TCPSocket.open(host,port)  # Connect to server
socket.print(request)               # Send request
response = socket.read              # Read complete response
# Split response at first blank line into headers and body
headers,body = response.split("\r\n\r\n", 2)
print body                          # And display it
```

HTTP is a complex protocol, and the simple code above only really handles straightforward cases. You might prefer to use a prebuilt library like Net::HTTP for working
with HTTP. Here is code that does the equivalent of the previous code:

```
require 'net/http'        # The library we need
host = 'www.example.com'  # The web server
path = '/index.html'      # The file we want

http = Net::HTTP.new(host)       # Create a connection
headers, body = http.get(path)   # Request the file
if headers.code == "200"         # Check the status code
                                 # NOTE: code is not a number!
  print body                     # Print body if we got it
else                             # Otherwise
  puts "#{headers.code} #{headers.message}" # Display error message
end
```

Similar libraries exist for working with the FTP, SMTP, POP, and IMAP protocols.
Details of those standard libraries are beyond the scope of this book.

Finally, recall that the `open-uri` library described earlier in the chapter makes fetching a web page even easier:

```
require 'open-uri'
open("http://www.example.com/index.html") {|f|
  puts f.read
}
```

9.9 Threads and Concurrency

Traditional programs have a single "thread of execution": the statements or instructions that comprise the program are executed sequentially until the program terminates. A *multithreaded* program has more than one thread of execution. Within each thread, statements are executed sequentially, but the threads themselves may be executed in parallel—on a multicore CPU, for example. Often (on single-core, single-CPU machines, for instance), multiple threads are not actually executed in parallel, but parallelism is simulated by interleaving the execution of the threads.

Programs such as image processing software that perform a lot of calculations are said to be *compute-bound*. They can only benefit from multithreading if there are actually multiple CPUs to run computations in parallel. Most programs are not fully compute-bound, however. Many, such as web browsers, spend most of their time waiting for network or file I/O. Programs like these are said to be *IO-bound*. IO-bound programs can be usefully multithreaded even when there is only a single CPU available. A web browser might render an image in one thread while another thread is waiting for the next image to be downloaded from the network.

Ruby makes it easy to write multi-threaded programs with the `Thread` class. To start a new thread, just associate a block with a call to `Thread.new`. A new thread will be created to execute the code in the block, and the original thread will return from `Thread.new` immediately and resume execution with the next statement:

```
# Thread #1 is running here
Thread.new {
  # Thread #2 runs this code
}
# Thread #1 runs this code
```

We'll begin our coverage of threads by explaining Ruby's thread model and API in some detail. These introductory sections explain things such as thread lifecycle, thread scheduling, and thread states. With that introductory material as prerequisite, we move on to present example code and to cover advanced topics such as thread synchronization.

Finally, it is worth noting that Ruby programs can also achieve concurrency at the level of the operating system process by running external executables or by forking new copies of the Ruby interpreter. Doing this is operating system-dependent, however, and is covered only briefly in Chapter 10. For further information, use *ri* to look up the methods `Kernel.system`, `Kernel.exec`, `Kernel.fork`, `IO.popen`, and the module `Process`.

Threads and Platform Dependencies

Different operating systems implement threads differently. And different Ruby implementations layer Ruby threads on top of operating system threads differently. The standard C implementation of Ruby 1.8, for example, uses only a single native thread and runs all Ruby threads within that one native thread. This means that in Ruby 1.8 threads are very lightweight, but that they never run in parallel, even on multicore CPUs.

Ruby 1.9 is different: it allocates a native thread for each Ruby thread. But because some of the C libraries used in this implementation are not themselves thread-safe, Ruby 1.9 is very conservative and never allows more than one of its native threads to run at the same time. (This restriction may be relaxed in later releases of 1.9, if the C code can be made thread-safe.)

JRuby, the Java implementation of Ruby, maps each Ruby thread to a Java thread. But the implementation and behavior of Java threads depends, in turn, on the implementation of the Java virtual machine. Modern Java implementations typically implement Java threads as native threads and allow true parallel processing on multicore CPUs.

9.9.1 Thread Lifecycle

As described above, new threads are created with `Thread.new`. You can also use the synonyms `Thread.start` and `Thread.fork`. There is no need to start a thread after creating it; it begins running automatically when CPU resources become available. The value of the `Thread.new` invocation is a `Thread` object. The `Thread` class defines a number of methods to query and manipulate the thread while it is running.

A thread runs the code in the block associated with the call to `Thread.new` and then it stops running. The value of the last expression in that block is the value of the thread, and can be obtained by calling the `value` method of the `Thread` object. If the thread has run to completion, then the `value` returns the thread's value right away. Otherwise, the `value` method blocks and does not return until the thread has completed.

The class method `Thread.current` returns the `Thread` object that represents the current thread. This allows threads to manipulate themselves. The class method `Thread.main` returns the `Thread` object that represents the main thread—this is the initial thread of execution that began when the Ruby program was started.

9.9.1.1 The main thread

The main thread is special: the Ruby interpreter stops running when the main thread is done. It does this even if the main thread has created other threads that are still running. You must ensure, therefore, that your main thread does not end while other threads are still running. One way to do this is to write your main thread in the form of an infinite loop. Another way is to explicitly wait for the threads you care about to complete. We've already mentioned that you can call the **value** method of a thread to wait for it to finish. If you don't care about the value of your threads, you can wait with the **join** method instead.

The following method waits until all threads, other than the main thread and the current thread (which may be the same thing), have exited:

```
# Wait for all threads (other than the current thread and
# main thread) to stop running.
# Assumes that no new threads are started while waiting.
def join_all
  main = Thread.main        # The main thread
  current = Thread.current  # The current thread
  all = Thread.list         # All threads still running
  # Now call join on each thread
  all.each {|t| t.join unless t == current or t == main }
end
```

9.9.1.2 Threads and unhandled exceptions

If an exception is raised in the main thread, and is not handled anywhere, the Ruby interpreter prints a message and exits. In threads other than the main thread, unhandled exceptions cause the thread to stop running. By default, however, this does not cause the interpreter to print a message or exit. If a thread **t** exits because of an unhandled exception, and another thread **s** calls **t.join** or **t.value**, then the exception that occurred in **t** is raised in the thread **s**.

If you would like any unhandled exception in any thread to cause the interpreter to exit, use the class method **Thread.abort_on_exception=**:

```
Thread.abort_on_exception = true
```

If you want an unhandled exception in one particular thread to cause the interpreter to exit, use the instance method by the same name:

```
t = Thread.new { ... }
t.abort_on_exception = true
```

9.9.2 Threads and Variables

One of the key features of threads is that they can share access to variables. Because threads are defined by blocks, they have access to whatever variables (local variables, instance variables, global variables, and so on) are in the scope of the block:

```
x = 0

t1 = Thread.new do
  # This thread can query and set the variable x
end
```

```
t2 = Thread.new do
  # This thread and also query and set x
  # And it can query and set t1 and t2 as well.
end
```

When two or more threads read and write the same variables concurrently, they must be careful that they do so correctly. We'll have more to say about this when we consider thread synchronization below.

9.9.2.1 Thread-private variables

Variables defined within the block of a thread are private to that thread and are not visible to any other thread. This is simply a consequence of Ruby's variable scoping rules.

We often want a thread to have its own private copy of a variable so that its behavior does not change if the value of that variable changes. Consider the following code, which attempts to create three threads that print (respectively) the numbers 1, 2, and 3:

```
n = 1
while n <= 3
  Thread.new { puts n }
  n += 1
end
```

In some circumstances, in some implementations, this code might work as expected and print the numbers 1, 2, and 3. In other circumstances or in other implementations, it might not. It is perfectly possible (if newly created threads do not run right away) for the code to print 4, 4, and 4, for example. Each thread reads a shared copy of the variable n, and the value of that variable changes as the loop executes. The value printed by the thread depends on when that thread runs in relation to the parent thread.

To solve this problem, we pass the current value of n to the `Thread.new` method, and assign the current value of that variable to a block parameter. Block parameters are private to the block (but see §5.4.3 for cautions), and this private value is not shared between threads:

```
n = 1
while n <= 3
  # Get a private copy of the current value of n in x
  Thread.new(n) {|x| puts x }
  n += 1
end
```

Note that another way to solve this problem is to use an iterator instead of a `while` loop. In this case, the value of n is private to the outer block and never changes during the execution of that block:

```
1.upto(3) {|n| Thread.new { puts n }}
```

9.9.2.2 Thread-local variables

Certain of Ruby's special global variables are *thread-local*: they may have different values in different threads. $SAFE (see §10.5) and $~ (see Table 9-3) are examples. This means that if two threads are performing regular expression matching concurrently, they will see different values of $~, and performing a match in one thread will not interfere with the results of a match performed in another thread.

The Thread class provides hash-like behavior. It defines [] and []= instance methods that allow you to associate arbitrary values with any symbol. (If you use a string instead, it will be converted to a symbol. Unlike true hashes, the Thread class only allows symbols as keys.) The values associated with these symbols behave like thread-local variables. They are not private like block-local variables because any thread can look up a value in any other thread. But they are not shared variables either, since each thread can have its own copy.

As an example, suppose that we've created threads to download files from a web server. The main thread might want to monitor the progress of the download. To enable this, each thread might do the following:

```
Thread.current[:progress] = bytes_received
```

The main thread could then determine the total bytes downloaded with code like this:

```
total = 0
download_threads.each {|t| total += t[:progress] }
```

Along with [] and []=, Thread also defines a key? method to test whether a given key exists for a thread. The keys method returns an array of symbols representing the defined keys for the thread. This code could be better written as follows, so that it works for threads that have not yet started running and have not defined the :progress key yet:

```
total = 0
download_threads.each {|t| total += t[:progress] if t.key?(:progress)}
```

9.9.3 Thread Scheduling

Ruby interpreters often have more threads to run than there are CPUs available to run them. When true parallel processing is not possible, it is simulated by sharing a CPU among threads. The process for sharing a CPU among threads is called thread scheduling. Depending on the implementation and platform, thread scheduling may be done by the Ruby interpreter, or it may be handled by the underlying operating system.

9.9.3.1 Thread priorities

The first factor that affects thread scheduling is *thread priority*: high-priority threads are scheduled before low-priority threads. More precisely, a thread will only get CPU time if there are no higher-priority threads waiting to run.

Set and query the priority of a Ruby `Thread` object with `priority=` and `priority`. Note that there is no way to set the priority of a thread before it starts running. A thread can, however, raise or lower its own priority as the first action it takes.

A newly created thread starts at the same priority as the thread that created it. The main thread starts off at priority 0.

Like many aspects of threading, thread priorities are dependent on the implementation of Ruby and on the underlying operating system. Under Linux, for example, nonprivileged threads cannot have their priorities raised or lowered. So in Ruby 1.9 (which uses native threads) on Linux, the thread priority setting is ignored.

9.9.3.2 Thread preemption and Thread.pass

When multiple threads of the same priority need to share the CPU, it is up to the thread scheduler to decide when, and for how long, each thread runs. Some schedulers are preempting, which means that they allow a thread to run only for a fixed amount of time before allowing another thread of the same priority to run. Other schedulers are not preempting: once a thread starts running, it keeps running unless it sleeps, blocks for I/O, or a higher-priority thread wakes up.

If a long-running compute-bound thread (i.e., one that does not ever block for I/O) is running on a nonpreempting scheduler, it will "starve" other threads of the same priority, and they will never get a chance to run. To avoid this issue, long-running compute-bound threads should periodically call `Thread.pass` to ask the scheduler to yield the CPU to another thread.

9.9.4 Thread States

A Ruby thread may be in one of five possible states. The two most interesting states are for live threads: a thread that is alive is *runnable* or *sleeping*. A runnable thread is one that is currently running, or that is ready and eligible to run the next time there are CPU resources for it. A sleeping thread is one that is sleeping (see `Kernel.sleep`), that is waiting for I/O, or that has stopped itself (see `Thread.stop` below). Threads typically go back and forth between the runnable and sleeping states.

There are two thread states for threads that are no longer alive. A terminated thread has either terminated normally or has terminated abnormally with an exception.

Finally, there is one transitional state. A thread that has been killed (see `Thread.kill` below) but that has not yet terminated is said to be *aborting*.

9.9.4.1 Querying thread state

The `Thread` class defines several instance methods for testing the status of a thread. `alive?` returns `true` if a thread is runnable or sleeping. `stop?` returns `true` if a thread is in any state other than runnable. Finally, the `status` method returns the state of the thread. There are five possible return values corresponding to the five possible states as shown in the following table.

Thread state	Return value
Runnable	`"run"`
Sleeping	`"sleep"`
Aborting	`"aborting"`
Terminated normally	`false`
Terminated with exception	`nil`

9.9.4.2 Altering state: pausing, waking, and killing threads

Threads are created in the *runnable* state, and are eligible to run right away. A thread can pause itself—enter the *sleeping* state—by calling `Thread.stop`. This is a class method that operates on the current thread—there is no equivalent instance method, so one thread cannot force another thread to pause. Calling `Thread.stop` is effectively the same thing as calling `Kernel.sleep` with no argument: the thread pauses forever (or until woken up, as explained below).

Threads also temporarily enter the *sleeping* state if they call `Kernel.sleep` with an argument. In this case, they automatically wake up and reenter the *runnable* state after (approximately) the specified number of seconds pass. Calling blocking `IO` methods may also cause a thread to sleep until the `IO` operation completes—in fact, it is the inherent latency of `IO` operations that makes threading worthwhile even on single-CPU systems.

A thread that has paused itself with `Thread.stop` or `Kernel.sleep` can be started again (even if the sleep time has not expired yet) with the instance methods `wakeup` and `run`. Both methods switch the thread from the *sleeping* state to the *runnable* state. The `run` method also invokes the thread scheduler. This causes the current thread to yield the CPU, and may cause the newly awoken thread to start running right away. The `wakeup` method wakes the specified thread without yielding the CPU.

A thread can switch itself from the *runnable* state to one of the *terminated* states simply by exiting its block or by raising an exception. Another way for a thread to terminate normally is by calling `Thread.exit`. Note that any `ensure` clauses are processed before a thread exits in this way.

A thread can forcibly terminate another thread by invoking the instance method `kill` on the thread to be terminated. `terminate` and `exit` are synonyms for `kill`. These methods put the killed thread into the *terminated normally* state. The killed thread runs any `ensure` clauses before it actually dies. The `kill!` method (and its synonyms `terminate!` and `exit!`) terminate a thread but do not allow any `ensure` clauses to run.

The thread termination methods described so far all force a thread to the *terminated normally* state. You can raise an exception within another thread with the instance method `raise`. If the thread cannot handle the exception you have imposed on it, it will enter the *terminated with exception* state. The threads ensure clauses are processed as they would normally be during the course of exception propagation.

Killing a thread is a dangerous thing to do unless you have some way of knowing that the thread is not in the middle of altering the shared state of your system. Killing a thread with one of the ! methods is even more dangerous because the killed thread may leave files, sockets, or other resources open. If a thread must be able to exit upon command, it is better to have it periodically check the state of a flag variable and terminate itself safely and gracefully if or when the flag becomes set.

9.9.5 Listing Threads and Thread Groups

The `Thread.list` method returns an array of `Thread` objects representing all live (running or sleeping) threads. When a thread exits, it is removed from this array.

Every thread other than the main thread is created by some other thread. Threads could, therefore, be organized into a tree structure, with every thread having a parent and a set of children. The `Thread` class does not maintain this information, however: threads are usually considered autonomous rather than subordinate to the thread that created them.

If you want to impose some order onto a subset of threads, you can create a `ThreadGroup` object and add threads to it:

```
group = ThreadGroup.new
3.times {|n| group.add(Thread.new { do_task(n) }}
```

New threads are initially placed in the group to which their parent belongs. Use the instance method `group` to query the `ThreadGroup` to which a thread belongs. And use the `list` method of `ThreadGroup` to obtain an array of threads in a group. Like the class method `Thread.list`, the instance method `ThreadGroup.list` returns only threads that have not terminated yet. You can use this `list` method to define methods that operate on all threads in a group. Such a method might lower the priority of all threads in the group, for example.

The feature of the `ThreadGroup` class that makes it more useful than a simple array of threads is its `enclose` method. Once a thread group has been enclosed, threads may not be removed from it and new threads cannot be added to it. The threads in the group may create new threads, and these new threads will become members of the group. An enclosed `ThreadGroup` is useful when you run untrusted Ruby code under the $SAFE variable (see §10.5) and want to keep track of any threads spawned by that code.

9.9.6 Threading Examples

Now that we've explained Ruby's thread model and thread API, we'll take a look at some actual examples of multithreaded code.

9.9.6.1 Reading files concurrently

The most common use of Ruby's threads is in programs that are IO-bound. They allow programs to keep busy even while waiting for input from the user, the filesystem, or the network. The following code, for example, defines a method `conread` (for concurrent read) that takes an array of filenames and returns a hash mapping those names to the contents of those files. It uses threads to read those files concurrently, and is really intended for use with the `open-uri` module, which allows HTTP and FTP URLs to be opened with `Kernel.open` and read as if they were files:

```ruby
# Read files concurrently. Use with the "open-uri" module to fetch URLs.
# Pass an array of filenames. Returns a hash mapping filenames to content.
def conread(filenames)
  h = {}                          # Empty hash of results

  # Create one thread for each file
  filenames.each do |filename|    # For each named file
    h[filename] = Thread.new do   # Create a thread, map to filename
      open(filename) {|f| f.read } # Open and read the file
    end                           # Thread value is file contents
  end

  # Iterate through the hash, waiting for each thread to complete.
  # Replace the thread in the hash with its value (the file contents)
  h.each_pair do |filename, thread|
    begin
      h[filename] = thread.value  # Map filename to file contents
    rescue
      h[filename] = $!            # Or to the exception raised
    end
  end
end
```

9.9.6.2 A Multithreaded Server

Another, almost canonical, use case for threads is for writing servers that can communicate with more than one client at a time. We saw how to do this using multiplexing with `Kernel.select`, but a somewhat simpler (though possibly less scalable) solution uses threads:

```ruby
require 'socket'

# This method expects a socket connected to a client.
# It reads lines from the client, reverses them and sends them back.
# Multiple threads may run this method at the same time.
def handle_client(c)
  while true
    input = c.gets.chop        # Read a line of input from the client
    break if !input            # Exit if no more input
    break if input=="quit"     # or if the client asks to.
    c.puts(input.reverse)      # Otherwise, respond to client.
    c.flush                    # Force our output out
  end
```

```
    c.close                  # Close the client socket
  end


server = TCPServer.open(2000) # Listen on port 2000

while true                   # Servers loop forever
  client = server.accept     # Wait for a client to connect
  Thread.start(client) do |c| # Start a new thread
    handle_client(c)         # And handle the client on that thread
  end
end
```

9.9.6.3 Concurrent iterators

Although IO-bound tasks are the typical use case for Ruby's threads, they are not restricted to that use. The following code adds a method conmap (for concurrent map) to the Enumerable module. It works like map but processes each element of the input array using a separate thread:

```
module Enumerable          # Open the Enumerable module
  def conmap(&block)       # Define a new method that expects a block
    threads = []           # Start with an empty array of threads
    self.each do |item|    # For each enumerable item
      # Invoke the block in a new thread, and remember the thread
      threads << Thread.new { block.call(item) }
    end
    # Now map the array of threads to their values
    threads.map {|t| t.value } # And return the array of values
  end
end
```

And here's a similar concurrent version of the each iterator:

```
module Enumerable
  def concurrently
    map {|item| Thread.new { yield item }}.each {|t| t.join }
  end
end
```

The code is succinct and challenging: if you can make sense of it, you are well on your way to mastery of Ruby syntax and Ruby iterators.

Recall that in Ruby 1.9, standard iterators that are not passed a block return an enumerator object. This means that given the concurrently method defined earlier and a Hash object h, we can write:

```
h.each_pair.concurrently {|*pair| process(pair)}
```

9.9.7 Thread Exclusion and Deadlock

If two threads share access to the same data, and at least one of the threads modifies that data, you must take special care to ensure that no thread can ever see the data in an inconsistent state. This is called *thread exclusion*. A couple of examples will explain why it is necessary.

First, suppose that two threads are processing files and each thread increments a shared variable in order to keep track of the total number of files processed. The problem is that incrementing a variable is not an *atomic* operation. That means that it does not happen in a single step: to increment a variable, a Ruby program must read its value, add 1, and then store the new value back into the variable. Suppose that our counter is at 100, and imagine the following interleaved execution of the two threads. The first thread reads the value 100, but before it can add 1, the scheduler stops running the first thread and allows the second thread to run. Now the second thread reads the value 100, adds 1, and stores 101 back into the counter variable. This second thread now starts to read a new file, which causes it to block and allows the first thread to resume. The first thread now adds 1 to 100 and stores the result. Both threads have incremented the counter, but its value is 101 instead of 102.

Another classic example of the need for thread exclusion involves an electronic banking application. Suppose one thread is processing a transfer of money from a savings account to a checking account, and another thread is generating monthly reports to be sent out to customers. Without proper exclusion, the report-generation thread might read the customers' account data after funds had been subtracted from savings but before they had been added to checking.

We resolve problems like these by using a cooperative locking mechanism. Each thread that wants to access shared data must first *lock* that data. The lock is represented by a Mutex (short for "mutual exclusion") object. To lock a Mutex, you call its lock method. When you're done reading or altering the shared data, you call the unlock method of the Mutex. The lock method blocks when called on a Mutex that's already locked, and it does not return until the caller has successfully obtained a lock. If each thread that accesses the shared data locks and unlocks the Mutex correctly, no thread will see the data in an inconsistent state and we won't have problems like those we've described.

Mutex is a core class in Ruby 1.9 and is part of the standard thread library in Ruby 1.8. Instead of using the lock and unlock methods explicitly, it is more common to use the synchronize method and associate a block with it. synchronize locks the Mutex, runs the code in the block, and then unlocks the Mutex in an ensure clause so that exceptions are properly handled. Here is a simple model of our bank account example, using a Mutex object to synchronize thread access to shared account data:

```ruby
require 'thread'  # For Mutex class in Ruby 1.8

# A BankAccount has a name, a checking amount, and a savings amount.
class BankAccount
  def init(name, checking, savings)
    @name,@checking,@savings = name,checking,savings
    @lock = Mutex.new        # For thread safety
  end
```

```ruby
  # Lock account and transfer money from savings to checking
  def transfer_from_savings(x)
    @lock.synchronize {
      @savings -= x
      @checking += x
    }
  end

  # Lock account and report current balances
  def report
    @lock.synchronize {
      "#@name\nChecking: #@checking\nSavings: #@savings"
    }
  end
end
```

9.9.7.1 Deadlock

When we start using `Mutex` objects for thread exclusion we must be careful to avoid *deadlock*. Deadlock is the condition that occurs when all threads are waiting to acquire a resource held by another thread. Because all threads are blocked, they cannot release the locks they hold. And because they cannot release the locks, no other thread can acquire those locks.

A classic deadlock scenario involves two threads and two `Mutex` objects. Thread 1 locks `Mutex` 1 and then attempts to lock `Mutex` 2. Meanwhile, thread 2 locks `Mutex` 2 and then attempts to lock `Mutex` 1. Neither thread can acquire the lock it needs, and neither thread can release the lock the other one needs, so both threads block forever:

```ruby
# Classic deadlock: two threads and two locks
require 'thread'

m,n = Mutex.new, Mutex.new

t = Thread.new {
  m.lock
  puts "Thread t locked Mutex m"
  sleep 1
  puts "Thread t waiting to lock Mutex n"
  n.lock
}

s = Thread.new {
  n.lock
  puts "Thread s locked Mutex n"
  sleep 1
  puts "Thread s waiting to lock Mutex m"
  m.lock
}

t.join
s.join
```

The way to avoid this kind of deadlock is to always lock resources in the same order. If the second thread locked m before locking n, then deadlock would not occur.

Note that deadlock is possible even without using Mutex objects. Calling join on a thread that calls Thread.stop will deadlock both threads, unless there is a third thread that can awaken the stopped thread.

Bear in mind that some Ruby implementations can detect simple deadlocks like these and abort with an error, but this is not guaranteed.

9.9.8 Queue and SizedQueue

The standard thread library defines the Queue and SizedQueue data structures specifically for concurrent programming. They implement thread-safe FIFO queues and are intended for a producer/consumer model of programming. Under this model, one thread produces values of some sort and places them on a queue with the enq (enqueue) method or its synonym push. Another thread "consumes" these values, removing them from the queue with the deq (dequeue) method as needed. (The pop and shift methods are synonyms for deq.)

The key features of Queue that make it suitable for concurrent programming is that the deq method blocks if the queue is empty and waits until the producer thread adds a value to the queue. The Queue and SizedQueue classes implement the same basic API, but the SizedQueue variant has a maximum size. If the queue is already at its maximum size, then the method for adding a value to the queue will block until the consumer thread removes a value from the queue.

As with Ruby's other collection classes, you can determine the number of elements in a queue with size or length, and you can determine if a queue is empty with empty?. Specify the maximum size of a SizedQueue when you call SizedQueue.new. After creating a SizedQueue, you can query and alter its maximum size with max and max=.

Earlier in this chapter, we saw how to add a concurrent map method to the Enumerable module. We now define a method that combines a concurrent map with a concurrent inject. It creates a thread for each element of the enumerable collection and uses that thread to apply a mapping Proc. The value returned by that Proc is enqueued on a Queue object. One final thread acts as a consumer; it removes values from the queue and passes them to the injection Proc as they become available.

We call this concurrent injection method conject, and you could use it like this to concurrently compute the sum of the squares of the values in an array. Note that a sequential algorithm would almost certainly be faster for a simple sum-of-squares example like this:

```
a = [-2,-1,0,1,2]
mapper = lambda {|x| x*x }          # Compute squares
injector = lambda {|total,x| total+x } # Compute sum
a.conject(0, mapper, injector)       # => 10
```

The code for this `conject` method is as follows—note the use of a `Queue` object and its `enq` and `deq` methods:

```
module Enumerable
  # Concurrent inject: expects an initial value and two Procs
  def conject(initial, mapper, injector)
    # Use a Queue to pass values from mapping threads to injector thread
    q = Queue.new
    count = 0                  # How many items?
    each do |item|             # For each item
      Thread.new do            # Create a new thread
        q.enq(mapper[item])    # Map and enqueue mapped value
      end
      count += 1               # Count items
    end

    t = Thread.new do          # Create injector thread
      x = initial              # Start with specified initial value
      while(count > 0)         # Loop once for each item
        x = injector[x,q.deq]  # Dequeue value and inject
        count -= 1             # Count down
      end
      x                        # Thread value is injected value
    end

    t.value    # Wait for injector thread and return its value
  end
end
```

9.9.9 Condition Variables and Queues

There is something important to notice about the `Queue` class: the `deq` method can block. Normally, we only think of blocking as happening with `IO` methods (or when calling `join` on a thread or `lock` on a `Mutex`). In multithreaded programming, however, it is sometimes necessary to have a thread wait for some condition (outside of the control of that thread) to become true. In the case of the `Queue` class, the condition is the non-empty status of the queue: if the queue is empty, then a consumer thread must wait until a producer thread calls `enq` and makes the queue nonempty.

Making a thread wait until some other thread tells it that it can go again is accomplished most cleanly with a `ConditionVariable`. Like `Queue`, `ConditionVariable` is part of the standard thread library. Create a `ConditionVariable` with `ConditionVariable.new`. Make a thread wait on the condition with the `wait` method. Wake one waiting thread with `signal`. Wake all waiting threads with `broadcast`. There is one slightly tricky part to the use of condition variables: in order to make things work correctly, the waiting thread must pass a locked `Mutex` object to the `wait` method. This mutex will be temporarily unlocked while the thread waits, and it will be locked again when the thread wakes up.

We conclude our coverage of threads with a utility class that is sometimes useful in multithreaded programs. It is called `Exchanger`, and it allows two threads to swap arbitrary values. Suppose we have threads `t1` and `t2` and an `Exchanger` object `e`. `t1` calls e.exchange(1). This method then blocks (using a `ConditionVariable`, of course) until t2 calls e.exchange(2). This second thread does not block, it simply returns 1—the value passed by t1. Now that the second thread has called exchange, t1 wakes up again and returns 2 from the exchange method.

The `Exchanger` implementation shown here is somewhat complex, but it demonstrates a typical use of the `ConditionVariable` class. One interesting feature of this code is that it uses two `Mutex` objects. One of them is used to synchronize access to the exchange method and is passed to the `wait` method of the condition variable. The other `Mutex` is used to determine whether the calling thread is the first or the second thread to invoke exchange. Instead of using `lock` with this `Mutex`, this class uses the nonblocking try_lock method. If `@first.try_lock` returns `true`, then the calling thread is the first thread. Otherwise, it is the second thread:

```ruby
require 'thread'

class Exchanger
  def initialize
    # These variables will hold the two values to be exchanged.
    @first_value = @second_value = nil
    # This Mutex protects access to the exchange method.
    @lock = Mutex.new
    # This Mutex allows us to determine whether we're the first or
    # second thread to call exchange.
    @first = Mutex.new
    # This ConditionVariable allows the first thread to wait for
    # the arrival of the second thread.
    @second = ConditionVariable.new
  end

  # Exchange this value for the value passed by the other thread.
  def exchange(value)
    @lock.synchronize do      # Only one thread can call this method at a time
      if @first.try_lock      # We are the first thread
        @first_value = value  # Store the first thread's argument
        # Now wait until the second thread arrives.
        # This temporarily unlocks the Mutex while we wait, so
        # that the second thread can call this method, too
        @second.wait(@lock)   # Wait for second thread
        @first.unlock         # Get ready for the next exchange
        @second_value         # Return the second thread's value
      else                    # Otherwise, we're the second thread
        @second_value = value # Store the second value
        @second.signal        # Tell the first thread we're here
        @first_value          # Return the first thread's value
      end
    end
  end
end
```

## CHAPTER 10

The Ruby Environment

This chapter is a catch-all for Ruby programming topics that have not been discussed elsewhere. Most of the features covered here have to do with the interface between Ruby and the operating system on which it is running. As such, some of these features are OS-dependent. Similarly, many of the features may be implementation dependent: not every Ruby interpreter will implement them in the same way. Topics covered include:

- The Ruby interpreter's command-line arguments and environment variables.
- The top-level execution environment: global functions, variables, and constants.
- Shortcuts for text processing scripts: global functions, variables, and interpreter options, usually inspired by the Perl programming language, that make it possible to write short but powerful Ruby programs for processing text files.
- OS commands: running shell commands and invoking executables in the underlying operating system. These are features that allow Ruby to be used as a scripting or "glue" language.
- Security: how to reduce the risk of SQL injection and similar attacks on with Ruby's tainting mechanism, and how to "sandbox" untrusted Ruby code with $SAFE execution levels.

10.1 Invoking the Ruby Interpreter

The standard C-based Ruby implementation is invoked from the command line like this:

```
ruby [options] [--] program [arguments]
```

options is zero or more command-line arguments that affect the operation of the interpreter. The legal arguments are described shortly.

program is the name of the file that holds the Ruby program to be run. If the name of the program begins with a hyphen, precede it with -- to force it to be treated as a program name rather than as an option. If you use a single hyphen as the program name, or omit *program* and *arguments* altogether, the interpreter will read program text from standard input.

Finally, *arguments* is any number of additional tokens on the command line. These tokens become the elements of the ARGV array.

The subsections that follow describe the options supported by the standard C-based Ruby implementation. Note that you may set the RUBYOPT environment variable to include any of the -W, -w, -v, -d, -I, -r, -K, -E, and -T options. These will automatically be applied to every invocation of the interpreter, as if they were specified on the command line, unless the command line includes --disable-rubyopt.

10.1.1 Common Options

The following options are probably the most commonly used. Most Ruby implementations can be expected to support these options or to provide a work-alike alternative:

-w

 This option enables warnings about deprecated or problematic code and sets $VERBOSE to true. Many Ruby programmers use this option routinely to ensure that their code is clean.

-e *script*

 This option runs the Ruby code in *script*. If more than one -e option is specified, their associated scripts are treated as separate lines of code. Also, if one or more -e option is specified, the interpreter does not load or run any *program* specified on the command line.

 To enable succinct one-liner scripts, Ruby code specified with the -e option may use the Regexp matching shortcut explained later in this chapter.

-I *path*

 This option adds the directories in *path* to the beginning of the global $LOAD_PATH array. This specifies directories to be searched by the load and require methods (but does not affect the loading of the *program* specified on the command line).

 Multiple -I options may appear in the command line and each may list one or more directories. If multiple directories are specified with a single -I option, they should be separated from each other with : on Unix and Unix-like systems and with ; on Windows systems.

-r *library*

 This option loads the specified *library* before running the specified program. This option works as if the first line of the program were:

```
require 'library'
```

 The space between the -r and the name of the library is optional and often omitted.

-rubygems

 This frequently used command-line argument is not a true option but simply a clever application of the -r option. It loads the module named ubygems (with no r) from the standard library. Conveniently, the ubygems module simply loads the real rubygems module. Ruby 1.9 can load installed gems without this module, so this option is only necessary in Ruby 1.8.

--disable-gems

 This Ruby 1.9 option prevents the addition of gem installation directories to the default load path. If you have many gems installed, and you are running a program that does not use those gems (or a program that explicitly manages its own dependencies with the gem method), you may find that your program startup time is reduced with this option.

`-d, --debug`

> These options set the global variables `$DEBUG` and `$VERBOSE` to `true`. Your program, or library code, used by your program may print debugging output or take other action when these variables are set.

`-h`

> This option displays a list of interpreter options and exits.

10.1.2 Warnings and Information Options

The following options control the type or the amount of information the Ruby interpreter displays:

`-W, -W2, --verbose`

> These are all synonyms for `-w`: they enable verbose warnings and set `$VERBOSE` to `true`.

`-W0`

> This option suppresses all warnings.

`-v`

> This option prints the Ruby version number. If no program is specified, it exits rather than reading a program from standard input. If a program is specified, run it as if `--verbose` (or `-w`) had been specified.

`--version, --copyright, --help`

> These options print Ruby version number, copyright information, or command-line help and exit. `--help` is a synonym for `-h`. `--version` differs from `-v` in that it never runs a specified program.

10.1.3 Encoding Options

The following options are used to specify the default external encoding of the Ruby process and the default source encoding for files that do not specify their own encoding with a coding comment. If none of these options is specified, then the default external encoding is derived from the locale and the default source encoding is ASCII (see §2.4 for more on source encoding and default external encoding):

`-K code`

> In Ruby 1.8, this option specifies the source encoding of the script and sets the global variable `$KCODE`. In Ruby 1.9, it sets the default external encoding of the Ruby process and specifies a default source encoding.
>
> Specify a *code* of a, A, n, or N for ASCII; u or U for Unicode; e or E for EUC-JP; and s or S for SJIS. (EUC-JP and SJIS are common Japanese encodings.)

`-E encoding, --encoding= encoding`

> These options are like `-K` but allow the encoding to be specified by name rather than by a one-letter abbreviation.

10.1.4 Text Processing Options

The following options alter Ruby's default text processing behavior, or are helpful when writing one-line scripts with the -e option:

-0 *xxx*

This option is the digit 0, not the letter O. *xxx* should be between zero and three octal digits. When specified, these digits are the ASCII code of the input record separator character and set the $/ variable. This defines "a line" for gets and similar methods. -0 by itself sets $/ to character code 0. -00 is special; it puts Ruby into "paragraph mode" in which lines are separated by two adjacent newline characters.

-a

This option automatically splits each line of input into fields and stores the fields in $F. This option only works with -n or -p looping options and adds the code $F = $_.split at the start of each iteration. See also -F.

-F *fieldsep*

This option sets the input field separator $; to fieldsep. This affects the behavior of split when called with no arguments. See -a.

fieldsep may be a single character or an arbitrary regular expression, without the delimiting slashes. Depending on your shell, you may need to quote or double the backslashes in any regular expression specified on the command line.

-i *[ext]*

This option edits the files specified on the command line in place. Lines are read from the files specified on the command line, and output goes back to those same files. If *ext* is specified, a backup copy of the files is made, adding *ext* to the filename.

-l

This option makes the output record separator $\ the same as the input record separator $/ (see -0), so that that line ending is automatically added to text output with print. This option is intended for use with -p or -n. When used with one of those options, it automatically calls chop to remove the input record separator from each line of input.

-n

This option runs the program as if it were enclosed in the following loop:

```
while gets            # Read a line of input into $_
  $F = split if $-a   # Split $_ into fields if -a was specified
  chop! if $-l        # Chop line ending off $_ if -l was specified
  # Program text here
end
```

This option works in Ruby 1.9 even though the global functions chop! and split are no longer available in that version of the language.

This option is often used with -e. See also -p.

-p

This option runs the program as if it were written in the following loop:

```
while gets              # Read a line of input into $_
  $F = split if $-a     # Split $_ into fields if -a was specified
  chop! if $-l          # Chop line ending off $_ if -l was specified
  # Program text here
  print                 # Output $_ (adding $/ if -l was specified)
end
```

This option works in Ruby 1.9 even though the global functions chop! and split are no longer available in that version of the language.

This option is often used with -e. See also -n.

10.1.5 Miscellaneous Options

The following options don't fit into any of the previous categories:

-c

This option parses the program and report any syntax errors, but does not run it.

-C *dir*, -X *dir*

These options change the current directory to dir before running the program.

-s

When this option is specified, the interpreter preprocesses any arguments that appear after the program name and begin with a hyphen. For arguments of the form -x=y, it sets $x to y. For arguments of the form -x, it sets $x to true. The preprocessed arguments are removed from ARGV.

-S

This option looks for the specified program file relative to the path specified in the RUBY_PATH environment variable. If it is not found there, it looks for it relative to the PATH environment variable. And if it is still not found, it looks for it normally.

-T *n*

This option sets $SAFE to *n*, or to 1 if *n* is omitted. See §10.5 for more.

-x *[dir]*

This option extracts Ruby source from the program file by discarding any lines before the first that starts #!ruby. For compatibility with the capital -X option, this option also allows a directory to be specified.

10.2 The Top-Level Environment

When the Ruby interpreter starts, a number of classes, modules, constants, and global variables and global functions are defined and available for use by programs. The subsections that follow list these predefined features.

10.2.1 Predefined Modules and Classes

When the Ruby 1.8 interpreter starts, the following modules are defined:

Comparable	FileTest	Marshal	Precision
Enumerable	GC	Math	Process
Errno	Kernel	ObjectSpace	Signal

These classes are defined on startup:

Array	File	Method	String
Bignum	Fixnum	Module	Struct
Binding	Float	NilClass	Symbol
Class	Hash	Numeric	Thread
Continuation	IO	Object	ThreadGroup
Data	Integer	Proc	Time
Dir	MatchData	Range	TrueClass
FalseClass	MatchingData	Regexp	UnboundMethod

The following exception classes are also defined:

ArgumentError	NameError	SignalException
EOFError	NoMemoryError	StandardError
Exception	NoMethodError	SyntaxError
FloatDomainError	NotImplementedError	SystemCallError
IOError	RangeError	SystemExit
IndexError	RegexpError	SystemStackError
Interrupt	RuntimeError	ThreadError
LoadError	ScriptError	TypeError
LocalJumpError	SecurityError	ZeroDivisionError

Ruby 1.9 adds the following modules, classes, and exceptions:

BasicObject	FiberError	Mutex	VM
Fiber	KeyError	StopIteration	

You can check the predefined modules, classes, and exceptions in your implementation with code like this:

```
# Print all modules (excluding classes)
puts Module.constants.sort.select {|x| eval(x.to_s).instance_of? Module}

# Print all classes (excluding exceptions)
puts Module.constants.sort.select {|x|
  c = eval(x.to_s)
  c.is_a? Class and not c.ancestors.include? Exception
}

# Print all exceptions
puts Module.constants.sort.select {|x|
  c = eval(x.to_s)
  c.instance_of? Class and c.ancestors.include? Exception
}
```

10.2.2 Top-Level Constants

When the Ruby interpreter starts, the following top-level constants are defined (in addition to the modules and classes listed previously). A module that defines a constant by the same name can still access these top-level constants by explicitly prefixing them with ::. You can list the top-level constants in your implementation with:

```
ruby -e 'puts Module.constants.sort.reject{|x| eval(x.to_s).is_a? Module}'
```

ARGF

An IO object providing access to a virtual concatenation of files named in ARGV, or to standard input if ARGV is empty. A synonym for $<.

ARGV

An array containing the arguments specified on the command line. A synonym for $*.

DATA

If your program file includes the token __END__ on a line by itself, then this constant is defined to be a stream that allows access to the lines of the file following __END__. If the program file does not include __END__, then this constant is not defined.

ENV

An object that behaves like a hash and provides access to the environment variable settings in effect for the interpreter.

FALSE

A deprecated synonym for false.

NIL

A deprecated synonym for nil.

RUBY_PATCHLEVEL

A string indicating the patchlevel for the interpreter.

RUBY_PLATFORM

A string indicating the platform of the Ruby interpreter.

RUBY_RELEASE_DATE

A string indicating the release date of the Ruby interpreter.

RUBY_VERSION

A string indicating the version of the Ruby language supported by the interpreter.

STDERR

The standard error output stream. This is the default value of the $stderr variable.

STDIN

The standard input stream. This is the default value of the $stdin variable.

STDOUT

The standard output stream. This is the default value of the $stdout variable.

```
TOPLEVEL_BINDING
```
    A `Binding` object representing the bindings in the top-level scope.
```
TRUE
```
    A deprecated synonym for `true`.

10.2.3 Global Variables

The Ruby interpreter predefines a number of global variables that your programs can use. Many of these variables are special in some way. Some use punctuation characters in their names. (The `English.rb` module defines English-language alternatives to the punctuation. Add `require 'English'` to your program if you want to use these verbose alternatives.) Some are read-only and may not be assigned to. And some are thread-local, so that each thread of a Ruby program may see a different value of the variable. Finally, some global variables (`$_`, `$~`, and the pattern-matching variables derived from it) are method-local: although the variable is globally accessible, its value is local to the current method. If a method sets the value of one of these magic globals, it does not alter the value seen by the code that invokes that method.

You can obtain the complete list of global variables predefined by your Ruby interpreter with:

```
ruby -e 'puts global_variables.sort'
```

To include the verbose names from the `English` module in your listing, try:

```
ruby -rEnglish -e 'puts global_variables.sort'
```

The subsections that follow document the predefined global variables by category.

10.2.3.1 Global settings

These global variables hold configuration settings and specify information, such as command-line arguments, about the environment in which the Ruby program is running:

`$*`
    A read-only synonym for the `ARGV` constant. English synonym: `$ARGV`.

`$$`
    The process ID of the current Ruby process. Read-only. English synonyms: `$PID`, `$PROCESS_ID`.

`$?`
    The exit status of the last process terminated. Read-only and thread-local. English synonym: `$CHILD_STATUS`.

`$DEBUG, $-d`
    Set to `true` if the `-d` or `--debug` options were set on the command line.

$KCODE, $-K

In Ruby 1.8, this variable holds a string that names the current text encoding. Its value is "NONE", "UTF8", "SJIS" or "EUC". This value can be set with the interpreter option -K. This variable no longer works in Ruby 1.9 and using it causes a warning.

$LOADED_FEATURES, $"

An array of strings naming the files that have been loaded. Read-only.

$LOAD_PATH, $:, $-I

An array of strings holding the directories to be searched when loading files with the load and require methods. This variable is read-only, but you can alter the contents of the array to which it refers, appending or prepending new directories to the path, for example.

$PROGRAM_NAME, $0

The name of the file that holds the Ruby program currently being executed. The value will be "-" if the program is read from standard input, or "-e" if the program was specified with a -e option. Note that this is different from $FILENAME.

$SAFE

The current safe level for program execution. See §10.5 for details. This variable may be set from the command line with the -T option. The value of this variable is thread-local.

$VERBOSE, $-v, $-w

True if the -v, -w, or --verbose command-line option is specified. nil if -W0 was specified. false otherwise. You can set this variable to nil to suppress all warnings.

10.2.3.2 Exception-handling globals

The following two global variables are useful in rescue clauses when an exception has been raised:

$!

The last exception object raised. The exception object can also be accessed using the => syntax in the declaration of the rescue clause. The value of this variable is thread-local. English synonym: $ERROR_INFO.

$@

The stack trace of the last exception, equivalent to $!.backtrace. This value is thread-local. English synonym: $ERROR_POSITION.

10.2.3.3 Streams and text-processing globals

The following globals are IO streams and variables that affect the default behavior of text-processing Kernel methods. You'll find examples of their use in §10.3:

$_

The last string read by the `Kernel` methods `gets` and `readline`. This value is thread-local and method-local. A number of `Kernel` methods operate implicitly on `$_`. English synonym: `$LAST_READ_LINE`.

$<

A read-only synonym for the `ARGF` stream: an `IO`-like object providing access to a virtual concatenation of the files specified on the command-line, or to standard input if no files were specified. `Kernel` read methods, such as `gets`, read from this stream. Note that this stream is not always the same as `$stdin`. English synonym: `$DEFAULT_INPUT`.

$stdin

The standard input stream. The initial value of this variable is the constant `STDIN`. Many Ruby program read from `ARGF` or `$<` instead of `$stdin`.

$stdout, $>

The standard output stream, and the destination of the printing methods of `Kernel`: `puts`, `print`, `printf`, etc. English synonym: `$DEFAULT_OUTPUT`.

$stderr

The standard error output stream. The initial value of this variable is the constant `STDERR`.

$FILENAME

The name of the file currently being read from `ARGF`. Equivalent to `ARGF.filename`. Read-only.

$.

The number of the last line read from the current input file. Equivalent to `ARGF.lineno`. English synonyms: `$NR`, `$INPUT_LINE_NUMBER`.

$/, $-0

The input record separator (newline by default). `gets` and `readline` use this value by default to determine line boundaries. You can set this value with the `-0` interpreter option. English synonyms: `$RS`, `$INPUT_RECORD_SEPARATOR`.

$

The output record separator. The default value is `nil`, but is set to `$/` when the interpreter option `-l` is used. If non-`nil`, the output record separator is output after every call to `print` (but not `puts` or other output methods). English synonyms: `$ORS`, `$OUTPUT_RECORD_SEPARATOR`.

$,

The separator output between the arguments to `print` and the default separator for `Array.join`. The default is `nil`. English synonyms: `$OFS`, `$OUTPUT_FIELD_SEPARATOR`.

$;, $-F

The default field separator used by `split`. The default is `nil`, but you can specify a value with the interpreter option `-F`. English synonyms: `$FS`, `$FIELD_SEPARATOR`.

$F

> This variable is defined if the Ruby interpreter is invoked with the -a option and either -n or -p. It holds the fields of the current input line, as returned by `split`.

10.2.3.4 Pattern-matching globals

The following globals are thread-local and method-local and are set by any `Regexp` pattern-matching operation:

$~

> The `MatchData` object produced by the last pattern matching operation. This value is thread-local and method-local. The other pattern-matching globals described here are derived from this one. Setting this variable to a new `MatchData` object alters the value of the other variables. English synonym: `$MATCH_INFO`.

$&

> The most recently matched text. Equivalent to `$~[0]`. Read-only, thread-local, method-local, and derived from `$~`. English synonym: `$MATCH`.

$`

> The string preceding the match in the last pattern match. Equivalent to `$~.pre_match`. Read-only, thread-local, method-local, and derived from `$~`. English synonym: `$PREMATCH`.

$'

> The string following the match in the last pattern match. Equivalent to `$~.post_match` Read-only, thread-local, method-local, and derived from `$~`. English synonym: `$POSTMATCH`.

$+

> The string corresponding to the last successfully matched group in the last pattern match. Read-only, thread-local, method-local, and derived from `$~`. English synonym: `$LAST_PAREN_MATCH`.

10.2.3.5 Command-line option globals

Ruby defines a number of global variables that correspond to the state or value of interpreter command-line options. The variables $-0, $-F, $-I, $-K, $-d, $-v, and $-w have synonyms and are included in the previous sections:

$-a

> `true` if the interpreter option -a was specified; `false` otherwise. Read-only.

$-i

> `nil` if the interpreter option -i was not specified. Otherwise, this variable is set to the backup file extension specified with -i.

$-l

> `true` if the -l option was specified. Read-only.

$-p

> `true` if the interpreter option -p was specified; `false` otherwise. Read-only.

$-W

> In Ruby 1.9, this global variable specifies the current verbose level. It is 0 if the -W0 option was used, and is 2 if any of the options -w, -v, or --verbose were used. Otherwise, this variable is 1. Read-only.

10.2.4 Predefined Global Functions

The `Kernel` module, which is included by `Object`, defines a number of private instance methods that serve as global functions. Because they are private, they must be invoked functionally, without an explicit receiver object. And because they are included by `Object`, they can be invoked anywhere—no matter what the value of `self` is, it will be an object, and these methods can be implicitly invoked on it. The functions defined by `Kernel` can be grouped into several categories, most of which are covered elsewhere in this chapter or elsewhere in this book.

10.2.4.1 Keyword functions

The following `Kernel` functions behave like language keywords and are documented elsewhere in this book:

```
block_given?   iterator?   loop    require
callcc         lambda      proc    throw
catch          load        raise
```

10.2.4.2 Text input, output, and manipulation functions

`Kernel` defines the following functions most of which are global variants of `IO` methods. They are covered in more detail in §10.3:

```
format    print    puts       sprintf
gets      printf   readline
p         putc     readlines
```

In Ruby 1.8 (but not 1.9), `Kernel` also defines the following global variants of `String` methods that operate implicitly on `$_`:

```
chomp    chop    gsub    scan    sub
chomp!   chop!   gsub!   split   sub!
```

10.2.4.3 OS methods

The following `Kernel` functions allow a Ruby program to interface with the operating system. They are platform-dependent and are covered in §10.4. Note that ` is the specially named backtick method that returns the text output by an arbitrary OS shell command:

```
`         fork    select  system  trap
exec      open    syscall test
```

10.2.4.4 Warnings, failures, and exiting

The following `Kernel` functions display warnings, raise exceptions, cause the program to exit, or register blocks of code to be run when the program terminates. They are documented along with OS-specific methods in §10.4:

```
abort   at_exit exit   exit!  fail   warn
```

10.2.4.5 Reflection functions

The following `Kernel` functions are part of Ruby's reflection API and were described in Chapter 8:

```
binding                      set_trace_func
caller                       singleton_method_added
eval                         singleton_method_removed
global_variables             singleton_method_undefined
local_variables              trace_var
method_missing               untrace_var
remove_instance_variable
```

10.2.4.6 Conversion functions

The following `Kernel` functions attempt to convert their arguments to a new type. They were described in §3.8.7.3:

```
Array   Float   Integer String
```

10.2.4.7 Miscellaneous Kernel functions

The following miscellaneous `Kernel` functions don't fit into the previous categories:

```
autoload               rand                 srand
autoload?              sleep
```

`rand` and `srand` are for generating random numbers, and are documented in §9.3.7. `autoload` and `autoload?` are covered in §7.6.3. And `sleep` is covered in §9.9 and §10.4.4.

10.2.5 User-Defined Global Functions

When you define a method with `def` inside a `class` or `module` declaration and do not specify a receiver object for the method, the method is created as a public instance method of `self`, where `self` is the class or module you are defining. Using `def` at the top level, outside of any `class` or `module`, is different in two important ways. First, top-level methods are instance methods of `Object` (even though `self` is not `Object`). Second, top-level methods are always private.

Top-Level self: the Main Object

Because top-level methods become instance methods of `Object`, you might expect that the value of `self` would be `Object`. In fact, however, top-level methods are a special case: methods are defined in `Object`, but `self` is a different object. This special top-level

---

object is known as the "main" object, and there is not much to say about it. The class of the main object is Object, and it has a singleton to_s method that returns the string "main".

The fact that top-level methods are defined in Object means that they are inherited by all objects (including Module and Class) and (if not overridden) can be used within any class or instance method definition. (You can review Ruby's method name resolution algorithm in §7.8 to convince yourself of this.) The fact that top-level methods are private means that they must be invoked like functions, without an explicit receiver. In this way, Ruby mimics a procedural programming paradigm within its strictly object-oriented framework.

10.3 Practical Extraction and Reporting Shortcuts

Ruby was influenced by the scripting language Perl, whose name is an acronym for Practical Extraction and Reporting Language. Because of this, Ruby includes a number of global functions that make it easy to write programs that extract information from files and generate reports. In the object-oriented paradigm, input and output functions are methods of IO, and string manipulation functions are methods of String. For pragmatic reasons, however, it is useful to have global functions that read from and write to predefined input and output streams. In addition to providing these global functions, Ruby follows Perl further and defines special behavior for the functions: many of them operate implicitly on the special method-local variable $_. This variable holds the last line read from the input stream. The underscore character is mnemonic: it looks like a line. (Most of Ruby's global variables that use punctuation characters are inherited from Perl.) In addition to the global input and output functions, there are several global string processing functions that work like the String methods but operate implicitly on $_.

These global functions and variables are intended as shortcuts for short and simple Ruby scripts. It is generally considered bad form to rely on them in larger programs.

10.3.1 Input Functions

The global functions gets, readline, and readlines are just like the IO methods by the same names (see §9.7.3.1), but they operate implicitly on the $< stream (which is also available as the constant known as ARGF). Like the methods of IO, these global functions implicitly set $_.

$< behaves like an IO object, but it is not an IO object. (Its class method returns Object, and its to_s method returns "ARGF".) The precise behavior of this stream is complicated. If the ARGV array is empty, then $< is the same as STDIN: the standard input stream. If ARGV is not empty, then Ruby assumes that it is a list of filenames. In this case, $< behaves as if it were reading from the concatenation of each of those files. This does not correctly capture the behavior of $<, however. When the first read request for $< occurs, Ruby uses `ARGV.shift` to remove the first filename from `ARGV`. It opens and reads from that file. When the end of that file is reached, Ruby repeats the process, shifting the next filename out of `ARGV` and opening that file. $< does not report end-of-file until there are no more file names in `ARGV`.

What this means is that your Ruby scripts can alter `ARGV` (to process command-line options, for example) before beginning to read from $<. Your script can also add additional files to `ARGV` as it runs, and $< will use these files.

10.3.2 Deprecated Extraction Functions

In Ruby 1.8 and before, the global functions `chomp`, `chomp!`, `chop`, `chop!`, `gsub`, `gsub!`, `scan`, `split`, `sub`, and `sub!` work like the same-named methods of `String`, but operate implicitly on `$_`. Furthermore, `chomp`, `chop`, `gsub`, and `sub` assign their result back into `$_`, which means that they are effectively synonyms for their exclamation-mark versions.

These global functions have been removed in Ruby 1.9, so they should not be used in new code.

10.3.3 Reporting Functions

`Kernel` defines a number of global functions for sending output to `$stdout`. (This global variable initially refers to the standard output stream, `STDOUT`, of the Ruby process, but you can alter its value and change the behavior of the functions described here.)

`puts`, `print`, `printf` and `putc` are equivalent to the same-named methods of `STDOUT` (see §9.7.4). Recall that `puts` appends a newline to its output if there is not one there already. `print`, on the other hand, does not automatically append a newline, but it does append the output record separator `$\`, if that global variable has been set.

The global function `p` is one with no analog in the `IO` class. It is intended for debugging, and its short name makes it very easy to type. It calls the `inspect` method of each of its arguments and passes the resulting strings to `puts`. Recall that `inspect` is equivalent to `to_s` by default, but that some classes redefine it to provide more developer-friendly output suitable for debugging. If you require the `pp` library, you can use the `pp` function in place of `p` to "pretty print" your debugging output. (This is useful for printing large arrays and hashes.)

The `printf` method mentioned earlier expects a format string as its first argument and substitutes the value of its remaining arguments into that string before outputting the result. You can also format into a string without sending the result to `$stdout` with the global function `sprintf` or its synonym `format`. These work like the % operator of `String`.

10.3.4 One-Line Script Shortcuts

Earlier in this chapter, we described the -e option to the interpreter for executing single-line Ruby scripts (often used in conjunction with the -n and -p looping options). There is one special shortcut inherited from Perl that is allowed only in scripts specified with -e.

If a script is specified with -e, and a regular expression literal appears by itself in a conditional expression (part of an if, unless, while, or until statement or modifier), then the regular expression is implicitly compared to $_. If you want to print all lines in a file that begin with the letter A, for example, you can write:

```
ruby -n -e 'print if /^A/' datafile
```

If this same script was stored in a file and run without the -e option, it would still work, but it would print a warning (even without -w). To avoid the warning, you'd have to make the comparison explicit instead:

```
print if $_ =~ /^A/
```

10.4 Calling the OS

Ruby supports a number of global functions for interacting with the operating system to execute programs, fork new processes, handle signals, and so on. Ruby was initially developed for Unix-like operating systems, and many of these OS-related functions reflect that heritage. By their very nature, these functions are less portable than most others, and some may not be implemented at all on Windows and other non-Unix platforms. The subsections that follow describe some of the most commonly used of the OS-dependent functions. Functions, such a syscall, that are particularly low-level or platform-dependent are not covered here.

10.4.1 Invoking OS Commands

The Kernel.` method expects a single string argument representing an OS shell command. It starts a subshell and passes the specified text to it. The return value is the text printed to standard output. This method is typically invoked using special syntax; it is invoked on string literals surrounded by backquotes or on string literals delimited with %x (see §3.2.1.6). For example:

```
os = `uname`              # String literal and method invocation in one
os = %x{uname}            # Another quoting syntax
os = Kernel.`("uname")    # Invoke the method explicitly
```

This method does not simply invoke the specified executable; it invokes a shell, which means that shell features such as filename wildcard expansion are available:

```
files = `echo *.xml`
```

Another way to start a process and read its output is with the `Kernel.open` function. This method is a variant on `File.open` and is most often used to open files. (And if you `require 'open-uri'` from the standard library, it can also be used to open HTTP and FTP URLs.) But if the first character of the specified "filename" is the pipe character `|`, then it instead opens a pipe to read from and/or write to the specified shell command:

```
pipe = open("|echo *.xml")
files = pipe.readline
pipe.close
```

If you want to invoke a command in a shell, but are not interested in its output, use the `Kernel.system` method instead. When passed a single string, it executes that string in a shell, waits for the command to complete, and returns `true` on success or `false` on failure. If you pass multiple arguments to `system`, the first argument is the name of the program to invoke, and remaining arguments are its command-line arguments. In this case no shell expansion is performed on those arguments.

A lower-level way to invoke an arbitrary executable is with the `exec` function. This function never returns: it simply replaces the currently running Ruby process with the specified executable. This might be useful if you are writing a Ruby script that is simply a wrapper to launch some other program. Usually, however, it is used in conjunction with the `fork` function, which is described in the next section.

10.4.2 Forking and Processes

§9.9 described Ruby's API for writing multithreaded programs. Another approach to achieving concurrency in Ruby is to use multiple Ruby processes. Do this with the `fork` function or its `Process.fork` synonym. The easiest way to use this function is with a block:

```
fork {
  puts "Hello from the child process: #$$"
}
puts "Hello from the parent process: #$$"
```

When used this way, the original Ruby process continues with the code that appears after the block and the new Ruby process executes the code in the block.

When invoked without a block, `fork` behaves differently. In the parent process, the call to `fork` returns an integer which is the process ID of the newly created child process. In the child process, the same call to `fork` returns `nil`. So the previous code could also be written like this:

```
pid = fork
if (pid)
  puts "Hello from parent process: #$$"
  puts "Created child process #{pid}"
else
  puts Hello from child process: #$$"
end
```

One very important difference between processes and threads is that processes do not share memory. When you call fork, the new Ruby process starts off as an exact duplicate of the parent process. But any changes it makes to the process state (by altering or creating objects) are done in its own address space. The child process cannot alter the data structures of the parent, nor can the parent alter the structures seen by the child.

If you need your parent and child processes to be able to communicate, use open, and pass "|-" as the first argument. This opens a pipe to a newly forked Ruby process. The open call yields to the associated block in both the parent and the child. In the child, the block receives nil. In the parent, however, an IO object is passed to the block. Reading from this IO object returns data written by the child. And data written to the IO object becomes available for reading through the child's standard input. For example:

```
open("|-", "r+") do |child|
  if child
    # This is the parent process
    child.puts("Hello child")        # Send to child
    response = child.gets            # Read from child
    puts "Child said: #{response}"
  else
    # This is the child process
    from_parent = gets              # Read from parent
    STDERR.puts "Parent said: #{from_parent}"
    puts("Hi Mom!")                 # Send to parent
  end
end
```

The Kernel.exec function is useful in conjunction with the fork function or the open method. We saw earlier that you can use the ` and system functions to send an arbitrary command to the operating system shell. Both of those methods are synchronous, however; they don't return until the command completes. If you want to execute an operating system command as a separate process, first use fork to create a child process, and then call exec in the child to run the command. A call to exec never returns; it replaces the current process with a new process. The arguments to exec are the same as those to system. If there is only one, it is treated as a shell command. If there are multiple arguments, then the first identifies the executable to invoke, and any remaining arguments become the "ARGV" for that executable:

```
open("|-", "r") do |child|
  if child
    # This is the parent process
    files = child.readlines   # Read the output of our child
    child.close
  else
    # This is the child process
    exec("/bin/ls", "-l")     # Run another executable
  end
end
```

Working with processes is a low-level programming task and the details are beyond the scope of this book. If you want to know more, start by using *ri* to read about the other methods of the Process module.

10.4.3 Trapping Signals

Most operating systems allow asynchronous signals to be sent to a running process. This is what happens, for example, when the user types Ctrl-C to abort a program. Most shell programs send a signal named "SIGINT" (for interrupt) in response to Ctrl-C. And the default response to this signal is usually to abort the program. Ruby allows programs to "trap" signals and define their own signal handlers. This is done with the Kernel.trap method (or its synonym Signal.trap). For example, if you don't want to allow the user to use Ctrl-C to abort:

```
trap "SIGINT" {
  puts "Ignoring SIGINT"
}
```

Instead of passing a block to the trap method, you can equivalently pass a Proc object. If you simply want to silently ignore a signal, you can also pass the string "IGNORE" as the second argument. Pass "DEFAULT" as the second argument to restore the OS default behavior for a signal.

In long-running programs such as servers, it can be useful to define signal handlers to make the server reread its configuration file, dump its usage statistics to the log, or enter debugging mode, for example. On Unix-like operating systems, SIGUSR1 and SIGUSR2 are commonly used for such purposes.

10.4.4 Terminating Programs

There are a number of related Kernel methods for terminating program or performing related actions. The exit function is the most straightforward. It raises a SystemExit exception, which, if uncaught, causes the program to exit. Before the exit occurs, however, END blocks and any shutdown handlers registered with Kernel.at_exit are run. To exit immediately, use exit! instead. Both methods accept an integer argument that specifies the process exit code that is reported to the operating system. Process.exit and Process.exit! are synonyms for these two Kernel functions.

The abort function prints the specified error message to the standard output stream and then calls exit(1).

fail is simply a synonym for raise, and it is intended for cases in which the exception raised is expected to terminate the program. Like abort, fail causes a message to be displayed when the program exits. For example:

```
fail "Unknown option #{switch}"
```

The `warn` function is related to `abort` and `fail`: it prints a warning message to standard error (unless warnings have been explicitly disabled with `-W0`). Note, however, that this function does not raise an exception or cause the program to exit.

`sleep` is another related function that does not cause the program to exit. Instead, it simply causes the program (or at least the current thread of the program) to pause for the specified number of seconds.

10.5 Security

Ruby's security system provides a mechanism for writing programs that work with untrusted data and untrusted code. There are two parts to the security system. The first is a mechanism for distinguishing safe data from untrusted, or *tainted*, data. The second is a technique for *restricted execution*, which allows you to "lock down" the Ruby environment and prevents the Ruby interpreter from performing potentially dangerous operations on tainted data. This serves to prevent things like SQL injection attacks in which malicious input alters a program's behavior. Restricted execution can be taken a step further so that untrusted (and possibly malicious) code can be executed without fear that it will delete files, steal data, or otherwise cause harm.

10.5.1 Tainted Data

Every object in Ruby is either tainted or untainted. Literal values in program source code are untainted. Values that are derived from the external environment are tainted. These include strings read from the command-line (`ARGV`) or environment variables (`ENV`) and also any data read from files, sockets, or other streams. The environment variable `PATH` is a special case: it is tainted only if one or more of the directories it contains is world-writable. Importantly, taintedness is contagious, so objects derived from tainted objects are also tainted.

The `Object` methods `taint`, `tainted?`, and `untaint` allow you to mark an untainted object as tainted, test the taintedness of an object, and untaint a tainted object. You should untaint a tainted object only if your code has inspected it and determined that it is safe despite its unsafe origin or derivation.

10.5.2 Restricted Execution and Safe Levels

Ruby can execute programs with *security checking* turned on. The global variable `$SAFE` determines the level of the security check. The default safe level is normally 0, but is 1 for Ruby programs that run *setuid* or *setgid*. (These are Unix terms for a program that runs with privileges beyond those of the user that invokes it.) Legal safe levels are the integers 0, 1, 2, 3, and 4. You can explicitly set the safe level with the `-T` command-line option to the Ruby interpreter. You can also set the safe level by assigning to

$SAFE. Note, however, that you can only increase the value—it is never possible to lower this value:

```
$SAFE=1              # upgrade the safe level
$SAFE=4              # upgrade the safe level even higher
$SAFE=0              # SecurityError!  you can't do it
```

$SAFE is thread-local. In other words, the value of $SAFE in a thread may be changed without affecting the value in other threads. Using this feature, threads can be sandboxed for untrusted programs:

```
Thread.start {       # Create a "sandbox" thread
  $SAFE = 4          # Restrict execution in this thread only
  ...                # Untrusted code can be run here
}
```

This discussion of Ruby's SAFE levels is specific to the reference implementation. Other implementations may differ. JRuby, in particular, makes very little attempt (at the time of this writing) to emulate the restricted execution modes of the reference implementation. Furthermore, keep in mind that Ruby's security model has not received the kind of careful and prolonged scrutiny that Java's security architecture has. The subsections that follow explain how restricted execution is supposed to work in Ruby, but bugs yet to be discovered may allow the restrictions to be circumvented.

10.5.2.1 Safe level 0

Level 0 is the default safe level. No checks are performed on tainted data.

10.5.2.2 Safe Level 1

In this level, potentially dangerous operations using tainted data are forbidden. You can't evaluate a string of code if the string is tainted; you can't require a library if the library name is tainted; you can't open a named file if the filename is tainted; and you can't connect to a network host if the hostname is tainted. Programs, especially networked servers, that accept arbitrary input should probably use this safe level. This helps catch programming errors that use tainted data in unsafe ways.

If you write a library that performs potentially dangerous operations—such as communicating with a database server—you should check the value of $SAFE. If it is 1 or higher, your library should not operate on tainted objects. For example, you should not send a SQL query to a database if the string containing that query is tainted.

Execution restrictions at safe level 1 include the following:

- Environment variables RUBYLIB and RUBYOPT are ignored at startup.
- The current directory (.) isn't included in $LOAD_PATH.
- The command-line options -e, -i, -I, -r, -s, -S, and -X are prohibited.
- Certain instance methods and class methods of Dir, IO, File, and FileTest are prohibited for tainted arguments.

- `test`, `eval`, `require`, `load`, and `trap` may not be invoked with tainted arguments.

10.5.2.3 Safe level 2

Safe level 2 restricts operations on tainted data just as level 1 does, but also imposes additional restrictions on how files and processes can be manipulated, regardless of taint. There is little reason for a program to set its own safe level to 2, but a system administrator might choose to run a program you have written at this safe level to ensure that it cannot create or delete directories, change file permissions, launch executables, load Ruby code from world-writable directories, and so on.

Methods restricted at this safe level include:

```
Dir.chdir          File.truncate       Process.egid=
Dir.chroot         File.umask          Process.fork
Dir.mkdir          IO.fctrl            Process.kill
Dir.rmdir          IO.ioctl            Process.setpgid
File.chmod         Kernel.exit!        Process.setpriority
File.chown         Kernel.fork         Process.setsid
File.flock         Kernel.syscall
File.lstat         Kernel.trap
```

In addition, safe level 2 prevents you from loading or requiring Ruby code or running executables stored in world-writable directories.

10.5.2.4 Safe level 3

Safe level 3 includes all of the restrictions of level 2, and in addition, all objects— including literals in program source code (but not including predefined objects in the global environment)—are tainted when they are created. Furthermore, the `untaint` method is prohibited.

Safe level 3 is an intermediate step toward level 4 and is not commonly used.

10.5.2.5 Safe level 4

This level extends safe level 3 by preventing any modifications to untainted objects (including calling `taint` on untainted objects). Code running at this level cannot modify the global environment, nor can it modify any untainted objects previously created by code running at lower safe levels. This effectively creates a sandbox in which untrusted code can be run without doing any harm. (In theory, at least—bugs in the implementation or deficiencies in the underlying security model may be found in the future.)

Calling `eval` on a tainted string is prohibited in levels 1, 2, and 3. In safe level 4, it is allowed again because the restrictions on level 4 are stringent enough that the evaluated string can do no harm. Here is a way to evaluate arbitrary code in a level-4 sandbox:

```
def safe_eval(str)
  Thread.start {          # Start sandbox thread
    $SAFE = 4             # Upgrade safe level
```

```
        eval(str)              # Eval in the sandbox
    }.value                    # Retrieve result
  end
```

In safe level 4, you may not use **require** to load another file of Ruby code. You can use **load**, but only in wrapped form, with **true** as its second argument. This causes Ruby to sandbox the loaded file in an anonymous module so that any classes, modules, or constants it defines do not affect the global namespace. This means that code running under safe level 4 can load, but cannot use, classes and modules defined in external modules.

You can further restrict a level-4 sandbox by placing the sandbox thread (before setting **$SAFE**) into a **ThreadGroup** and calling **enclose** on that group. See §9.9.5 for details.

As part of the sandbox it creates, safe level 4 prohibits additional operations including the following:

- **require**, unwrapped **load**, **autoload**, and **include**
- Modifying **Object** class
- Modifying untainted classes or modules
- Metaprogramming methods
- Manipulating threads other than current
- Accessing thread local data
- Terminating the process
- File input/output
- Modifying environment variables
- Seeding the random number generator with **srand**

Index

Symbols

! operator, 30, 102, 107, 306
!= operator, 55, 79, 106
    object equality and, 77
!~ operator, 102, 106
" (quotation marks), 47
    expressions, interpolating into strings, 308
(hash)
    comments and, 2, 26, 36
    string interpolation and, 48
#{ } interpolation in regexps, 311
$ (dollar sign), 87
    global
        variables and, 30
    keywords prefixes and, 31
    regexp anchor, 315
$! global variable, 158, 398
$$ global variable, 397
$& global variable, 400
$' global variable, 400
$* global variable, 397
$+ global variable, 400
$, global operator, 399
$-d global variable, 397
$-I global variable, 398
$-K global variables, 398
$. global variable, 399
$/ global variable, 399
$: global variable, 253, 398
$; global variable, 399
$< global operator, 358, 399
$> global operator, 399
$? global variable, 397
$@ global variable, 398

$\ global variable, 399
$_ global variable, 360, 399
$` global variable, 400
$~ global regexp variable, 318
$~ global variable, 316, 400
% (percent sign)
    modulo operator, using as, 44, 96, 102
    %Q sequence, using as, 51
    %r delimiter, 310
    %x syntax, 53
%= operator, 102
%q sequences, 64
%Q sequences, 64
& (ampersand)
    method invocation and, 191
& operator, 66, 102, 104
&& operator, 102, 107
&&= operator, 96, 102
&= operator, 96, 102
' (single quotes), using for string literals, 46
( ) (parentheses)
    functions/methods, using, 3
    if statements and, 119
    method declarations, 33, 90, 183
    optional, 183
    parallel assignment and, 99
    required, 184
* (asterisk), 115
    matching characters, 352
    multiplication operator, 5, 44, 102
    repetition (strings), 304
    variable-length method argument lists,
        setting, 186
** (exponentiation) operator, 44, 102, 103
**= operator, 96, 102

We'd like to hear your suggestions for improving our indexes. Send email to *index@oreilly.com*.

object creation and initialization, 242
private/protected methods and, 232
singleton classes and, 247
initialize method (Class), 73
initialize_copy method, 83, 243–245
inject iterator, 205
inject method (Enumerable), 132, 334
input/output, 356–366
input functions, 403
random access methods, 365
streams, writing to, 364
inspect method, 12, 346
installing gems, 14
instance variables, 8, 30, 88
assigning, 93
classes, 231
inheritance and, 239
instance_eval method (Object), 234, 270, 279
instance_exec method (Object), 270
instance_of? method (Object), 74, 267
Integer function, 321
Integer function (Kernel), 81
integers
literals, 43
intern method (String), 71
internal iterator, 137
internal_encoding method (IO), 359
internationalization, 308
interpreter (Ruby), 11–15, 390–394
lexical structure and, 26
syntactic structure and, 34
introspection (see reflection)
invert method (Hash), 346
invocations, 89–92, 176
IO object, 356–366
IO-bound programs, 373
IO.bytes enumerator, 363
IO.chars enumerator, 363
IO.copy_stream method, 362
IO.each iterator, 360
IO.each_byte iterator, 363
IO.each_char iterator, 363
IO.each_line iterator, 360
IO.foreach method, 361
IO.lines enumerator, 360
IO.new method, 356
IO.open method, 356
IO.pipe method, 356
IO.popen method, 356

IO.read method, 361
IO.readlines method, 361
IOError, 235
irb (interactive Ruby) tool, 11, 13, 269
IronRuby, 12
is_a? method (Object), 75, 267
iterators, 3–4, 130–140
classes/methods and, 10
concurrent modification and, 140
custom, writing, 133–135
external, 137–140, 330
numeric, 131
Set class and, 349
strings, 58

J

Java programming language, using equality operators, 77
JRuby, 12

K

-K command-line option, 37, 63
Kanji characters, 29
$KCODE global variable, 398
Kernel module, 81, 90, 251, 266
looping, 138
Kernel.eval method, 268
Kernel.lambda method, 193
Kernel.proc method, 194
Kernel.rand method, 325
keys, 67
storing in hashes, 342
keyword literals, 86
keywords, 30
kill method, 379
kill! method, 379
kind_of? method (Object), 267

L

-l command-line option, 393
lambdas, 147, 192–200
invoking, 195
literals, 194
length method (Array), 64
length method (String), 56, 59
less than (<) operator, 55, 79, 102, 105
less than or equal (<=) operator, 55, 79, 102, 105

About the Authors

David Flanagan is a computer programmer who spends most of his time writing about programming languages. His other books with O'Reilly include *JavaScript: The Definitive Guide* and *Java in a Nutshell*. David has a degree in computer science and engineering from the Massachusetts Institute of Technology. He lives with his wife and children in the U.S. Pacific Northwest between the cities of Seattle, Washington, and Vancouver, British Columbia.

Yukihiro Matsumoto ("Matz"), the creator of Ruby, is a professional programmer who worked for the Japanese open source company netlab.jp. Matz is also known as one of the open source evangelists in Japan. He's released several open source products, including cmail, the Emacs-based mail user agent, written entirely in Emacs lisp. Ruby is his first piece of software that has become known outside of Japan.

Colophon

The animals on the cover of *The Ruby Programming Language* are Horned Sungem hummingbirds (*Heliactin bilophus*). These small birds are native to South America, living mainly in Brazil and Bolivia. They prefer dry, open habitats such as grasslands, and they avoid dense or humid forests.

Hummingbirds have the fastest wingbeat of all birds, and the Horned Sungem is capable of 90 wingbeats per second. (Contrast that with the vulture, the slowest of all birds, capable of just 1 wingbeat per second.) Because hummingbirds are so fast and light, they are able to hover in mid-air by rapidly flapping their wings. They can also fly backward (the only birds who can do so) in order to keep position as they drink nectar from flowers. Their long, thin bills allow them to reach deep within blossoms. Fittingly, the Portuguese word for hummingbird is *beija-flor*, or "flower kisser." The English word, of course, comes from the hum made by its fast-moving wings.

The male Horned Sungem has tufts of red, blue, and gold feathers on either side of its head. Its back is iridescent green, its throat and breast are black, and its belly is white. It has a long, pointed tail. The female looks similar to the male but lacks the dramatic crown pattern. Because of the hummingbird's vibrant colors, early Spanish explorers named it *Joyas voladoras*, or "flying jewel."

There are many myths about hummingbirds. In Brazil, a black hummingbird is a sign of a death in the family. The ancient Aztecs honored them, and priests used staffs covered with their feathers to remove curses. The hummingbird is also a symbol of resurrection, as Aztecs believed that dead warriors were reincarnated as these birds. The Aztec god of the Sun and war, Huitzilopochtli, was represented as one; his name means "Hummingbird from the south," the south being the location of the spirit world.

Related Titles from O'Reilly

Web Programming

ActionScript 3.0 Cookbook

ActionScript 3.0 Design Patterns

ActionScript for Flash MX: The
Definitive Guide, *2nd Edition*

Advanced Rails

AIR for JavaScript Developer's
Pocket Guide

Ajax Design Patterns

Ajax Hacks

Ajax on Rails

Ajax: The Definitive Guide

Building Scalable Web Sites

Designing Web Navigation

Dynamic HTML: The Definitive
Reference, *3rd Edition*

Essential ActionScript 3.0

Essential PHP Security

Flash Hacks

Head First HTML with CSS &
XHTML

Head Rush Ajax

High Performance Web Sites

HTTP: The Definitive Guide

JavaScript & DHTML Cookbook,
2nd Edition

JavaScript Pocket Reference,
2nd Edition

JavaScript: The Definitive Guide,
5th Edition

Learning ActionScript 3.0

Learning PHP and MySQL,
2nd Edition

PHP Cookbook, *2nd Edition*

PHP Hacks

PHP in a Nutshell

PHP Pocket Reference,
2nd Edition

PHP Unit Pocket Guide

Programming ColdFusion MX,
2nd Edition

Programming Flex 2

Programming PHP, *2nd Edition*

Programming Rails

Rails Cookbook

Upgrading to PHP 5

Web Database Applications with
PHP and MySQL, *2nd Edition*

Web Scripting Power Tools

Web Site Cookbook

Webmaster in a Nutshell,
3rd Edition

Our books are available at most retail and online bookstores.

To order direct: 1-800-998-9938 • *order@oreilly.com* • *www.oreilly.com*

Online editions of most O'Reilly titles are available by subscription at *safari.oreilly.com*